D0821223

THE PRICE WE PAY

The Case Against Racist Speech,
Hate Propaganda, and Pornography

■

Edited by

Laura J. Lederer and Richard Delgado

Hill and Wang

NEW YORK

A division of Farrar, Straus and Giroux

IN GRATITUDE

To John Foster-Bey and Jean Stefancic, whose sustained support made this book possible.

To Lianna and Kara Foster-Bey, for their patience and love, and to Miroslava Vyteckova, for her childcare.

To Dorchen Leidholdt, Evelina Giobbe, Loretta Ross, Morrison Torrey, Mary Becker, Cass Sunstein, Kathleen Barry, Catharine MacKinnon, Frank Michelman, john a. powell, Andrea Dworkin, and numerous other colleagues who encouraged us along the way.

To the Butler Family Foundation, the Shaler-Adams Foundation, the Joe and Emily Lowe Foundation, the Directors' Discretionary Fund of the Jessie Smith Noyes Foundation, and several anonymous donors for their financial support.

To Devona Futch and Bonnie Kae Grover for their fast, efficient research and proofreading.

To Lori Hewitt and Bettyann Reed for typing the manuscript.

To Sara Bershtel, Ariel Kaminer, Linda MacColl, and Elisabeth Sifton of Hill and Wang for their encouragement and editing, and to Esther Kaplan for her copyediting. And finally, to Sydelle Kramer of the Frances Goldin Literary Agency for her good sense, good humor, and guidance throughout the production of the book.

CONTENTS

Chapter Three: Conceptualizing Harm

PART II: THE REMEDIES

Chapter Four: Formulating Strategies under Current Law

Chapter Five: New Legal Paradigms

FOREWORD

Many of the essays in this anthology were presented at a conference on "Speech, Equality and Harm" held at the University of Chicago Law School in March 1993. This event brought together some of our nation's most creative, provocative, and engaging scholars to address a series of highly complex issues that cut to the very core of our commitment to such fundamental values as equality, free expression, and individual dignity.

In examining the connections among speech, equality, and harm, these articles explore the outer limits of causation and individual responsibility, probe the meaning of discrimination and the contours of protected expression, and address the limits of both tolerance and our tolerance of intolerance. Although there remain deep and often searing disagreements about the proper ways to deal with hate speech and pornography, almost everyone agrees that our ultimate resolution of these issues will speak volumes about who we are as individuals and as a community.

This book represents a valuable contribution to our understanding of these extraordinarily difficult and important issues and should be read by all those who care about freedom of speech, equality, and human rights.

GEOFFREY R. STONE, PROVOST
The University of Chicago

THE PRICE WE PAY

INTRODUCTION

- A Stanford Medical School professor resigns from the faculty, claiming sexual harassment: she cites the use of pornographic photos to illustrate lectures as an example of the sexism that pervades the school. Male faculty members insist that she is "overreacting."

- An African-American worker is repeatedly subjected to racist speech on the job. A noose is hung in his work area. His coworkers joke about the Ku Klux Klan and direct racial slurs and death threats at him. His employer dismisses the incidents as "horseplay."

- A young secretary's male coworkers place on her desk dozens of drawings depicting a naked woman with exaggerated sexual parts. The drawings, titled "Hot and Horny," all bear her initials. When she complains, her male employer tells her she is "doing this to herself."

- In San Francisco, a swastika is found on the desks of Asian-American and African-American inspectors in the newly integrated fire department. The battalion chief's official explanation is that the swastika was a "joke" gift to him many years earlier which he had just kept around the office.

- In Eureka, California, a Hmong family twice finds a four-foot-high cross burning on their lawn. Local police dismiss each incident as a "prank."

- In Jacksonville, Florida, a welder at Jacksonville Shipyards presses charges when her male coworkers, who outnumber her by more than a hundred to one, hang photographs of women posed in full labial display. In retaliation for the charges, her coworkers posted a "Men Only" sign on the door of the workroom and covered the walls with pornographic images of women. The company later admits that it regularly distributes pornographic calendars, which are sent by its major suppliers, to its male employees.

- A young college student finds the words "Nigger go home!" scrawled on his dormitory door the first day of school. "No Blacks Allowed" is spray-painted in a law student's dorm at the University of Wisconsin. The schools disavow responsibility.

• A female nurse is asked, and agrees, to critique an educational film during an important meeting of male administrators. The film turns out to be a pornographic movie about the rape of a young nurse. The woman sues the administrators but loses in court.

• A gay high school student arrives at school one morning to find the word "Faggot" printed in red on his locker with a line through it.

• A Jewish woman is repeatedly harassed by her next door neighbors, who scream "Die Jewish bitch," hang swastikas and "Nazi Power" signs in their windows, and telephone her house with death threats.

• An African-American man and a Latino man are confronted in a bowling alley by a group of white men who begin hurling racial slurs at them. When the two men reply angrily, one of the white men draws a knife and stabs the Latino man.

These are only a few of the thousands of incidents from the last few years that reflect growing bias and hatred against women, people of color, Jewish people, and gay men and lesbians in this country. Other countries that have experienced similar recent rises of racist speech, hate propaganda, and pornography, such as Germany and Canada, have taken swift legal action to criminalize this speech and conduct. But until recently the United States' tradition of absolutism regarding free speech and the First Amendment has precluded serious discussion of how to address harmful speech and conduct in America.

The Harm of Hate Speech

This book is about harm, the First Amendment, and legal change. Written during a time of ferment, it is intended to help the reader understand some of the issues at stake in the controversy about hate speech and pornography. In our country, *acts*—assault, battery, vandalism, arson, murder, lynchings, physical harassment—are punishable under our criminal and civil rights laws. But *words*, like kike, faggot, nigger, spic; *pictures*, like those in pornographic magazines depicting women being degraded, bound, raped, tortured, abused or murdered for sexual stimulation; and *symbols*, such as the burning of a cross on a black family's lawn, the desecration of a synagogue with Nazi signs, the wearing of a KKK hood or the flying of a confederate flag, are frequently protected by the courts as acts of individual expression. Speech or conduct aimed at a group of historically disenfranchised people; speech that reviles, ridicules, or puts in an intensely negative light a person or group on account of who they are—this is what we are calling "racist speech" or "hate propaganda." *Pornography* we define as the graphic, sexually explicit subordination of women through pictures or words, including the presentation of women in a dehumanized way as sexual objects or commodities; as enjoying pain, rape, or humiliation; as body parts (such as breasts, vaginas, or buttocks); or in any other way that sexualizes degradation, pain, or subordination. We use the term "harmful speech" or "hate speech" as a catch-all to refer to all forms of racist speech, hate propaganda, and pornography.

The old adage holds that "sticks and stones can break your bones, but names will never hurt you." This book questions the truth of that belief from a number of perspectives. First-person accounts, social science research, and new legal theories all suggest that hate speech is harmful—it harms the individual who is the target of the hate speech and it perpetuates negative stereotypes, promotes discrimination, and maintains whole groups of people as second-class citizens, hampering their participation in our democracy.

Just how hate speech harms is the subject of much debate. The contributors to this book argue that *the purpose of hate speech is the subordination of one people by another.* The mechanisms of this subordination are different in every case—but, in any event, they usually include a complex, interlocking series of acts, some physical, some verbal, some symbolic. For instance, rape, woman battering, catcalls, whistles, leers, and the proliferation of violent and degrading pornography all contribute to the subordination of women by making them fearful and by inviting others to think of them as targets. In the same way, gay bashing, harassment on the street, and name-calling—from "faggot" to "sissy"—help to mark all gay men and lesbians as "other." The early campaign of lynchings, racial slurs, and epithets directed against African Americans crippled that group's development by creating an atmosphere of fear, intimidation, harassment, and discrimination. Physical acts—lynchings, battery, rape, murder, vandalism, and arson—are the most noticeable forms of assault and receive the harshest sanctions from the courts, but verbal and symbolic acts can also be assaults and may be more insidious. Most physical wounds can heal, but psychological wounds are often carried for life. The ubiquity of harmful racial, sexual, and religious depictions is the source of their virulence.

The First Amendment and Hate Speech

The First Amendment was designed to insure that debate on public issues is "uninhibited, robust, and wide open." Civil libertarians often argue that the amendment should protect speech we hate as much as speech we hold dear. They note predemocratic struggles against censorship by king and church, and more recent battles to protect dissident political speech and art. They quote Oliver Wendell Holmes's famous dissent in *Abrams* v. *United States*, that "the best test of truth is the power of the thought to get itself accepted in the competition of the market. . . ." Originating in this dissent and rooted in laissez-faire economics, the "marketplace of ideas" became a concept by which to encourage the free dissemination of ideas and the rational process by which citizens could choose the best ideas and discard the others.

In recent years, however, this "marketplace of ideas" metaphor has increasingly been called into question. Some scholars argue that it has little relation to the way ideas are actually circulated. They note that rather than free and fair competition, there has always been an inequality in the power to communicate ideas, with those already in power having greater access to the means of dissemination and the appearance of credibility. Women, people of color, and other historically disenfranchised groups have never been able fully to "display their wares" in this hypothetical market. Critics contend that a truly open "marketplace of ideas" will exist only if people enter it as equals and are afforded equal respect. They argue that the government has a constitutional obligation to address the obstacles that prevent equal participation. Racist speech, which demoralizes and silences its victims while denying them credibility in the eyes of the public at large, will need to be regulated. Pornography, which has the same effect on women, will need redress.

But can this be done within our system of law and politics? Civil libertarians argue that the First Amendment prohibits any regulation of speech. But a closer examination reveals that the First Amendment guarantee has never been absolute. The courts have always recognized that the right to free speech can be overcome by a "compelling state interest" in protecting citizens from harm. Courts have ruled that the harm of many kinds of speech outweighs the good that might result from their protection. They have carved out dozens of "exceptions" to the free speech guarantee, including: speech used to form a criminal conspiracy, speech that disseminates an official secret, speech that defames or libels someone, speech that creates a hostile working place, speech that violates a trademark or plagiarizes another's words, speech that creates a clear and present danger (for instance, shouting fire in a crowded theater), speech used to defraud a consumer, speech used to fix prices, speech used to communicate a criminal threat (for example, "stick 'em up"), untruthful or irrelevant speech given under oath or during a trial, and disrespectful words aimed at a judge or a military officer. Each of these is a case of "pure" speech (i.e., words alone as opposed to symbols or acts) in which the Court has decided that the right of free expression must be balanced against some other right— such as safety from harm, or equal protection of the law. In each case, the Court has weighed two rights and found that the social interest represented by the other right was more important than the free speech right. And though some of these "exceptions" to the First Amendment were once hotly debated, all are now commonly accepted.

The question today is whether the social interest in equality for people of color, women, gays, lesbians, and Jewish people is somehow less compelling than those interests that justified such exceptions. Hate speech and pornography are beginning to emerge as new exceptions to the First Amendment, although not without sharp resistance from many quarters.

Interestingly, once as a society we agree that a certain category of speech is harmful, we are likely to give it a label other than speech: e.g., "stick 'em up" becomes robbery; shouting fire in a crowded theater becomes incitement to riot; speech violating a trademark is an intellectual property matter; and so on. One could, then, say that the real question is whether hate speech and pornography are forms of harassment or discrimination, rather than kinds of speech. The questions then become more difficult: in what forums should one regulate such practices (public, private, university settings)? Who will regulate? How will regulation take place? What remedies will be available?

The Current Debate

The current debate revolves around two very different constitutional paradigms. One, pressed by civil libertarians and traditional free speech advocates, puts freedom of expression at the center. These activists cite the First Amendment guarantee that "Congress shall make no law . . . abridging the freedom of speech" and require that those who would regulate hate speech provide strong justification for doing so.

The other paradigm, embraced by civil rights advocates and "First Amendment realists," places equality and equal rights at the center. They quote the Fourteenth Amendment to the Constitution, which requires equal protection of the law, and they contend that hate speech is an abuse of the First Amendment, that it harms people, and that it should not be protected as speech, but rather punished as a form of discrimination. They believe that the government has the duty to recognize the problems of historically vulnerable populations, and they demand that civil libertarians demonstrate why hate speech should be protected.

Civil libertarians respond that while pornography and hate speech are abhorrent, the First Amendment forbids any action against them. They call for "more speech" as a cure for the problem, and support debates in which both sides present their arguments and the audience can make up its own mind. But to realists, "more speech" can be a response only to rationally constructed arguments. Harmful speech, however, can very rarely be countered rationally. Racial and sexual epithets are often flung without notice, immobilizing the target and rendering him or her literally speechless. In addition, as the reader will see in Chapter One, harmful speech is often delivered in a cowardly, anonymous fashion—a cross burned on a lawn at night, a temple desecrated in darkness, an anonymous letter slipped under a doorway, a dead dog left on a mailbox. Other times it is delivered in a situation where the power imbalance is so great (e.g., five male CEOs forcing one working woman to watch a pornographic movie, a dozen heterosexual males pursuing one lone gay man and screaming epithets at him, a fraternity house of twenty white males yelling racial slurs at two black females) that to "talk back" would be to risk one's job, one's health, or one's life. For all these reasons, First Amendment realists argue, "more speech" is not a viable response; the speech it would purportedly counter too often silences its victims and deepens inequality, thus paradoxically diminishing, rather than contributing to, the vigorous debate and dialogue all civil libertarians desire.

Legal Responses to Hate Speech

To date, few legal initiatives have addressed the harm of hate speech and pornography. Reflecting a growing awareness of these issues, in 1990 Congress passed the Hate Crimes Statistics Act, designed to establish a means for gathering data on these incidents. The bill contained no preventive or punitive measures.

Some attorneys are using federal civil rights laws to prosecute hate speech. For example, women who have been subjected to pornography on the job have successfully pressed civil rights charges under Title VII of the Civil Rights Act, which prohibits discrimination in the workplace. And minorities have successfully sued people who conspire to deprive them of their civil rights, including equal protection of the laws.

Several states and municipalities have also drafted statutes and ordinances that prohibit hate speech and pornography, but a number of recent Supreme Court and U.S. district court decisions have tested these laws. The most important case is *R.A.V.* v. *St. Paul*, based on an incident in which a seventeen-year-old white youth burned a cross on a black family's front lawn. He was charged with violating a St. Paul, Minnesota, ordinance that prohibited the use of symbols or objects such as Nazi swastikas or burning crosses to arouse anger based on race, color, creed, religion, or gender. In 1992 the U.S. Supreme Court held the ordinance unconstitutional. Scholars are still debating that decision, and several contributors to this book argue that the case was incorrectly decided. A short time after, in 1993, in *Wisconsin* v. *Mitchell*, the Supreme Court upheld penalty enhancement (i.e., longer prison sentences) for hate-related crimes. In that case, Greg Mitchell, a young black man, went to see the movie *Mississippi Burning* with several friends. Afterward, they discussed a scene from the picture in which a white man beats a young black boy who was praying. Mitchell then said, "Do you all feel hyped up to move on some white people?" When a white youth walked by, Mitchell and the group jumped and beat him, leaving him in a coma for four days. The Court held that the First Amendment allows for penalty enhancement if the defendant intentionally picks out his victim because of his race. But this case, which deals solely with violent physical *acts*, does not address the question of hate speech.

Two early cases do weigh free speech guarantees against the harm of hate speech. In *Beauharnais* v. *Illinois* (1952), the head of the White Circle League organized the distribution of a leaflet proclaiming that "the Negro" would invade white neighborhoods and mongrelize the white race with "rapes, robberies, knives, guns and marijuana." He was convicted under a statute prohibiting the dissemination of materials promoting racial or religious hatred. The Court ruled that libelous statements aimed at groups, like those aimed at individuals, fall outside First Amendment protection. Civil libertarians question whether *Beauharnais* would be decided the same way by today's courts, but First Amendment realists argue that the case has never been overruled and it is still good law. In a famous trilogy of cases outlawing hate speech, the Canadian Supreme Court cited *Beauharnais* as the U.S. case it felt best dealt with the problem of group libel.

In *Chaplinsky* v. *New Hampshire*, the U.S. Supreme Court first articulated the doctrine of *fighting words*. In this case, Chaplinsky, who was a member of the Jehovah's Witnesses, was preaching about the Bible. Some citizens complained that he was denouncing religion and sent the city marshall to investigate. Chaplinsky called him a "God damned racketeer" and "damned Fascist." The marshall sued and the court upheld his complaint, noting that

". . . it is well understood that the right of free speech is not absolute. . . . There are certain well-defined and narrowly limited classes of speech the prevention and punishment of which have never been thought to raise any Constitutional problem. These include . . . the libelous, and the insulting or 'fighting words'—those which by their very utterance inflict injury or tend to incite an immediate breach of the peace." Many proponents of hate speech regulation argue that hate speech falls in the category of "fighting words" and therefore can be regulated.

Finally, some scholars support tort law as another mechanism for responding to hate speech. Torts are wrongs inflicted by one person or institution on another. Scholars argue that individuals who have been harmed by hate speech could sue under defamation laws, intentional infliction of emotional distress laws, or assault and battery laws. If hate speech occurs in the workplace, state or federal laws prohibiting bias-motivated harassment could also be used to redress it.

The legal treatment of pornography has pursued a somewhat similar course. Until about mid-century, certain types of anti-women books and films were forbidden under obscenity statutes. A leading U.S. Supreme Court decision, *Roth* v. *United States* (1957), held that obscenity—material that appeals to prurient interest—lies outside First Amendment protection. A later decision by the same Court, *Miller* v. *California* (1973), modified this approach slightly. For a work to be defined as obscene, an average person, applying contemporary standards, must find the work, taken as a whole, to appeal to prurient interest. Moreover, the work must lack serious literary, artistic, political, or scientific value.

Feminists criticized these approaches because they were morals-based; that is, based on the idea of community offensiveness. Works were designated illegal only because of their effect on community sensibilities or moral standards, not because they harmed or degraded women.

In 1985, the Seventh Circuit Court of Appeals considered an ordinance drafted by two of the contributors to this book, Andrea Dworkin and Catharine MacKinnon, that provided for civil suits by women who could demonstrate that they were injured by pornography. The court declared the ordinance, which had been approved by voters in two cities, unconstitutional. The court found that the law would have penalized much material that was not obscene. Moreover, it would have discriminated against forms of expression based on their content. The case (*American Booksellers* v. *Hudnut*, 1984) was summarily affirmed by the Supreme Court. Despite this setback, developments occurred elsewhere. A Canadian Supreme Court decision (*Regina* v. *Butler*, described in the chapter by Kathleen Mahoney) upheld a Canadian antipornography law, emphasizing that graphic pornography harms women and injures the ideal of equality. And as we go to press, Congress, state legislatures, and legal scholars are exploring new approaches to curb material that degrades and injures women.

Several of the first-person accounts in this book include descriptions of legal battles using state ordinances, federal statutes, or tort law to attempt to redress the harm of hate speech and pornography. But while a few plaintiffs have prevailed, many loopholes in the law allow severe harassment and discrimination to continue under the rubric of free speech.

A new generation of scholars, practitioners, and activists argue that these loopholes should be closed. They contend that First Amendment absolutism leads to a license to harm; that bigoted assault should be punished, not protected; and that the First Amendment must be balanced against other constitutional requirements—especially the Fourteenth Amendment, which guarantees equal protection under the law to all citizens.

In the United States, women's organizations and communities of color have made parallel progress in analyzing the impact of pornography and hate speech on their respective communities, but until now there has been little if any exchange among the various groups working on these related issues. The movements against hate speech and pornography both arose in response to continuing and unrelenting discrimination, exacerbated by widespread acceptance of racist and sexist speech and conduct. Both take as their starting point the real-life experiences of the members of their communities. On the basis of these experiences, both have developed an increasingly sophisticated analysis of how particular kinds of expression work in our culture to reinforce long-standing patterns of inequality and subordination. Both have proposed new "harms-based" and "equality-based" legal strategies for combating harmful speech and conduct. And finally, both have faced enormous opposition from disseminators of racist speech and pornography, and—unexpectedly—from civil libertarians who in many other arenas have been their political allies.

This book is organized in two parts. Part One, entitled "The Harm," presents first-person accounts, empirical research, and new legal and social analyses of the harm of racist speech, hate propaganda, and pornography. Because of a growing sense that theories and action must be grounded in the lived experience of actual people, Chapter One in this section presents the stories of women, minorities, Jewish and gay people who have been the targets of verbal and physical abuse. Olivia Young and Emmit E. Fisher recount early efforts to obtain protection and redress from the law for harassment they suffered on the job. More current accounts are provided by Russ and Laura Jones, the black family in whose yard a cross was burned (*R.A.V.* v. *St. Paul*); Wanda Henson, whose neighbors tried to force her and her lover Brenda off their Mississippi land; and Ann Simonton, a *Sports Illustrated* cover model who gave up fashion modeling when she realized the extent to which it commodified and dehumanized women's bodies. In the same section, Native American Fred Veilleux describes the ridicule and mockery that find expression in Native American team names and sports mascots.

Simply recording these real-life experiences, however, is not enough to change the conditions that produced them. These accounts, then, are followed in Chapter Two by social science research that interprets and assesses such experiences. We have included current documentation of the incidence of racist speech and hate propaganda, as well as laboratory research, attitudinal surveys, and retrospective studies on the individual and social effects of pornography and hate speech.

In Chapter Three, we turn to law. Here, legal scholars develop "harms-based" and "equality-based" theories of hate speech and pornography. In urgent, intense arguments, they make the case for the need to eliminate hate speech and pornography.

Part Two of the book, "The Remedies," analyzes remedies for harmful speech. While all the contributors in this book believe that pornography, racist speech, and hate propaganda are harmful, some believe that effective action can be taken within the current First Amendment framework. Thus, in Chapter Four, scholars address currently available legal strategies including the use of obscenity, hate crimes, and civil rights law; tort actions for individual victims; improving compensation for victims; and increasing the voice and authority of women and minorities in legislative and other settings.

Finally, in Chapter Five, contributors argue that current First Amendment law cannot address the damage done by racist speech, hate propaganda, and pornography. They note that while harmful speech is often aimed at an individual, it disrupts far more than that individual's life. Hate speech and pornography are tools for creating and maintaining a caste system in our country, and the First Amendment, which has been called the "jewel" in our Bill of Rights, is being used by pornographers and hate mongers to protect hate speech and pornography and to perpetuate systems of discrimination and second-class citizenship. Arguing that nothing less than a rethinking of our legal framework can adequately address harmful speech, these scholars point toward a new First Amendment paradigm—one that balances free speech against harms to equality and other constitutional values.

Throughout this book, a number of themes emerge: whether and how speech can harm; how to assess the harm; what to do about the harm; whether it is better to use current law or to create new law; whether and when speech is action; how to reconcile the tensions between freedom of speech and equality; how to weigh individual liberty against a larger sense of community; how to balance civil liberties and civil rights; and, finally, how to envision the future.

Just as American society will look different in the next century, our political and legal systems will need our sober reconsideration if they are to serve the needs of that emerging society. It is in that spirit that we offer this book.

PART I: THE HARM

I [do not] find the wisdom, foresight and sense of justice exhibited by the framers [of the Constitution] particularly profound. To the contrary, the government they devised was defective from the start, requiring several amendments, civil war and momentous social transformation to attain the system of constitutional government and the respect for individual freedoms and human rights we hold as fundamental today.

—THURGOOD MARSHALL

CHAPTER ONE

Experiencing Hate

How does it feel to be the target of hate speech? In this chapter, ten contributors relate their experiences. They are a diverse group—women, Jewish people, people of color, and gays and lesbians—and the hate speech they suffered takes different forms—from cross-burnings to pornographic movies to racial epithets. But their responses are remarkably similar: fear, humiliation, degradation, illness, terror, fury, anger, and rage.

They have something else in common too: they realized during the attacks that hate speech has a purpose and a message. It demeans, debases, and debilitates. It says to the recipient, "You are different," "You don't belong here," "You are not as good as I am," "You belong back—in the black part of town, on your back sexually serving us, on the reservation where we put you, in the closet, in the ovens of fifty years ago, silent, enslaved, second class, or dead—as you were before."

These contributors have one other trait in common. No matter what the cost, they said no to the hate and enlisted others—neighbors, citizens, the law—to help them.

Here they tell their own stories in their own words.

A WEAPON TO WEAKEN
Pornography in the Workplace

Olivia Young

On March 31, 1980, Olivia Young, a young black nurse, attended a business meeting at St. Louis University Medical Center. The other participants were the CEO of St. Louis University Hospital and four of his assistants. During the meeting, the CEO asked Young to critique an "educational film" that he said was being used to train doctors and nurses. She was then shown a pornographic movie. She sued for infliction of emotional harm and took her case all the way to the U.S. Supreme Court. Her case was an early, and unsuccessful, effort to press the legal system to recognize harmful speech as workplace harassment.

■

I was born into a low-income family. My parents migrated from the south to East St. Louis in 1945. My father and mother broke up when I was in the second grade, and we went from poor to very poor. We struggled economically, but my mother gave us a great deal of love, and I worked hard to make something of myself. I put myself through college, and by the time I was married and the mother of two sons, I had a degree in community nursing from the University of Illinois and was a home nursing administrator in Janna Medical Systems, a large medical center in St. Louis.

When my husband and I celebrated our tenth wedding anniversary on March 31, 1977, we looked back with a sense of satisfaction and forward to reaping the benefits of so much effort. Thus, on March 31, 1980, when I went into a meeting with the four top administrators of St. Louis University Hospital at around 4:30 p.m., my biggest concern was expediting the business as quickly as possible. My husband and I had dinner reservations at 7 p.m. to celebrate our anniversary.

The meeting was an important one. It was one of a series arranged by Janna's president, in which the St. Louis University Medical Center CEO, Richard Stensrude, and I could explore the possibility of using the hospital as a training site for student nurses. I had been recruited by Janna to develop advanced management training programs for nurses, and at this meeting, which was also attended by three hospital administrators (all of them men with whom I'd been working on the project), we were to get to know one another, to discuss the training course I had developed, and to settle the costs involved. My boss, Mrs. Ardith Grandbouche, was present at the start of the meeting but left shortly after introductions were over. I was in the middle of giving the others an overview of the proposed course of training when Richard Stensrude interrupted to ask if I would view "one of the films we use to educate our nurses." I agreed to review it, and I continued my discussion, but the men began laughing and Stensrude's assistant jumped up and left the room. I paused in my presentation and said, "What's so funny?" The men laughed harder. "What's the name of the film?" I asked. "*Deep Throat*," said one of the men. The others giggled and laughed again. I guess I just didn't get the "joke." There were no credits at the beginning of the film, and no one in the room said anything about what was to come. Even the first scene was normal looking. A woman who was a home nurse was driving a car down the street. She turned into the driveway, got out of the car, and walked into the house with a bag of groceries. She looked as though she were going to fix a meal for a sick person. She walked over to a kitchen cabinet on the far wall. Then, suddenly, the camera swung to a different wall of the kitchen. A woman was seated on the counter. She had her dress hiked up over her hips. She had her legs spread. A man was seated on a chair in front of her performing cunnilingus. With this graphic image, the men's giggling and laughter stopped and they began to hoot, "Look at that sucker suck," "Look at him suck," "Suck! Suck!," "We can make you feel that way, Olivia," "Look at her, Olivia," "Look at that dick," "Olivia, they say black men have really big dicks," "I'll bet you've never seen one this big before, have you?" and "It'll make you really . . ." "Stop!" I said. But they continued. Then I started crying and sobbed, "Why are you doing this to me?" At this point, Richard Stensrude hit his fist on the table and said, "This film represents the price of doing business with Dick Stensrude!"

Later, people asked me, "Why didn't you just get up and walk out?" But I just couldn't believe this was happening to me. I was shocked, stunned, horrified. I didn't know how to get out of Stensrude's conference room because it was in an isolated area of the hospital and the one other time I had been there, I had been escorted through the halls by a security guard. I was sitting there with five men I didn't know, in a high-pressure business meeting. I felt a combination of shock, fear, anger, and rage sweep through me and, most of all, a paralyzing sense of powerlessness. No sane man would do this, I reasoned, and, if they would do this to me, what would they do next? On the screen, the actress was obviously suffering, gagging as she was forced to perform oral sex. Tears were coming out of her eyes; her nose was running. In the next scene, she got attacked by several men at once. I felt assaulted. How could any woman confronted with that much power protect herself? As all this was racing through my head, a secretary walked into the room and said to the men, "Oh, you're at it again." I jumped up and said, "I have to go" and left with her. I don't know how I got to my car. I had one moment of clarity as I was getting off I-40 onto I-270—I must *not* tell my husband. I walked around in a stupor for about two and a half weeks.

When I finally told my husband what had occurred, his response mirrored the general one I received—to blame me, question my integrity and my intelligence. "Why would men in that position do something like that if you hadn't done something to make them think it was okay?" people asked. "You should have cursed them out!" "You should have slapped their faces." "You should have destroyed that film." "I wouldn't have tolerated that kind of treatment." "Didn't you know better than to put yourself in that position in the first place?" Even more hurtful was the incredulous "A *black female* was traumatized by something like that? A sister?" "A registered nurse couldn't handle seeing sex? You're a weak woman to let something like that freak you out." Occasionally, however, someone would say, "Not even one of those men objected? That's disgusting. You must have been horrified!"

After the incident, my husband and I had arguments about it. I felt alone, abandoned—as if no one, not even the person closest to me, understood. My husband was angry. He said things like "The white man has taken everything from me and now he's ruined my wife too." Despite counseling, my marriage ended in 1983. Following that, I was fired from my job. I lost my sense of well being and security; the ability to function in a normal way as a person, wife, mother; the ability to concentrate; my sense of being free, joyous, and happy; my marriage and sexual response and my home.

I was angry and traumatized by this incident and determined that these men would not get away with this. I spent ten years in litigation trying to bring them to justice. I sued Dick Stensrude, the CEO who had instigated the pornography movie. He was a trustee of St. Louis University Center, a board member of several hospitals, and a well-known and prosperous businessman. The case was David and Goliath all over. I didn't understand that the men, the hospital, and the university system would circle the wagons to protect Stensrude. I didn't realize that most lawyers would be afraid to take on an important businessman and top university administrator.

I brought a tort action for emotional distress against St. Louis University, the St. Louis University Medical Center, and Richard L. Stensrude, Jr., chief executive officer of the St. Louis Hospitals, charging that the defendants reck-lessly, intentionally, and willfully subjected me to emotional distress by showing me a pornographic film after representing to me that that film was educational and needed to be reviewed for business purposes. My lawyers argued that I suffered emotional shock and mental and physical embarrassment resulting in medical care and medical expenses and the loss of my job. They also argued that there was racial motivation in the incident, since I was black and the other five people attending the meeting were white male professionals. The trial court dismissed the suit on grounds that I had failed to state a claim, but the appeals court reversed that decision, and the case went to court. The trial was a kind of zoo. My attorney had to bring in psychiatrists to prove the claim of emotional distress, so the opposing side brought in psychiatrists too. Since I was suing a medical center, they had an arsenal of doctors testifying on their behalf. Their psychiatrists testified, after examining me for an hour, that I suffered from paranoid schizophrenia and therefore any "emotional distress" I might have had was not due to being forced to view this film with five white male administrators.

My attorney argued that I had successfully held a job for many years, had been married for thirteen years, was successfully raising a family, and had a family life "basically without problems" until the incident. We tried to explain to the jury my anger, rage, fear, and pain at being targeted by Dick Stensrude—that Stensrude obviously saw me as a sex object—as a female he could use for his sexual kicks. I recounted him shouting sexual obscenities to me in front of the other men while this film ran. I explained the rage and fear I felt when I realized what he had done to me and why. I described the resulting problems with my superiors, who just wanted me to shut up and not rock the boat—which, by the way, would have allowed Stensrude to force this movie upon yet another unsuspecting female sometime in the future. When I would not just keep quiet, I was fired. I described the turmoil it caused my family when I lost my $28,000 job—at that time very good money—the anger my husband had at me and at the situation, the sexual problems I had with my husband following my viewing part of the movie—the scenes of anal intercourse and group rape which kept recurring in my head every time we tried to make love—the anger and rage my husband had when I withdrew from physical intimacy. I described the atmosphere at work and home. But to no avail. The jury deliberated for several hours before denying me any damages. We later found out that over half of the jurors had already seen the film *as entertainment* before this case, so there was no way I got a fair and impartial hearing. If so many of the jurors saw a pornographic film as an evening's entertainment, they were probably going to be hard-pressed to understand the way the film was used to intimidate, humiliate, and harass me. We also had another problem common in small towns and cities: the judge, the judge's father, the judge's son, the opposing side's attorneys, and my attorney had all graduated from St. Louis University. SLU was a family tradition for the judge. In fact, there was a scholarship in his father's name at the university. The case should have been removed to another jurisdiction for a fair trial, but it was not.

After many years of litigation at the trial level, the court found the men not liable. I appealed, but I lost at the appellate level and was rejected for consideration by the Missouri State Supreme Court and the U.S. Supreme Court. I was forced to accept that as a woman and an African American, I do not enjoy the full protection of the law. After my loss at the state court level, I was contacted by women's groups, such as the National Organization for Women and Women Against Pornography. They, along with friends and new colleagues, have helped me to understand—and try to change—this system that denied me protection or redress.

ONE MAN'S DIGNITY
An Interview with Emmit E. Fisher

Richard Delgado

Emmit E. Fisher was the plaintiff in *Fisher* v. *Carrousel Motor Hotel* (424 S.W.2d 627), a landmark racial discrimination case. In 1965, Fisher, a black NASA mathematician, was attending an electronic equipment demonstration in Houston, Texas, when he was accosted by the white restaurant manager of the Brass Ring Club—a whites-only private club. While Fisher was waiting in the serving line, the manager snatched an empty plate from his hand and told him in a loud voice that he could not eat in the cafeteria. The plaintiff alleged that he was "highly embarrassed and hurt" by the manager's actions in the presence of Fisher's associates. The jury awarded him $900. The judge, however, denied him any recovery. The Texas Court of Appeals affirmed the trial court's decision. Fisher appealed once again and the Texas Supreme Court reversed, finding that the plaintiff could recover under the tort of assault and battery because the employee's seizure of the plate supplied the required offensive touching. The court further held that because battery law is designed to protect dignity as well as physical security, the plaintiff was not required to show physical harm to recover damages. This case is typical of a small number of early cases in which the court strained to find a cause of action for "words that wound."

■

RD: Tell me what you were doing at the meeting when the tort occurred.

EF: I was a mathematician working for NASA. I was attending a meeting sponsored by two vendors [Defense Electronics and Ampex Corporation] to hear presentations concerning electronic equipment they wanted to sell to the government. We met at the Carrousel Motor Hotel for the presentation, but we went to lunch at the restaurant in the Brass Ring Club, a private, for-whites-only club that was affiliated with the hotel.

RD: What happened at the restaurant?

EF: I was in the line with the other attendees waiting to be served. A waiter, who was African American, had just offered me hot soup, which I declined. Soon after that someone who turned out to be the manager of the restaurant came up and, without any warning, snatched the plate from my hand. Then, in a very harsh voice, he told me that they did not serve Negroes and I could not eat there.

RD: Then what happened?

EF: The whole place fell silent. You could hear a pin drop.

RD: Did anyone speak up for you?

EF: Yes, the host representatives and the club manager then engaged in a very heated argument, but to no avail. The club refused to apologize for the incident and insisted they would not serve me. There was one other person, who turned out to be a graduate student from Rice University, who became upset over the incident. He said, "If he can't eat here, then I won't either." I left the club and the two of us returned to the meeting room.

RD: Was the student white or black?

EF: He was white.

RD: And did he actually leave with you?

EF: Yes, we walked out together.

RD: Do you remember if you were the only black person in the restaurant at the time?

EF: Yes, I was, other than the waiters.

RD: Did you have any trouble getting a lawyer?

EF: I did. Most lawyers wouldn't take the case because they didn't think I had a chance of winning. Then I met Ben Levy, a civil rights attorney, who agreed to take the case.

RD: Did you have any difficulty deciding whether to seek legal relief?

EF: Not really. I'm a fighter, and what they did at the restaurant was wrong. Soon after the incident, I filed a grievance with NASA. The government investigated and found that there had been discrimination. Later, I learned that the government required firms who wanted to conduct demonstrations to the government to hold them in a government facility. But I never felt those two companies were at fault. They didn't check with the hotel and were caught off guard when the restaurant manager did what he did and refused to serve me.

RD: Tell me a little about the trial and your legal strategy.

EF: I brought a tort action for assault and battery by the hotel manager. In assault and battery you have to prove that you were assaulted and that you were damaged by the assault. This was not the average assault and battery case. I didn't testify that I was hit or punched or even actually touched. Nor did I testify that I feared that the manager was going to hurt me physically. These are the usual elements of assault and battery. Instead I testified that the manager yanked the plate forcibly from my hand and that I was embarrassed, humiliated, and hurt by his conduct in the presence of my associates. What was distinctive about my case was that the court held that I could claim damages for mental suffering due to unpermitted and intentional invasion of my "person," that is, my personal space. They also held that personal indignity is the essence of an action for battery and that the manager was liable for contact with me that was offensive or insulting. Thus the court recognized that the real pain I suffered wasn't the fact that the manager grabbed the plate out of my hand, but the fact that he embarrassed, humiliated, and insulted me based on my race.*

RD: Anything else you remember about the trial?

EF: Well, we had trouble getting people to testify. Only two people did, even though a room full of people saw what happened, including three of my coworkers who attended the meeting with me. They were in line directly behind me at the time of the incident, yet insisted they saw nothing, which is what they told the government investigators. The ones who agreed to testify were the Rice student and the black waiter. The waiter was so disgusted over the incident that he quit his job about a week later. Some time later, I was told that my case affected all hotels and businesses in the Houston area that catered to government meetings. Because this resulted in a loss of business, the Carrousel Hotel was blackballed by other hotels and eventually went out of business. Not only that, the manager who perpetrated this incident died of a heart attack a short time after our lawyers took depositions.

RD: Sounds like the other side's behavior brought them no good, either. What kind of jury did you have?

EF: It was all white. We had asked for $15,000. At first I wanted more, because I thought what the restaurant did was really outrageous. But Ben Levy convinced me that when we went to trial, it would most likely be an all-white jury, and, even if we won, an all-white jury was not going to give a Negro a large sum of money. He convinced me that by asking for this smaller amount, it became more likely that the jury would

---

* This case is one of the earliest cases in which the court recognized that words can harm, and that the harm is serious enough to warrant damages. Compare this case to the research in Ehrlich, Larcom, and Purvis's piece, "The Traumatic Impact of Ethnoviolence," p. 62, this volume, in which the authors document the negative effects of hate speech.—Eds.

find for us. They would see that we were in it not to make money but to vindicate principle.

RD: How did you feel when the incident happened? And how did you feel when the jury found in your favor?

EF: At the restaurant, I was shocked and mad. After hearing the verdict I felt better. However, when they awarded me only $900, I was quite disappointed. Then two weeks later, the judge overturned the jury's ruling—something I didn't know could happen. I was perturbed. That's when we decided to appeal. The Texas Court of Appeals affirmed the judge's decision, so we appealed again. The Texas Supreme Court reversed and gave a ruling that attracted national attention—that assault and battery charges were designed to protect dignity too.

RD: What happened at work?

EF: For days afterward, I was a celebrity. People would parade by my office, looking in, stopping and staring. Eventually, I closed the door. Later, my performance ratings began to drop no matter how good my work was. I had a difficult time with some of my white coworkers. It was a very difficult time for me at work during that period. That included being given bottom-of-the-barrel assignments. Most of my black friends and coworkers supported me; most of the others didn't. Many of the NASA employees never really forgave me for filing the complaint and for years after still made demeaning remarks about the lawsuit.

After I won in the state supreme court, it was on the national news, and I received calls from people all around the nation. Later, when my case hit the casebooks, law students, law professors, and others around the country began calling. I get calls from time to time even now.

RD: Did your lawyer experience any repercussions?

EF: I heard that some other local lawyers gave him a hard time.

RD: Did the restaurant or hotel ever apologize to you or admit wrongdoing?

EF: Not at all.

RD: Did you ever have any doubts about what you did?

EF: Never. I'm a cantankerous, strong-willed kind of person. I'd do it all over again, if I had to.

THE CASE OF THE CROSS-BURNING
An Interview with Russ and Laura Jones

Laura J. Lederer

On June 20, 1990, six young white men burned a cross on the lawn of Russ and Laura Jones, the only black family on the block in the overwhelmingly white east side of St. Paul. They were charged with violating a 1982 ordinance that barred the display, on public or private property, of any "symbol, object, appellation, characterization or graffiti, including but not limited to a burning cross or Nazi swastika, which one knows or has reasonable grounds to know arouses anger, alarm or resentment in others on the basis of race, color, creed, religion or gender." The case, known as *R.A.V.* v. *St. Paul*, went to the United States Supreme Court, where a five-justice majority, led by Antonin Scalia, declared the ordinance unconstitutional. In this interview, Russ and Laura Jones describe their experiences and reactions in the wake of the cross-burning.

■

LJL: Tell me what led to R.A.V. v. *St. Paul.*

LJ: We had lived in a part of St. Paul that was considered the black neighborhood. In 1990, we moved to a part of St. Paul that was infamous in the black community. It was considered the "white" part of town, mainly working-class white. Even though a few blacks had recently begun to move in, Russ didn't want to move there.

LJL: Why not?

RJ: I had always lived in St. Paul. I grew up here. When you're involved in sports, you get a feel for all the areas of the city. The atmosphere in the east side of St. Paul was clear—the students didn't like black folks. There was always an attitude—a "We're going to beat these kids" type of thing. They made the games competitive in a racial kind of way. As the years went by we saw more black kids play on the east side teams, but every so often we still heard on the news that some racist graffiti had been spray painted on a fence or a house—nothing big—just enough to tell you that there were still problems. We liked the houses in the east side neighborhood, and our house was situated on the very edge of the area, so my wife convinced me that we wouldn't have a problem.

LJ: But within the first month of living here our tires were slashed. At the time we thought it was just random vandalism. We didn't think too much of it until the second incident.

RJ: The next month, I bought a new station wagon. I parked it out in front of the house a couple days later and that night the tailgate window was smashed. One of the police officers who took the report mentioned that there were some skinheads in the area who'd been causing trouble.

LJL: Did you ever catch the people who broke the tailgate window?

RJ: No. There were no witnesses. The police took the report and told us that they could do nothing unless we had more information or evidence. A couple of weeks after that, we were going out to a meeting with our children. I had just come out the front door when we saw three teenagers on the sidewalk. We started walking down the sidewalk toward the car and as we passed them, one of them said to my son, "What are you looking at, nigger?" At first my wife didn't believe my son when he told her what they said, but I had heard him too and I told her, "Yes that's what they said, all right." After that we became more aware of what was going on around us.

Then, on the night of June 20, just about three months after we had moved into the house, we were lying in bed when we heard several kids outside the house. There were some young people in a car on the corner having car trouble. They were quite loud for a few hours. While trying to sleep we noticed their voices seemed to be getting closer to the house. Then, along with what sounded like hushed voices inside our fenced yard, we also heard footsteps. It sounded as if people were running away from the house. Even though we were half asleep, it was the footsteps that got us up, not their voices. I opened my eyes and saw this unnatural glow in the window. I thought, "Oh no—now they've set the car on fire!" When I got over to the window I couldn't believe my eyes: there was a large cross burning right there in my yard.

LJL: How did you feel at that moment?

RJ: I felt a combination of anger and fear. At first I felt anger—like someone had violated me—my space—like they were challenging me. Then I thought of my family sleeping in the next rooms and I felt fear. I was going to go out there and confront whoever was threatening us, but that would have been a pretty stupid thing to do.

LJ: We called the police and they responded in about ten minutes. We heard later that someone else drove by the house, stopped, looked at the cross burning there, and then drove around the corner and called the police, too. When the police came, we went outside. Some of the neighbors were out too. They were appalled that this was happening in their neighborhood and wanted to help. When they arrived, the police themselves didn't seem to know what to do. They seemed shocked by the cross, but after asking the usual questions, they packed up to leave saying they didn't have any suspects because there were no witnesses.

LJL: What about the cross itself? Did they take that as evidence?

RJ: No. I asked them what to do about it, and they said, "Throw it away." I didn't even want to touch it, but I had to take it apart myself and throw it in the back by the trash cans, still smoldering.

LJ: After they left we stayed up for a while. At about 4:20 a.m. after going back to bed we saw another fire across the street. They had come back and lit another cross in front of the apartment building across from us! We felt very vulnerable. We were the only black family there, and because our house is on the corner, we felt like we were sitting out in the open.

LJL: How were those responsible caught?

LJ: One of them, Robert Viktora [R.A.V. in the Supreme Court case] started bragging to his friends about what he had done. Apparently someone overheard him and turned him and his friends in—five of them in all. It was all done anonymously.

LJL: When you heard they had caught him, did you want to prosecute? How did you decide on the legal strategy you would take?

RJ: We didn't decide. The county prosecutor talked to us and told us that he would be prosecuting them under the new St. Paul Hate and Bias Crime Ordinance. But when I heard that bias crimes were only misdemeanors, I didn't want to take that route. I wanted them prosecuted under terrorist threats, which is a felony. But the prosecutor had his mind made up.

After that everything turned into a circus. It seemed like the violation to our family was pushed to the back burner, and the entire case was focused on this skinhead's "free speech" right to burn a cross in our yard. We were hounded by the media, who twisted our words to fit their purpose. I can't tell you how many interviews I did with reporters in which I explained what had happened to us, and how we felt, and then saw on the evening news a chopped-up, edited version of the interview which completely misrepresented our position.

A *Life* magazine article made it seem like the kid who burned the cross was the victim, instead of presenting him as he was—a criminal who had terrorized our family. Being minorities, and also Jehovah's Witnesses, we are of course tremendous believers in the First Amendment. We couldn't believe it when we were characterized as against freedom of speech—as if burning a cross on our front lawn was free speech! For us, it wasn't an issue of freedom of speech. As far as we were concerned this was a violation of our rights as citizens of the United States. The Constitution should protect us from violence, terrorism, and prejudice. All we wanted was for this criminal to be shown that he and his friends had done something wrong—that they had threatened us and should be punished for it. But the media and others used *R.A.V.* to push their own agenda about the First Amendment. They tried to turn the criminal into the hero—focusing on his rights to the exclusion of ours. It made me really mad. And when the Supreme Court decision was announced, we felt disappointed. It was as if the Court was saying "Of course, we don't condone cross-burning, *but . . .*" It almost seemed to be saying, "Well, it's okay to burn crosses on black people's lawns."

LJ: No one seemed to care what the message of the cross-burning was, or what effect it had on us. When I saw that cross burning on our lawn, I thought of the stories my grandparents told about living in the South and being intimidated by white people. When a cross was burned down there they either meant to harm you or to put you in your place. It was a clear threat. So for us the Court's decision was more than disappointing. We almost felt like there was some kind of conspiracy—it was as if the Ramsey County prosecutor didn't really care about the actual crimes that had been committed, or about convicting those teenagers. His main concern seemed to be going to the Supreme Court with this case. Otherwise we felt he would have chosen a different legal strategy, prosecuted under other laws—like terroristic threats.*

RJ: You should have seen how excited they were. This was their Super Bowl—that's how they talked about it, as if it were a big game they were preparing for. They kept saying that arguing before the Supreme Court was a once in a lifetime opportunity.

LJ: It almost seemed like the prosecutor and the defense attorney were using our case in order to make names for themselves. After we lost the case in the Supreme Court, that was it. The prosecutor never bothered to try to get Viktora on any other grounds.

---

* See "The Prosecutor's Dilemma," this volume, p. 194, for an explanation of why the prosecutor chose the legal strategy he did. —Eds.

LJL: When the case was over what did you do?

RJ: We were relieved that the circus was over. Our lives had been interrupted. Our children were afraid. We wanted to try to repair the damage,
to get our lives back to normal. But it was impossible. The skinheads
wouldn't let us alone. Now we started to see them gathering right across
the street from our house. They did it blatantly, even tauntingly, flaunt-
ing it in our faces—as if to say, "We won. We can do whatever we
want to." They were letting us know that even the Supreme Court was
going to protect them.

LJ: They had a rally on one sunny Sunday afternoon, wearing their masks,
wielding their baseball bats and clubs, waving their Confederate flags.
They absolutely terrified us and the neighbors. It was awful. I felt trapped
in my own home. We didn't go anywhere because I would have had
to face them and could never tell what they would do. That evening I
had a coworker pick me up for work. A couple of times we called the
police, but they just said, "We'll keep an eye on them." Before the
Supreme Court decision the skinheads were anonymous—we had never
really seen them. But afterward, they were right in our faces. And you
could see the hate in their eyes.

RJ: So I decided we had to do something—otherwise these people were
going to drive us out of our own home. When an attorney with the
Justice Department called me and asked if we wanted them to prosecute
under federal civil rights laws, we said yes. They charged the three
skinheads with a violation of our civil rights. Within a couple of months
they had convictions for all five of them. Since they were juveniles,
they were sent to the workhouse. Viktora got twenty-seven months. The
others got one year to eighteen months.

LJ: This was what we had wanted all along. We just wanted them convicted
for the crimes they had committed. The convictions themselves produced the biggest message: after that the skinheads stopped gathering
across from our house. They knew if they threatened us, they would go
to jail.

LJL: If you had it to do over again, would you?

RJ: Yes, we would. But we wouldn't let the media take advantage of us like
they did.

LJL: What advice do you have for others who might find themselves in similar
situations?

RJ: Take whatever legal means necessary, but don't allow yourself and your
family to be drawn into the middle of a media circus.

LIKE A SMACK IN THE FACE
Pornography in the Trades

Barbara Trees

In 1990 the New York City Human Rights Commission held hearings on sex and race discrimination in the New York City building trades. Barbara Trees helped organize those hearings in the hope that they would lead to public acknowledgment of the plight of tradeswomen. Forty women and people of color testified about their treatment. A major point of the testimony was that pornography is used as a weapon to push women out of the trades.

■

I want to tell you a bit about myself and construction work because most people who don't work in construction have no idea what it's like. I am a carpenter in New York City. I applied to the Carpenters' Union in 1978 and began my four-year apprenticeship in 1980. I am college educated and was thirty years old at the time. There were maybe ten women—tops—and 20,000 men in the union at the time.

I wanted to be a carpenter because it was daring, well paid, and out of the mainstream. I thought women merely had to prove we could do the work and then many more women would join us.

It made perfect sense to see the building trades as a great opportunity for women to achieve equality with men. Jobs were available, and the apprenticeships were open to people with limited educations. But, in spite of the possibilities, this field has not really opened up for women. And the mistreatment of women in construction is a horror story which has not been adequately told.

A woman who is sent to a job at a construction site can usually expect to be the only one on a crew of hundreds of men. For the first five or six years I went through the motions of fitting in. I guess we all did, we "first women." It was so very important to get along. The job sites were dirty and dangerous and the work was hard; we all got the difficult jobs, not the "tit" jobs, as easy work is called. The men we were supposed to learn the trade from usually had no intention of teaching us. They thought it was the most preposterous thing that women actually wanted to do this work.

These men found ways to push us out, and they were *not* nice about it. They were scary and belligerent and did not want "girls" around (the lone woman on a job or crew is always called "the girl"). The atmosphere was and is horrible. There is filthy language. There is total contempt for women and wives. The men piss and shit out in the open and on the floor instead of in toilets. Women are given the worst jobs to do, made to work alone at a job two or three men would do, and laid off first without cause. There are no changing facilities or bathrooms with locks for women. The men use binoculars to look for women in nearby buildings, and when they spot one in a bathroom or undressed, they yell, "There's one, there's one!" In addition to all this harassment, physical violence is common. I know of several women who were hit or punched by fellow construction workers, and nothing was done about it.

Pornography is commonplace on construction jobs. You see it in the locker rooms; on drinking fountains, on and inside lunchboxes, on and inside toolboxes, on tools, on walls in management, union, and other offices. It is often posted on job sites or on half-constructed buildings. I found it humiliating. I began to avoid areas where I found it and tore it down when I saw it. After that, it had a funny way of showing up where I was working or walking—just one little dirty picture, like a smack in the face—and nobody around to take the credit. The men feel they have an absolute right to display these pictures. It is very risky to complain about pornography in the construction industry. You can get harassed. You can get hurt. You can get fired, and once fired, you have no recourse. The contractor does not have to say why you were fired. The union stewards don't want to hear about it. There is no grievance procedure. I was fired from a job after politely asking a foreman to remove a beaver shot from our shanty, but only found out a year later that that was why I was fired.* But losing your job is not the only threat. The mafia, some of whom deal in prostitution and pornography, lurk everywhere. Most of us who are activists have nightmares about construction workers chopping our doors down to get into our homes. We fear for our lives.

Many women in the trades try to ignore the pornography, but I could not do that and survive. I had listened to filthy woman-hating "jokes," had co-

---

* See Dorchen Leidholdt, "Pornography in the Workplace," in this volume, p. 216, for other stories about how men use pornography to harass and intimidate women in the workplace.

workers "accidentally" touch my breasts or ass, and put up with the idea of women as funny—the mere mention of breasts or anything about women's bodies bringing smirks. I just couldn't take it anymore.

So I got sick, quite seriously sick, and stayed out of work for two years. For women, this is not an uncommon reaction to these pressures in the non-traditional work world. But during the time I was ill, I thought about the situation, and when I went back I vowed that I would practice pro-woman self-defense. It worked. It gave me a sense of entitlement—to dignity, to the job, to fight for the women in my union as if we are the most important people on earth. It meant that I refused to listen to men bad-mouthing women, that I took these "jokes" and remarks for the insults they were, and that I responded accordingly.

In 1989, I founded New York Tradeswomen, a support group for women in the building trades. We formed a Women Carpenters Committee in the New York City District Council. I was appointed a shop steward in my local union in 1990, the first woman in my 2,000-member local to hold this position. As a steward, the union representative for the carpenters on a particular job site, I've battled pornography for the last three years. The union office gave me the protection to fight it and not be fired. But I still have problems. I've had long pornographic phone messages placed on my answering machine from men who boasted of being in my local. I've had a contractor tell me to go fuck myself when I asked him to remove the pornography from the trailer where, as a steward, I had to go to call my union. I told a teamster that I wouldn't hang a door in his shanty until he removed a nude picture. Later he chased me around waving a nude picture, yelling, "This is beautiful, this is good!" Once a pornographic picture showed up on the cooler. I saw it and took off my hard hat and bashed the closest guy to me over the head with it and said, "Is that yours?!" He may not even have put it there, but I didn't care, I was so mad. When I asked a tin knocker to simply turn his large toolbox, which was covered with beaver shots, away from the door so that I wouldn't have to see them, he accused me of being ridiculous and said that I should know better, that these pictures are everywhere, that this is the way it is in the construction industry, that I had to fit in, and that I would be to blame if he got fired over something so "minor." After I complained to union officials, this same guy followed me, glaring, to the subway.

I thought that women could change these job sites, but so far we haven't. There aren't enough of us, and the men are picking us off, one by one, both the weak and the strong. Using pornography and other forms of sexual harassment, men have successfully kept women out of construction in any significant numbers. Now that the recession has hit, we are devastated.

BIBLE BELT LESBIANS FIGHT HATE

Wanda Henson

What happens when a committed lesbian couple settle near a small traditional Mississippi farming community? Wanda Henson recounts the har-
rowing experiences she and her partner Brenda have endured in Ovett,
Mississippi. Their story demonstrates a common pattern in which verbal
harassment—name-calling, use of symbols, threats and hate speech—is
combined with physical harassment—assault, vandalism, attempted
murder—in order to intimidate, harm, and, in this case, drive out those
targeted.

■

Brenda and I have been a committed couple in love almost since the day we
met. Our life's work is to take care of ourselves, to take care of each other, to
take care of the earth. We have never turned our heads the other way when
faced with adversity, no matter how great.

In 1989, we founded an IRS-recognized, all-volunteer non-profit charitable
organization named Sister Spirit Incorporated. Our fourth project, now in the
development stage, is Camp Sister Spirit, a feminist educational and cultural
retreat center. After fundraising for four years and searching for land for two,
we finally found 120 acres of cut-over land, with six buildings in need of
extensive repair, five soil types, and water, all for the price of $60,000. It was
an incredible buy, and only a few miles from the Mississippi coast.

Being a native of Mississippi and having lived on the coast my entire life, I
was reluctant to move from where I was. Southerners teach their children,
"Don't fall far from the tree." The land in Jones County was perfect: not too
far from the coast and five miles out from Ovett. Rural, peaceful, and serene:
a dream come true. On July 29, 1993, we signed the papers and began to
develop the land.

On November 8, Andrea [Brenda's daughter by birth] received a phone call
from the post office. The mail carrier said he would not deliver our mail
because there was a dead dog on the mailbox. Andrea walked down to see. A
female dog had been shot once in the abdomen and was draped across the

mailbox; two sanitary napkins were attached to its side; a nine-millimeter bullet hole was shot through the mailbox. The message was clear: *die bitches*. The sheriff's deputy who investigated found two gun shell casings on the ground and took them as evidence. He asked if there were "any blacks in your organization."

For three days we talked about the meaning behind the dead dog. If the perpetrator could kill a dog for the sole purpose of frightening us, what else would he do? All my life I have been a committed pacifist. But three days later, we purchased a rifle, prepared to fight back if necessary. We are not violent people, but we will defend ourselves.

We were contacted by a representative of a local TV station, who informed us they had received our newsletter, *The Grapevine*, anonymously in the mail. We were later told the newsletter had been altered and was being passed out in grocery store parking lots and churches for miles around. We had sent the newsletter only to our organization's volunteers, but anyone else could have gotten one just by reaching into our mailbox and taking one that had been returned. We had already gotten back several in the mail from women who had moved. We went on the radio immediately in an attempt to explain to the public who we are and to head off the fury. We were not surprised when we began to see the local paper printing letters to the editor about the lesbians coming to town. The sheriff's deputy was quoted in the newspaper as saying we were "filth" and "all your violent crimes are committed by homosexuals." Most of the newspapers misquoted or oversimplified what was happening to us. We began to receive harassing phone calls. Our appeals to the sheriff met with snickers.

A few weeks later, we received an announcement that there was to be a town meeting to explore ways to "run us off our land." When we called the sheriff, he assured us he was going to tell those at the meeting, "The Hensons are American citizens. They have the right to be here and I must enforce the law." We later found out that he actually said, "I support y'all [what is now called Mississippi for Family Values] 100 percent, but I must uphold the law."

After the meeting, we received a call from a former participant in our educational programs who had gone to see what these people were saying. She was in tears, and said she was terrified for our lives. She begged us to leave the area for our own safety, saying in all her life she had never been in such a hate-filled space as she had at that meeting. She had heard some of the men at the meeting say it was "time to get out the white sheets again."

The next hours and days confirmed her fears, as we watched and read news accounts of the meeting. We stared in disbelief at the angry faces on the TV screen as they called us "satan" and spoke of possible attempts by us to "convert our women into lesbians" and to "take our little girls" and do God knows what to them.

We began to see more and more angry faces as we went to town. Children screamed "faggots" at us as their school bus drove by. The driver blew the horn in seeming agreement with the children, teaching them hate on their way home from school. At the grocery store cashiers peered around their registers and bag-boys giggled. The women at the local general store were careful not to touch us when giving back our change. The friendly smiles and questions given to most newcomers were gone. In the following months we were called "cuntlickers," "cracksmackers," "lesbos," "devil worshippers," "faggots," and "worthy of death." A billboard went up at the end of our road overnight saying "Lickersville" with a picture of a man with his tongue hanging out.

There were only three of us on the land at the time. We stayed up as late as we could every night, then went to bed praying for morning. Each morning as we opened our eyes, we smiled: we had made it through another night! Concerned neighbors began phoning to warn us of plans to burn us out, to kill us, and to scare the hell out of us. Some callers gave names, some identified themselves as "someone in Ovett" or "someone at the power station."

We were shot at on several occasions, and heard shots fired on a regular basis just outside our property. We found large square-headed nails—but only after they had disabled eight vehicles—that someone had poured in our drive-way, and we found men with guns trespassing on our land. Planes flew low over our property so the pilots could photograph us. Explosions shook our buildings three times in one night, and people came to the edge of our property and yelled obscenities and made lewd gestures. We received two bomb threats through local radio stations, a death threat on the phone, and a bomb threat in the mail. Someone even threatened to shoot our dog.

A second town meeting was held where the terrible *Gay Agenda* film [a religious-right propaganda piece] was shown to further incite the hate and prejudice against us. A woman who said she was a member of Concerned Women of America pointed her finger directly at us and warned, "There is nothing to protect you!" We will never forget the menacing look on her face.

We live in fear such as we have never known before. All the other caretakers on the land have pledged that if something happens to one of us, the others will stay and fight. We are now beginning to get support from around the world in donations and well wishes from the lesbian and gay community and human rights allies. People are coming to the land to help build fences and walls and install lights and alarms.

Laws must be enacted to protect the lives and dignity of gays and lesbians.

We have a right to love and to live in partnership with those we love. We have a right to live our lives in freedom. We want an end to the hate and vitriol that gays and lesbians are subjected to all over this country. We want equal rights and civil rights as citizens of this great nation. Nothing more and nothing less.

DESECRATION IN DARKNESS

Marshall Levin

In 1982, Shaare Tefila, a Jewish congregation in Silver Spring, Maryland, filed suit against eight men for defacing its synagogue walls with huge paintings of anti-Semitic symbols, slogans, and pictures. Marshall Levin, at that time the executive director of the synagogue, championed an unusual community action and a unique lawsuit which called attention not only to the desecration, but also to the congregation's precedent-setting response to the crime.

■

On the night of November 1, 1982, the eve of Election Day that year, I was attending the monthly meeting of the congregation's Board of Directors at Shaare Tefila synagogue in Silver Spring, Maryland. Religious school classes were going on that same evening, so there had been a great deal of activity in the building until about 9 p.m. The board meeting continued from 8 p.m. until a little past 11 p.m., at which time I went back to my office with one of the custodians. As was customary, he went outside to check the building before locking it for the night. After making his rounds, he came back in to get me. He was visibly shaken and could hardly speak to describe what he had seen.

The president of the congregation and I went outside with him and, one by one, we discovered half a dozen seven-foot-tall murals spray painted in red enamel on various panels of the building's white walls, each defacement more detailed and ominous than the last. There were a huge swastika, a skull and crossbones, a flaming cross, an American Nazi eagle, and anti-Semitic slogans [such as "death to the Jude"] in both English and German. Around the back of the synagogue, on the door that was used by our nursery children to enter the outdoor play area, we found the most frightening slogan of all, "TAKE A SHOWER, JEW," painted in large block letters that spanned the full height and width of the door, with an accompanying graphic picture of a gas chamber.

Immediately we went back inside and called the rabbi of the congregation to join us in deciding what next steps we should take. While waiting for the rabbi, it occurred to me that if the building had been defaced, perhaps cars in the synagogue's parking lot may also have been sprayed. In fact, we did find that one car had been spray painted with a swastika, and the owner of that car was deeply afraid for himself and his family because the parking lot had been filled to capacity and yet his was the only car defaced. "Is this a personal message?" he wondered. "Why have I been targeted?"

Decisive action needed to be taken immediately. The next day was Election Day, and polling machines were due to arrive at the synagogue by 6 a.m. because the congregation served as a public polling station. Soon after daybreak the synagogue would be a hotbed of activity. People would discover and be frightened, perhaps traumatized, by the shocking defacement. Should we leave it up or take it down before anyone could see it?

First, we would need to notify the police. As far as we knew, never before had murals of this magnitude or sophistication been seen in a public act of defacement anywhere in America. Clearly, this was not just some childish prank or amateur act. The Ku Klux Klan had just been denied permission to stage a march in Washington, D.C., and we thought that perhaps we had been chosen to serve as the KKK's billboard for the nation. Several weeks earlier, the Anti-Defamation League of B'nai B'rith contacted all Washington-area synagogues to say that the KKK and several international terrorist organizations were threatening to target synagogues and national Jewish organizations during the High Holy Day season of that fall. The Anti-Defamation League sent a formal, though unpublicized, set of instructions advising that if there were any crimes against property (as distinct from crimes against persons) such as incidents of defacement or other vandalism to buildings, the graffiti should be removed immediately. They reasoned that we did not want to spur crimes of imitation, or give free publicity to the hate mongers. Thus, they urged everyone to take quick action to remove the evidence and downplay the issue, indeed to literally make the problem disappear.

We disagreed with this policy. I felt that this was a crime against the whole community, not just against our synagogue, nor even just against Jewish people. I argued that this desecration would offend the moral sensibilities of everyone, and that rather than hiding it or making it seem as though we bore any responsibility for it being there—as if we had brought it on ourselves—we should leave it up, call attention to it, and enlist the help of the larger community.

In any event, by the time the defacement had been discovered and our small decision-making group had convened, it was after midnight. If we were going to have people come on an emergency basis and sandblast through the night, we would have to call them right away. After much discussion, the other members of our small group agreed with me and we decided that, instead of sandblasting the defacement away in the dark of night, we would devise a plan to invite the community and the media to join the children of our congregation to remove the spray-painted slogans and pictures on the coming Sunday morning. We decided that we would roll up our sleeves, take buckets and scrub brushes, and—led by our children—hundreds of people would wipe away in daylight what a handful of people had put there in darkness.

We knew that the message of the perpetrators was, "You should fear us, whoever we are and wherever we are, because we know who you are and we know where you live. We can find you in your homes. And if you think that Hitler will not be granted any posthumous victories, you are wrong. We are still alive and you will never be safe from us." This message was not directed solely at Jews; it was also directed at African Americans, because there were symbols and words about Aryan power and the KKK on our synagogue. I am sure that the perpetrators intended to instill a sense of fear, not only among the members of our congregation, but also throughout the community at large. People tend to individualize feelings of fear because they feel personally violated, personally vulnerable. When we feel most intimidated, we feel most isolated. Isolating us is a key part of the hate mongers' plan.

There was also fear that this may not have been the act of a single person, but that there was actually a militant gang out there—an army of racist vigilantes who might return and escalate their crime by causing physical harm to the children and adults of our congregation. Members of the congregation felt that we had been targeted—not just as a billboard for hate messages, but as the next victims, the next casualties. People were saying, "How could they do this and leave the scene undetected?"; "We were in the building; what if they had come in and attacked us?"; "They know who and where we are, and we don't even know who they are"; "This is our place of worship, a place to gather and be with God. If we aren't safe here, how can we be safe anywhere?"

We wanted to express these fears, to discuss them, to communicate them to our neighborhood friends. I believed that doing this would be like turning on giant floodlights around the building. When hate mongers realize they're in bright light, that they can be seen, they scurry—like cockroaches—for cover. They don't even venture out anymore.

So we convened meetings and discussion groups within the congregation during that week. I led a series of leadership training workshops to ensure that the members of the congregation did not feel more threatened than necessary, that they understood our plan of positive response, and that each of us would give the right message to the public via the media. We met with children from three years old (in our nursery school) up through high school age (in our religious school). We also met with the older people in our congregation, including a number of survivors of Nazi Europe and the Holocaust, to reassure them of their safety. If *The Price We Pay* had been on the shelves at that time, we would surely have used it as a text during that week. We knew that national attention would focus on our synagogue once the media learned of the incident, and we wanted our members to transform this horrible event into a positive learning experience for themselves and for people in communities across the country.

When the media called, we were ready for them. They came because, after voting, people called them, and, as we knew it would, the word spread like wildfire. They wanted to turn the incident into an "anti-Semitism and racism on the rise" story and sensationalize it. But we felt it important to frame the story, not from their point of view, but from ours. I asked them to agree that if they came now, they had to come back on Sunday, since we knew that we wanted the story to focus on the community's response to the problem. One by one they agreed.

At the time, our decision to leave the defacement in place did not seem so momentous, but later we discovered that we were the first congregation in the United States not to withdraw and turn inward. The next day on local radio and television, reporters invited the whole community to come and express their outrage. And they did. We had over a thousand people at the synagogue on Sunday. We had media coverage by local, regional, and national news, as well as by German television and Soviet, French, and Israeli newspapers. A week later, the Anti-Defamation League and B'nai B'rith changed their official policy on desecration and defacing of synagogues. Our action had changed the way religious groups respond to hate violence in the U.S.

Many good things happened as a result of our decision to leave the slogans up. After the story appeared on television, a tipster fund was set up by the Montgomery County Council to reward anyone who came forward with a tip. Shortly after, the police did get a lead that ultimately led to the arrest of seven of the eight men involved. The eighth man was never apprehended. The police believe he fled to somewhere in Europe.

We wanted to use the incident as an educational tool, so, in concert with the Human Relations Commission and several other organizations, we assisted in launching Sensitivity Awareness Symposium (SAS) Day. The County Council, Human Relations Commission, and the Montgomery County public schools put SAS Day into every Montgomery County school to teach children and teens that there is a real "price we pay" for inaction and to show them the gains we made individually and communally by initiating positive action. In addition to visiting the schools, we also spoke at local community meetings.

We wrote and produced a documentary film about the event, including interviews with County Council members, congregation members, clergymen, police officers, community members, congressional representatives, and children. The film has since won an international award and has become a valuable action catalyst for communities under siege. We attempted to cast everything in the following light: that good can come out of evil. As Mike Barnes, congressional representative of Silver Spring, said, "The people who did this didn't intend to do a favor for the community, but it was a wake-up call and a rallying point for the community." It was a shocking act which galvanized them to positive action. So the memory of this incident is now not just what the criminals did, but, more important, what the community did in response.

When one of the congregation members who was a Holocaust survivor said that the major difference between the U.S. and Nazi Germany during World War II is that now there are laws on the books that we can use to protect us, we decided to press legal charges against the perpetrators. It became apparent to us that the absence of legal recourse in pre–World War II Germany may have been a fateful factor in the unbridled Holocaust that followed. Once we decided to press charges, we were surprised to find that actions like this had never been successfully litigated before in this country. Apparently Jewish people had turned to the courts before for protection, but because Judaism is, strictly speaking, a religion and not a race, we are not covered under general civil rights legislation. We filed a landmark lawsuit in Baltimore federal court seeking damages from the eight men under an 1866 civil rights law. The law is a post–Civil War race-discrimination statute which provides, among other things, that "all persons within the jurisdiction of the United States shall have the same right in every State and Territory to the full and equal benefit of all laws and proceedings for the security of persons and property as is enjoyed by white citizens."

Our attorneys argued that while Jews do not regard themselves as a separate race, the perpetrators of the vandalism perceived us as "racially distinct," and were motivated by "racial animus," and therefore the statute should focus on the motivations and perceptions of the perpetrators rather than on the vandalism. Some said, "How can you figure out what is in the minds of the perpetrators? How will you be able to prove that their actions were motivated by racial animus?" But the court held that we could prove racial animus through the drawings, symbols, and words scrawled on our synagogue. For example, the perpetrators left the slogan "Toten, Kampf, Verband" on one wall. This translates as "The Skull Association" and was the slogan of the Waffen SS in Nazi Germany, who were directly responsible for the murder of many Jewish people; it helped us prove that this had been a planned, premeditated event. Clearly, there was substantial historic knowledge on the part of these hate mongers, a historic knowledge that arose from extreme animus against the Jewish people.

We asked for compensatory and other damages, but we agreed from the beginning that any money above the $3,000 it would take to remove the slogans and pictures from the walls would be given to the Montgomery County Human Relations Commission.

I believe that Shaare Tefila illustrates a congregation chosen, through no action of its own, to play an important role in history. The congregation certainly did not realize the significance of their decision about how to handle the incident until after they had taken the action. We had a unique collection of people there at that time who were able to make innovative, against-the-current decisions and to see them through. The congregation stayed together through the entire series of events which followed the incident. The incident happened on November 1, 1982. The film was completed in 1984. The Supreme Court agreed to hear the case in 1986, and decided in our favor in 1989, when the justices unanimously held that the real issue at stake is the nature of prejudice, and awarded us damages.

Looking back now, it is gratifying to see that our actions, undertaken without any guarantee of success or long-term impact, changed the way that many communities deal with hate-motivated speech, violence, and vandalism. If I had to choose the one aspect of which I feel most proud, it would be the community-affirming lesson and legacy, both moral and legal, that the Shaare Tefila response has left for our children.

INDIANS ARE A PEOPLE, NOT MASCOTS

Fred Veilleux

Fred Veilleux, a member of the Leech Lake band of the Chippewa Indians, located in Minnesota, relates how he became engaged in the Native American effort to eliminate the use of Indian mascots and team names at educational institutions and in the professional sports world.

■

In 1987, a colleague of mine, Phil St. John, a Dakota from Sessiton, South Dakota, who now lives and works in the Twin Cities, attended a high school basketball game with his family. During the game, a match between the Southwest High School Indians and the Osseo High School Orioles, a white student paraded around wearing his version of Indian dress and regalia with painted face and headband, acting out his version of how an American Indian behaves, all presumably to show school spirit.

Phil and I worked together at a community clinic located in the heart of the urban Indian community in Minneapolis. Upon arriving at work the next day Phil told me how the Southwest student's behavior had caused his eight-year-old son to shrink down behind him in humiliation. Phil stated that he himself didn't know how to deal with it and concluded that there's no reason why we should have to deal with it. The sight of this war-whooping student-fan struck him as mockery of his ethnicity and religious beliefs.

He asked if I would help him compose a letter to send to the school and the Minneapolis School Board, demanding that the school change its team name. Phil and I and a third friend presented our case before the board. It took two months to convince them to change the name (they are now called the Southwest High Lakers). It was at this point that Phil founded the Concerned American Indian Parents organization. We then decided to take this issue to the Minnesota State Board of Education and confront the remaining fifty schools that use Indian names or characters for their mascots, names like "Chiefs," "Braves," "Redmen," "Redskins." We argued that "Indian" is clearly the name of a race group and, while it may be neutral in some cases, when it is used as a team mascot, it is degrading and exploitive.

To help educators acquire a perspective on this issue, we reviewed a little U.S. history. For example, it was not at all uncommon for early American writers to denigrate the Indian people by calling them "heathens," "savages," and "cannibals" in order to lend Christian justification to the genocide of Indian people. Making the indigenous people less than human helped make killing them seem to be no more than killing wild animals. When Europeans first came to the shores of Indian country some 500 years ago, the estimated population of Indian people in this land, now called the United States, was 15 million. By 1900, it was 250,000. The majority of lives lost were due to diseases brought here by Europeans, ones for which Indian people had no immunity, such as smallpox, bubonic plague, tuberculosis, malaria, yellow fever, and influenza, but there is historical evidence that the U.S. Cavalry deliberately provided Indian people with blankets that were infested with small-pox. The white man's relentless hunger for Indian land and westward expansion threatened the lives and way of life of the Indian people. The Indian people bravely defended their homelands against this Euro-American invasion in bat-tles at Sand Creek, Washita, and Wounded Knee—all massacres of Indians. Yet it is the Indians who are characterized as warlike aggressors. This false characterization is one of the factors we are fighting against in the mascot issue.

Consider, for example, the origin of the term "redskin." Many colonial leaders followed an express policy of extermination. General George Wash-ington wrote a letter ordering his men to clear the New England area of its Indian population by killing as many of them as possible. In 1755, his excel-lency, William Shirly, esquire, captain general and governor in chief of the province of Massachusetts Bay, issued a proclamation promoting the murdering of American Indians, and placing bounties on their heads, scalps, and skin. The term "red skins" was first used to describe this bounty placed on Native Americans. For every male Indian prisoner above the age of twelve brought to Boston, fifty pounds in currency was offered. For every male Indian scalp brought in as evidence of someone being killed, forty pounds was paid. In 1764, the governor of Pennsylvania also offered a reward, "for the scalp of every male Indian enemy above the age of ten years, one hundred and thirty-four pieces of eight." For the scalp of every female above the age of ten years, the sum of fifty pieces of eight was paid. Once you know the history of this term, it is easier to understand why we object to its use as a sports team name.

Schools and educational institutes also played a role in destroying Indian culture. In 1819 Congress directed the Federal Indian Service, a branch of the War Department, to teach Native children. In the 1870s the Bureau of

Indian Affairs of the U.S. government began building its own system of boarding schools. From the start, boarding schools maintained a stern military tone. Richard Pratt, who established Carlisle Indian School, the first off-reservation school, was a military man. This system of education was often referred to as "schooling the savage." Pratt always thought the best way to domesticate the Indians was to make them into European-style farmers. The government's first target was language, the heart of any culture. Hundreds of Native languages and dialects were replaced by English. Children were whipped or had their mouths washed with soap for speaking their Indian language. Kids ran away almost every day. Historians say that many Indian families became eager for their children to get a boarding school education. But other families refused. In the early years, government agents withheld rations of food and clothing, forcing their cooperation. In other places, Indian children were taken from reluctant families at gunpoint. Parents were thrown in jail. Nearly a half million Indian children went to those schools. Virtually every Indian family has boarding school stories to tell. So while public schools were instituting Indian mascot names and logos, real Indians were undergoing the experience of cultural genocide. Little wonder that Indians resist racism at schools.

The majority of mascot names were adopted in the early 1900s, a period when racism against Indians was rife. Many high schools throughout the United States were named after American historical figures—few of whom are American Indian. Instead, we were bestowed the dubious honor of being foolish-looking mascots for Washington, Lincoln, and Franklin high schools. Approximately 1,500 high schools, ninety colleges and universities, and five professional sports teams currently do us this form of "honor."

It took us a year to convince the school board of the inappropriateness of using the name of a race of people for a school mascot. We were joined in this effort by the Minnesota Civil Liberties Union, which argued that it is unconstitutional to single out a race group in a public school for any purpose other than an educational one. The MCLU threatened to file suit against those schools who refused to change their team names. Since then, thirty-three of the fifty schools have changed their names either voluntarily or by order of their local school board.

The purpose of a mascot in sports is to serve as a focal point for fans to express allegiance to the home team or opposition to the visiting team. Sports fans, students, and faculty wear banners, T-shirts, and buttons to identify themselves. When the target or mascot is a race of people, the buttons and banners say, for example, "Scalp the Indians," "Skin the Chiefs," or "Hang the Redskins." On one side of the stadium, fans with painted faces and chicken-feather headdresses do the tomahawk chop, while on the other side, the bleachers ring with cheers like "Kill the Indians!" This activity represents a form of institutional racism. It also distorts our identity, the identity of our ancestors, and an honest depiction of American history. In addition, it creates an environment where Indian people, families, and children become targets for mockery and ridicule.

It is our understanding—hope, really—that this kind of mistreatment stems from society's miseducation. Public school textbooks came into use in the late 1800s when Indians were depicted as savage and less than human. These characterizations continued throughout public education and were compounded with the onslaught of dime novels and Hollywood westerns. Although these images are gradually being replaced by more benign ones, educational institutions continue to perpetuate racial stereotypes, misleading the public and providing a basis for the provocation of racist slander and behavior. For example, in Illinois there is a high school sports team called the Naperville Redskins. Their 1987 yearbook devoted an entire page to insulting American Indians. An article entitled "Eighty-Seven Uses for a Dead Redskin" listed such items as "maggot farm; doormat; redskin rug; coat hanger; punching bag." The yearbook also included cartoons displaying an Indian man used as a rope in a tug-of-war, another tarred and feathered, and a third serving as a lamp stand with a lamp shade on his head. The American Heritage Dictionary defines "redskin" as "offensive slang"—the same phrase they use to define "nigger," "spic," "wop," and "kike." None of these terms would ever be used as a sports mascot or a team name. So why redskin?

In 1992, the Illinois Board of Education decided the name Redskin had to be eliminated. In reaching this decision, the board examined school yearbooks dating back forty-five years, concluding: "Naperville Central High's yearbooks and other sources to which local school authorities have provided access [show that] over a period of at least forty-five years, the name 'redskins' has been used in that school in association with many insulting visual and verbal caricatures."

How would white Americans feel about having to send their children to a school called "Palefaces"? Imagine a place where the majority of students are people of color and the administration and staff encourage the active use of white images as mascots in all of their school events, i.e., homecoming, pep rallies, skits, yearbooks, athletic competition, etc. Imagine a picture of George Washington wearing knickers and a white-haired wig, sporting a silly grin with two front teeth missing, while holding a Bible in one hand and a sword in the other, emblazoned on the school walls, the gym floor, athletic jackets, jerseys, and the school yearbook. Imagine yourself attending a game with your family to watch your son or daughter compete while being surrounded by people of color, some with faces painted white in mockery of white people. I realize that it may be difficult for white Americans to empathize with this scenario because they have never experienced the centuries of racist persecution American Indians have, both as a group and on a personal level. As Phil would say, they can't know the pain because they've never felt it. Nevertheless, compassionate people should measure offensiveness from the viewpoint of those being offended, and not those doing the offending.

One part of the offensiveness is religious desecration. Both Indians and non-Indians have cultural and religious symbols that are important to them. Whites, for example, generally exhibit great respect for their national flags; witness the role of the flag in parades and in battle, and the furor that results when protesters try to burn the flag. Indians exhibit and demand similar respect for their special symbols, such as the eagle feather. In Indian culture, the headdress of eagle feathers was and continues to be reserved for our most revered and respected chiefs and spiritual leaders. Each feather is earned through a lifetime of service and sacrifice. The markings on the face are an important part of the spiritual ceremonies of most Indian nations, such as reaching adulthood, wedding ceremonies, and that time when one is returned to the bosom of Mother Earth and starts the spiritual journey into the spirit world. Our music is either social songs, prayer songs, or honor songs, all parts of a culture that is thousands of years old.

Real headdresses can't be bought—they must be constructed one feather at a time, over a period of perhaps ten, twenty, or thirty years. Historically, a warrior who "counted coup," that is, spared an enemy when he could have destroyed him, might be rewarded with an eagle feather. To many Indian people, the eagle feather is comparable to the Congressional Medal of Honor.

When a white person sees someone dancing in feathered costume, he sees innocent fun and wonders what is making Indian people so upset. But when an Indian person sees the same scene, for example, Atlanta Braves fans in headdresses doing the tomahawk chop, he knows that the headdresses and bustles aren't just ornamentation—they're parodies, mockeries of the greatest signs of respect tribe and family can bestow on a young man. The Indian reacts as the white man would react to someone burning the American flag.

Suppose a team such as the New Orleans "Saints" decided to include religious rituals in their half-time shows. For instance, could you imagine that whenever a touchdown is made the public address system and the organist break into a rendition of Ave Maria while cheering fans dressed as the Pope sprinkle holy water while toasting one another with chalices full of beer or wine? The Catholic church and the American public would be outraged.

What if the Cleveland "Indians" or the Atlanta "Braves" were called the Cleveland "Negroes" or the Atlanta "Cotton Pickers," whose fans are encouraged to cheer on their team by mimicking their idea of African Americans, painting their faces black and throwing balls of cotton in the air every time someone hits a home run? Or maybe they would dress in grass skirts and do the "Spear Chuck Romp" in place of the "Tomahawk Chop." Imagine the caricature of a black man's head, larger than life on the front of the stadium, with this same caricature plastered on millions of hats each year.

Of course these things do not happen in America—the very thought is repugnant. But recall the Cleveland Indians' moronically grinning, fire engine red caricature of a generic Injun, complete with triangular eyes, perpendicular cheek bones, and the enlarged proboscis, called, of all things, "Chief Wahoo." Why is it inconceivable to caricature any other ethnic group, yet somehow acceptable to demean the original people of this continent? In response to a letter sent to the Cleveland baseball organization by pastors and members of the United Church of Christ requesting that they discontinue use of the Indian mascot and logo, the Cleveland president responded:

> I have reviewed your comments concerning the Indians' long-standing club logo, Chief Wahoo. I am sure you realize, as do I, that there is much tradition in Baseball, and certainly when the club logo was designed it was not designed with any intention of in any way being offensive to the Indians, or to demean them in any fashion. Now that it is almost a part of Cleveland tradition, we think it would be very difficult to change.

Following game two of the recent World Series in Minneapolis, and following a massive march and two days of protesting outside the Metrodome organized by the American Indian Movement (AIM), I decided to catch a bus to Atlanta and join a group of Indians protesting the Braves' use of an Indian logo and the "tomahawk chop" for game five of the World Series. I knew there might be trouble. Before I left Minneapolis, six Indian youths had been arrested after they confronted a group of about twenty Braves fans who were wearing Indian headdresses and carrying foam tomahawks outside the stadium. There was shouting back and forth. Fans threw beer at the kids. The kids went after them and were arrested. Clyde Bellecourt, the AIM leader, compared the Braves fans' actions to "dressing up like Little Black Sambo and walking in the ghetto of Atlanta."

After taking my seat in center field, I turned around to see four police officers standing in the doorways to my left and right. Each time the fans would stand and do the tomahawk chop, encouraged by the public address system, I would stand and lift my sign up above the tomahawks. My sign said, "Indians are a people, not mascots. We deserve respect." After a few innings I left my seat to make a phone call and walk the halls. I was followed by the police guard. When walking down the corridor someone spat at me. Upon stepping over legs when taking my seat someone in the crowd behind me yelled out, "Sit down, chief." I yelled back, "My name is Fred, not Chief." Around the fifth inning I realized the police guard had gone. A little later, I decided to take a stroll. As I walked through the corridor around the stadium I discovered that there wasn't a barricade between the outfield and the infield ticket holders as there is in Minneapolis. I found myself directly behind home plate.

I said to myself, "I came to Atlanta to protest—well, here goes." After an usher had walked someone to their seat, I began a long walk down the stairway that ends up just behind the backstop. People booed, hissed, and yelled, "Get a job," "Hey chief," and "Get a haircut." When I reached the bottom of the staircase the usher told me I had to go back up and that I wasn't allowed down there. As I turned to walk back up, a group of about ten chicken-feathered tomahawk choppers came walking by. As they passed, I raised my sign to their tomahawks. One of them shoved me while another hit my sign with his six-foot tomahawk. The usher told me I could follow them out. I did. In the midst of all the hoopla, mockery, and ridicule, a black brother reached out his hand and gave me a high five.

As I walked through the city streets back to my hotel, the streets rang out with the sound of horns honking, Hollywood chants, and *woo woo woo woo* tomahawk chopping, and I had a feeling of loneliness in a city full of cele-bration. In reflecting upon my life, this was truly my worst nightmare. You know, in all the commotion and everything I didn't catch the score of the game. I asked a passerby: What was the score? He said, Braves won, Indians nothing. The following day I filed a complaint with the U.S. Justice Depart-ment Civil Rights Division.

Indian activists have also enlisted the help of Senator Ben Nighthorse Camp-bell and a Minneapolis law firm to take action on two fronts. First, Senator Campbell introduced an amendment to the Stadium Act of 1957.* The bill prohibited the use of the Washington, D.C., stadium by any person or orga-nization exploiting racial or ethnic characteristics of Native Americans. Jack Kent Cooke, owner of the Washington Redskins, then simply took his team to another location. But, at the same time, a coalition of Native American leaders filed suit to remove federal trademark protection from the name "Wash-ington Redskins." The legal basis for the action is a provision in federal trade-mark law stating that federal trademark registrations cannot be issued for words

---

* See Senator Campbell's article, "Homage to Heritage: Native Americans Say No to Racial Stereotyping," this volume, p 237. —Eds.

that are "scandalous, immoral or disparaging." Because the word "redskin" is a derogatory term, we are arguing that patent registrations should never have been granted and should be canceled. The lawsuit is still pending, following several rulings in the Native Americans' favor. The court has already held that there is a "public policy" interest in addition to the interests of the Native American leaders. If we are successful, the Redskins lose exclusive ability to use their name on shirts, jackets, caps, banners, buttons, cups, or any other such item. It will have a tremendous negative economic impact on their organization and, we hope, will convince them that it is not worth it to keep a pejorative name for their team.

Our Indian ancestors were not savages. Their culture, their languages, and their spiritual ways reflected their connectedness to mother earth and the natural order of things—a tradition that present-day Indian people live by and pass on to our children, one rich in history, philosophy, and spirituality based upon thousands of years of living in this land now called the U.S.A. We developed the idea of democracy, of checks and balances, and of government by the consent of the governed, hundreds of years before the colonials did. But the misguided negative stereotyping of which I have written erases all of this. Racism is an insidious disease. Not only does it affect amateur and professional sports and the institutions and organizations that continue to perpetuate this condition, it adversely affects all the American people, children and old alike.

Please allow me to close with an obvious display of racial bigotry and insensitivity with the hope of giving you a more visceral understanding of the problem with Indian-named mascots and logos. The example is taken from a paper submitted to the National Coalition on Racism in Sports and the Media by Spencer Lonetree, a Winnebago Indian.

ALL-AMERICAN MASCOTS COMPETITION
LADIES AND GENTLEMEN AND FANS OF ALL SPORTS!!

Welcome to the Hubert H. Humphrey Metrodome in Minneapolis, Minnesota, where you are about to witness the first All-American Mascots Competition. This exciting event calls for your participation, where you the audience will decide the winner. Your applause and cheers will be measured on a meter and you can wave your homer hankies too to determine the winner. This extravaganza—hosted by RACISTS-BIGOTS AMERICANA—is sure to be entertaining. RACISTS-BIGOTS AMERICANA has pulled out all the stops to bring you a cast of characters so real you'll just hate them . . . We are sure bleeding heart liberals and open-minded people, the various racial and ethnic groups, and devout Christians will find this great show offensive and in bad taste. But who cares, right? However, those close-minded racist ignoramuses are sure to appreciate the great effort put forth by RACISTS-BIGOTS AMERICANA. The mascots represent various sports teams from throughout the country. Here is just a sampling of what you will see.

The Los Angeles A-RABS soccer team will send their emissary, or Camel Jockey, dressed in a turban and a long robe and he will enter the dome riding a camel and pulling a miniature oil well. He will try to pump 100 gallons of oil in a terroristic fashion in less than a minute. Wow! *** Again from out west, the Honolulu GOOKS hockey team will be represented by—you guessed it! A little slant-eyed host person wearing a cone-shaped straw hat riding a water buffalo. We'll be sure to show a close-up as he demonstrates how to eat rice with chopsticks. Ah-soo-vely interesting. *** From the New Jersey DAGOS boccie team comes a mascot who will arrive in a black chauffeured limo dressed in a dark suit and a dark shirt with a white tie and wearing sunglasses. He will throw spaghetti against a wall from fifty feet using only a ladle. We'll amplify the sound so you can hear the sound WOP! Doesn't that just sound exciting?

Not to be outdone, the San Antonio WETBACKS baseball team mascot will attempt to crawl and sneak through a maze of fences past a half-dozen guards, all while wearing a large sombrero and eating burritos. Ay, Chihuahua! Eet should be fun, no? *** We can't forget the north country and we won't. The Duluth SWEDES curling team will be well represented with a big blonde-haired dumbo called "Ole Olson." Yah, he will try to see if he can beat Milwaukee's Polock and try to count to ten without using his fingers or toes. Noo—he vill bring his own ten lutefisk and use them to count with. Oh yes, he vill be dressed as a lumberjack and vill bee accompanied by a blue ox. Go get 'em Ole! *** You don't think we're done yet, do you?

You're free to boo at anyone if you really hate them. We believe the following may be the crowd favorite, though. From the Houston RED-NECKS basketball team comes the "Duke." This white dude wears a cowboy hat, chews tobacco while swigging beer, and drives a pickup truck. He wears cowboy boots, tight-fitting Levi's, and silver-tinted sunglasses and swaggers when he walks. As soon as he enters the arena in his truck, he will start shouting every conceivable racial obscenity at each and every one of the competitors until the veins of his neck turn red. A crowd-pleaser and crowd favorite for sure. *** Wait a minute, wait a minute, there seems to be a racial group missing. Let's see, okay, we got it, for a minute we almost forgot about those savages that used to own this country. That's right, folks, the Injun. We didn't know what mascot to choose, since there are so many of them. Let's see, we have the Atlanta BRAVES, Cleveland INDIANS, Kansas City CHIEFS, Chicago BLACKHAWKS, North Dakota FIGHTING SIOUX, Illinois FIGHTING ILLINI, and the Washington RED-SKINS, just to name a few. We decided on the REDSKINS.

Next year, sports fans, RACISTS-BIGOTS AMERICANA will bring you even more enjoyment with other mascots. You will see characters from the Buffalo BLACKSKINS, Yonkers YELLOWSKINS, Wilkes-Barre WHITESKINS, and the Baton Rouge BROWNSKINS. Stay tuned for further details.

Maybe now you know how American Indians feel when they see themselves and caricatures of their honorable ancestors mocked by sports teams' logos and fan behavior.

IN THE BELLY OF THE BEAST
The Selling of Sexuality

Ann Simonton

Everyone knows about the privileges of being a fashion model, but few hear about the penalties of being an object. Ann Simonton, once on the "coveted" cover of *Sports Illustrated*'s swimsuit issue, abandoned her modeling career to speak out publicly about the harm of media images which sexualize women. Here she writes about the similarities between fashion modeling and pornography. She also reflects on her own commodification, describes in graphic detail how even the most highly paid models are treated as sexual objects—subjected to unwanted leers, catcalls, stares, and propositions—and argues that fashion modeling constitutes the upper end of a continuum of sexual exploitation, and pornography the lower end—a continuum that creates within the public mind the idea that women are ornaments, objects, or things to be used.

■

I began modeling at age fourteen, in a banner-draped swimsuit as a trophy girl for a car race. The man who won the race was twice my age. He shoved his tongue in my mouth, and the crowd cheered as I struggled backward. My next job was as Miss Teen Covina in a rigged beauty contest in Hollywood. When it was my turn to parade the runway in a two-piece bathing suit before a live TV audience, I was so terrified and humiliated that my whole body shook. I knew that my pale freckled skin and flat chest were not the ideal being sought.

Somewhere between the racetrack and a nationally syndicated teen show I learned to fake confidence. I could convincingly invite the stares, swallow the terror, accept unwanted kisses, and keep smiling. Outwardly, I pretended to be a happy exhibitionist, while inside I was still a shy, sensitive girl who despised being gawked at. In the middle of my first semester in college I moved to New York City, as aspiring models do.

Two and a half months later, on my way to an afternoon modeling job at Columbia University, I got off at the wrong subway stop in Spanish Harlem and was gang raped at knife point. When I tried to prosecute the men, one of whom I could identify positively, I was told I needed a witness. My agent, Eileen Ford, never warned me about dangerous neighborhoods. She encouraged her models to use subways. Years later, I interviewed her, to request that she warn her new models about dangerous areas in the city. She responded, "Every area is dangerous in New York. Why, just the other day a woman was shot on Sutton Place." She and her two daughters took subways to attend Columbia University and *they* were never raped, she added.

After the rape, I became withdrawn and calloused. I focused on gaining financial independence. To survive in the business, fashion models, like pornographic models, learn to divorce themselves from their bodies—bodies that are under constant scrutiny and judgment or are being physically acted upon. Models from both industries have a propensity to use drugs and alcohol to maintain the separation. I numbed my feelings, ignored the humiliation, and smiled constantly. I convinced myself that the joke was on them for paying me thousands to do such inane work.

Stripping down to a bikini in front of a group of male judges and then being asked to read scripted lines into a camera for an interview wasn't rare, especially during my years in Hollywood. I've had grown ad executives ask me to bend over so they could assess my rear end. Photographers have had me lift my dress higher, higher, higher. Working in New York meant changing clothes behind a towel in the middle of Central Park and dressing rooms that were never private. Hairdressers, photographers, and makeup men came and went as they pleased. Street harassment was common since many job interviews took place in the garment district, where trucks were backed onto loading docks. The ever-present men got close enough to whisper their obscenities. I learned that by wearing children's sunglasses and a sneering expression, and holding my elbows up ready to shove, I could pass for a "crazy" and be left alone.

Models are easy prey, especially young ones who want to succeed in this highly competitive field. I heard stories of models who were raped by photographers and of one who became catatonic on the runway and had to be carried off. Supermodel Gia-Marie Carangi, part of New York's drug scene, had to have her needle marks airbrushed out on the April 1982 cover of *Cosmopolitan*. She died four years later from an AIDS-related disease. My friend and colleague Laura Collins, responding to a call for models, became the first murder victim of the Hillside Strangler, who filmed his victims as they were being killed.

According to *60 Minutes*, modeling agents in Paris have been accused of forcibly drugging and raping their teen models and forcing them to have sex in exchange for work. A New York fashion photographer, Joel Schoenfeld, was killed by a model's boyfriend because the model had accused the photographer of raping her. At the time of Schoenfeld's death, he was on probation for attempted rape of another model and had at least four separate complaints of sexual abuse against him.

Sexual harassment is accepted as an inevitable part of a model's job which makes it more difficult for society and the legal system to take it seriously. As a director of a prominent New York modeling agency put it: "Women have a tough time with rejection. And 90 percent of all [sexual] harassment cases are created [by women who feel rejected]."

If it's hard for fashion models to have their complaints taken seriously, the situation is even worse for those in the sex trades, where verbal and physical abuse are endemic. Can a strip tease dancer object to harassment or a prostitute claim she was raped? Fashion models are made into idols; pornographic models are dismissed as trash. Their lower status means their stories of abuse and victimization, though very common, go unheard and unprosecuted in court.

During those eleven years in New York, Los Angeles, San Francisco, and Europe, it was clear to me that modeling was a form of glamorized prostitution and I was a high-class whore. I sold my body for money. My agent/pimp was paid first, then I got my cut—and it was all perfectly legal. While I was never *forced* to disrobe in front of the camera or actually perform coitus with strangers, it was my job to occasionally provide masturbatory material for men and boys. Fashion models keep their clothes on, but their legs open and their lips parted: the come-on in both industries is pornographic.

Women deserve to have work that does not degrade or compromise their self-worth. Our global free-market economy offers its highest rewards to women who act as objects and orifices, performing jobs like modeling, stripping, acting in pornographic films, and prostitution. The financial rewards make it difficult for most people to sympathize with the lack of dignity that being on display requires or what it feels like to be an animal in the zoo. I, myself, found it difficult to turn away from the monetary benefits. I felt "crazy" and alone for hating what modeling had done to me. Being bought and sold like a hunk of meat had successfully annihilated my self-esteem. Even after graduating from the University of California with double honors, I sadly believed my true worth was best realized through displaying my beauty publicly. But slowly I realized I was being made to feel like a freak and an animal. Eventually, I found people who openly agreed that humans aren't meant to be paraded, stripped, and judged. I finally understood how the media's portrayal of women as sex objects promotes and perpetuates violence, because it is much easier to hurt an object or a "piece of ass" than it is to hurt a real human being. Ending my lucrative modeling career was a small sacrifice compared to the social contribution I could make to the survival of all women—including myself.

THE BARGAIN BASEMENT IN THE MARKETPLACE OF IDEAS

Evelina Giobbe

Evelina Giobbe is the founder of WHISPER (Women Hurt in Systems of Prostitution Engaged in Revolt), an organization of women who have survived systems of prostitution. She considers pornography a form of prostitution. According to Giobbe, the function of pornography, like that of the institution of prostitution, is to allow males unconditional access to females, limited solely by their ability to pay. "Being in the sex industry affects every aspect of a woman's life," says Giobbe. "It affects you physically, psychologically, emotionally, spiritually. It is like a prison without walls. Prostitution takes away your humanity—you are left with nothing. The effects of prostitution are irrevocable. You can't turn it back; you can't undo it. All you can do is try to rebuild, an impossible task that no one does fully." In this article, she contrasts the abstract discussions about pornography as free expression with the real-life pain of the women who are used in pornography.

In intellectual discourse, the "marketplace of ideas" is a figure of speech that we use to frame discussions about where, how, and with whom we have discussions. It is a metaphorical place and time where the democratic exchange of ideas occurs. But for many women, women like myself in particular, the marketplace of ideas is a very concrete space where we are walled into a compound built on the illusion of a slippery slope; where brick upon brick is mortared together with the specious rhetoric of free expression and the door is bolted shut with the First Amendment.

In the bargain basement of the marketplace of ideas, men's fantasies are projected onto the blank screens of women's lives.

In the bargain basement of the marketplace of ideas, women's experiences are captured in camcorders, frozen on reels of thirty-five-millimeter film, trapped in the tangle of yards and yards and yards of video tape.

In the bargain basement of the marketplace of ideas, human beings are transformed into pictures and words, sealed in the plastic shrink wrap of the Constitution, and carried away in unmarked graves of plain brown paper wrappings.

I live in the bargain basement of the marketplace of ideas. A red tag special, tossed on the sale rack, picked up and picked over by countless sweaty palms, the pages of my life thumbed through by anonymous hands and sticky fingers. I am a woman whose youth is frozen in time, frame by frame, in the technological recycling bin of prostitution: I am a woman who has been used in pornography.

If you peruse the racks of this very real marketplace, you will find me sandwiched somewhere between my sisters in the video section, among such titles as *Abused Runaway, Teen Street Slut,* and *Call Girl.* You can buy us; rent us; or, if you don't want to take us home, you can stroll over to the peep show booth, drop a quarter in the coin box, and watch us caught in an endless pornographic loop of sexual humiliation and abuse. With a pocketful of change you can see us bend, twist, turn, and spread our legs for your pleasure. Drop in another coin and watch us lie with any manner of man or beast, and if there is no living thing within reach, any common household object will do. Another coin and you can hear us beg for more. Reach in your pants for just one more quarter, quickly though, before the metal curtain snaps shut on the object of your desire, a tortured smile captured in a freeze frame, dead eyes staring out at you.

Or walk back to the magazine section and you can see me as a child, painted and dressed in a garish pornographic parody of a woman. Pick up a later edition, and you can see the woman I'd become, genitals shaved and exposed, hair in pigtails, a grotesque parody of the nymph child. One of a thousand pseudo-Lolitas whose market appeal declined before her twenty-first birthday.

Raised in a brothel by pimps and johns, pornography is my family photo album. If you lay the pictures end to end you can track the destruction of a human being, the death of a woman, and her reconstruction and resurrection as a whore: desired, despised, discarded.

I've been out of the sex industry for about two decades. I've survived the prostitution; outlived a good many of the johns. But the pornography that was made of me still exists. Somewhere some pimp masquerading as a publisher is packing up a shipment of magazines, while some other pimp, somewhere else, masquerading as a film distributor, is filling a truck with pornographic video cassettes. Waiting for these deliveries on the other end is some sticky-fingered john, with a pocketful of quarters, waiting to buy yet another piece of my youth, in the bargain basement of the marketplace of ideas. I want them to stop. I want us to stop them.

CHAPTER TWO

How Hate Harms

What are the effects of hate and disparagement on individuals? Until recently, there was little empirical evidence one way or the other. But in the last ten years, social scientists have begun to study racist speech, hate propaganda, and pornography. In general this body of research shows that all three forms of expression have discernible effects on their targets and on society in general. The studies included in this chapter add to this body of information and explore a number of new dimensions: How are racial insults different from nonracial ones? How does pornography affect women and children? What happens when pornography includes both racial and sexual elements? Are anti-Semitism and antigay violence growing? And if so, why?

THE TRAUMATIC IMPACT OF ETHNOVIOLENCE

Howard J. Ehrlich, Barbara E. K. Larcom, and Robert D. Purvis

Until recently, there was very little, if any, research on the effects of hate speech on individuals and on society. In an effort to fill this gap, The Prejudice Institute carried out a study of the traumatic effects of prejudice. Their definition of ethnoviolence, which they pioneered, includes acts motivated by prejudice that are intended to do physical or psychological harm to persons because of their actual or perceived membership in a social category. Ethnoviolent acts range from brutal assaults and arson to everyday expressions of prejudice such as insults, epithets, threats, acts of harassment or physical intimidation, graffiti and vandalism, and displays of commonly identified symbols of prejudice and group hatred. Groups typically victimized by ethnoviolence are those identified by ethnicity, skin color, religion, national origin, or sexual orientation.

■

A Prefatory Note

Central to the program of research begun in 1986 at the National Institute Against Prejudice and Violence, and continuing at The Prejudice Institute/Center for the Applied Study of Ethnoviolence, has been our attempt to assess the impact of being victimized for reasons of group prejudice. Ethnoviolence is a term we introduced to delimit prejudiced behavior which causes, or is intended to cause, physical and psychological harm to its victims.

While there are valid conceptual questions concerning the intent of the actors and the perceptions of the target persons, these will not be discussed here. At the empirical level, we have found the classification of incidents and false claims of victimization to be surprisingly easy to deal with. Substantial protocols exist for verifying an incident as one motivated by prejudice.* Furthermore, for both law enforcement and scientific purposes, one can always partition the verified reports from the unverified or erroneous ones. As to false claims of victimization, our impression—after eight years of monitoring ethnoviolent incidents—is that they are likely to occur with a frequency well below one percent. Interestingly, half of the false reports we have seen were contrived in order to bring community attention to other real and verifiable incidents.

In our studies we have focused on the perceptions of the people we interviewed or to whom we administered questionnaires. That is, if a person reported being victimized for reasons of prejudice, we were inclined to accept that statement as an honest perceptual report. However, in both our national telephone survey and in our corporate workplace case study, we were able to build in methodological safeguards against false reports, such as asking multiple variations of the same question as well as reviewing questionable cases with our interviewers. We found very few questionable cases. In the course of private interviews (conducted by highly skilled, mature interviewers), almost everyone responded openly and, quite often, wtih gratitude for the opportunity to review and "work through" their experience of ethnoviolence and its trauma.

A full discussion of the research designs and methodological issues are presented in the original reports cited in our notes and references.

The National Ethnoviolence Victimization Survey

In 1989, we undertook the first national assessment of the extent and consequences of ethnoviolence and other forms of victimization in the United States. We conducted phone interviews on a stratified random sample of 2,078 people. Of these, 918 were white and 1,013 were black; 1,302 were women and 776 were men.

To get a clear picture of people's experiences we asked several different series of questions. Initially, we asked our respondents whether they had been victimized by various types of verbal and physical violence or abuse during the previous twelve months. Next came questions about co-victimization, that is, whether anyone close to the respondent had experienced violence or abuse during the same period. In a third series we asked whether the respondents had experienced group insult—operationally defined as insults based on their backgrounds or those of persons with whom they were identified. Fourth,

---

* See, for example, Federal Bureau of Investigation, 1990; National Gay and Lesbian Task Force Policy Institute, 1992; National Institute Against Prejudice and Violence, 1993.—Authors.

respondents were asked whether they had been mistreated in various ways at work or school. Each series was followed by asking the respondents if their experiences were based on prejudice of some kind.

In addition, respondents answered questions about other important life events during the past year; physical and psychological symptoms they had experienced, as well as behavioral changes they had made in the same period; and demographic, family, work, and school information.

The Basic Findings

VIOLENCE   The survey results show that violence and abuse are very common in the United States. Thirty-five percent of the sample (726 respondents) reported having been the victim of at least one incident of violence or abuse during the preceding twelve months. Of those, seven out of ten experienced more than one incident. The most frequent type of incident reported was a verbal attack: abusive language (15 percent) and harassing telephone calls or mail (13 percent). A notable proportion of all respondents said their homes had been broken into (13 percent) or their property destroyed or damaged (6 percent). In addition, respondents were sexually harassed (5 percent) or threatened with physical harm (5 percent). Other kinds of violent incidents were mentioned, too, but not in significant numbers.

Seventy-eight percent of victims said they had discussed the incident with friends, neighbors, or relatives. Many fewer, however, reported the incident to an official source. For example, only 36 percent called the police. This figure is consistent with National Crime Survey estimates that only one-third of all crimes are reported to the police.

For each incident of victimization, we asked if the incident was motivated by prejudice. Respondents who said yes were asked to name all the types of prejudice involved (a list of examples was given). At least 135 persons (6.5 percent of the sample) experienced incidents of violence or abuse that they believed to be the result of prejudice. Of victims providing definite responses, 15.4 percent reported that the most salient incident in their experience was definitely or possibly motivated by prejudice; an additional 13.4 percent reported that at least one other incident was prejudice-based.

All respondents victimized in the preceding year answered follow-up questions regarding at least one incident which happened to them. If more than one incident was reported, respondents were asked to select for discussion the "primary" incident—the one that had the greatest effect on their lives.

Among the 107 primary incidents motivated by prejudice, nearly one-third were based on the respondent's race and these were divided almost evenly between white and black respondents. Twenty-eight persons reported an incident based on gender prejudice. None of the other bases of prejudice were reported in large numbers.

We have already noted that a low percentage of victims, overall, report their incidents to the police. Our survey data also show that persons victimized for reasons of prejudice are even less likely than other victims to report incidents—less than 24 percent compared to 39 percent.

Another form of violence is group defamation: verbal, written, or symbolic statements (for example, a spray painted "KKK") that are not directed individually at the respondent. Rather, these are statements about the group to which an individual belongs or with which she or he is identified. We asked our respondents whether, because of their own background or that of someone close to them, they had been insulted by either leaflets or posters, spray painted signs or slogans, radio or television programming, newspaper or magazine materials, teasing or jokes or other comments.

Of the 2,078 people interviewed, 530 (25.5 percent) reported experiences of group defamation. Of that number, seventy-six also reported other ethnoviolent experiences, leaving 454 new cases. If we add these 454 to our roster of at least 135 victims of ethnoviolence, the total becomes 589. This amounts to at least 28.3 percent of the total sample who were victims of a prejudice-motivated action during the preceding year.

Those reporting group defamation were asked to specify the basis of prejudice. The major bases of prejudice that these victims identified were skin color or race, gender, nationality or ethnic group, and religion, in that order.

THE TRAUMATIC EFFECTS   Being victimized can cause serious psychological damage. Debilitating effects may last for years or recur sporadically. Our experience indicates that an observer cannot predict the effects of an incident solely from knowledge of the incident itself. What is of consequence to one person may elicit only passing notice from another. Also, a given act can change its meaning depending on the social setting in which it takes place.

In this analysis, we compared four major subgroups: people who had not been victimized during the preceding twelve months; people who reported group defamation and no other victimization; people who reported violence or abuse, but with no perceived basis in prejudice; and persons who reported violence or abuse that they believed was based on prejudice.

We developed two checklists of responses in order to measure the consequences of the various categories of victimization. In the first checklist, we asked respondents to indicate whether they had experienced any of nineteen psychophysiological symptoms of post-traumatic stress during the preceding year. In the second, we asked respondents about twelve social and behavioral changes that they might have made over the course of the previous year.

The findings of this analysis, presented in tables 1 and 2, are quite striking and important. On both checklists, victims of ethnoviolence show the greatest average number of symptoms and behavioral changes, while people who had not experienced any incident display the lowest average. Persons who experienced group defamation and those victimized by violence not based on prejudice ("personal victims") show an intermediate number of symptoms and behavioral changes. These differences in the average number of symptoms are of substantial proportions and translate into dramatic differences in the quality of life for the persons involved (see table 1).

In order to understand the findings more fully, we also performed a detailed item analysis, comparing nonvictims, personal victims, and ethnoviolence victims. The results of these comparisons are found in table 2.

A clear overall pattern appears: ethnoviolence victims reported symptoms more often than personal victims, and personal victims reported them more frequently than nonvictims. For eighteen of the nineteen psychophysiological symptoms, there were statistically significant differences among the three groups. The one exception was the item, "felt as if you didn't want to live any longer." For all other items, victims reported the symptom more frequently than nonvictims. Moreover, for a number of these items—nervousness, trouble waking up, trouble concentrating or working, anger and desire to retaliate against the perpetrator, fear of having more trouble in one's life, and feeling exhausted or weak for no reason—ethnoviolence victims reported the symptom significantly more often than other victims.

The comparisons using the checklist of social and behavioral changes are similar, though not identical. In nearly all items, there were significant differences among the three groups in the percentages of persons who reported the changes. The two exceptions were the items "pay more attention to where you walk" and "stay home at night more often" (responses to these probably reflected a more universal concern with safety). For all other items, victims reported changes more frequently than did nonvictims. In addition, ethnoviolence victims noted changes significantly more often than did other victims for the items "had difficulty with a spouse or significant other" and "took a self-defense class."

ETHNOVIOLENCE IN THE WORKPLACE   We decided to focus special attention on persons who reported violence and abuse occurring in the workplace. We did so for three interrelated reasons: adults spend a great deal of time at work; intergroup contacts are more likely to occur at the workplace and to be of longer duration than in any other setting; and workplace intergroup contacts

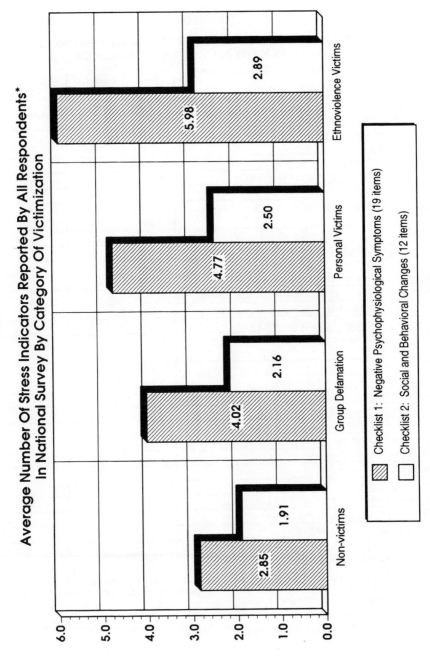

TABLE 1

Average Number Of Stress Indicators Reported By All Respondents* In National Survey By Category Of Victimization

Non-victims: Checklist 1 = 2.85, Checklist 2 = 1.91

Group Defamation: Checklist 1 = 4.02, Checklist 2 = 2.16

Personal Victims: Checklist 1 = 4.77, Checklist 2 = 2.50

Ethnoviolence Victims: Checklist 1 = 5.98, Checklist 2 = 2.89

Checklist 1: Negative Psychophysiological Symptoms (19 items)

Checklist 2: Social and Behavioral Changes (12 items)

* Note: The above figures are based only on black, white, and Hispanic respondents.

TABLE 2

THE PERCENTAGE OF ALL RESPONDENTS REPORTING STRESS INDICATORS IN NATIONAL SURVEY BY CATEGORY OF VICTIMIZATION

Response Items	Non Victims	Personal Victims	Ethnoviolence Victims
Felt depressed or sad	37%	52%	56%
Felt more nervous than usual	31	43	54
Thought over and over again about the same problem or incident	26	44	52
Pay more attention to where you walk *	45	45	50
Worried more about the safety of your family	36	43	47
Stay home at night more often *	50	48	46
Had physical problems like headaches, stomach aches, shortness of breath	26	36	41
Did something to make your home more secure *	30	43	40
Lost or gained weight without intending to	30	37	40
Lost people you thought were friends *	21	29	38
Felt afraid of having more trouble in your life	14	24	37
Felt very angry, wanted to hurt the people who hurt you	9	23	34
Had sleep problems, trouble falling asleep, bad dreams	21	33	33
Had trouble concentrating, couldn't work well	13	23	32
Had difficulty or broke up with your spouse or significant other *	9	19	29
Felt helpless	13	23	27
Felt exhausted or weak for no reason	14	17	26
Had trouble waking up, slept more than usual	9	17	26
Felt ashamed, lost confidence in yourself	9	16	22
Tried to be less visible, not to let people notice you *	9	14	21
Used more alcohol, prescription drugs, or other drugs	10	13	19
Moved to another neighborhood *	10	15	18
Felt afraid to be alone	8	14	16
Became withdrawn	5	10	16
Felt afraid to answer the phone or leave the house	2	8	9
Felt as if you didn't want to live any longer	4	5	8
Bought a gun or started carrying a gun *	4	7	7
Took a self-defense class *	1	2	7

* Starred items were included in Checklist 2 (social and behavioral changes); all other items were part of Checklist 1 (psychophysiological symptoms). Three items from Checklist 2 were omitted from this table because the number of cases was too small to permit comparisons among groups.

often result from involuntary assignments made by the employer. As it turned out, the workplace was the single most frequent site of ethnoviolent incidents.

There were 1,372 people in our sample who worked for pay during the year preceding the national survey. Of these, 105 experienced some direct form of work-related violence, with 39 of them attributing the act to prejudice of some kind. In addition, twenty-one persons also indicated that insulting jokes or comments based on their background were made to them personally at work.

Among the 105 persons who experienced work-related violence, those who believed the incident was based on prejudice were much less likely to report it to someone in authority (usually the first-line supervisor) than workers who perceived no prejudice in the event (38 percent versus 68 percent, respectively).

In an analysis similar to the one already described, we compared four groups of workers on their psychophysiological symptoms and their social and behavioral changes during the preceding year. The four groups were nonvictims; people reporting group insult directed at them in the workplace, but no other incidents; personal victims of work-related violence with no basis in prejudice; and victims of ethnoviolence. The results are found in table 3.

The results show significant differences in stress indicators among the groups. They suggest that at least in workplace settings, prejudice-based incidents of all kinds—including personally directed group insults—produce considerably more psychological trauma, physical symptoms, and defensive behavioral change than other incidents. These findings prompted us to take a more in-depth look at ethnoviolence in the workplace.

The Traumatic Impact of Ethnoviolence
in the Corporate Workplace

"Eastern Corporation"—the pseudonymous site of this study—is located in a thriving metropolitan area in the Middle Atlantic states. It employs over 4,300 people in a range of semiskilled, skilled, managerial, and professional jobs. In the first stage of the study, which we report here, we interviewed 327 first-line workers in private settings at their work sites. These face-to-face interviews averaged forty-five minutes.

We started the interviews with standard background questions, followed by specific questions about the respondents' jobs, their evaluation of their work, and their attitudes toward their coworkers. We then asked a series of questions designed to determine whether a person had been differentially treated because of prejudice. In one question, for example, we asked, "How often do you think people at work treat you negatively because of your . . .?" The categories of

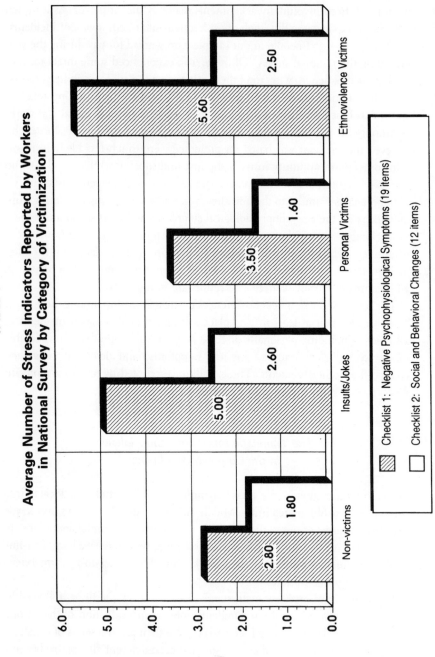

TABLE 3

Average Number of Stress Indicators Reported by Workers in National Survey by Category of Victimization

Checklist 1: Negative Psychophysiological Symptoms (19 items)

Checklist 2: Social and Behavioral Changes (12 items)

response were sex, education, skin color/race, ethnic background, age, religion, sexual orientation, and handicap/illness. Respondents were asked to indicate the frequency of such treatment: often, sometimes, or never. In a second key question we asked, "In the past three years, have you ever been mistreated at work in this company? Did anyone. . . ." Here people were given twelve categories of response, for example: "call you names or make insulting jokes or comments," "attack or threaten you physically?" Those who replied "yes" to any category were then questioned about when the incident occurred, whether they perceived it to have been motivated by prejudice, and how they responded to the incident—what they did and how they felt.

THE BASIC FINDINGS   The results of this survey indicate that expressions of prejudice and discriminatory mistreatment are ubiquitous at Eastern Corporation. Fifty-six percent of the sample reported that they had experienced at least one incident of prejudice-motivated mistreatment in the previous three years (half of them reported three or more events). The violent acts most frequently perceived were name-calling and insulting jokes and comments (21 percent), being treated as a nonperson (18 percent), sexual harassment (11 percent), physical threats or attacks (9 percent), property damage (8 percent), and insulting phone calls or mail (6 percent).

One out of every five workers had suffered major forms of discrimination, which included the denial of raises, promotions, or transfers and the differential granting of privileges. In addition, many workers felt that they had been set up for failure (13 percent) and kept from getting the training they needed (12 percent).

Race and gender were the central focuses of these discriminatory and ethnoviolent acts. Ethnicity, age, and education were secondary. Almost one-fourth of victims indicated three or more categories as a basis for their mistreatment, for example, race, gender, and education. Sample reports from the interviews are presented in table 4.

Most victims were able to identify the perpetrators: they were supervisors or other managers in 55 percent of the cases and coworkers in 34 percent of the cases. Coworkers were primarily involved in assaultive acts (physical or verbal), while supervisors were primarily involved in various acts of discrimination. For ethnoviolent incidents typically there was more than one perpetrator, and they were reported mainly as being white males around forty years of age.

Most victims talked with friends or relatives about their experience, but only three out of ten reported the incident to company or even union officials. "Wouldn't have done any good" or "would have made matters worse" were the major reasons given for not reporting the incident.

TABLE 4

EXAMPLES OF ETHNOVIOLENT INCIDENTS AT "EASTERN CORPORATION" AS REPORTED BY RESPONDENTS

FROM BLACK RESPONDENTS SPEAKING OF RACIAL INCIDENTS:

A White guy who's in a rifle club brought a target in of a Black person and showed it around our department.

My supervisor brought in pictures of a Halloween party where his friends were dressed as Ku Klux Klan and he thought it was funny. Personally, I thought it was an insult and I told him about it.

My co-workers treat me as if I do not exist....I never see any general conversation other than someone telling me what I need to be doing on my job. Another secretary is going through the same situation. We are both the only Black secretaries in this group. The other secretaries leave me and my co-worker letters instead of talking to us face to face. Most letters or notes from the secretaries are nasty.

New sets of computers have come in twice. Everyone has their new computer. I've been given a used computer from another desk. The new computer was placed on the empty desk!

For three months I had no idea who I was to report to. I was never even instructed how to do a time sheet. For a month and a half, no one even spoke to me! People would pass me and not speak. I went to the director asking for work to do, and to be assigned to someone. He said he couldn't do this at the time. Eventually a team leader approached me with a small amount of work to do. He really did not have the authority to do this. It paid off. I've been with him ever since....For three months I sat idle!

This man asked me about Blacks and pancakes and said that one day I was going to come in looking like Aunt Jemima. One day when one of my co-workers and I were in the snack room, another man came in and joined in the conversation, and said he was tired of "offbeat minorities."

I was socializing with people on the job and went out with two White co-workers to see Nutcracker. They were talking and referred to a site: "You know that's where all those dirty Black people are."

A guy in my work group told me that Blacks talked jive and were not intelligent. Afterwards, he told me he was kidding. However, I did not appreciate it.

The supervisor called me "nigger" to my face, reported me for minor things, while other people's minor offenses were ignored. I was also called "nigger" by the union president.

I was once sent a picture of Buckwheat....Although my co-workers are basically friendly, they take liberties in making stereotypical remarks to me that really bother me. This happens several times a month and the focus is generally on Black music and Black food stereotypes. I really like contemporary jazz music but no one recognizes my taste in this music. They assume because I am Black that I like rap music and break dancing and always refer to me in discussions regarding rap music....Comments are also made about my assumed preference for fried chicken and watermelon. I get really tired of the stereotypes — why can't they get to know me and my personal tastes in music, food, etc. What is frustrating is that as soon as someone gets friendly with me, they begin to take liberties at insulting me. So now I have to be careful about how friendly I am and yet if I'm not friendly my co-workers will hold that against me too....When I first came to this department, I heard some of my co-workers comment, "See, he is a normal guy," referring to me. Well, what did they expect!

A group of guys I work with horse around a lot, and were throwing paper balls at me. One White man tried to hit me with the door to the refrigerator when I was behind him to get something out of the refrigerator. The same guy kept throwing stuff at me, and one day about a month ago he threw a large roll of duct tape at me twice....An argument ensued with swearing and yelling. Later in the lunch room when I saw him, I hit his cup out of his hand. This was witnessed by my foreman and co-workers, who said it was a racial attack on my part against this White co-worker. I tried to tell him of all the stuff he did to me prior to that but he didn't care. Now every one of my co-workers thinks it was a racial incident. I don't think it was racial when the argument happened or even when he threw the tape — but others perceive it as that now and so it has become that, especially since there was another incident that happened in my small group the same week, which has been handled as a racial incident.

There was a White girl who had a lot less time, and there were seven Blacks who had a lot of seniority. They hired her. I went to the union steward and threatened to go to EEOC.

TABLE 4 (CONTINUED)

FROM HISPANIC RESPONDENTS:

Co-workers put a poster of Mariachis, a Mexican group, on the fridge and put my name on it — and had some insulting comments written on it. They say I dress like a faggot because I wear Spandex; they call me "wetback," "spic"....I was warned by my brother who works here about my supervisor, on the first day. My supervisor told my brother not to date a fellow co-worker. He said to me, "Are you an alien? Did you come over the river?" I said I was born here. He asked me if [my brother]...was dating [the co-worker]. So I asked what that had to do with my job? He said, "You spics are all the same."

I get called "Chico" or "wetback." Sometimes when it is not said in a joking manner I get mad. About a year ago, I told a man I didn't appreciate it, and he doesn't talk to me anymore.

FROM WHITE RESPONDENTS TALKING ABOUT RACIAL ISSUES:

A stenographer is permitted to sleep on the job, turn in work late, come and go as she pleases. The supervisor allows this because she is Black. He is afraid of her. I have to do her work. I am not afforded these privileges.

I was reprimanded for making phone calls during my father's illness and subsequent death, while others, Blacks, are able to talk often on the phone and nothing is said. I am also reprimanded for talking loud. When two of the Black employees got into an altercation, shouting at each other, obscenity, etc., and all the supervisors did was say quiet it down.

Once I'm told what to do, the [Black] acting supervisor then accuses me of doing it wrong....The Black acting supervisor accuses the White employees that they are not doing their jobs correctly....This is done only to White employees in the group. The majority of the workers in the group are Black....There is also an attitude of Black co-workers toward their White co-workers. The shop steward is Black and is no help at all.

FROM WOMEN DISCUSSING INCIDENTS/DISCRIMINATION BASED ON GENDER:

After maternity leave, when I came back my supervisor gave me a low rating for the year. I should have received a "no rating." I complained to him and his supervisor. They wouldn't change it.

Several male co-workers always make comments about me being a woman and that's why I got my job.

It's been insinuated that because I was working with a male in a project that we were sleeping together.

My co-worker's wife had surgery, and he was telling me his sexual fantasies.

I have a male co-worker who touched me where I did not want to be touched. He assumed that since I am single that I need someone. I wrote him a note and told him that I did not appreciate his actions.

When I first started working, my foreman, who was a lot older, came onto me and hugged me inappropriately. I reported him to the union and the union told me to tell them if it happens again. It did, so I reported my foreman again. The union threatened to fire the foreman so he in turn threatened to fire me if I so much as looked at him wrong.

FROM MEN TALKING ABOUT GENDER ISSUES:

There is ongoing talking amongst the females [in my work group], such as "All men are dogs."

Females get a lighter workload than the rest of us. One female who doesn't do any work was rated [the highest rating]. The foreman was also unhappy because he was told to give her [the highest rating].

There were two men and two women who bid for the same jobs as instructor, and both women were hired. It really felt like discrimination towards me because of being male. I feel the females were not equally qualified as me — they didn't have as much educational experience. I and the other man had passed a certification exam and the females had failed. They told me that the reason I was not given the job is that there was a higher level job that I was qualified for but I was not given this higher level position until last year.

THE TRAUMATIC EFFECTS   Following the series of questions designed to uncover prejudice, we asked people for their overall response to their mistreatment. When asked how it affected their job performance, more than half indicated that the incident had at least some effect, while 28 percent indicated that it had "a very big effect." We asked how it affected their job, and it was evident from their self-reports that these victimized workers had become deeply alienated, primarily from their jobs and secondarily from the people they worked with. The ninety-seven codable responses were distributed as follows, by percentage:

Felt bitter, developed a bad attitude 27
Didn't want to come to work or do job 24
Did less work 17
No longer trusted coworkers, supervisor. 16
Asked for transfer 9
Lost self-confidence 7

Next, we examined the self-reported symptoms of stress that resulted from the incidents. Respondents were presented with sixteen standard indicators of post-traumatic stress and queried: "Because of this mistreatment, did you experience any of the following . . . ?" Table 5 presents the distribution of the responses. This table displays the stress-induced symptoms and behavior of ethnoviolence victims and of persons whose victimization was not motivated by prejudice (personal victims).

The data are extraordinarily revealing of the impact of victimization, and ethnoviolent victimization in particular, on the mental and physical health of those victimized. Not only does a pattern of psychological response emerge from the data, but they show that these workplace events have a significant impact on the outside social relationships of workers, resulting in difficulties within the family and a disruption of friendships.

To begin with, the patterns of response for personal victims and ethnoviolence victims are virtually identical (the rank correlation between them is .99). This means that regardless of the motivational bias of their victimization people experienced the same set of stress responses.

On the other hand, critical differences separate the two sets of responses. In fifteen of the sixteen categories of stress-related behavior, ethnoviolence victims reported experiencing stress behavior with greater frequency than personal victims (in the remaining item, there was no difference between the two groups). For example, while 66.7 percent of the personal victims "felt very angry," over 80 percent of the prejudice victims felt that way; while 24.4 percent of the personal victims "became withdrawn," 37.4 percent of the victims of prejudice

TABLE 5

The Percentage of Respondents Reporting Stress Indicators in "Eastern Corporation" by Category of Victimization

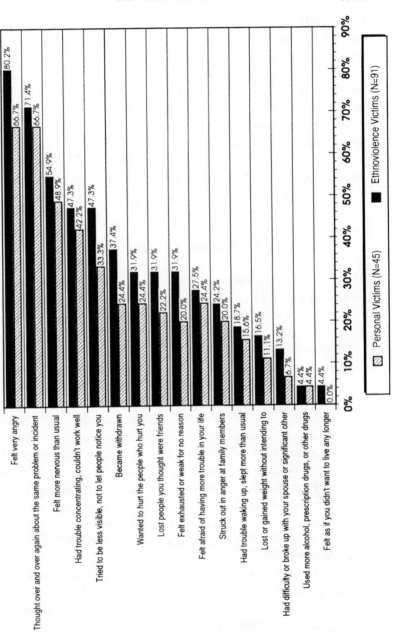

reported withdrawal. Further, the difference in the average *number* of symptoms reported by personal violence and ethnoviolence victims is statistically significant.

The leading symptoms presented here are those commonly associated with post-traumatic stress: anger, mental replay of the incident, nervousness, difficulty in concentrating, withdrawal, and trying to become invisibile. The trauma took its toll on interpersonal relations as well: respondents experienced loss of friends, anger with family members, and difficulties with significant others. Victims also reported problems in maintaining their weight, in sleeping, and in their energy level. As these findings demonstrate, events of discrimination and ethnoviolence are psychologically important in the lives of workers.

Ethnoviolence on College Campuses

The data from college campus studies are considerably more limited than those we have already reported. Since the data are from a younger population (the average student age is twenty), and since they offer a complementary perspective, we thought it worthwhile to summarize the relevant findings here.

THE BASIC FINDINGS   In 1986, at the University of Maryland in Baltimore County, we initiated the first of what was to become a series of studies of ethnoviolence on college campuses (Ehrlich, Pincus, and Morton, 1987; Ehrlich, 1992). In that first study, we administered and completed 347 student questionnaires. Ten percent of the students (including white, nonminority students) indicated that they had been the victim of an ethnoviolent incident: that is, they had been called names, insulted, harassed, threatened, physically attacked, or had their property damaged. Further, one out of four victims had experienced more than one incident during the school year. Replication studies were also conducted at Rutgers (Peterson, 1990) and at State University of New York College at Cortland (Taylor, 1990). These, among other studies, are reviewed in Ehrlich (1992). Related research on gay and lesbian student victimization is reviewed in Berrill (1992).

There is substantial variation in the proportion of students reporting ethnoviolent victimization. That is, different groups (black, Latino, Asian/Pacific, Jewish, etc.) are targeted with different frequencies on different campuses. Further, structural dimensions of the campus appear to have influenced the rate of ethnoviolence. For example, residential campuses appear to have had more incidents than commuter campuses. Unfortunately, there has not yet been enough research to determine reliably the sources of variation.

There are, however, some substantial findings. First, the median percentage of minority students who are ethnoviolence victims during a single school year is most likely 20 percent to 25 percent. (If we include white nonminority students, the rates are much lower.) Second, this high level of campus ethnoviolence has been hidden by the failure of between 80 percent and 94 percent of ethnoviolence victims to report their experience to campus officials. This finding points to the need for sociologically sophisticated research while casting serious doubts on the adequacy of collection techniques that rely on reported incidents. Third, the major form of ethnoviolent behavior among students is verbal aggression: name-calling, insults, harassment, and threats.

THE TRAUMATIC EFFECTS In the UMBC study we asked the victimized students, "How do you feel about what happened?" Two major patterns of response accounted for 52 percent of all replies. In the first, respondents felt angry, upset, disturbed, and disgusted. In the second, they felt helplessness and shame.

While two-thirds of the students felt that the incident had not affected or changed their social life on campus, the remaining one-third described having withdrawn from campus life. "I try to blend into backgrounds," said one Chinese-American senior woman. A black woman, also a senior, expressed a similar reaction to her encounter with ethnoviolence: "I attend my classes and go straight home. I do not participate in any on-campus activities." This common pattern of withdrawal is not limited to minority victims. One white male senior student who was harassed by several black students commented: "I am now disinclined to foster relationships and friendships with most Blacks. . . . I used to be quite friendly."

Five years after the UMBC study, we assisted in the collection of data for nine New York colleges and universities, a sample that included public and private, elite and nonelite, small and large institutions. In this study, conducted both in more heterogeneous settings and at a time when there was considerably more media attention given to campus ethnoviolence, only 31 percent of the student victims of ethnoviolence said that they had not been affected by their experience.

In table 6 we have displayed the responses to our stress-symptoms checklist. Students were asked, "As a result of this event or events, did any of these things happen to you?" As the table indicates, many students were seriously disturbed by their experiences of ethnoviolence. Once again we can observe the post-traumatic stress responses of anger, perseveration with the event, fear, and revenge fantasies. And, as in our national survey and workplace case study, we observed how the trauma of ethnoviolence affected the victims' interpersonal relationships and their ability to fulfill their role expectations.

While the student responses are substantial, workers in the Eastern Cor-

TABLE 6

THE PERCENTAGE OF STUDENTS REPORTING STRESS INDICATORS
IN RESPONSE TO ETHNOVIOLENCE AT NINE COLLEGES

Response Item	%
Felt very angry	54.1
Thought over and over again about the same problem or incident	42.6
Felt more nervous than usual	39.2
Felt afraid of having more trouble in your life	30.3
Tried to be less visible, not to let people notice you	29.6
Wanted to hurt the people who hurt you	28.1
Became withdrawn	26.1
Had trouble concentrating, couldn't work well	24.8
Lost people you thought were friends	19.6
Struck out in anger at family members	19.0
Felt exhausted or weak for no reason	17.1
Lost or gained weight without intending to	16.9
Had trouble waking up, slept more than usual	16.8
Had difficulty or broke up with your spouse or significant other	16.1
Used more alcohol, prescription drugs, or other drugs	13.2
Felt as if you didn't want to live any longer	12.2

Note: Students were sampled at nine colleges and universities in New York State. The total number of students in the surveys was 2,340. The number of students who were victimized and responded to these questions varied, by question, between 410 and 423.

poration were even more likely—in eleven of the sixteen categories—to have experienced stress (compare tables 5 and 6). We can only speculate on the meaning of these differences, but it is clear that the social context of ethnoviolence does affect the way that people respond to it.

Summary

In this summary analysis of our research program, we have identified three findings of critical significance to an understanding of ethnoviolent victimization.

1. Ethnoviolent victimization occurs at substantially high rates in society. The rates vary by social setting (community, work, school) and by target group (black, white, gay, Latino, etc.).

2. Most ethnoviolent acts are not reported to "official" sources. As a consequence, the magnitude of ethnoviolence and its aftermath has been obscured from public scrutiny.

3. Ethnoviolence victims suffer greater trauma than do victims of other types of violence that is committed for other reasons.

THE EFFECTS OF PORNOGRAPHY ON WOMEN

Wendy Stock

Ten years ago research into pornography was still overwhelmingly concerned with its effects on men. Social scientists were busy in the laboratory
measuring penile erections, in the street doing attitudinal surveys on what
males thought about pornography, and in the jails doing retrospective
studies on rapists and child molesters. While that research has its place,
to our mind the most important research in the last decade has focused
on the effects of pornography on women, adolescents, and people of color.
Here Wendy Stock reports on findings from four areas of research on the
effects of pornography on women's lives. First, she examines responses to
violent pornography and demonstrates that it does not sexually arouse
women. Second, she reports on female reactions to two types of nonviolent
pornography—one in which the woman is degraded and one in which the
woman is sexually available. Third, she reports on pornography consumption patterns of men and women. And fourth, she describes an attitudinal
study she did on how women feel about the presence of pornography in
their homes and the use of pornography by their husbands or boyfriends.

■

I began researching the effects of pornography on women with the naive belief
that I could use paradigms developed for studies on adult men, usually white
men. It quickly became evident that these research models would not be useful
with women, and I began to tailor my research according to new feminist
definitions. Old research paradigms, for example, did not distinguish between
violent pornography (images of women being bound, raped, tortured, or murdered for sexual stimulation), degrading pornography (where women are depicted as being subordinate to men), erotica (where men and women are
depicted in equal and loving sexual relationships), and sex education materials.
Early studies of the effects of pornography on men typically lumped together
all sexual images under the heading of "sexually explicit materials" or "por-

nography," and, as a result, much of the data (which, naturally, find that "pornography" is harmless) are flawed. My laboratory research examining women's reactions to pornography recognizes the distinct categories I mentioned above. And in my most recent research I have left the laboratory altogether to conduct attitudinal surveys on how women feel about pornography when it appears in their homes, when their partners use it, and when they experience it personally.

Stage One: The Effects of Violent Pornography on Women (1982)

We all know, and research proves, that rape is highly traumatic—both physically and psychologically—for its survivors. Yet some research documents a high frequency of rape fantasies among women. In these fantasies, the imagined experience of rape is an erotic encounter (Hariton and Singer, 1974). I found this puzzling at best—and disturbing at worst—and decided in 1982 to examine women's responses to and feelings about eroticized depictions of rape. How did the prevalence of the rape myth affect women's sexuality? Did it socialize women to conform with the pornographic version of rape, in which women are turned on rather than harmed? How might this contribute to women's vulnerability to sexual coercion? I was concerned that if these images and depictions shape women's attitudes about rape, then extended exposure could serve to discourage women from reporting and prosecuting rape. After all, if women are "asking for it," how can it be a crime?

I used what was then the prevailing dichotomy between violent (harmful) and nonviolent (benign) pornography to measure women's emotional reactions and genital arousal response during exposure to pornography. The categories were inconsistent with my own reactions to nonviolent pornography, but they were all that was available to researchers at the time.

Seventy-five undergraduate women (average age, twenty years) participated in the research. Before the experiment, I asked them standardized questions about their past experience of sexual coercion, their body image, their acceptance of rape myths, how much violence there was in their personal lives, how often they had force-oriented sexual fantasies, and how much pornography they had been exposed to.

Participants first heard one of four audiotapes including (1) a direct transcript from a rape myth scenario, taken verbatim from pornography (what I call a "rape myth"), (2) a realistic rape depiction in which the woman suffers and is not aroused, (3) a mutually consenting sexual interaction, and (4) a neutral male-female conversation.

The rape myth tape was taken from a letter, entitled "Trapped," which appeared in *Variations* magazine (August 1981). The letter is an account by a young woman who goes to a bar dressed very provocatively. On her way to the restroom, she encounters a man who grabs her breasts, twists her nipples painfully, and drags her into the men's room, locking the door behind her. He ties her up and proceeds to assault her sexually. At first she is terrified, and fights. But as he proceeds through an array of sexual acts, she becomes extremely sexually responsive, enjoying her tight bonds and the feeling of being ground against a cement wall. By the end of the encounter, she is having a wonderful time. She leaves the restroom glowing from her experience, hoping it will happen again in the future.

The tape of the realistic rape used the same setup as the rape myth scenario, but in it the woman's initial, negative reaction lasts throughout the encounter, rather than changing to pleasure and gratitude.

The mutual consent scenario used the same setup as the rape myth, but portrayed the woman as interested and willing throughout.

The neutral scenario featured the initiation of a short neutral conversation between the characters with no sexual contact at all.

As the participants in the study listened to the audiotapes, I measured the degree of the women's physiological sexual arousal with a vaginal photoplyths-mograph, a tampon-shaped lucite probe with a sensor in it, which the partic-ipants had inserted in private. I also measured self-rated sexual arousal by survey after the audiotape.

The highest levels of genital and self-rated sexual arousal resulted from hearing the rape myth scenario; they were significantly higher than the realistic rape and the neutral conversation, and higher (but not significantly so) than the mutual consent scene. There was no difference between the arousal level for the realistic rape and the neutral tape, indicating that actual rape was not sexually arousing to the study's participants.

Women's emotional responses to the tapes showed a number of significant differences. The rape myth group had the highest self-ratings of sexual arousal, positive feelings, embarrassment, and sensuous feelings. The mutual consent group had equally high levels of positive feelings, sexual arousal, and sensuous feelings, without the embarrassment observed in the rape myth group. The realistic rape group had the highest ratings of frustration, anxiety, and anger.

In general these findings indicate that women are not sexually aroused by representations of rape, and do not enjoy depictions of it that include the victim's pain and suffering. It appears that women, like men, can be sexually aroused by the depiction of a woman enjoying being raped. We do not yet know how exposure to these depictions affects women's beliefs about what constitutes sexual coercion.

Stage Two: Differential Responses of Women and Men to Violent Pornography, Degrading/Dehumanizing Pornography, and Erotica*

My findings in this study were consistent with the majority of existing research into the matter. In early studies, women had a variety of negative subjective reactions to pornographic materials. Mosher and Greenberg's study (1969) found women to be anxious after reading an erotic passage. Mosher (1973) reported women became disgusted, benumbed, anxious, embarrassed, and less serene and peaceful after viewing a film portraying heterosexual sex. (In an exception, Heiman [1975] found women and men equally sexually aroused by erotic scenarios, but these were scripts that Heiman had written herself, not commercially available pornography.) Krafka (1985) found that after being exposed to depictions of violence against women, female viewers were less likely to sympathize with rape victims. After exposure to standard, nonviolent pornographic films, women expressed increased acceptance of the rape myth. Thus the literature to date suggests that women can become sexually aroused by sexually explicit materials, but that standard pornography may cause female viewers to experience attitudinal shifts.

Faith in the assumption—which guided my 1982 study—that pornography could be usefully categorized as either violent or nonviolent has shaped all research in the field for years. But this division fails to capture the feminist conviction that all representations of the dehumanization, degradation, and subordination of women, *even without explicit physical violence*, injure women in general. Feminists who oppose pornography are interested in how it works, not only what it shows, and are aware that degrading representations of women are more common than violent depictions. They define pornography conceptually as any material that depicts an unequal balance of power and shows the objectification, denigration, or brutalization of a person for the purpose of sexual stimulation and entertainment (Dworkin, 1985).

Early data on men's responses to pornography are striking. A small number of studies demonstrated that *nonviolent* pornography had a negative effect on men. In 1982 Zillmann and Bryant showed that men who viewed pornography

---

* "Degrading/dehumanizing" pornography is a term used by social science researchers to describe pornography that does not have overt violence but does portray women as subordinate sex objects. Playboy centerfolds, for example, would fall into this category of pornography.—Eds.

were less sympathetic toward women who had been raped and that they triv-ialized the trauma of rape. They also showed decreased support of the women's movement. In 1978 both Donnerstein and Barrett and Donnerstein and Hallam demonstrated that after two months' exposure to pornography, men demon-strated marked declines in their sense of a rape victim's worth and the severity of her injury. In 1984 Donnerstein and Linz demonstrated that males are more likely to accept rape myths after exposure to pornography. The results were shockingly clear and could have had a great impact. But researchers pulled their punches and reserved their critique for the effects of *violent* pornography, nearly ignoring the effects of nonviolent materials.*

In the last decade, however, new researchers have begun investigating the effects of a broader range of pornographic materials (Check, 1989; Senn and Radtke, 1990; Weaver, 1987; Buchman, 1989; and Zillmann and Bryant, 1989). In 1989, researchers Check and Guloien proposed a new typology that avoids the simplistic violent/nonviolent distinction. They divided sexual ma-terials into the four categories I mentioned at the beginning of this essay:

1. *Sexually violent pornography*, which includes the overt infliction of pain and use of force, or the threat of either.
2. *Degrading/dehumanizing pornography*, which does not include physical violence, but in which men or women are verbally abused or portrayed as having animal characteristics. In it, women are often shown as lacking any human character or identity and are depicted as mere sexual playthings, instantly responsive to male sexual de-mands. They worship male genitals and their own value depends on the quality of their genitals and breasts.
3. *Erotica*, which portrays positive, affectionate human sexual inter-action between consenting individuals participating within a balance of power.
4. *Sexual education materials*, which are neutral, scientific descriptions of the male and female body and the sexual act.

Recently Cowan (1993) prompted a reevaluation of the category of "degrad-ing/dehumanizing" pornography. Noting that the criteria for this category of pornography are more ambiguous than those for violent or erotic materials, she points out that in the only other study on this material Zillmann (1989) defines degrading material as that which depicts "women as sexually insatiable, as socially nondiscriminating in the sense that they seem eager to accommodate

* See "The Costs of Denial," in this volume, p. 104, which describes the self-censorship of some U.S. male researchers.—Eds.

the sexual desires of any man in the vicinity . . ." Cowan argues that because such portrayals often show women not as a sexual object, but rather as a sexual agent, Zillmann's definition confuses the eroticization of female inequality with depictions of female availability. She suggested that there be at least two subgroups of degrading/dehumanizing pornography—one including male dominance and power-asymmetric relations, and the other depicting women as actively and assertively pursuing sexual gratification.

SEX DIFFERENTIAL EFFECTS OF DEGRADING PORNOGRAPHY On the basis of Cowan's work, I conducted studies examining the effects of viewing four types of sexual videos: violent pornography, two types of degrading pornography (female-unequal and female-available), and erotica. *Unequal* degrading materials included depictions of females worshiping penises, unreciprocated sex (i.e., where male desires are satisfied but female desires are not), male dominance, status inequality, status reduction of females, and submission of females. *Available* materials depicted women who were insatiable, available, and constantly responsive. We categorized as *violent* any material that featured eroticized rape, i.e., where women are portrayed as resisting but eventually enjoying forced sex. *Erotic* materials portrayed mutually consenting, enjoyable sexual interactions, without violent or dehumanizing content.

In my study, ninety-three male and fifty-nine female undergraduate students, ages eighteen to thirty-eight, participated. Before and after viewing the videotapes, we gave all of the participants tests measuring their mood (states such as anxiety, depression, hostility, vigor, fatigue and confusion, distress); we also gave them a pretest to assess their use of pornographic materials prior to the experiment. I included seven questions for the women pertaining to the coercive use of pornography. And when the participants—both male and female—had viewed the videotapes, they answered questions about how the tapes had made them feel. Women responded most negatively to the unequal material, and more negatively than men to both the unequal and violent tapes. Those women who viewed only the unequal material indicated the most severe resultant distress, depression, anxiety, hostility, and confusion, and described the women in the videos as suffering pain. The nonviolent pornography, then, was very damaging, more so even than the violent material. This finding provides support for the validity of Cowan's observations.

In contrast, women who viewed the *available* material had predominantly positive responses. They rated the material as sexually arousing and exciting, and saw the women in the tape as assertive, not dominant or degraded. Men, on the other hand, rated the sexual pleasure of male characters as lowest in those scenarios where women exhibited sexual agency, which suggests a general sense of male discomfort with women who initiate sex.

PORNOGRAPHY CONSUMPTION PATTERNS   As part of this study, I collected information on how people use pornography. Ninety-three men and fifty-nine women filled out a questionnaire asking about the kinds of pornographic materials they used. The results were: *Playboy/Penthouse*, men 41 percent, women 8.5 percent; *Hustler*, men 13 percent, women 1.7 percent; hardcore pornography magazines, men 10 percent, women 1.7 percent; adult pornographic paperbacks, men 6.5 percent, women 10.2 percent; X-rated movies, men 8.6 percent, women 5.1 percent; X-rated videotapes, men 27 percent, women 11.9 percent; and romance novels, men 0 percent, women 44.1 percent.

In terms of frequency of pornography use, the male median was once a month (12.9 percent) with the largest percentage (21.5 percent) indicating use six times a year. For females, the median was "never" (54.2 percent), with the next highest percentage at once a year (20.3 percent). Only 17 percent of the female sample used pornography once a month or more.

Males tended to use pornography most often by themselves (39.8 percent), and commonly, though less frequently, with a group (24.7 percent). In contrast to the men, women tended to use pornography as a partner-related activity. Most women (66.1 percent) do not use pornography at all, but of those who do, 22 percent use it with a partner, 8.5 percent by themselves, and 3.4 percent with a group; 18 percent use it by mutual choice with a partner, 3 percent when their partners initiate it, and 10.2 percent initiate it alone.

Of men, 21.6 percent at least occasionally use pornography with sadistic themes: 18.3 percent use some sadistic pornography, 2.2 percent use mostly sadistic pornography, and 1.1 percent exclusively use sadistic pornography. Only 8.5 percent of women surveyed indicated any use of sadistic pornography.

My additional questions for women only about coercive use of pornography drew telling responses. Sixteen out of fifty-nine women in this sample (27.1 percent) answered affirmatively the question, taken from Russell (1980), "Have you ever been upset by anyone trying to get you to do what they had seen in pornographic pictures, movies, or books?" In this subgroup of sixteen women, 23.7 percent had experienced attempted oral, anal, or vaginal intercourse in such a context; 15.3 percent completed intercourse, and for 8.5 percent, this was accompanied by physical force. Also, 5.1 percent of the women had been shown pornographic material by a man who then asked them or forced them to act out the depiction; 16.9 percent had partners describe pornographic acts and then ask or force them to act these out; and 6.8 percent of these women had been forced to pose for pornographic pictures. The most frequent setting in which the women had been exposed to pornography was with a partner, which was also indicated as the most common setting in which pornography was used in a coercive fashion.

Stage 3: Women's Experiences of Pornography in Real Life

My most recent research examines how 500 women from different age, ethnic, geographic, and educational groups feel about the presence of pornography in their homes, in their partner's hands, and in the media marketplace.

Results of the questionnaire indicate that women had a variety of negative responses upon viewing pornography. They felt: upset, 30 percent; discomfited 75 percent; nauseated, 27 percent; confused, 19 percent; angered, 25 percent; embarrassed, 73 percent; repulsed, 41 percent; degraded, 39 percent; objectified, 30 percent; rendered unattractive, 26 percent, or inadequate, 26 percent; and exposed, 20 percent.

Seven percent of the women reported using pornography by themselves, and 12 percent use it with a partner. Thirty-seven percent do not allow pornography in their homes.

Data on how pornography affects women's relationships with men demonstrate that women feel: emotionally distant, 15 percent; sexually distant, 14 percent; as if they are being negatively compared to other women, 42 percent; bad about their bodies, 33 percent; sexually inadequate, 19 percent; pressured to perform, 22 percent; as if sex were a performance, 24 percent; and pressured to try sex acts, 15 percent.

Twelve percent answered that they had "been upset by someone trying to get you to do what they had seen in pornographic pictures, movies, or books." Women who complied with requests or demands to enact behaviors shown in pornography did so most often (17 percent) out of a desire to please their partner. Typical behaviors men asked for included talking dirty, 9 percent; providing oral sex, 11 percent; providing "deep throat" oral sex, 7 percent; having sexual intercourse in uncomfortable positions, 8 percent; having anal intercourse, 9 percent.

As Diana Russell (1993) has recently argued, "We cannot deceive ourselves that more definitive research verifying the harmful effects of pornography will break through the wall of many men's self-interested attachment to material that denigrates women." Men who consume and defend pornography will not voluntarily abandon it. Those who benefit from their dominant position will not relinquish it voluntarily. As the body count of battered, molested, raped, and murdered women mounts, Russell calls for direct political action, including civil disobedience and violent resistance to combat widespread violence against women and its valorization and perpetuation by pornography.

Direct action cannot succeed only on the strength of a few brave women.

It requires a critical mass of support—not a majority, but a sizable, informed, and politicized minority. Further research from more quarters on the effects of pornography in women's lives, and the return of that information to women, will enable this critical mass to form.

Women are not used to talking with one another about their experiences with pornography. Unless they have more information, women in our culture are likely to see their negative feelings about pornography as simply their own problem, evidence of their own prudishness and inhibitions. Breaking through this isolation will facilitate the development of a broad-based movement of resistance to pornography. For these reasons, it is imperative to continue to conduct research on women's experiences of pornography.

TEENAGE TRAINING
The Effects of Pornography on Adolescent Males

James Check

Although the law prohibits the sale of pornography to minors, most young men say that long before their parents spoke with them about sex, they got their real education on the curb with other nine- and ten-year-olds, or in a back room with a dog-eared copy of *Playboy*. What are the effects of this early exposure to pornography? James Check is the first social scientist to focus on this important population.

■

An important subject missing in the research on pornography is how it affects children. Not those who are *depicted* in pornography, but those who are *consumers* of pornography. People who sell and distribute pornography call it "adults-only material." In a host of legal cases against pornography distributors the defense has made much of the existence of a "No Minors Allowed" sign. It turns out, however, that pornography is not "adults only."

For nine years now I have been seeing evidence of that in my research. I studied Canadians ranging in age from four to twelve—a survey of eleven hundred children—and found that about 39 percent of the children in the survey said that they watched pornography at least once a month. When I presented these findings, many people were incredulous. They said, "Children don't know what pornography is," or "They didn't understand the question," or "You must have counted incorrectly," etc. So I decided to collect more data. I conducted the survey again, with an even clearer questionnaire. We administered it at many different locations where children are commonly found: shopping malls, theaters, schools. In each case the results were the same: 39 percent.

In the last of a series of studies, we asked 275 teenagers (with an average age of fourteen) from a local high school in a middle-class Toronto neighborhood a number of simple questions, including, "How often do you watch pornography?" Because people had been skeptical that children know what pornography is, we inserted a long sentence that listed every phrase we could possibly imagine that would make the teenagers think "pornography": *sex video, video porn, X-rated, adults-only, movies of people having sex, lots of nudity, naked bodies,* and so on.

This is what we found: nine out of ten boys (90 percent), and six out of ten girls (60 percent) had seen at least one pornographic movie. One-third of the boys, but only 2 percent of the girls, watched pornography at least once a month. Our data suggest the girls watched once because a boyfriend or somebody wanted them to, or because they were curious, and then didn't want to watch again. So while six out of ten girls have actually seen one pornographic movie, very few girls consume regularly. We then provided a list of six possible sources of information about sex (teachers, peers, parents, books, schools, and magazines) and asked if pornography was an important source. Because the girls did not consume it regularly, they did not find pornography the most significant source of sex information in their lives. Twenty-nine percent of the boys, however, said that pornography was *the most significant source* among those listed. These are two important findings: About one in three fourteen-year-old males is a regular consumer of pornography, and almost the same proportion say that pornography is a significant source of sex information.

Does pornography have any effect on children? I suggest that it has a much greater effect on children than it does on adults. Fourteen-year-olds are exploring sexuality, desperate for information, and pornography provides what they think is useful information about sex. But as my next study shows, the lessons these children learn are not always what society would like.

Children cannot be exposed to pornography in laboratory experiments for obvious legal, ethical, and logistical reasons. So researchers must conduct studies that correlate several sets of statistics. We asked, "What do children learn from pornography?" If pornography is harmless, children should be having a positive learning experience—for instance, how to make love and have sex, how to relate in positive, affectionate ways. On the other hand, if pornography is harmful, children will have a negative learning experience, connecting sex to exploitation, force, or violence. Not surprisingly, in our study, many young boys indicated that they learned from pornography to connect the use of force during sex with excitement, with feeling stimulated. They also learned that force was justified if the female was at all active, i.e., if she took the initiative.

The condition that produced the most acceptance of force during sex was when the female sexually excited the male. We used a scale, from "not at all okay" to "maybe it was okay," all the way to "definitely okay." Forty-three percent of the boys and 16 percent of the girls said holding a girl down and forcing her to have intercourse if a boy has been sexually excited is at least "maybe okay" or said "I'm not sure." On the bottom end of the scale, only 71 percent of the girls and 35 percent of the boys said it's *"definitely not okay."* These data have been replicated in studies in California and Rhode Island.

Now, consider those boys who said that it is okay to hold a girl down and force her to have intercourse. Our study demonstrates that overwhelmingly they are the male teenagers who are reading and watching pornography. This is not a causal link, but it is a statistical link between the amount of pornography male teenagers watch and the belief that it may be okay to use force with sex. This is very important.

I have five data sets now, all pointing in the same direction: children are major consumers of pornography and they are learning from watching it. And restricting children's access to pornography while it is so ubiquitous in our culture is as likely to be effective as restricting their access to alcohol. Teenagers have access to pornography in their homes from parents, brothers, sisters, and friends. They can easily copy a friend's videotape or buy or rent one in a store. Age is simply not a significant barrier for a motivated youngster.

In conclusion, pornography is far from "adults-only" material. Let us reconsider our analyses, keeping in mind that children are watching pornography. For these children—some of them as young as six, seven, eight, nine, or ten years old—pornography *is* their sex education. In factual sex education materials, you get plumbing lessons: here's what a vagina looks like, here's a Fallopian tube. Here's what the penis looks like, here's the glans. You do not get rape scenarios. You do not get force or domination connected with pleasure. You do not get exploitation of one sex by the other. So as long as pornography is this readily available, sex educators cannot hope to compete. That is the main message of my research.

RACISM AND SEXISM IN PORNOGRAPHY

Gloria Cowan

Videocassettes are an important mode of pornography production and distribution today. In 1989, 395 million X-rated videos were rented, representing 12 percent of all rentals. Researchers have examined pornographic videos for sexual violence and exploitation, but little attention has been paid to interracial pornography and to the messages it conveys about people of color. Gloria Cowan describes her study analyzing the content of pornography for racism and sexism.

■

While some researchers make incidental references to particularly racist pornography, to date no one has undertaken systematic research on the prevalence and content of racial themes in pornography. To investigate this important and complex arena, we analyzed 476 characters in fifty-four black/white interracial pornography videos noting evidence of physical and verbal aggression, intimacy, inequality, and the perpetuation of racial stereotypes. Of the characters we saw, there were 119 white females, 133 black females, 98 white males, and 126 black males. In particular, we were interested in racial-sexual combinations of white women with black men, and black women with white men.

Hypothesizing that we would find both sexism and racism in interracial pornography videos, we began by delineating markers of them in pornography. We identified sexism as the disproportionate representation of women as inferior to men or as targets of physical and verbal aggression. We identified racism by reliance on racial stereotypes and the presentation of blacks as lower in status and less intimate than whites.

Measures

We set up a number of scales for measuring racial and sexual inequality. *Physical aggression* consisted of six indicators: hitting, pinching, slapping, hair pulling, holding down, and rape (which we defined as a sexual attack by a male in which the female does not eventually submit).

We measured *verbal aggression* by noting verbal orders, name calling, racial insults, and coercion (threats or inducements such as drugs or money, used to compel a character to engage in sexual activity). We measured *inequality* by such power imbalances as clear age difference, role and occupational inequalities (pimp/whore, master/slave, boss/secretary, etc.). We also noted other inequalities, such as one character being presented as stupid, or one character appearing to be less than human or to serve merely as an ornament.

We measured the degree to which *race* was a salient factor by recording any mention of race, the use of racial names (such as Sapphire or Ebony), racially specific insults or compliments, stereotyped speech, ethnic background music, and so on.

We measured *intimacy* by how often characters kiss, use their partner's name, caress, have face-to-face intercourse, or talk during sexual activity.

In addition, we catalogued the frequency of particularly loaded sex acts. To register the submissiveness of the female characters, we counted the number of times a woman was shown performing fellatio while on her knees. To chart the sexual stereotype of the "big black buck," we recorded each mention of the size of a male character's penis, and whether his penis was larger than average. Finally, we recorded all instances of anal sex, fellatio, intercourse, cunnilingus, and use of the female face or mouth as a receptacle for male ejaculation.

Results

Racism and sexism are prevalent in interracial pornography, combining to produce an effect distinct from that caused by their individual presence. Race seems to exaggerate sex roles in pornography; for example, all female characters are dominated, but in the case of black female characters the domination is particularly extreme. In general, dehumanization and depersonalization are pervasive in interracial pornography.

The sexism of pornography has been extensively explored by other researchers, and it was corroborated by this study. Male characters registered high on the aggression scales, both physical and verbal, and their aggression was largely directed at their lower-scoring female counterparts. White men were depicted as perpetrating more acts of aggression against black women than against white women. Black men perpetrated more acts of aggression against white women than black women. The incidence of rape was not frequent enough to be analyzed, but of the five rapes we counted, four of the targets were white women. Both women and men exhibited more verbal aggression toward partners of a different race than toward partners of their own race.

Thus, our prediction that women would be portrayed in pornography as physically and verbally subordinate to men was supported. But our prediction that women would be depicted as uniformly subordinate to men was less accurate. The status of black men and women was not significantly different: both were subordinate to white men, as were white women. In all, this may be a function of white men being the material's intended audience; the material may betray a deliberate effort to cater to their fantasies of their own dominance, and their fantasies about black sexuality (Mapp, 1982; Santiago, 1990).

Racial inequality was no less in evidence than gender-based inequality. Black characters were consistently presented as subordinate to white characters. For instance, more black women (68.3 percent) performed fellatio while on their knees than did white women (53.1 percent). (Though it is interesting to note that white women were ejaculated on in the face more often than black women; subordination may take different forms for white and black women.) Black women were also the victims of a greater number of acts of physical and verbal aggression than white women, regardless of the race of the perpetrator. More of the black women were treated as objects by white men than by black men (34 percent versus 17 percent), while more white women were treated as objects by black men than by white men (40 percent versus 19 percent).

Pornography reinforces racially specific sexual stereotypes. Black men were portrayed as having unusually large penises, and as being mere sex machines —incapable of or uninterested in such intimate gestures as kissing, caressing, and talking—rather than full human beings. It should be noted, however, that black men were no more aggressive than white men.

Discussion

Our findings support bell hooks's (1990) view of racism and sexism as interlocking systems of domination that maintain each other.

A number of writers have discussed racism in pornography as a historical consequence of slavery and racism in this country (Gardner, 1980; hooks, 1990; Teisch, 1980; Walker, 1980). They note that it is not the mere presence of

African-American people in pornography that makes it racist, but rather its exploitation of the history of slavery and the mythology of racial oppression (Gardner, 1980). White male domination of or aggression toward black women derives historically from the antebellum status of female slaves as chattel, entirely the property of their owner, and this consistency gives meaning to much of the interracial material we viewed. For example, an extremely racially derogatory scene in one of the pornography videos, *Let Me Tell Ya 'Bout Black Chicks*, portrayed a black woman willingly having simultaneous vaginal and anal sex with two white men in Ku Klux Klan hoods. Having found her in her bedroom, masturbating to gospel music, these men say, "Let's f____ the s____ out of this darky." In this scene, it is the sociohistorical *context*—provided by our knowledge of the KKK and the lie that the oppressed wants to engage in sex with her oppressor—that makes the scene degrading and racist.

Another possible explanation for the prevalence of interracial sexual aggression in pornography is that it is used to play out societal outrage at the existence of interracial sex in the real world. Female characters who violate our society's taboo against interracial sex may lose the protection of society; indeed, they may be seen as losing all their rights, deserving to suffer whatever aggression their nonsanctioned partner inflicts. In this way, black male characters in pornography serve as they have throughout mythology and literature: as the punishers of sexually active white women. Paul Hock (1979) traced the archetypes of black beast, white hero, and white goddess as far back as ancient Greece, finding the theme of erect-black-buck-threatening-chaste-white-lady to have been dominant in mythology for more than three centuries.

Alice Walker suggests that many black men see pornography as progressive because in it the previously forbidden white woman is available to them. Others, like hooks and Santiago, have theorized that pornography may provide a sort of bond between white and black men, uniting them in a common goal—the sexual domination of women—that momentarily supersedes the racial differences that otherwise divide them.

In truth, however, pornographic representations do not unite black men and white men in a common struggle, not even one as perverse as sexual domination. Black male characters are consistently reduced to the basest racial stereotypes, subordinated to their white counterparts, and "defined solely by the size, readiness, and unselectivity of [their] penis" (Walker, 1980). The "frothing-at-the-mouth for a white woman, strong-backed, sixty-minute hot black" (Lincoln, 1970) may simply be an exaggerated continuation of pornography's depiction of all men, or it may be a surrogate figure exploitively used by white men to commit the sexual violence about which they fantasize, but which they hesitate to act out themselves. In any case, Andrea Dworkin (1989), noting the consistency with which racially vilified groups have been imagined as demonstrating a bestial sexuality, has shown that, far from being an empowering image of strength, the hypersexualized representation of black men is a tool used to justify their oppression.

The representation of black women is often particularly disempowering, as it manipulates their double legacy of race and gender oppression. For example, the simultaneous depiction of black women as seductresses and as objects available for exploitation by any male has recurred in Hollywood for many years (Mapp, 1982), through images of them as sexually uncivilized or promiscuous, or as whores (Dworkin, 1989; Gardner, 1980; hooks, 1990). Again, the roots of the stereotype in the U.S. begin in slavery—an institution that made the black woman particularly vulnerable to sexual exploitation (Mapp, 1982). Thus, it is no surprise that the degradation, dehumanization, and aggression directed toward women in pornography is seen more strongly with black than white women.

Conclusion

It is clear from this brief examination that racism and sexism are intertwined in pornography. We need more research investigating the functions of pornography in general, and of racist pornography in particular. Is the purpose of pornography to reinforce racial and sexual stereotypes? Does it function as a bond between men, regardless of race? If it plays on racial and sexual oppression, is it doubly damaging to women of color?

Pornography has often been labeled a women's issue; a feminist issue; and, more specifically, a white feminist issue (Gardner, 1980). Some have suggested that black women may have hesitated to address its harms because they see it as a racially divisive issue (Davis, 1981). But this study demonstrates that pornography is not racially or ethnically neutral. If people become more aware of the negative depiction of African Americans in pornography, perhaps it will cease to be a white women's issue and will be recognized as a matter of equal concern to all people of color.

HATE ACTIVITY AND THE JEWISH COMMUNITY

Alan Schwartz

For fifteen years the Anti-Defamation League has been monitoring incidents of violence, harassment, threats, assault, and vandalism directed against Jews in the United States. Their latest audit notes an increase of 23 percent in acts of assault, threat, or harassment from 1992 to 1993. As sobering as these figures are, social scientists estimate that the real figures may be as many as eight times higher because of incomplete reporting.

■

In 1993, the Anti-Defamation League catalogued a total of 1,167 anti-Semitic incidents against property and persons in forty-four states and the District of Columbia. This figure, the second-highest in fifteen years, represents an increase of 8 percent over the year before. Acts of personal assault, threat, or harassment rose by 23 percent, while incidents related to property—e.g., vandalizing synagogues, spray painting anti-Jewish slogans—decreased by 8 percent.

The 1993 findings document several trends:

1. For the third straight year, acts of anti-Semitic hostility against individuals far outnumbered incidents of vandalism against institutions and other property. There was a total of 1,079 acts against individuals.
2. The disturbing upward trend in on-campus anti-Semitic incidents continued in 1993. In the past six years, campus incidents have more than doubled. The most well-known events are the verbal anti-Semitic attacks by such bigots and demagogues as Louis Farrakhan and his followers, whose presentations at numerous schools have fostered a sense of outrage, intimidation, and harassment among Jewish students.
3. Finally, in the vandalism category, the number of anti-Semitic incidents (352) committed against public property—e.g., buildings, bridges, signposts, etc.—was more than twice that committed against synagogues, schools, and other Jewish institutions (161).

Harassment, Threats, and Assaults

The number of personal incidents surpassed instances of vandalism in 1993 for the third consecutive year. In addition to outright crimes, such as physical violence, this category includes a variety of acts, which, though not prohibited by law, constitute overt and painful expressions of anti-Semitic hatred. Such acts include slurs directed at Jews on their way to synagogue or campus gatherings, neo-Nazi literature mailed to Jews, and threatening phone calls placed to synagogues or Jewish schools.

While all incident totals increased steadily between 1986 and 1991, the category of harassment, threats, and assaults rose most dramatically in the five years prior to 1992, a staggering 193 percent. After an 8 percent decline in 1992, the rate of increase has resumed, and the new total is the second highest ever reported. In the 1990s alone, these incidents have risen 42 percent. This trend confirms the impression of many observers across the nation that confrontational, "in-your-face" acts of violence, intimidation, and incivility have been growing and spreading. Overall, anti-Semitic acts of personal harassment and assault have risen 245 percent in the seven years since 1986. In the worlds of politics, culture, and education, anti-Jewish conspiracy theories have become not only more common, but more casually tolerated and rationalized—a trend some observers have called the "mainstreaming" of anti-Semitism, signaling a new willingness by those inclined toward anti-Semitism to engage in direct, provocative confrontations with Jews, and an erosion of the taboo against open bigotry.

Here is a representative sampling of 1993 incidents of anti-Semitic harassment in Washington, D.C., and the ten states reporting the highest totals of such acts:

• Boynton Beach, Florida, March—A Jewish middle school student, who was taunted for months with anti-Semitic remarks by two older boys, was severely beaten by them when he got off his school bus (state total, 139).

• The Bronx, New York, October—Four Jewish students, around thirteen years old, were surrounded by a large gang of teenagers who punched the Jewish boys, called them "dirty Jews," and knocked their skullcaps off. Three of the attackers were arrested (state total, 128).

• Framingham, Massachusetts, June—"Jew!" was yelled by a man in a passing truck at a Jewish woman mourner leaving a cemetery (state total, 118).

• Santa Cruz, California, August—Anti-Semitic remarks, threats, and obscenities, including "We kill Jews. Fuck you," were left on a Jewish family's telephone answering machine (state total, 116).

• Westfield, New Jersey, March—Anti-Semitic obscenities—"You fucking Jews, we're gonna get you"—were yelled by several men in a passing car at an individual in front of a synagogue (state total, 88).

• Skokie, Illinois, November—A threatening anti-Semitic message was left on a synagogue answering machine, including, "We are skinheads and we have the upper hand" (state total, 66).

• Toledo, Ohio, August—A telephone call was made to the Toledo Jewish Federation and Jewish Community Center containing anti-Semitic remarks and threatening, "No Jew in Ohio is safe" (state total, 64).

• Houston, Texas, February—Anti-Semitic hate group material was mailed to a Jewish family's home, referring to "the jew-sponsored [sic] 3rd world immigration Invasion" (state total, 20).

• Washington, D.C., September—On a city bus, a man called a Jewish woman "a kike," said "We hate Jews," and pulled her hair (district total, 18).

• Denver, Colorado, June—A threatening anti-Semitic letter was sent to a newly elected Denver City Council member who is Jewish, calling her "a kike voice" and warning that "the sound of jack boots is never far away" (state total, 10).

• Albuquerque, New Mexico, August—A woman was assaulted and told: "You fucking Jew bitch, you should have all burned in the oven" (state total, 11).

Campus Incidents

Anti-Semitic acts on American college campuses increased for the sixth straight year in 1993, to a total of 122 at eighty-one campuses—7 percent more incidents on twenty-one more campuses than the year before. Since 1988, the rise has been 126 percent. Paralleling the audit's findings for the general community, far more of the incidents on campus involved personal harassment, threat, and assault than the vandalism of property, by a ratio of about 8 to 1. A major portion of this activity consisted of paid advertisements in campus newspapers that maintain the Holocaust never occurred. The central figure in this propaganda campaign is Bradley R. Smith, who submitted an ad to eighteen major university newspapers in the past year. Five newspapers rejected the ad outright, seven published it as received, four ran it as an op-ed piece or in letter form, and two printed parts of it in other forms. (It may be noted that Smith also sent the ad to a high school newspaper in Portland, Oregon. After it appeared, school authorities there ordered that it not be reprinted by any of the other schools in the area.) Other incidents include:

• At the City University of New York's LaGuardia Community College an article appeared in the school's newspaper, *The Bridge*, declaring: "Jews don't own the United States but some act as if they do . . . Jews immigrated here after over 4.5 million were killed in Hitler's concentration camps. If it wasn't for the presence of an all-Black army unit, many more Jews would have died . . . their race was almost extinct. Now they are trying to 'extinct' Blacks out of everything, including existence." Although campus officials denounced the article as inflammatory propaganda, they took no punitive action. The student who wrote the tract later became news editor; the editor who published it was promoted to editor-in-chief.

• At Wellesley College in Massachusetts, several students lodged a complaint against Anthony Martin, a professor in the African Studies Department, for assigning *The Secret Relationship between Blacks and Jews* as required reading in his introductory class on African-American history. The book, written by members of Louis Farrakhan's Nation of Islam, is an anti-Semitic diatribe that maintains that Jews played a controlling role in the African slave trade. Responding to criticism of his use of this tract (from figures including Selwyn Cudjoc, chair of the department), Martin charged that anti-Semitism had become "a bludgeon" used against African Americans by "the privileged and powerful U.S. Jewish leadership and their unthinking Negro stooges." He published a book entitled *The Jewish Onslaught*, alleging a campaign of "lies, distortion and scurrilous attacks" against him, mostly by Jews. Wellesley president Diana Chapman Walsh denounced the "innuendo and . . . racial and religious stereotype" contained in the professor's charges.

• Many incidents of anti-Semitic graffiti took place on campuses. On February 7, 1993, at Florida Atlantic University, a spray-painted message was found in a men's room: "Anti-Semitism is alive and well at FAU—we will hang the Jews in the University Center on Saturday." On March 7, 1993, a swastika and the words "Fuck the Jews" were discovered on a wall in an entry to Lowell House at Harvard University. On April 17, 1993, numerous swastikas were found on buildings at Tufts University. On September 29, 1993, vandals painted a series of swastikas on the campus of George Washington University.

On December 5, 1993, vandals scrawled "Jews burn in Hell" on the steps of a predominantly Jewish fraternity at Colorado University.

Vandalism

In 1993 there were one incident of arson and two of attempted arson, one bombing and two attempted bombings, and twenty-five cemetery desecrations—a combined total of thirty-one particularly serious acts of vandalism. In 1992, this total was twenty-nine. The breakdown of cemetery desecrations was: Ohio, eight; Massachusetts, three; New Jersey, three; Washington State, three; California, two; Connecticut, two; Arizona, one; Minnesota, one; Montana, one; and New York, one. Jewish cemeteries generally cover a vast physical area and are therefore the hardest facilities to secure. The increase in these incidents over the last three years suggests that as hate crime laws, law enforcement action, and Jewish institutions' own security measures have all increased, perpetrators of anti-Semitic hate crime are increasingly targeting those locations that are hardest to protect.

Skinhead Incidents

In recent years, the Anti-Defamation League has monitored the activities of neo-Nazi skinhead gangs around the United States. In 1993, the ADL published its seventh and most extensive fact-finding report* on the worrisome phenomenon of these organizations, noting the existence of about 100 groups, with between 330 and 3,500 members in forty states.

The ADL document reports that neo-Nazi skinheads have been implicated in twenty-eight homicides as well as many other destructive, antisocial acts during the past six years, though in 1993 comparatively few of these criminal acts were committed against Jews, Jewish institutions, or Jewish property. Far more were committed against black, Hispanic, or gay targets, or against other rival skinheads.

In 1993 neo-Nazi skinheads perpetrated a dozen anti-Semitic incidents in eight states. One notorious incident on this list was the plot by eight white supremacists from Southern California to blow up a black church and assassinate black and Jewish leaders. Christopher Fisher, leader of the Fourth Reich Skinheads and a codefendant, Carl Boese, received prison sentences of eight

---

* "Young Nazi Killers: The Rising Skinhead Danger," ADL Special Report, 1993.

years and four years, nine months, respectively, for their roles. Another was the extensive cemetery desecration in Everett, Massachusetts; at least one of the culprits had neo-Nazi skinhead ties. Other skinhead-related incidents (including graffiti on synagogues, hate messages on telephones, and neo-Nazi fliers in mailboxes) were reported in Arizona, Florida, Georgia, Illinois, New Jersey, and New York.

Skinhead-related anti-Semitic incidents have declined substantially (by about 90 percent) over the past five years; since 1989, when the high mark of 116 such episodes was reported, the number has dropped steadily to 87 in 1990, 62 in 1991, 19 in 1992, and 12 in 1993. This decline is likely due to at least three factors: growing law enforcement awareness and attention to the skinhead problem around the country; a steadily improving program of preventive security measures by Jewish institutions; and, as noted, the availability of several other more readily recognized target minorities who are being victimized by these young neo-Nazi thugs.

These findings indicate that as skinhead gangs have proliferated they have grown less satisfied with small-scale vandalism and harassment. Tough law enforcement seems to deter skinhead crime. Consequently, appropriate resources must be directed to that effort.

In summary, these findings reveal trends consistent with similar, more broadly based developments in American society: the widely reported ethnic tensions on our college campuses; the spread of Holocaust denial propaganda; the bigotry of some demagogues claiming leadership within the black community (including Louis Farrakhan and Leonard Jeffries); the palpable loosening of taboos against anti-Semitic, racist, homophobic, and misogynistic stereotyping in the public arena; and the increasingly violent imagery and declining standards of decency in our cultural life, especially in music, on TV, and in films.

All of these general trends find their parallels in the episodes of anti-Semitic violence, bigotry, and insensitivity revealed by the present report. In effect, the audit presents a microcosm of many of our nation's social ills.

In general, our Constitution protects everyone's right to hold and promote even the most obnoxious and offensive views. Thus, expressions of hate conveyed through speech (overt or symbolic) or other forms of communication, including print, telephone, television and computer, present a complex challenge in terms of effective, constitutionally sound response. ADL opposes censorship, and believes that the best answer to "bad" speech is more and better speech, by the decent majority who do not hate.

The 1993 audit does not bring welcome news. The problem of anti-Semitism will not disappear tomorrow. For the Jewish community, as well as other minority communities, and for their allies in the public and private sectors, much work remains to be done.

THE COSTS OF DENIAL
Self-Censorship of Research on Degrading/Dehumanizing Pornography

Gloria Cowan and Wendy Stock

After the publication of the report of the Attorney General's Commission on Pornography in 1986, pornography became an important focus of research. A spate of social science investigations followed, including attitudinal surveys, laboratory experiments, and retrospective studies, mostly focused on proving a causal link between pornography and violence against women. But in the early eighties, several leading social scientists shifted the focus of their research from pornographic films and magazines to violent films—for example, mainstream B-grade slasher films. Some researchers recanted their original findings on the effects of pornography. Rumors abounded that at least one leading researcher was receiving funds from pornographers. Researchers reported that federal and private grant monies were available only to those whose research shifted attention away from the harm of pornography. Here, Gloria Cowan and Wendy Stock discuss the cost of research not done and results denied.

■

Pornography research has been colored by a great deal of controversy and mutual accusations. Researchers have strong views about this area because it brings into play many deeply held values. In addition, because research findings on pornography often have immediate policy implications, many researchers have been concerned that their findings might be used to support an ideological position with which they do not agree.

In this article, we consider three ethical issues: first, the lack of attention paid to degrading/dehumanizing pornography; second, the imprecise selection of sexual materials in research studies; and third, the distortion of findings by some researchers and inconsistencies in their statements.

The first issue is the unwillingness of most researchers to focus their studies on sexually explicit material that degrades and dehumanizes. Antipornography feminists have proposed that sexually explicit material that portrays the sexual subordination, domination, or objectification of women has negative effects on male consumers and on the status and well-being of women. But at present, most researchers recognize only the distinction between violent and nonviolent pornography. Many recent studies emphasize the harmful effects of *violent* pornography, but rarely deal with the possible harmful effects of pornography that is degrading and dehumanizing, but *not* explicitly violent. As a result, we know very little about how imagery that depersonalizes and dehumanizes women (such as the centerfolds of the major "men's entertainment magazines") contributes to the devaluation of women; whether it renders women as sex objects in the eyes of readers; or if it fosters violence or increases sexual harassment by those exposed to it. Because it is as important to examine factors that may contribute to misogyny and discrimination against women as it is to investigate factors that support rape and battery, the researchers' refusal to examine such effects has deep ethical implications.

Some researchers have indicated that "degrading/dehumanizing" pornography is hard to define. But the surveys Cowan and Dunn conducted among college students demonstrated that (1) to a large extent, women and men agree on which types of images are more and less degrading to women, (2) dominance and objectification are the two themes viewed as most degrading by both women and men, and (3) sex without subordination is not seen as degrading. For an example of degrading material, consider the following description from the cover of *Gang Bang 4*, an example of the new popular genre of amateur videos. These videos are not made by professionals, but are rented and sold alongside those from established studios.

> Ginger takes it all—this video has Ginger being fucked over twenty-five times and taking over nineteen facial cum shots. Ginger strips for fun at a Bachelor party where she is the entertainment. First she goes to the floor with cocks everywhere, one in her pussy, one in her mouth, and one in each hand. From there she is carried to a desk to let everyone cum in her mouth or on her face. But this is only the beginning. She lays naked in front of the men and masturbates with a huge double dildo. This means she passes the dildo to each guy to see who can shove it deeper into her pussy until she takes over 18″ deep into her pussy. This leads to more fucking and a wild cum shower. Lucky she wore her glasses as they are totally covered as is her face with hot wet cum. But this isn't the end as four more men fuck her and cum on her hot body. She licks ass, licks their balls and takes it in her ass. Enough? Not for Ginger as

she ends the video by emptying the cum from three condoms into
her hungry mouth licking up every drop (two hours).

Like this cover description, which is meant to appeal directly to those who are
aroused by images of women being used and objectified, a great deal of pornography falls into the "degrading/dehumanizing" category.

Unfortunately, experimental research on the effects of pornography has been
damagingly split into two main camps. Donnerstein, Linz, and Penrod (1987)
have argued that it is the violence in pornography that is a problem. Zillmann,
Bryant, and Weaver (1989), on the other hand, argue that the most harmful
influence on viewers' attitudes is repeated exposure to images of women as
"sexually insatiable, as nondiscriminating and as hypereuphoric about any kind
of sexual stimulation."

The implication of the argument that only violent material is harmful is
that since most pornography is not violent, most pornography can be dismissed
from scrutiny. Further, the question is begged of why one should bother
examining pornography at all, since violence is everywhere in the mass media.

On the other hand, the researchers who focus on the harm of hypersexual
female representations are also doing a disservice to women. Identifying female
promiscuity as the main problem with pornography feeds dangerously into a
moralistic critique of female sexuality in general, and suggests, in any case,
the specious belief that *all* sexually explicit material may be harmful. In both
cases, the framing of the issue diverts attention from the specific ways that
pornography subordinates women.

It is difficult to understand why the role of degrading and dehumanizing
pornography has been downplayed when so much material features the domination and exploitation of women. (Cowan's investigation of X-rated videos
found that dominance and exploitation were major themes in 54 percent of
the sexually explicit scenes.) Moreover, feminist theorists have been writing
about the issue of subordination in pornography for years. Researchers must
challenge the accepted paradigms of the field if they are to meet the real needs
of women.

The second problem in studies on the effect of degrading or dehumanizing
pornography is the selection of stimulus materials. For example, a 1988 study
by Linz, Donnerstein, and Penrod entitled "The Effects of Long Term Exposure to Violence and Sexually Degrading Depictions of Women" found no
negative attitudinal changes in men who viewed the selected X-rated films.
But the researchers chose material that is relatively low in the degradation or
subordination of women. In two of the films, *Debbie Does Dallas* and *Indecent
Exposure*, the main female characters engineered their own sexual encounters

and stayed in control of their outcomes; *Indecent Exposure* depicts an unusual number of acts of intimacy. This material is simply not characteristic of the most damaging kinds of pornography, and cannot be used to disprove theories about its harmfulness.

The intransigence of most researchers has resulted in significantly distorted data. Instead of presenting findings and reviewing the literature in a balanced and impartial way, they politicize the field by pursuing their traditional agenda and devaluing the work of their dissenting peers. The work of Zillmann, Check and Guloien, and Weaver, for example, which found that after viewing nonviolent pornography people were more likely to trivialize rape or display proclivity to rape, has gone unquoted and unrecognized.

The third problem in understanding the effects of degrading or dehumanizing pornography is the tendency of some researchers to reverse or revise previous statements. During the Minneapolis hearings on pornography in 1983, for example, Edward Donnerstein stated, on the basis of his own previous decade's worth of research, that the long-term effects of X-rated material without violence included "increases in sex stereotypes and . . . the same attitudes that you get in the violent material. The only difference is the immediate increase in aggression. That is where the differences occur." He made clear that degrading or dehumanizing pornography has negative effects on those who view it. But two years later, Donnerstein stated that "sexually explicit material has no effects on behavior attitudes. Take away the violent element, no effects." It is unlikely that this change is the result of new data collected between 1983 and 1985.

Perhaps, as psychologist Stewart Page has suggested, such reversals are entirely motivated by politics. He speculates that ideological differences between researchers and the highly partisan Meese Commission on Pornography led researchers to downplay—even deny—the results of their own research lest it be used to justify the commission's legislative agenda.

Not only is this behavior unethical, unscientific, and unprofessional, it is also dangerous to women. The fear of being identified with Jessie Helms, Phyllis Schlafly, or the religious right should not lead researchers to deny their findings, but rather encourage them to continue research and present findings with all their complexities and contradictions. Merely because degrading or dehumanizing pornography may not be the only cause of violence against women, and just because it may lead to negative changes in attitudes and beliefs and not to extreme violent behavior, it does not follow that it is inconsequential.

Linz and Donnerstein say that they have shifted their approach because they are concerned about safeguarding freedom of expression. But what about the safety of women? Linz and Donnerstein disregard the high rates of violence against women, both reported and unreported. Our society is not a safe place for women—certainly it is much less safe for women than for pornography researchers. Social scientists should include consideration of harm to women as well as concern for freedom of expression and fear of censorship in their set of responsibilities and professional ethics.

Researchers cannot tell the public how to weigh free speech against women's well-being, safety, and social status, but they do have the responsibility to provide up-to-date and unbiased accounts of the evidence to help individuals make their own decisions. In our research on attitudes toward the regulation of pornography, we consider both how damaging the material is and how much people value free speech. Individuals will not be able to make rational and thoughtful decisions about these important issues if researchers are unwilling to conduct unbiased studies, if they distort their findings, or if they shift like weather vanes with every new political breeze that blows. Researchers must expand their perspectives and modify their preferred research models to consider the very real harm that is done by degrading and dehumanizing pornography.

ANTI–GAY AND –LESBIAN VIOLENCE, VICTIMIZATION, AND DEFAMATION
Trends, Victimization Studies, and Incident Descriptions

Martin Kazu Hiraga

From offices in six cities around the United States, the National Gay and Lesbian Task Force monitors anti-gay incidents of violence, hate speech, intimidation, and vandalism. In the group's ninth annual survey, they note the continuation of widespread violence against gay men and lesbians in this country. Their report demonstrates once again that hate speech and hate crimes are inextricably intertwined—that assault is often accompanied by or preceded by verbal epithets and that this hate speech is itself part of a larger campaign of intimidation and terrorization.

■

Victim service agencies in six cities documented 1,813 incidents of harassment in 1993—including threats, physical assault, vandalism, arson, police abuse, kidnapping, extortion, and murder—directed against lesbians or gay men because of their sexuality. The highest number of such episodes was recorded in New York City (587), followed by San Francisco (366), Minneapolis/St. Paul (240), Denver (229), Chicago (204), and Boston (187).

A few examples of the variety of anti-gay incidents reported in 1993 include:

• Staten Island, New York: A gay man was chased for several blocks by thirty youths and hit in the face with an object. When the attackers caught up with the victim they assaulted him, shouting, "We should kill you, faggot" (*The Washington Blade*, July 23, 1993).

• Washington, D.C.: A gay man was thrown to the ground and robbed by an assailant who pretended to be romantically interested in him. The attacker called the gay man a "stupid faggot-ass" and threatened to shoot him (*The Washington Blade*, May 28, 1993).

• Woodhaven, Michigan: A man hiding in the back seat of a car forced a lesbian to drive to a nearby field, punched her in the face, and raped her twice. Over the course of the two-hour attack the assailant told the victim, "This should teach you not to be a queer . . . It's wrong . . . This is what you need" (*Heritage* newspaper, December 1, 1993).

• Anchorage, Alaska: A gay couple holding hands was attacked by three teen-agers wielding baseball bats and a pipe in February. The assailants called the men "queers" and "faggots" (*Anchorage Daily News*, February 16, 1993).

• Riviera Beach, Maryland: Vandals spray painted the word "Queer," other anti-gay epithets, and swastikas on a gay man's car and property (*The Washington Blade*, July 16, 1993).

• Boston, Massachusetts: Obscene, threatening, and harassing calls to the Boston Bisexual Community Center soared after group members appeared on a talk show (*BiWomen*, February/March 1993).

• Willacoochee, Georgia: A burning cross was planted on the front lawn of a gay couple's residence. One week earlier the couple had found their mailbox vandalized (*Southern Voice*, August 5, 1993).

• Hillcrest, California: A mechanic yelled "God-damned faggot! You sorry cocksucker" at a gay man and told him to "get out of our office, faggot!" when the gay man tried to register a complaint about an anti-gay epithet on the auto shop's computer system (*Gay and Lesbian Times*, February 4, 1993).

• Orlando, Florida: Thirty skinheads protested gays in the military in front of a gay bar. The skinheads confronted lesbian and gay counter-demonstrators, calling them "faggots" and making the Nazi stiff-arm salute. The white supremacists yelled "Spic" and "Seig Heil" when a Latino bystander demanded to know what they were doing (*Orlando Sentinel*, February 28, 1993).

• Colorado Springs, Colorado: The Society to Remove All Immoral Gross Homosexual Trash (STRAIGHT) hung posters at gay, lesbian, and bisexual bars and businesses calling for the "death of homosexuals as prescribed in the Bible." Some of the signs also recruited new members for the Ku Klux Klan (*Rocky Mountain News*, March 28, 1993).

Because victims frequently choose not to report their experiences—because they don't know the procedure, don't see the purpose, or fear public disclosure—these figures almost certainly reflect only a fraction of the actual number of incidents. Moreover, while fewer incidents were reported in 1993, more of those who reported them reported multiple criminal acts committed against them during each incident. For example, while in 1992 some complainants reported having been harassed because of their sexual orientation, in 1993 survivors were more likely to report they had not only been harassed, but were assaulted and robbed during the same incident. Nationwide, the number of anti-gay incidents including multiple offenses rose 22 percent from 1992 to 1993.

Anti-gay arson was the most serious form of offense to increase this year—from two such incidents in 1992 to six in 1993. Vandalism also rose 10 percent, from 141 incidents in 1992 to 155 in 1993. Bomb threats increased 8 percent, from thirteen incidents in 1992 to fourteen in 1993. Harassment—personalized, confrontational incidents in which lesbians, gay men, and bisexuals are intimidated face-to-face, on the phone, or by mail—rose 35 percent from 1,230 incidents in 1992 to 1,665 in 1993.

Reports of threats and deliberate intimidation dropped 9 percent, from 667 incidents to 605. Physical assaults (gay bashing) fell 16 percent in the six cities, from 848 incidents in 1992 to 710 in 1993. Robberies declined 28 percent, from eighty-five to sixty-one. Reports of police abuse dipped 36 percent, from 248 to 161. Anti-gay murders fell from fourteen to seven. Murders in which the victim's sexual orientation was one of several motivating factors declined 25 percent, from twenty-four to eighteen.

During the campaign for Colorado's Amendment 2, a bill that sought to deny lesbians and gays legal protection from discrimination, backers blanketed communities with literature and videos that portrayed lesbians, gay men, and bisexuals as degenerate, privileged, sexually perverse, and subhuman. The amendment was passed,* as have similar initiatives in Cincinnati, Ohio; Lewiston, Maine; Portsmouth, New Hampshire; and several cities and counties in Oregon. Initiative backers in all four campaigns asserted that the initiatives sought only to prevent lesbians, gay men, and bisexuals from gaining "special rights." By early 1994, far-right organizations had filed anti-gay ballot initiatives in Idaho, Oregon, Arizona, Missouri, Michigan, Florida, Washington, and Nevada. As the experiences in Colorado and Oregon demonstrated, these campaigns provide unparalleled opportunities for hate-mongering and harass-

---

* The amendment's enforcement is currently barred by injunction.—Eds.

ment that community leaders, public officers, church officials, and citizens of conscience must take great efforts to counteract.

In 1993, federal, state, and local authorities made progress in countering hate violence. The U.S. Supreme Court ruled unanimously that states may enhance penalties for crimes in which victims were singled out because of their race, religion, sexual orientation, or other such group status. After the Supreme Court's decision, the Federal Hate Crime Sentencing Enhancement Act was introduced and passed in the House of Representatives.

Taken together, the data and descriptions in this report show that homophobic violence and victimization continue to be a widespread and critical problem. As with other bigoted attacks, each anti-gay episode sends a message of hatred and terror intended to silence and render invisible not only the particular victim, but all who are like him or her. The effect, then, of such violence is to deny gay people their full measure of equality, including the rights to speak out, associate, and assemble. It is not a coincidence that anti-gay hate propaganda and violence occur simultaneously with pervasive attacks against Jews, people of color, and women. Given how extensive bigotry is and the all-encompassing hatred of those who commit such crimes, it is imperative that measures to address the problem include all those who are the targets of hatred.

Some leaders in government, law enforcement, and religion actively oppose violence and discrimination based on sexual orientation. Too frequently they, like the victims of hate speech and hate crimes themselves, encounter fierce resistance from those seeking to deny lesbian and gay people the same protections accorded other groups in our society. But these leaders cannot give up in that struggle, nor can the citizens whom they represent. The continued denial of such protections is a legal and moral disgrace that must be challenged and overcome.

CHAPTER THREE

Conceptualizing Harm

Activism against hate speech and pornography grew out of the larger civil rights and women's rights movements—movements that are first and foremost efforts to gain equality and justice for people who have been historically excluded from the mainstream. In their early days, the civil rights and women's rights efforts struck many as dangerous, as going too far. They challenged established notions of property and rights, of neighborhood and school patterns, of electoral politics, of equality and justice. Just as these earlier efforts required that society learn to think differently about the treatment of women and people of color, the anti-pornography and anti-hate speech movements challenge us to do the same today. Like the activists who preceded and inspired them, they seek to teach society to reconceive its notions of harmful speech and conduct.

In this chapter, ten contributors refer to the experiences of people of color, women, and other marginalized populations in formulating new conceptual frameworks for understanding the harm of racist speech, hate propaganda, and pornography. Their descriptions of silencing, objectification, and exclusion supply the essential bridge between experience and reform, and lay the foundation for a legal response.

CROSS-BURNING AND THE SOUND OF SILENCE
Anti-subordination Theory and the First Amendment

Charles R. Lawrence III

The legal decision in *R.A.V.* v. *St. Paul*, the celebrated cross-burning case, is a complicated, even convoluted one. The Minneapolis Supreme Court found St. Paul's ordinance against hate bias to be constitutional because it regulated only speech that fell under the category of "fighting words." But the U.S. Supreme Court reversed this decision, holding that even fighting words can convey ideas, and cannot be prohibited based on the content of their message. In other words, said the Supreme Court, an ordinance prohibiting "fighting words" is constitutional, but one prohibiting *racist* fighting words is not. How the Supreme Court took a case of white hooligans terrorizing a black family and turned it into a free speech case is the subject of this article.

■

In the early morning hours of June 21, 1990, long after they had put their five children to bed, Russ and Laura Jones were awakened by voices outside their house. Russ got up, went to his bedroom window, and peered into the dark. "I saw a glow," he recalled. There, in the middle of his yard, was a burning cross.*

The Joneses are black. In the spring of 1990 they had moved into their four-bedroom, three-bathroom dream house on Earl Street in St. Paul, Minnesota. They were the only black family on the block. A few weeks after they had settled into their predominantly white neighborhood, their car tires were

---

* For a more complete account of the Jones family's experience leading up to the *R.A.V.* case, see The Case of the Cross-Burning, p. 27. —Eds.

slashed. A few weeks later, one of their car's tailgate windows was shattered. A couple of weeks after that, a group of teenagers walked past their house and called their nine-year-old son a "nigger." And then came the burning cross. Russ and Laura Jones did not have to guess at the meaning of this symbol of racial hatred. There is not a black person in America who has not been taught the significance of this instrument of persecution and intimidation, who has not had emblazoned on his or her mind the image of black men's scorched bodies hanging from trees, and who does not know the story of Emmett Till.* One can only imagine the terror that the Joneses felt as they watched the flames and thought of how vulnerable their family was.

This assault on the Jones family begins the story of *R.A.V.* v. *City of St. Paul*, the "hate speech" case recently decided by the United States Supreme Court. The Joneses, however, are not the subject of the Court's opinion. The constitutional injury addressed in *R.A.V.* was not this black family's right to live where they pleased[1] or to associate with their neighbors,[2] or not how this attack might impair the Joneses' constitutional right to be full and valued participants in the political community. Instead, the Court was concerned with the alleged constitutional injury to those who assaulted the Joneses, that is, the First Amendment rights of the cross-burners.[3]

Much is deeply troubling about Justice Scalia's majority opinion in *R.A.V.* But its utter disregard for the silenced voice of the victims is the most frightening. Nowhere in the opinion is any mention made of the Jones family or of their constitutional rights. Nowhere are we told of the history of the Ku Klux Klan or of its use of the burning cross as a tool for the suppression of speech. By describing cross-burning as a kind of speech that must therefore be protected, Justice Scalia turns the First Amendment on its head, transforming an act intended to silence through terror and intimidation into an invitation to join a public discussion.[4] In so doing, he clothes the cross-burners' terroristic act in the legitimacy of protected political speech and invites them to burn again.

"Let there be no mistake about our belief that burning a cross in someone's front yard is reprehensible,"[5] writes Justice Scalia at the close of his opinion. But I am skeptical; these words seem little more than an obligatory genuflection to decency. For even in this attempt to assure the reader of his good intentions, Justice Scalia's words betray his inability to see the Joneses or hear their voices. "Burning a cross in *someone's* front yard is *reprehensible*," he says—reprehensible, but not injurious or immoral, not a violation

---

* Emmett Till, a fourteen-year-old boy from Chicago, was killed while visiting relatives in Mississippi in 1955. His murderers claimed that his alleged "wolf whistle" at a white woman provoked them.—Eds.

of civil rights and certainly not of the Joneses' rights. For Justice Scalia, the identity of that "someone" is irrelevant. As is the fact that it is a *cross* that is burned.

When I first read Justice Scalia's opinion, I felt as if another cross had just been set ablaze, this one on the pages of the U.S. record. Such a cross was set on fire in 1857, when Justice Taney held that African Americans were not included and were not intended to be included under the word "citizen" in the Constitution,[6] and another burned in 1896 when Justice Brown ruled that "separate but equal" was a constitutionally viable standard.[7] The message was the same each time: You have "no rights which the white man [is] bound to respect" or protect. If you think a white man has injured you, it is a figment of your imagination that this Constitution will not recognize.

For the past couple of years I have been struggling to find a way to talk to my friends in the civil liberties community about the injuries that are ignored in the R.A.V. case. I have tried to articulate the ways in which hate speech harms its victims, and how it harms all of us by undermining core values in our Constitution.[8]

One of these values is full and equal citizenship as expressed in the Fourteenth Amendment's Equal Protection Clause. People who are told, through unmistakable threats and intimidation, that they are and shall stay second-class citizens, cannot enjoy the full range of their rights. When hate speech is employed with the purpose and effect of maintaining systems of caste and subordination, it violates the core value of equal rights. The other constitutional value threatened by hate speech is free expression itself. Hate speech frequently silences its victims—more often than not, those people already least heard in the public arena. An understanding of both of these injuries is aided by feminism and critical race theory, which give special attention to structures of subordination and the voices of the subordinated.[9]

My sense of the need to inform First Amendment discourse with the insights of antisubordination theory began a few years ago with the debate over regulation of hate speech on campuses. As I lectured at universities throughout the United States, I heard about serious racist and anti-Semitic hate incidents. Students told me of swastikas painted during Jewish holy days, of cross burnings, racist slurs, and vicious verbal assaults. Universities have long been sites of institutional racism, papered over in euphemisms and high ideas, but now, it seemed, they were a home to racism in its worst gutter forms. In 1990, the Chronicle of Higher Education reported that approximately 250 colleges and universities had experienced serious racist incidents since 1986. The National Institute Against Prejudice and Violence estimates that 25 percent of all minority students are victimized at least once during an academic year.

I urged my colleagues to hear these students' voices. I argued that the anti-discrimination principle at the heart of *Brown* v. *Board of Education* identified these students' constitutional injury and the need to remedy it.[10] We do not usually think of *Brown* as a case about speech. Most narrowly read, it is about the rights of black children to equal educational opportunity. But *Brown* teaches us another lesson: that the harm of segregation is achieved by the message it conveys. The Court's opinion declared that racial segregation is unconstitutional not because the physical separation of black and white children is bad or because resources were distributed unequally among black and white schools. *Brown* held that segregated schools were unconstitutional primarily because of their *meaning*, the message they send that black children are an untouchable caste, unfit to be educated with white children. Segregation is unconstitutional because it stamps a badge of inferiority upon blacks, signaling their exclusion from the community of citizens.[11]

"Whites Only" signs at lunch counters, swimming pools, and drinking fountains convey the same message. The anti-discrimination principle articulated in *Brown* presumptively entitles every individual to be treated as a participating member of organized society. This is the principle upon which our civil rights laws rest, the guiding principle of the Fourteenth Amendment's requirement of nondiscriminatory government action in its Equal Protection Clause.[12]* In addition, this principle has been applied in regulating private discrimination.

The words "Women Need Not Apply" in a job announcement, the racially exclusionary clause in a restrictive covenant, and the racial epithet scrawled on the locker of the new black employee at a previously all-white job site all convey a political message. But rather than protect these forms of speech under the First Amendment, we treat them as discriminatory practices and outlaw them under federal and state civil rights legislation. More than mere speech, they are integral elements of historically ingrained systems of social discrimination.[13] Because they work to keep traditionally victimized groups in socially isolated, stigmatized, and disadvantaged positions through the promotion of fear, intolerance, degradation, and violence, the Equal Protection Clause prohibits such practices. And the First Amendment does not prevent such prohibitions simply because those discriminatory practices are achieved through words and symbols.[14]

Under Title VII† the courts have recently recognized that racist or sexist

---

* The Fourteenth Amendment's Equal Protection Clause provides that no state shall deny citizens equal protection under the law or any other government action. In particular, the Supreme Court has held that discrimination based on race or sex is inherently suspect. —Eds.
† Title VII is a section of the Civil Rights Law of 1964 that outlaws certain types of discrimination in the workplace. —Eds.

verbal harassment in the workplace can create a "hostile environment," especially in situations where there has been recent or tokenistic integration, and that this environment denies its victims equal access to employment. As one of the few female craft workers employed by Jacksonville Shipyards, Lois Robinson was constantly subjected to the sight of pornographic pinup photos and the degradation of viciously sexist remarks by her male coworkers and supervisors. When she brought suit under Title VII, a U.S. District Court decided *Robinson v. Jacksonville Shipyards* in her favor.

The case presents a clear example of the tension between the law's commitment to free speech and its commitment to equality. The U.S. District Court found that the presence in the workplace of pictures of women in various stages of undress and in sexually suggestive or submissive poses and the remarks made by male employees and supervisors that demeaned women constituted a violation of Title VII "through the maintenance of a sexually hostile work environment."[15] Much of District Court Judge Howell Melton's opinion is a recounting of the indignities that Robinson and five other women experienced almost daily while working with 850 men over the course of ten years. In addition to mentioning the omnipresent display of sexually explicit drawings, graffiti, calendars, centerfold-style pictures, magazines, and cartoons, the trial record details a number of incidents in which sexually suggestive pictures and comments were directed at Robinson.* Male employees admitted that the shipyard was "a boys' club" and "more or less a man's world." The local chapter of the American Civil Liberties Union appealed the District Court's decision, arguing that "even sexists have a right to free speech."[16] However, when one reads the trial record one is amazed at the civil libertarians' lack of concern for Robinson's right to do her work without being subjected to assault. Robinson's male colleagues weren't interested in advancing the cause of erotic speech when they made her the target of pornographic comments and graffiti. They wanted to put her in her place, remind her of her sexual vulnerability, and send her back home where she belonged.

But it is not sufficient to describe the injury occasioned by hate speech only in terms of the countervailing value of equality. We must also consider the injury to the First Amendment itself. When the Joneses moved to Earl Street in St. Paul, they were expressing their individuality. When they chose their house and their neighbors, they were saying, "This is who we are. We are a proud black family and we want to live here." When the Joneses looked out their window and saw that burning cross, they heard a message that

---

* For the other stories of women subjected to a sexually hostile work environment, see Dorchen Leidholdt, "Pornography in the Workplace," p. 216 this volume.

said, "Shut up, black folks, or risk harm to yourselves and your family." Maybe the Joneses will speak even more loudly in the face of this threat; perhaps they are especially brave, or especially foolhardy. But most victims of such an act will be silenced, and the greater community will lose the benefit of their voices.

According to Lawrence Tribe, the First Amendment preserves two fundamental values.[17] The first is its intrinsic value: speech as self-expression, as the manifestation of our humanity and our individuality. The second is its instrumental value: the First Amendment protects dissent in order to maximize public discourse, and to promote the flowering of debate essential to democracy.

For African Americans, the intrinsic value of speech as self-expression and self-definition has been particularly important. Suppressing a "black voice" was one of the most important means by which European-American racism denied Africans their humanity and thereby justified their enslavement.[18] African-American slaves were prevented from learning to read and write, prohibited from speaking freely, and denied all opportunity to express themselves in any way that might either instill in them a sense of self-worth or display evidence of their humanity. Their silence and submission were taken as proof that they were subhuman. People who burn crosses on their neighbors' lawns understand that to silence a person is to dehumanize him or her, and this is part of their purpose.[19] When one has been threatened into self-censorship, when one is afraid to give full expression to one's individuality, one no longer enjoys the liberties guaranteed by the Constitution, and the oppressor has won.

The instrumental value of speech was likewise threatened by the terrorist attack on the Joneses. Whether at the voting booth or in conversations with their neighbors, Russ and Laura Jones brought new voices to the discourse of their mostly white St. Paul community. Ideally, they would vote and talk politics with their neighbors; they would bring new experiences and perspectives to the discussion. But a burning cross silences people like the Joneses—and thereby impoverishes the democratic process and renders our collective conversation less informed.[20]

First Amendment doctrine and theory have no words for the injuries of silence imposed by private actors. There is no language for the damage that is done to the First Amendment when the hateful speech of the cross-burner or the sexual harasser silences its victims. In fair housing laws, public accommodations provisions, and employment discrimination laws, we recognize the necessity of regulating all discriminating behavior—whether by the government or by private actors—that threatens the values of equal citizenship. We know that we could not hope to realize the constitutional ideal of equal citizenship if we pretended that the government was the only discriminator.

But there is no recognition in First Amendment law of the systematic private suppression of speech. To some extent, courts and scholars have worried about the heckler's veto,[21] and in limited-access speech fora we have given attention to questions of equal time and the right to reply.[22] But, for the most part, we act as if the government is the only entity that ever limits anyone's speech.[23] We valorize the marketplace of ideas as if all its voices were equal, as if none were ever silenced.[24] First Amendment discourse does not accommodate an understanding of how those who are silenced are always less powerful than those who do the silencing. First Amendment law ignores the ways in which patriarchy silences women and racism silences people of color. When a husband threatens to beat his wife the next time she contradicts him, a First Amendment injury has occurred.[25] When a gay-basher forces gays and lesbians into the closet, he denies us *all* the insight and beauty of their voices.

Professor Mari Matsuda has spoken compellingly of this problem in a personal story about an early professional experience. She was working on an article she subsequently published in the *Michigan Law Review* entitled "Public Response to Racist Speech: Considering the Victim's Story," when a mentor at Harvard Law School warned her not to publish anything about hate speech until she had gained tenure. "It's a lightning rod,"[26] he told her. She followed his advice, publishing the article years later, after securing her position and attracting visiting offers from prestigious schools.

"What is the sound of a paper unpublished?" she now asks. "What don't we hear when some young scholar chooses tenure over controversial speech? Every fall, students return from summer jobs and tell me of the times they didn't speak out against racist or anti-Semitic comments. They tell of the times they were invited to discriminatory clubs and went along in silence. What is the sound of all those silenced because they need a job? These silences, these things that go unsaid, aren't seen as First Amendment issues. The absences are characterized as private and voluntary, beyond collective cure."

In the rush to protect the "speech" of cross-burners, champions of the First Amendment must not forget the voices of their victims. If First Amendment doctrine and theory is truly to serve First Amendment ideals, it must recognize the injury done by private suppression of speech; it must take into account the historical reality that some members of our community are less powerful than others and that those persons continue to be systematically silenced by those who are more powerful. If we are truly committed to free speech, First Amendment doctrine and theory must be guided by the principle of antisubordination. There can be no free speech when there are still masters and slaves.

SILENCING WOMEN'S SPEECH

Michelle J. Anderson

Does pornography silence women? Many authorities have taken positions on one side or the other of this controversy based on hunches or a priori principles, failing to notice that it has an empirical dimension. Michelle Anderson explores this dimension, analyzing what is known about the way watching pornography affects young adults, male and female.

■

During the past decade, pornography has become the most profitable form of media, soaring ahead of all nonpornographic films and records combined.[1] Pornographic films now outnumber other films three to one.[2] As documentary filmmaker Harriet Koskoff has observed, "Porn is everywhere; we live in an environment that's saturated with it."[3] This is not true just for the adult world either: schoolteachers have confiscated issues of *Hustler* magazine from third-graders.[4] Nine out of ten boys and six out of ten girls have seen at least one pornographic video in their lives and one-third of boys and 2 percent of girls consume pornography more than once a month.[5]

Pornography's influence extends into many forms of mainstream media such as popular movies in which women derive pleasure from sexual abuse; interactive computer pornography which allows users to insert knives into the vaginas of the female characters, books in which women are tortured, mutilated, and killed for sexual pleasure; "high art" and fashion photos which eroticize the abuse of women; rock and rap group album cover art and lyrics which are violently misogynist; popular slasher films in which scantily clad girls and women are murdered with various implements. The depictions of abusive sex and violence in these "nonpornographic" slasher movies, in particular, have become increasingly graphic, especially in the feature-length films shown in theaters.[6] Millions of people, mostly adolescent and young adult males, consume these films as entertainment.[7] As a consequence, "For the first time in history, children are growing up whose earliest sexual imprinting derives not from a living human being, or fantasies of their own . . . [but from] mass-produced, deliberately dehumanizing and inhuman [images]."[8]

Pornography's apologists defend its expansion and influence on mainstream media on the basis of its producers' right to free speech. Pornography is a medium of communication, they say, and regulating it would threaten the fundamental values that the First Amendment is designed to protect—individual self-expression and collective self-determination. The marketplace of ideas, the argument goes, must welcome all ideological positions and include everyone, even pornographers. Only in such a democratic marketplace of ideas can truth emerge.

In fact, however, the marketplace that welcomes pornographers has been neither free nor democratic. We have become so accustomed to the presence of pornography that we have almost lost the ability to imagine an alternative —a market in which pornography does not monopolize sexual speech and quash dissent. We lose sight of the fact that a blanket defense of pornography does not protect individual self-expression, but rather protects the corporate propagation of imagery that is anti-democratic. "Hard core" pornography, "far from being a bold critique of conventional morality, is economically motivated and 'entrenches and embodies society's most repressive and anti-egalitarian norms.' "[9] Promoting pornography distorts public discourse and enforces silence.[10]

Mass media can reduce their consumers to political lethargy. The impact of pornographic mass media is even more anti-democratic: its harm is directed toward a specific, disadvantaged group—women—whose political participation is hampered by historic patterns of discrimination. The silencing pornography does is inextricably tied to what social science has documented are pornography's "nonspeech" harms: its contribution to sexist attitudes, its encouragement of rape myths, its sexualization of dominance, and its reduction of men's inhibitions to rape.

Female/Male Communication

A man tells a woman a joke:

> A patient goes into a doctor's office and the doctor says, "I've got some good news and some bad news."
> The patient says, "Give me the bad news first."
> The doctor says, "OK. You've got three weeks to live."
> "Three weeks to live! Doctor! What is the good news?!"
> And the doctor says, "Did you see that secretary out front? I finally fucked her."[11]

The female listener falls silent after the man finishes his telling.

Sociolinguists have researched the differences between men's and women's speech patterns, and the results are of considerable use to legal scholars interested in the First Amendment. Principally, data point to aspects of men's speech patterns that "chill" women's speech, and reveal pornography as a mechanism by which that chilling effect occurs. Similarly, research shows that after viewing pornography, women have less to say and men hear less of what women do say.

At puberty, girls become especially conscious of strong social cues that they should remain subordinate to men in their speech.[12] Male speakers often drown out women by dominating conversations.[13] Men use interruptions and "delayed minimal responses" (pauses, monosyllabic utterances, and blank stares) to control discussions:[14] interruptions, in particular, silence women.[15] In mixed-sex groups, women speak less than men—in number of words, frequency, and duration of turn.[16] Men present their ideas in more depth than women, employing more background references and other information.[17] Women generally indicate more support for the primary speakers in conversations and are more verbally accommodating.[18] Thus, women criticize and express unique or dissenting opinions less than men do.[19]

If women talk as women usually do, they are discredited as speakers. Women are significantly more likely than men to use hedges (beginning sentences with self-effacing comments such as, "I may be wrong, but . . .") and tag questions (ending sentences with equivocations such as, "Isn't that right?"), while males lead in such indicators as assertiveness, verbal commands, and opinions.[20] Thus, women appear more tentative and deferential in their parlance; men more confident. Sometimes a woman will introduce an idea in a mixed-sex group and the idea will be ignored; when a man then introduces the same idea, the group will discuss it and attribute it to him. Men thus carry more legitimacy as speakers.[21]

If women talk as *men* usually do, they lose even more credibility. Studies indicate that if women talk in groups for the same amount of time as men do, people think that women have dominated the conversation. If women use what are traditionally male speech patterns, they are seen as masculine, overbearing, and arrogant. This creates for women the frustrating dilemma: "If they speak in ways expected of women, they are seen as inadequate leaders. If they speak in ways expected of leaders, they are seen as inadequate women."[22]

Men feel more comfortable using a "public speaking" style—which they employ not only with formal speeches delivered to an audience, but also in informal, mixed-group discussions. "Study after study," one linguist notes, "finds that it is men who talk more—at meetings, in mixed group discussions, and in classrooms." Other linguists have concluded that men tend to speak "competitively" while women tend to speak "cooperatively." Their research reveals that the speech of some may indeed censor or block the speech of others. Those whose speech silences others are largely male; those who are silenced are largely female.

These preexisting patterns are exacerbated when pornography enters the picture. Men employ "obscene"* language—which often deprecates women, female bodies, and female sexuality[23]—much more than women do. This language can serve as a form of social control,[24] since all verbal put-downs can and do silence others.[25] In addition, a number of studies reveal a causal relationship between men's exposure to pornography and their insensitivity to women's speech. One study by two Canadian psychologists attempted to gauge the impact of viewing nonviolent pornography upon males' cognitive and behavioral sexism toward women in a professional setting.[26] Sixty male undergraduates were told that they were going to participate in three experimental studies. The male experimenter in the first study said that he was researching censorship. Half of the subjects then viewed a nonviolent pornographic film depicting explicit heterosexual sex while the rest viewed a nonpornographic film. Afterwards each subject filled out a questionnaire about his reactions to the film. Proceeding to the second study, each was then met by a female experimenter and seated on a standard rolling office chair. The female experimenter said that in this study she was researching the methods by which students adapt to university life; she described the research for a few minutes and then the subject filled out another questionnaire. After each student exited, the female experimenter recorded whether the subject stared at her body and measured how closely he moved his chair toward her. In the third study, a male experimenter told the student he was researching memory patterns. The subject was asked to describe the last study, the experimenter herself, and the room in which the experiment took place.

The subjects who viewed the pornography displayed an inattentiveness to the woman's speech and an overattentiveness to her body—especially those participants who had been categorized through a prescreening as "strongly masculine." After viewing pornography only 4 percent of this group was able to recall what the female speaker had said.[27] The results for the other participants were quite different—24 percent.

That men scrutinize women's bodies more closely after viewing pornography

---

* The author puts *obscene* in quotation marks because feminists take issue with the courts' definition of obscenity. —Eds.

is, at first blush, a neutral point in terms of free speech. But this scrutiny is not separable from the fact that, in a professional setting, men *hear less of what women have to say* after viewing pornography.[28] Other studies confirm that pornography has the ability to delegitimize women. After viewing either traditional pornography or nonpornographic slasher films, men have been shown to view women as significantly less than equal and to display less sympathy with statements about sexual equality than they had before.[29] Exposure to aggressive pornography also inclines men to disbelieve survivors' allegations of rape, and to believe instead rape myths, including the myth that women tend to lie about sexual assault.[30] With such deleterious effects on women's ability to be taken seriously and treated fairly, pornography can harm women when it is introduced into the school, the home, or the job site.

Education: Speech in the Locker Room, Silence in the Classroom

Pornography is often the first exposure children have to sexually explicit subject matter, so it can set the standard for normal or appropriate sexual behavior. Teenage boys are the biggest consumers of pornography. Teenagers don't just look; they learn from pornography. Twenty-nine percent of boys rated pornography over parents, teachers, books, school, and peers, as their source for the most useful information about sex. And what do they learn? Forty-three percent of boys and 16 percent of girls think it is okay or are not sure if it is okay for a boy to hold down a girl and force her to have sex if she sexually excites him.[31]

Schoolboys, further, learn to produce their own pornography, using bathroom stalls as soapboxes from which to exercise their free speech rights. Much of the graffiti they generate on bathroom walls sexually humiliates female classmates (or women in general). A lone insult becomes the starting point for a collectively written pornographic narrative, as was the case recently at one Minnesota high school bathroom wall. A single comment was scrawled: "Katy Lyle is a whore." Then the taunts escalated. "Katy Lyle is a slut" appeared, along with "Katy Lyle fucks farm animals" and then "Katy Lyle is a dick-sucking brother-fucking whore."[32]

The immediate victim of such graffiti is, of course, its subject—in this case Katy Lyle. While her family requested unsuccessfully that the school remove the graffiti, she was left to wonder why she had been singled out for such vicious treatment, to fear her classmates, and to hate going to school. But these kinds of messages are more broadly injurious: they can create an atmosphere of socially sanctioned contempt for women.

An extremely misogynist atmosphere may lead to physical violence. In the case of *D.R.* v. *Middle Bucks Area Vocational Technical School*, a group of boys forced D.R., an "almost totally hearing impaired" sixteen-year-old girl, whose "powers of articulation [were] seriously limited, into the bathroom."[33] They grabbed her breasts, pushed her down, forced her to masturbate them and perform fellatio on them, molested her, and sodomized her. The boys repeated this abuse two to four times per week for five months. They forced D.R. to watch the same thing being done to other female students. On one occasion, one of the boys made a videotape in the chaotic classroom, recording the sexual abuse of numerous girl students.[34] D.R. shouted "No!" but the boys disregarded her. D.R. told school officials of her plight but they ignored her requests for help.[35]

Sexually abusive speech like that the boys scrawled on bathroom stalls about Katy Lyle is an ordinary occurrence in schools, and, like much pornography, it normalizes sexual degradation. Most girls do not speak up when boys express themselves in this way on bathroom stalls, lest their protest occasion more abuse. Most learn to remain silent when they are victimized. Lyle, however, tried to speak up. The abuse is normal; her voice is *exceptional*. Her complaints about the graffiti were dismissed by school officials sixteen times in eighteen months. D.R., a hearing-impaired girl, who already had diminished speech capacity, also tried to speak to school officials of her abuse, but her words fell on deaf ears. To speak and yet remain unheard is not free speech. Without legal intervention, these girls' dissenting speech about their sexual denigration would have been squelched. Moreover, if education affords one the tools to speak, to participate in the polity, then diminishing girls' educational opportunities decreases their speech throughout their lives.

Employment: Speech on the Dartboard, Silence in the Boardroom

Pornography is frequently used to sexually harass women at work.[36] Many traditionally male employment enclaves—construction sites, police stations, electrical companies, bus lines, and so on—are marked by the exhibition of pornography at the job site. Displaying pornography in the workplace is a graphic and effective way for male workers to let their female colleagues know they are not welcome and are considered inferior. As scholar Robert Allen explains:

> [T]housands of women are sexually harassed every day, a great many of them women of color and poor women who are most vulnerable.

. . . The majority of crimes against them are not reported because women fear revenge from employers or know that their complaint will be dismissed. They are doubly oppressed: subjected to abuse and constrained to remain silent about it. . . . Incidents of sexual harassment are not unrelated to the flood of pornography that has invaded even the corner market.[37]

Sexual harassment affects women both physically and psychologically. It can cause high blood pressure, nausea, sleeping disorders, headaches, and eating disorders, as well as stress, dread of work, anxiety, depression, feelings of guilt and humiliation. Sexual harassment decreases women's self-esteem and life satisfaction, which in turn decreases their ability to respond to harassment in an assertive manner.[38] As a result, many women who are harassed with pornography on the job become quiet.[39] The main reason for this silence is fear: fear that they are somehow responsible, fear that they will not be believed or that the problem will be trivialized, and fear of reprisals.[40] Thus pornography in the workplace can muzzle women who want simply to keep their jobs.

Relationships: Speech on the Coffee Table, Silence in the Bedroom

Pornography's effects can be seen in the most intimate of settings. Research indicates that many men model their own sexual behavior on the acts they see in X-rated movies or magazines. Two studies asked female respondents, "Have you ever been upset by someone trying to get you to do something which they had seen in pornographic magazines, movies, or books?" Ten percent of women responded yes in a random sample study in San Francisco, and 24 percent said yes in a survey of college undergraduates.[41] Sometimes these interchanges are not simply requests. Three percent of women in one survey and 8.5 percent in another said that they had been physically coerced into sex by someone inspired by pornography.[42]

One woman who was raped by her husband testified that her husband "read the pornography like a textbook, like a journal. When he finally convinced me to be bound, he read in the magazine how to tie the knots and bind me in a way that I couldn't escape. Most of the scenes where I had to dress up or go through different fantasies were the exact same scenes that he had read in the magazines."

The San Francisco study noted that "the frequent comment that women in pornography are portrayed as enjoying abusive or forceful sex may be the source of, or may reinforce, many men's beliefs that women's refusals to engage in sex should not be taken seriously. The normalization of abusive sex acts is but one of the many destructive messages in pornography."[43]

Rape: Speech on the Billboard, Silence on the Street Corner

In a 1988 study of 114 undergraduate men, 91.3 percent admitted they "like[d] to dominate a woman"; 86.1 percent said they "enjoy[ed] the conquest part of sex"; 83.5 percent agreed that "[s]ome women look like they're just asking to be raped"; 63.5 percent said they "get excited when a woman struggles over sex"; and 61.7 percent decided that "[i]t would be exciting to use force to subdue a woman."[44] In a 1988 survey of young teenage males, 25 percent deemed rape justified if a boy spent ten to fifteen dollars on a girl and two-thirds of them deemed rape justified if he dated her for more than six months.[45] As boys consume more pornography, they become more firmly convinced of these ideas. Research indicates that exposure to pornography increases male subjects' acceptance of violence against women, significantly increases men's sexual callousness, decreases their compassion for women as rape victims, increases their propensity to trivialize rape, and increases their aggression against women.[46] It is no wonder. In many aggressive pornographic depictions, the woman is portrayed as desiring to be raped and deriving sexual gratification from it.[47] After exposure to aggressive pornography, male students report they are more likely to rape and engage in coercive sex acts.[48] As indicated above, exposure to this kind of pornography decreases men's assessment of a rape victim's credibility and increases men's belief in rape myths, such as that women routinely lie about sexual abuse.[49]

There are three types of silencing that rape can cause. First, there is the silencing that often occurs during a rape—ignoring her "no," the hand over her mouth, the knife at her throat daring her to scream. This type stops an individual woman from speaking or being heard for the duration of the rape, and haunts her for years later. Second, there is the long-term residual silencing caused by the experience of rape—she doesn't talk or laugh as much as she used to. Many women walk around as only shadows of their true selves because of the sexual abuse they have suffered. Their expressions are muted. Their deep grief strips them of their vitality. Third, there is the silence that comes from not telling anyone of the experience—society and the legal system respond as if the rape were her fault or as if she is lying, so she keeps quiet. Most women who endure rape remain silent. National statistics reveal that rape is the most underreported of all major crimes.[50] One of the reasons women don't

report their violations is that they know they will be subjected to the biases
that pornography helps perpetuate.

Speaking the Silence

> If men's freedom of speech requires the silencing of women, there
> is only partial freedom and surely no justice.
> —Michael S. Kimmel, *Men Confront Pornography*

> What would feminist silence sound like? What would genuine free
> speech say?
> —Robin Morgan, *The Politics of Silence*

The public hearings before the Minneapolis City Council on the Dworkin/
MacKinnon civil rights ordinance in December of 1983 were "the first time
in history that victims of pornography testified directly before a governmental
body."[51] For women who have been coerced in the production of pornography,
forced to view or imitate it, or assaulted by men incited by it, these hearings
were one of the first opportunities to tell of their abuse. The hearings thus
opened up space for women to speak of what pornography had done to them.
We need more such hearings so that women may come forward and address
the courts and the legislatures. Some confident, others stammering at first,
they may begin to say, "Pornography has hurt me," "His gun made me smile
to the camera," "He forced me to imitate what he had seen," "He raped me
like it said to do." These women may tender some proof: their words, an
affidavit, a language of grief for describing the unspeakable.[52] The governmental
body will weigh the evidence, and truth may yet emerge.

PORNOGRAPHY AND RACIST SPEECH AS HATE PROPAGANDA

Laura J. Lederer

What do pornography and racist speech have in common? In this essay, excerpted from a longer article, Laura Lederer argues that both may be seen as hate propaganda. Using the phrase as a term of art, as legal scholars have in Canada, Lederer contends that hate propaganda functions solely as a mechanism to separate people and to create hierarchies based on race, sex, religion, and sexual orientation.

■

In a landmark article, law professor Mari Matsuda notes that violent pornography and anti-gay and anti-lesbian hate speech require a separate analysis from that of racist speech because of the complex and violent nature of gender subordination, and the differences between sexuality-based and race-based oppression. Racist speech, she writes, "comprises the ideology of racial supremacy and the mechanisms for keeping selected victim groups in subordinated positions."[1] She argues for a legal response to this phenomenon. But she does not contend that pornography and hate speech aimed at gays or lesbians require the same legal treatment.

This paper argues that pornography and racist speech have the *same* locus of oppression, and that that locus is actually *differentness* (rather than sex or race or religion or sexual preference). The implements or tools used may differ based on the racial or religious or sexual group under attack, but their function is the same: to exclude, subordinate, discriminate against, and create second-class citizenship for entire groups of people. Thus, just as the purpose of racist speech is to keep selected groups in subordinated positions, so is the purpose of pornography to keep women subordinated. Racist speech and pornography function similarly, then, as sophisticated forms of hate propaganda that both create and prop up a system of inequality and exclusion.

As French political philosopher Jacques Ellul observes, propaganda, though difficult to define precisely, aims to intensify existing ideological trends, to exploit them, and above all, to bring about action. He describes propaganda as a modern technique with five basic characteristics:

- simultaneous manipulation of the individual
  and mass populations;
- totality of reach;
- power brokering;
- organization, continuity, and duration; and
- orthopraxy.

This complex set of attributes accurately describes the operations of both pornography and racist speech. Taking them in order, it is possible to see how racist speech and pornography function as forms of propaganda.

Manipulation of Individuals and Masses

As Ellul points out, propaganda addresses itself to the crowd but appeals to each individual as a member of that group—and plays on the reliance of each one on group identity for strength. Pornography and racist speech both have these characteristics. Pornography appeals to difference based on sex. While the purchase of pornography magazines is an individual act, the publications —billed as "Entertainment for Men," "the Magazine for Men," or "Men's Entertainment"—promise a collective identity. The men who read these magazines get not only the explicit entertainment of the photos and text, but the implicit reassurance that they belong to a community of readers who are moved by the same motives, receive the same impulses and impressions, find themselves focused on the same centers of interest. In short, they are a psychological, if not a biological, mass.

Racist hate speech, similarly, appeals to a category of "difference," race; and, while aimed at individual white people, it forms the basis of a shared story about white supremacy that links the individual participant with the common cause. The more entrenched this story becomes, the more it sets the terms for all related discourse and shapes the lives of both white people and people of color in this country, affecting rich and poor, smart and stupid. Charles Lawrence has demonstrated how conscious racism helps to create a country in which unconscious racism flourishes.[2] Richard Delgado notes that racist hate speech benefits not just the person who practices it, but all white people in the culture.[3]

Totality of Reach

Ellul notes that propaganda must use all possible techniques at its disposal to reach the individual. The press, radio, TV, movies, posters, meetings, door-to-door canvassing, computers, graffiti—each medium has its own particular audience and method of penetration, specific but at the same time "localized and limited."[4] And indeed, both pornography and racist speech are ever expanding the media through which they spread their message of hate. In the mid-1980s, Klansmen and neo-Nazis discovered that cable television could be an efficient forum through which to address the public and recruit new members. By mid-1991, more than thirty U.S. cities carried white supremacist programming. In addition, white supremacists publish newsletters, magazines, and leaflets, and now have highly sophisticated computer networks that link them nationally and internationally with other neo-Nazi, white supremacist, and Aryan Nation groups.[5] In the same way, pornographic images, expressions, and messages are now transmitted through magazines and newspapers, television, cable TV, videos, mail order magazines, 900-number telephone calls, books, computer networks, X-rated software, posters, graffiti, electronic mail, answering machine messages, and personal ads;[6] many larger cities have districts that can easily be identified as "porn strips." The effect of such a diversified assault is clear: as Ellul says, propaganda will "leave no part of the intellectual or emotional life alone; . . . [it will] surround [one] on all sides . . . by all possible routes."

Power Brokering

This use of mass media is paired with careful political organizing and strategic alliances. For example, one of the most effective propaganda techniques pornographers have developed is their alliance with anti-censorship organizations and civil libertarians. Through this coalition, pornographers have successfully shifted the debate over their product from one of sexual exploitation and abuse to one of free speech and First Amendment rights.[7] Pornographers who were defended by such groups as the ACLU during the late fifties and early sixties have donated liberally to civil libertarian and progressive causes over the past two decades. By the midseventies, the Playboy Foundation, for instance, was a well-known funder of social justice organizations. In this way, it won the loyalty of many grass-roots groups, from prisoners' rights advocates to government reform groups to proponents of military disarmament. They even funded some carefully selected women's issues such as reproductive rights.[8] This technique has been effective in buying the support—or at least the silence—of many constituencies that might otherwise have opposed them.

Hate groups have also learned how to broker power by using money. For example, far right activists have campaigned steadily in the farm belt to recruit financially troubled farmers by offering them low-interest loans and lobbying assistance in Washington, D.C., for small-farm subsidies. This much-needed financial relief is combined with hate messages about "international Jewish banking conspiracies" and white supremacy.[9]

Organization, Continuity, Duration

To be effective, Ellul points out, propaganda must be continuous and lasting, and propagandists must develop sophisticated methods of organization and dissemination.[10] In Southern and rural areas and now in the Pacific Northwest, promoters of "Christian Identity" use theology to recruit "soldiers" for what they see as the upcoming "war of Armageddon." New sects and leaders bring groups of people into these movements. They hold rallies and conduct electoral campaigns to build grass-roots support and collect millions of dollars. No longer isolated as they were in the 1970s, they now claim large constituencies and exert a noticeable impact on public policy. It is estimated that the white supremacist movement includes approximately 25,000 activists and another 150,000 to 200,000 sympathizers who attend meetings and conferences, buy literature, and make donations.

Pornographers have also made crucial inroads into public consciousness in the past thirty years, using psychology rather than theology. With the advice of prominent marketing firms, pornographers have steadily increased the reach of materials that portray sexual exploitation, sadomasochism, bondage, and child pornography—through publications in the U.S., through international editions, and, recently, through expansion into such mainstream markets as cable, video, and late night television.[11] They have developed large followings. The latest figures indicate that upwards of 10 million men consume pornography on a regular basis.

Orthopraxy

The last crucial element of propaganda is orthopraxy, which Ellul defines as an action that in itself leads *directly* to a goal. In other words, hate propagandists do not attempt to convince people of their views by rational argument.[12] They are, instead, concerned first and foremost with action, with *a concerted mass psychological reflexive response*, and "seek to short circuit all thought and decision. It [propaganda] must operate on the individual at the level of the unconscious. [The individual] must not know that he is being shaped by outside forces, [yet] some central core in him must be reached in order to achieve the cooperation and appropriate action the propaganda desires." The purpose of this propaganda, according to Ellul, is to prepare a person psychologically for *action*, "to get him [or her] into condition for the time when he will effectively, and without delay or hesitation, participate in an action."

According to Ellul, reflex and myth are the two great routes propaganda takes. "Propaganda tries first of all to create conditioned reflexes in the individual by training him so that certain words, signs, symbols or even people or facts provoke unfailing reactions." In addition, the propagandist tries to create "myths by which we will live—these myths are all encompassing, activating images which include all that he feels is good, just and true." Ellul gives examples: Hitler's myth of a superior race, or the Communist myth of the proletariat.

Certainly racial supremacy is a very powerful myth. White supremacists, for instance, will assert almost anything to reinforce it: that the high percentage of black men in prison is the result of a genetic predisposition to criminality, that blacks are more violence-prone than whites, or that they are less intelligent than people of other races. And recent research demonstrates how pornography works to change attitudes through the "short-circuiting" Ellul describes. Researchers have discovered that pornography desensitizes men to the pain women experience in sexual assault; encourages sexism, pro-rape attitudes, sexual harassment, and various forms of sexual assault; and increases men's self-reported likelihood to commit sexual assault.[13]

Building on Ellul's work, James A.C. Brown, in his book *Techniques of Persuasion*, lists eight techniques that are universally employed in propaganda campaigns. They are:

- use of stereotypes;
- name substitution;
- selective presentation of facts;
- lying;
- repetition;
- bold assertion of a single idea;
- creation of an enemy; and
- appeal to authority.[14]

In a landmark article, "The Propaganda of Misogyny," Beverly LaBelle uses these techniques to demonstrate how pornography functions as a form of indoctrination for male supremacist attitudes. Pornography and racist speech both make extensive use of these eight techniques.[15]

USE OF STEREOTYPES   The National Institute Against Prejudice and Violence has documented thousands of hate speech incidents that use stereotypes. A few include: white students placing rings in their noses and painting themselves black at a fraternity "jungle party"; a University of Michigan radio station caller stating that the most famous black woman is Aunt Jemima; white students jeering black students with the chant "Buckwheat!"; a Sambo-like defacing of a poster of Beethoven placed in a black dormitory; an American company using Japanese samurai as part of an ad campaign against its Japanese competitors; pictures of "Frito Bandito" being hung near a Mexican-American student's locker; Jewish people being referred to as part of a complex controlling the media, banking, certain political parties, and other industries; and white students holding an "Indian pow-wow."

Pornography, too, depends on stereotyping. In pornography magazines women are portrayed as sex-loving phallus worshippers who are carnal, submissive, and promiscuous; at once whores and Madonnas. Women who object to pornography are also stereotyped: as prudes with unhappy childhoods, sad rape victims, or Nazis looking to force everyone into some rigid sexual order. Recently, *Playboy* referred to major feminist researchers as moral majority types with "a pathological fear of anything that causes arousal."[16]

NAME SUBSTITUTION   As members of any disenfranchised group know, name calling plays a special role in denigrating people. There are dozens of pejorative terms for females: "cunt," "twat," "bitch," "whore," "piece of ass." Women are frequently referred to by animal names: the *Penthouse* centerfold is called the Penthouse "pet"; Playboy waitresses are known as "bunnies"; women have been referred to as "chicks," "dogs," "cows," and "sows," as well as "kittens" and "lambs." Pornographic movies often feature female characters named after food, such as Taffy, Candy, or Cookie. There are as many derogatory names for people of color: "nigger," "coon," "spic," "spade," "gook," "jap." For Jewish people there is "kike"; for gay people, "faggot," "queer," and "fairy" are common epithets.[17]

SELECTION   Propagandists typically select certain images and pass them off as representative of a whole group. In pornography, the only women depicted—who therefore stand in for all women—are young, buxom, and "attractive," not to mention airbrushed, plastic, and painted.[18] There are no images of older women, mothers, pregnant women, menstruating women, working women.[19] Women are presented strictly as sexual objects, stripped and sexually accessible at any and all times.[20]

Hate mongers also use selected images to portray people of color, Jews, and gay people as inferior. A December 1990 survey conducted by the National Opinion Research Center at the University of Chicago examined levels of racism in the United States. The survey demonstrated that white Americans thought blacks, Latinos, and Asians were lazy, violence-prone, less intelligent, and less patriotic than white Americans.[21] The Center for Democratic Renewal documents the teachings of the KKK, the Aryan Nation, Christian Identity, the Third Position, the Order, skinheads, the Christian Patriots, neo-Nazis, and other leading white supremacist groups, who portray people of color as not fully human and without souls; Jews as the children of Satan; Jewish banking conspiracies, Hollywood mafias, and media monopolies as the basis of many of the world's problems; Jews and other "non-whites" as aliens in the United States; and people of color as parasites on the economy. This selective use of denigrating—and false—images buttresses a worldview in which the targeted group is less than human.

LYING   A propaganda technique related to selection is the consistent repetition of false information. In *Beauharnais* v. *Illinois*, for example, the president of the White Circle League organized the distribution of a leaflet calling on the mayor and city council of Chicago to "halt the further encroachment, harassment and invasion of white people, their property, neighborhoods and persons, by the Negro." The leaflet noted that "If persuasion and the need to prevent the white race from becoming mongrelized by the negro will not unite us, then the aggressions, [rapes], robberies, knives, guns and marijuana of the negro surely will." The court held that this was defamation, calculated to perpetuate racism and discrimination.[22]

Pornography lies about women in similar ways. In "The Propaganda of Misogyny," Beverly LaBelle notes that violent pornography portrays women as enjoying rape, torture, and brutal sex. As an example, she uses "Columbine Cuts Up," a photo montage in *Chic* magazine in which a young woman is portrayed thrusting a large butcher knife into her vagina and cutting off her nipples with a sharp scissors. In the photo, blood is spurting from the wounds, but the woman is smiling.[23] It is not unusual for pornographers to portray women asking for painful beatings, torture, and rape and enjoying it. Andrea Dworkin has documented dozens of pornographic novels in which the female victim is whipped, chained, forced into anal or oral sex, burned, stuck with needles, or brutally stabbed. Throughout, these victims ask for the pain and humiliation and often confess their love for their torturer.[24] Pornography also lies about women's bodies by airbrushing away moles, birthmarks, stretch marks, and other imperfections; by exaggerating breast measurements and diminishing waist and hip measurements; and by replacing women's real thoughts, cares, hopes, fears, and desires with statements that portray women as purely sexual beings. These lies create and perpetuate the sexual objectification of women.

REPETITION   Both pornographers and hate mongers make extensive use of repetition. In pornography, the theme of women's sexual accessibility is played out over and over again. Racist speech employs the constant reiteration of a few themes: white supremacy, mongrelization, stupidity, laziness, and genetic inferiority.[25]

BOLD ASSERTION   Hate mongers and pornographers have become experts at disseminating their messages through aggressive promotion campaigns. They use newsletters, tabloids, magazines, brochures, posters, call-in phone lines, rallies, graffiti, acts of vandalism like cross burnings, radio, television and video programs, and computer networks.[26] Pornographers are even more adept at this promotion, due to their greater resources. They use top market research firms, advertising firms, lobbying firms, and distribution companies to market their message. In the late seventies, for example, *Playboy* hired market researchers to test a wide range of sexual themes, including child pornography and child molestation, on focus groups composed mainly of men. Hate groups, by contrast, tend to depend on grass-roots organizing campaigns, which nevertheless have proved highly effective.

CREATION OF AN ENEMY   An enemy or scapegoat is of prime importance in any propaganda campaign because it serves to direct aggression away from the propagandist and to strengthen feelings of solidarity within the group. Hatred is a powerful unifying emotion[27] and propagandists use it without apology.

For pornographers, women are the enemy to be conquered and controlled. In pornography, there are two levels at which this takes place. Most pornographic scenarios consist of women who initially resist a rape, but eventually succumb. Often, this conquest is accompanied by hateful comments (e.g., "You deserve this, bitch"). With this moment of conquest forever on the page or video, the male pornography consumer can live and relive it as often as he likes.

In addition, as LaBelle points out, both soft- and hard-core pornography directly pinpoint as the enemy feminists who critique pornography. For example, Dorchen Leidholdt was labeled a "piece of shit" in *Hustler* magazine. A major pornography magazine published an "interview with Gloria Steinem's clitoris," which was illustrated and virulently anti-feminist. Andrea Dworkin was defamed in *Hustler* magazine. Susan Brownmiller was portrayed as a "thrilling cock-fondler." After every major feminist protest against pornography, *Playboy* magazine has run several articles calling feminists prudes, censors, sexual fascists, or sad women with badly damaged childhoods.[28]

Hate mongers also demonize their enemies with racist speech. People of color, Jewish people, and gay people are often portrayed as the cause of economic, social, and political problems. For example, a recent sign in the Midwest farm belt read "Jews rape farmers." The Third Position, the political ideology of the White Aryan Resistance, strangely blames immigrants and third world people for capitalist exploitation. Aryan Nation members in Seattle recently portrayed gay leaders as the cause of deteriorating values in this country.[29]

APPEAL TO AUTHORITY   Hate mongers and pornographers refer to higher authorities, famous people, experts, scholars, and other leaders to gain respectability. For example, the Ku Klux Klan, the Christian Patriots, and other white supremacy organizations make many references to the Bible and God to buttress their hate campaigns. The new Institute for Historical Review, an organization formed to "disprove" the Holocaust, claims a board of "distinguished scholars" from France, Australia, Germany, Argentina, and the U.S.

Pornographers also fashion clever programs to support their campaign of female subordination. Perhaps the most famous is *Playboy* magazine's Playboy Interview, which has featured presidents, legislators, athletes, authors, artists, major sports figures, psychiatrists, Hollywood stars, scholars, and many other luminaries, whose presence legitimizes the rest of the magazine's content.

In *The Second Sex*, Simone de Beauvoir hypothesized that men have placed women in a subordinate position by making them into the Other: "[S]he is simply what man decrees; thus she is called 'the sex' by which is meant that she appears essentially to the male as a sexual being. For him she is sex—absolute sex, no less. She is defined and differentiated with reference to man and not he with reference to her; she is the incidental, the inessential as opposed to the essential. He is the Subject, he is the Absolute—she is the Other," a category that is quite profitable for the subject who asserts it. "Men profit," she says, "in many . . . ways from the otherness. . . . Here is miraculous balm for those afflicted with an inferiority complex, and indeed no one is more arrogant toward [the other], more aggressive, or scornful, than the man who is anxious about his virility." Moreover the subject, once he posits an other, lives in a world not of women or people of color, but of cooks, matrons, prostitutes, and bluestockings serving functions of pleasure or usefulness. That is to say, such others then have no existence in and for themselves, but only as functions in and for the subject. This is a very powerful concept, which creates a hierarchy that, once in place, is not easily dislodged.[30]

Propaganda is one of the methods used to create this otherness. Employing the techniques documented by Ellul and Brown, pornography and racist speech help to separate people into groups and to create differentness. This "otherness" or "differentness" then functions as the locus of oppression from which ideologies of sexual, ethnic, and racial supremacy are mounted. These ideologies are directly connected to the inequality, discrimination, and violence oppressed groups experience.

THE GAY "MALE" SYNDROME
Gay Male Pornography and the Eroticization of Masculine Identity

Christopher N. Kendall

One of the more troubling splits between the feminist and gay movements began in the late 1970s. The first wave of the feminist anti-pornography movement was in full bloom; the gay movement was just finding its voice. In 1978, Harvey Milk was elected to the city council in San Francisco, gay organizations began to form on college campuses, and a new gay culture sprang up in big cities. But feminists, among others, noted disturbing new developments: the popularity of a hypermasculine aesthetic among gay men and the explosion of the industry of gay male pornography. From the beginning, those who protested that gay pornography had the same unacceptable characteristics as heterosexual pornography were chastised or silenced. Here Christopher Kendall, a young gay legal scholar, argues that gay pornography has no place in gay culture because it buttresses compulsory heterosexuality and male dominance and encourages violence within gay relationships.

■

Gay males confuse me. As gay men they live with the fear and reality of the baseball bat and the crowbar. They know hate and what it means to be the victims of violence. So why the gay response to *Butler*—the supreme court of Canada's most recent, and successful, effort to address the harms of pornography?[1]* In Canada, when the Butler decision was released, gay men expressed outrage. As a white gay male, this reaction leaves me confused and, sadly, desperately in search of a community. For I consider gay male pornography an issue of power, a source of social inequality—including my own.

---

* R. v. *Butler* is the now famous Canadian case in which the Canadian Supreme Court held that pornography is harmful to women and children, and that the production and distribution of pornography undermines social equality, and therefore regulation of pornography is legal. Butler was a pornography dealer who had hundreds of pornography magazines, books, and videos seized from his store, the Avenue Video Boutique in Winnipeg, Manitoba, Canada.—Eds.

Some view gay male pornography as integral to the formation of gay male identity, as something that challenges heterosexuality as a compulsory social construct. But gay male pornography is neither. It is hate speech. It is integral, indeed central, to the formation of a misogynist and heterosexually defined gay male identity. Gay male pornography does not challenge compulsory heterosexuality and male dominance. It supports it. When I see gay male pornography, I see the underbelly of current identity politics—a gay identity that rejects compassion, affection, and caring between two men, and that instead promotes internalized homophobia, hate, and the harming of others. Gay male pornography presents hypermasculinity, what it means to be a socially defined "male." These images ensure that white male dominance is maintained and that those who have historically been denied equality will continue to be the victims of hatred and violence.

Let me emphasize that I am speaking about gay male pornography, not lesbian pornography. While I have little doubt that many of the issues I raise today apply equally to lesbian pornography, I do not intend to address it here. Rather, I will speak about what for me is closest to home.

In Canada, we are fortunate to have a supreme court that, in 1992, broke precedent and in the process reaffirmed its commitment to equality as the central Canadian right. The case of R. v. *Butler* does not represent the first time the court has been asked to rule on the claimed values and expressed harms of pornography, but it is the first time that the court has explicitly upheld laws against pornographic materials because their distribution and production undermine "respect for all members of society, and non-violence and *equality* in their relations with each other."[2]*

In *Butler*, the court recognized that pornography equals harm:

> The clear and unquestionable danger of this type of material is that it reinforces some unhealthy tendencies in Canadian society. The effect of this type of material is to reinforce male-female stereotypes to the detriment of both sexes. It attempts to make degradation, humiliation, victimization, and violence in human relationships appear normal and acceptable. A society which holds that egalitarianism, non-violence, consensualism, and mutuality are basic to any human reaction, whether sexual or other, is clearly justified in controlling any medium of depiction which violates these principles.[3]

---

* For a full discussion of the groundbreaking developments in Canada, see Kathleen Mahoney, "Recognizing the Constitutional Significance of Harmful Speech: The Canadian View of Pornography and Hate Propaganda," p. 277 of this volume.—Eds.

Applying this analysis, the court specifically rejected previous case law in which it was held that pornography should be regulated in order to maintain moral standards. Instead, it recognized that not all speech is equal and that some speech is, in fact, the very source of inequality. The court thus provided a new judicial standard for the evaluation of speech freedom—a standard that will assist the ongoing struggle for equality.

Canada is also home to Chris Berchell, a writer for Toronto's largest lesbian and gay "news" magazine, who, following *Butler*, expressed the following:

> Canada's pre-eminent feminist law-reform organization, the Legal Equality Action Fund (LEAF) seems determined to curtail Canadians' newly enshrined right to freedom of speech before most of us ever get a chance to exercise it. . . . The fact that public and expert witnesses believe that porn causes harm is due to the success of the past decade's anti-porn propaganda campaign, carried out by a dubious alliance of right-wing Christians and such feminist and anti-sex crusaders as Andrea Dworkin and Catharine MacKinnon, who helped develop LEAF's strategy in the Butler case. Thousands of dollars have gone to support women's groups which actively spread this misinformation. . . . It is a sad comment on our time that a moral panic about sexual imagery is led by feminists; that their energy is channeled into an anti-sex backlash that hits queers first and hardest![4]

Berchell believes that gay male pornography should *not* be "censored." Her arguments are based on the assumption that gay male pornography does not harm—that is, that it does not result in behavioral and attitudinal changes that lead to actual physical harm and which undermine social equality. To my mind, this analysis is both politically naive and socially regressive.

For all the effort expended on defending gay male pornography, it is telling that there is little description or documentation of what gay pornography *is*— that is, what it looks like, what it does, and what it says. If gay male pornography were liberating, then an analysis of how it is produced, by whom, and a description of who and what it represents as the source of that liberation would prove useful. Unfortunately, advocates of gay male pornography have failed to provide even basic information about that which they so adamantly defend. Focusing more on its perceived positive effect, they have tended to evade any realistic analysis of that from which this effect is derived. This, in turn, has tended to legitimize those arguments which, having ignored the reality of what is promoted, overlook its resulting harm.

Very little research has been done in the area of gay male pornography, but it seems to be an enormously profitable industry, with most profits going directly to the same people who produce straight pornography. (So much for a distinctly gay discourse, by us and for us!) In 1985 alone there were ten or more companies producing approximately one hundred gay pornographic films a year, each retailing for approximately forty dollars. No one knows for certain how many of these films are sold each year, but in 1985 alone, William Higgins, the self-acclaimed "king of the gay porno industry," grossed more than $2 million. That same year, gay pornographic magazines, which sell for seven to fifteen dollars each, had a distribution of more than 600,000 magazines a month. That's more than 7 million magazines in one year.

Gay male pornography boasts cover titles like *Nazi Torment, Slant Eyed Savages, Teen Bootlicker, Leather Rape Gang, Big Black Cocks, Stud Daddy, Oriental Guys, Inches, Bear: Masculinity . . . Without the Trappings,* and *Slaves of the S.S.* Once inside, you get spreads with names like "Be My Sushi Tonight," "Caught Sniffing First Playmate's Dad's Uniform," "More Prison Violations: Spick Muscle Enslaves Anglo Cellie," "I was a Substitute Vagina," and "I Slapped Him Until He Came."

What one sees in gay male pornography is an almost pervasive glorification of the idealized masculine/male icon. Cops, truckers, cowboys, bikers, and Nazis are eroticized. Racial stereotypes are sexualized and perpetuated. Muscle, "good-looks," and youth are glorified. Ostensibly straight or at least "straight-acting" men rape and/or humiliate descriptively (frequently stereotypically) gay men. Sadism, bondage, watersports, fisting, bootlicking, piercing, slapping, whipping, incest, branding, burning with cigarettes, torture of the genitals and nipples with hot wax, clamps, and the like, rape, and prison rape are presented as erotic, stimulating, and pleasurable. In most of these materials, it is the white, physically more powerful, more dominant male who is romanticized and afforded role model status. In those scenarios where male sexual partners "take turns" being the "top," the characteristics of dominance and non-mutuality remain central to the sexual act. The result is a hierarchical and rarely compassionate or mutual sexuality.

This is gay male pornography. *This* is what pro-porn advocates are defending. *This* is their identity politics. While content and presentation may vary in degree and explicitness from one medium to another, what one gets from the above is an overview of what gay male pornography *is.* If we take ourselves seriously, and if we take seriously the question of identity politics, then we owe it to ourselves to examine what this politics consists of.

The identity politics that can be culled from gay male pornography is one of degradation, exploitation, assertiveness linked with aggression, strength equated with violence, physical power and the right to overpower, intimidation, control of others, lack of mutuality, and disrespect. If you defend gay male pornography, you also defend these qualities as central to gay male identity. You defend aggressive, nonconsensual behavior as normal, even liberating and promoted as such.

The question to be asked then is whether the gay male politics it puts forward is supposed to result in my eventual liberation. I do not believe so. Rather, the identity politics will result in considerable harm—precisely the types of harms addressed in *Butler,* which have been so readily dismissed as nonexistent within *gay* pornography.

Given the description above, it is perhaps not surprising that gay pornography frequently places its "models" in scenarios that promote violence, cruelty, degradation, dehumanization, and exploitation. While deemed merely repesentational, hence "fictional," the "fantasy" offered in gay male pornography utilizes real people, a factor most pro-porn advocates overlook. The men used in gay male pornography are frequently involved precisely because they are psychologically and financially at their most vulnerable. They are easily exploited by an industry driven by its ability to manipulate those least likely to possess real life choices. Indeed, the lives and experiences of these young men are very much removed from the "fantasy" they invoke.

It is a disturbing reflection of the state of gay male relations that so little is known about, and ultimately done to assist, the men held out as the images from whence gay male identity is derived. Note, for example, the description of one young man (interviewed in 1985) involved in the production of gay male pornographic films and magazines:

> Jim Y. was raised by abusive, alcoholic parents. When Jim told his parents he was gay, at age 13, his father tried to kill him with a large kitchen knife. Jim left home at 17. At 19 he met Frank H., about ten years his senior, who was to become his lover. Frank was making a porno film at the time he met Jim, and convinced Jim to appear in it. Jim played a new arrival to the big city who engages in S&M, including bootlicking, bondage, beating with a belt, fisting, and implied murder. This film was the first film to show fisting and Jim says he is convinced that it created the gay interests in fisting as a sexual behavior. The film also reflected the S&M relationship that Jim and Frank were to share for the next decade. . . . Jim has been seeing a psychiatrist for three years now. He has been trying to avoid

S&M sex, and believes that his sexual behavior was a way he sought out contact with his abusive father. He also recognizes that much sexual "fantasy" can be destructive; when asked where it comes from, he said, "Well, to some extent, from me; from my films, that is." About one month ago Jim was diagnosed with AIDS, and now fears that he has lost whatever chance he might have had to turn his life around.[5]

The daily reality of the young men used in gay male pornography should, at a minimum, indicate that the industry does not afford protection to the people it uses for profit. Many of these men, already susceptible to the effects of past emotional, physical, and sexual abuse, are further endangered by an industry that, to date, has done little if anything to promote safe sex practices and, as a result, does very little to protect the people who are supposed to "present" positive and safe sexual practices. In addition, the industry is inextricably connected to the prostitution of these men, resulting in the increased risk of exposure of AIDS and the physical violence and exploitation commensurate with prostitution generally.

Similarly, it does not require too much insight to infer that scenarios of sexual violence and pain presented as pleasurable are in fact documentations of real degradation, which are neither pleasurable nor fictitious. While it is easy to articulate a liberation theory that overlooks or ignores the reality of what is speciously presented as "fantasy," the use and abuse of young men in scenarios of degradation, dehumanization, and violence cannot be justified, particularly by those who view their presentation as integral to the sexual and political awareness of *all* gay men. If anything violates a person's freedom and integrity more than direct sexual and physical abuse, it is the mass marketing of that abuse as sexual entertainment.

The gay male community has been reluctant to acknowledge that gay men do actually hurt each other, that this might be encouraged by pornography, or that there is anything inherent in the values expressed in gay male pornography that undermines equality. If these gay male publications were heterosexual ones, however, and presented women and men rather than men and men, the Canadian courts would acknowledge that they are substantially harmful to women and society, based on research indicating that the production and distribution of heterosexual pornography increases the risk of violence against women and that the stereotypes and gender hierarchies promoted in pornography undermine equality. The last decade of research additionally indicates that heterosexual pornography harms women by negatively influencing individual and group behavior and by being used as a tool to force people to participate in nonconsensual, nonegalitarian power relationships.

Do these harms result from gay male pornography as well? Or does the "gay" in gay male pornography make the pornography less pornographic? That is, is there something qualitatively different about pictures of men violating other men that makes gay male pornography harm-free, or outside the constraints of *Butler*?

Although research thus far has relied only on heterosexual pornography, I suggest that these findings are equally applicable to gay male pornography—that is, that the presentation of real people in scenarios of violence and degradation (not to mention the exploitation involved in the production of these images) can in this case, too, lead to increased violence against real people. I do not argue that the harm and the degree of it are exactly the same, since men are not socially in the same position as women. But an analogy can be drawn—that in both cases certain images cause behaviors that harm real people.

Supporters of gay male pornography will reply that heterosexual pornography is damaging because it depicts men harming women—that it is the biological difference that renders women unsafe and unequal. Hence, gay male pornography eliminates the risk of harm because no women figure into its presentation. Any analysis that rests on biology, however, is misleading, as well as essentialist. It assumes that when men hurt and violate men it is not harmful—an assumption that only reinforces dominant assumptions about acceptable male behavior and male aggression generally. More important, the danger inherent in straight pornography is not just its presentation of the biological male violating the biological female. Its danger also stems from the model of behavior afforded the biological male and sexualized as normal behavior. The legitimation of power for those who exhibit aggression and dominance reinforces male violence and systemic inequality for those who become their victims.

The maleness presented in pornography is in fact not a biological but a social trait. Two men can be made unequal if one man is viewed as a real man and his partner is not. Gay male pornography, like heterosexual pornography, creates a gender hierarchy in which masculinity equals power. It promotes male dominance, and this, in turn, results in considerable harm.

A 1991 study on gay male domestic violence reports that there are 350,000 to 650,000 victims of gay male domestic violence in the United States each year, the third largest health problem facing gay men in that country today. What is most interesting for an analysis of gay male pornography are the study's findings about the types of men who batter and how they perceive themselves and their partners.

Gay men who batter and abuse their partners have specific ideas of masculinity and what it means to be "male." This is the result of a near-complete lack of positive gay role models, a homophobic environment in which being gay means being nonmasculine, hence inferior, and the internalization of self-hatred and societal rejection. These men overcompensate for their sense of nonworth by seeking out value systems that they hope will provide control, power, and more social acceptance. The gay male batterers in the study interpret assertiveness to mean aggression (and hence ignore the rights and feelings of others), think of strength as a license to be violent, see power as a license to terrorize, and view mutuality as a threat. Gay male batterers "act out" what they perceive as appropriate masculine behavior, follow a recipe for that masculinity and, when they beat their partners, excuse their behavior by claiming that this is just how men act.

Gay male pornography promotes "values" like power, brutality, and non-mutuality, exactly the same as those held by gay male batterers. Gay male pornography thus supports and sexualizes a view of masculinity that daily results in gay men abusing and killing the men who love them.

While no research has been done to determine if gay men who abuse their partners use gay pornography, there is no evidence that they do not. For many pro-porn advocates, gay male pornography serves as a learning resource, particularly in a society where gay male expression is suppressed. To these people I ask whether it is unreasonable to assume that a learning resource that promotes masculinity, taken to its extreme, once interpreted by men who feel they do not fit the desired norm and feel that they should, has the potential to trigger already severe feelings of insecurity and result in some particularly destructive behaviors.

In sum, gay male pornography encourages all that is masculinity (read "male" socially defined). Thus, in addition to encouraging male aggression resulting in physical harm, it also goes a long way in maintaining systemic inequality by promoting rather than undermining a gender hierarchy in which "male" is top and "female" (read all women and those gay men who fail or choose not to conform to the male construct and who are thus socially feminized) is bottom. Like heterosexual pornography, it thus glorifies those in our society who have always had the most power and who have benefited from male dominance and social inequality: white, able-bodied straight men. The result for society is a sexual politic based on a male/female dichotomy, a split between power and powerlessness, top and bottom.

By referring to gay men as feminized and therefore "female," I am *not* suggesting that gay men and women are equally oppressed. As Andrea Dworkin explains, "devalued males can often change status, escape; women and girls cannot."[6] Nor am I suggesting that all gay men are equally oppressed. What I am saying, however, is that to the extent that some gay men *do* reject socially defined male behavior (as they must if systemic equality is ever to be attained) and express a sexuality and politics which have the potential to subvert male supremacy, their behavior is deemed unacceptable and devalued as such. The gay male who does so is, as John Stoltenberg explains, "stigmatized because he is perceived to participate in the degraded status of female" and, as such, assumes a position inferior to those who, not feminized, reap the benefits of male/female polarity.[7] He is, in essence, penalized for not "changing status" —that is, for not adopting those values and attitudes that maintain male dominance and the inequality that results from it.

Lesbian organizer Suzanne Pharr observes that when gay men break ranks with male roles through mutual bonding and display affection for other men, they are perceived as not being "real men" and are identified with women— the "weaker sex" that must be dominated, and which is the object of male hatred and abuse. Misogyny, she explains, gets transferred to gay men with a vengeance. It is increased by the mainstream fear that gay sexual identity and behavior will challenge male dominance and compulsory heterosexuality.[8]

The gay male, socially feminized, internalizes this misogyny and seeks to mimic those behaviors that will, he hopes, allow him to pass for the man he is supposed to be. Masculinity, for those who have been penalized for failing to meet its criteria, promises privilege and a safety net with which to find social existence.

This assumed safety net is exactly what makes gay pornography the homophobic threat to equality that it is. Rather than encouraging gay men to subvert oppressive gender constructs, it tells gay men that every sexual relationship must be hierarchical and that male power is at the top of that hierarchy. It promises the gay male a false sense of security that he too can gain more power if he can become that which epitomizes power—masculinity taken to its extreme. Unfortunately the power promised is a façade and does a great deal to further maintain male dominance—the very source of all that is anti-gay, anti-woman, anti-equality.

One does not defeat one's enemy by simply mimicking him. Mimicry only ensures invisibility. By dissuading the public expression of a sexuality that has the potential to undermine patriarchy, gay male pornography serves as little more than another homophobic source with which to silence gay men and reinforce an already deeply entrenched system of sex discrimination and social inequality.

Gay men state with conviction that "silence equals death." For many, this represents a call to action. To these same men I say: silence does equal death, and gay male pornography is your muzzle. Now let me see some real action.

HATE GROUPS, AFRICAN AMERICANS, AND THE FIRST AMENDMENT

Loretta J. Ross

What is the connection between hate speech and hate crimes? In this thought-provoking essay, Loretta Ross argues that hate speech can be compared to death threats, libel, or fraud: it is an abuse of the First Amendment that should not be protected. "Hate groups know that current interpretations of the First Amendment allow them to denigrate individuals and groups of people they do not like," says Ross. She notes that some supremacist organizations have begun to refer to the First Amendment as "our amendment" and argues that hate speech unchecked by law is a powerful weapon in their arsenal.

■

In July 1993, Anthony Griffin, an African-American attorney for the NAACP in Galveston, agreed to represent the Texas Knights of the Ku Klux Klan in a First Amendment case. The dispute arose from Klan efforts to prevent the court-ordered integration of an all-white housing project in Vidor, Texas. The Klan had conducted a year-long campaign of resistance against the court decision, including sixteen different rallies and direct intimidation: the Texas Commission on Human Rights says the life of Vidor's mayor was threatened, and four men in Klan military garb threatened to burn the housing project down if blacks moved in. Finally, the commission ordered the Klan to turn over its membership records to facilitate the investigation of possible criminal acts by Klan members. When the Klan refused, a judge jailed Grand Dragon Charles Lee for contempt of court. Enter Griffin.

Griffin rationalized his decision to defend the KKK by arguing that the Klan had First Amendment rights that, as an ACLU volunteer lawyer, he was compelled to defend: "The Klan has a right to meet and organize, and they have a right to say as many abhorrent, horrible, nasty, violent, vicious things as they want to say," he said. Griffin did not see race as relevant to the case. The Texas NAACP dismissed Griffin on the grounds that it was impossible for NAACP general counsel to represent the organization and the Klan at the same time.

The case illustrates the troublesome and misconceived relationships among the First, Thirteenth, and Fourteenth Amendments. In theory, the Thirteenth and Fourteenth Amendments to the Constitution can serve as limitations on the power of racist groups like the Klan to exercise traditional First Amendment rights of free speech and association. The Thirteenth Amendment, passed after the Civil War, outlawed slavery and prohibited depriving African Americans "of the basic rights that the law secures to all free persons." The amendment was intended not only to eliminate slavery, but also to eradicate the "badges of slavery," i.e., racism. The Fourteenth Amendment prohibited denying to any person equal protection of the law. Klan activity in Vidor directly denied African Americans the right to live where they pleased. Whites who favored integration were also threatened. All of the victims' equal protection of the law was denied by racist activities prohibited by the Constitution.

African Americans nervously applaud the First Amendment, thankful for its protections that sometimes, but not always, extend to the struggle against racial oppression. However, their support is tempered by the way the amendment has been used to protect anti-black racial terrorism. Do racists have a constitutional right to express their views in ways that severely restrict the rights of African Americans to be, live, and go where they please? When does a racist threat, veiled and anonymous, become a hate crime—and should such a threat be protected by the First Amendment?

Many who oppose restricting First Amendment protections for hate groups view hate speech apart from its actual cost in terms of human suffering. By not placing their arguments against the reality of white privilege in America, they decontextualize the freedom to express one's beliefs from the speaker's power to impose those beliefs on others. As Lani Guinier pointed out during her nomination to head the civil rights division of the Justice Department, this social and historical denial implies that "the remedy for racism is to simply stop talking about race," as if America were truly a race-neutral society. First Amendment absolutism prevents serious public debate about racial fairness and justice by casting the victims of racism as censors.

In their preoccupation with abstractions, absolutists fail to understand that America's lynching past is not over. Contemporary racist violence against African Americans reflects the stark brutality of earlier periods, and African Americans disproportionately shoulder the burden of keeping the First Amendment (selectively) unrestricted. For example, Michael Donald, a twenty-one-year-old college student, was lynched in Mobile, Alabama, by Klansmen in 1981. Gangs of white youths were responsible for the deaths of Michael Griffith in New York City in 1986; Tony Montgomery in Reno, Nevada, in 1988; Timothy Moss in California's Simi Valley in 1992; and the lynchings of William Brooks and Carlos Stoner in North Carolina in 1992. On New Year's Eve in 1993, freelance racists in Florida kidnapped Christopher Wilson, a black tourist, and set him on fire. These are only a few of the thousands of hate crimes that have been experienced by African Americans in the last decade. According to statistics from the Department of Justice, 75 percent of all racially motivated hate crimes were directed at African Americans in 1992—the first year hate crimes were counted by the federal government. Extremist activity targeting people of color continues to undermine democratic participation, because when people are intimidated or harassed, they tend to hide, withdraw, and become angry. White supremacists are doing the dirty work of other racist segments of the population, who themselves may not want to physically intimidate African Americans, but who like the results of that intimidation.

Hate Groups and the First Amendment

Hate speech is an integral part of white supremacists' campaigns. They use it to rally support, to cement solidarity, to threaten their victims—not to generate oppositional speech. Its purpose is to intimidate, humiliate, assault, and defame, but also, very importantly, to silence. Hate speech can be compared to death threats, libel, or fraud more easily than to the remarks of someone who, for example, dislikes smokers. Hate speech directed toward one black person is an injury to all African Americans. When civil libertarians insist that, although they abhor racist speech, it is private, and protected under the First Amendment, they deny its public harm and its ability to limit the human and civil rights of an entire targeted group.

Hate groups use a combination of legitimate and illegal activities to pursue their goals. Hate speech is one powerful weapon in their arsenal. Public rallies and demonstrations help them to gain visibility and provoke public controversy, which in turn increases media coverage and attracts recruits. It is common for them to rally peacefully in public during the day, and then commit hate crimes under cover of darkness. For example, after a 1993 neo-Nazi concert in Pennsylvania, which attracted over 300 skinheads from around the country, at least five hate crimes occurred, including an incident in which skinheads leaving the concert attempted to run over a black cyclist.

A large proportion of hate crimes directed toward African Americans are called "move-in" violence because they are designed to keep blacks out of white jobs, communities, and schools.* Because of segregation and fear, whites see blacks as "hordes" invading their communities, and they make this sentiment very clear. Klan rallies in neighborhoods undergoing integration in housing or in the public schools send an unmistakable message to African Americans in those communities. And these expressions are matched by more violent ones: in January 1993, Frank Scire of Brooklyn, New York, received an eight-year prison term for the 1991 firebombing of an "integrationist" real estate firm. The Prejudice Institute recently reported that 27 percent of all racist violence takes place at work because of increased minority representation in the work force, and that 20 percent of minority college students at predominantly white institutions are assaulted or harassed each year.

An infrequently mentioned consequence of hate speech is that it encourages those who are not even members of hate groups to commit hate crimes. Violent freelance racists look to the Ku Klux Klan and to neo-Nazi organizations for inspiration. The symbols and methods of the independent racist are often those of the KKK and the neo-Nazis: the burning cross, the swastika, anonymous vandalism in the night. The U.S. Civil Rights Commission reported that organized white supremacist groups provide the rhetoric of justification for other violent racists, who act on impulse.

Klan marches through small towns polarize residents, often provoking racist violence long after the event. Shortly after a 1992 Klan rally in Lenoir, North Carolina, for example, two white students stabbed two of their black classmates to death. When arrested, the students confessed that they had been influenced by the heightened racial tension in the town and had been given hate literature that was made widely available both before and after the Klan rally.

The Courts, Hate Speech, and Hate Crimes

In the past decade, forty-six states have passed laws prohibiting hate crimes and denying them constitutional protection; municipal laws and campus speech codes have been adopted; and 1990 brought passage of the Federal Hate Crimes Statistics Act. These measures were passed because an epidemic of hate crimes—many initiated with hate speech—is sweeping the nation. At the same time, civil suits have begun to gain success. For example, when Tom Metzger, of the White Aryan Resistance, encouraged young skinheads to murder an Ethiopian immigrant student in 1988, he was not criminally charged with the

---

* See "The Case of the Cross-Burning: An Interview with Russ and Laura Jones," p. 27, this volume. —Eds.

murder. The skinheads actually responsible are serving long prison terms for that. But a civil court jury found Metzger liable for his encouragement of the skinheads and awarded the student's family a $12.5 million judgment against Metzger—though some argued that he was merely exercising his First Amendment rights. Some of the debate over hate group activity and bigoted violence has finally moved into the public policy arena, as the judicial system has been forced to examine the connection between hate speech and hate crimes.

In 1992, the Supreme Court invoked the First Amendment to prevent the state of Minnesota from censoring "speech" (in this case, a burning cross) just because the idea expressed was offensive. Yet only one year later, in *Wisconsin* v. *Mitchell*, the Supreme Court ruled that a black teenager who said "there goes a white boy; go get him" to initiate a brutal attack against a white teenager in 1989 could be given an enhanced sentence in accordance with the state's hate crime laws. This conflicting set of messages has affected decisions in lower courts. For example, on August 27, 1993, the Maryland Court of Appeals overturned a law that made cross-burning a felony in Maryland, ruling that it restricted constitutionally protected speech. The law, enacted in the mid-1960s during a rash of violence against African Americans in the state, required cross-burners to first obtain the permission of property owners and to notify local fire officials. The case stemmed from a 1991 incident in which Brandon Sheldon, a white supremacist, burned a cross on the lawn of a black family in Upper Marlboro. The Maryland Court of Appeals ruled that cross-burning, even when done on someone else's property, qualifies as free speech. The charges against Sheldon were dismissed.

Can Hate-Speech Regulation Deter Hate Crimes?

Anti-racists do not naively expect hate-speech and hate-crime regulations to eliminate racism. One cannot even outlaw the entire realm of racist speech because so often speech is ambiguous. The California raisin commercials were found offensive by some African Americans; humorous by others. Rush Limbaugh must be tolerated; so must tasteless humor. Similarly, one cannot and should not suppress discussion of racial differences and characteristics. It is when speech is used to rationalize discrimination and prejudice that it moves beyond mere offense into undeniable injury.

This is an essential distinction. One may be offended by scholars who seek to prove racial superiority or inferiority. As pseudoscience these theories should receive the same credence as those who insist that $2 + 2 = 5$. But African Americans are injured—threatened—when a KKK member who lives next door to a black family displays a sign in his yard that caricatures a black man with a gun at his head. The wording on this actual sign in Gainesville, Georgia, read: "A mind is a terrible thing to waste; that's why niggers don't have any." It was a reference to the Christian Identity belief that blacks are nonhuman or "pre-Adamic" beasts created before God created Adam, the first human. Thus, Christian Identity leaders argue, only whites can be true Christians, and, moreover, they can murder African Americans without any consequences to their Christian souls because they are merely practicing "animal control." Propagation of these beliefs has had deadly consequences.

Many who desire hate speech regulation have legitimate concerns about the role of the government in its regulation. They see the government as inherently hostile to the interests of oppressed minorities and assume that, no matter what hate-speech laws are passed, these laws will be enforced in a racist manner. They fear that hate speech regulation will become another tool for whites to use in perpetuating racism, that whites will find ways to define themselves as America's victims. But whether or not hate-speech regulation will harm the victims of racism will be determined by the strength of the social movement to eliminate hate speech. That movement will influence how the law is used, now and in the future. Civil rights laws historically have only been as effective as the political movements behind them. As the lack of enforcement in the 1980s proved, civil rights laws become ineffective when they lack a social movement to ensure that racism does not win in the contest of competing rights.

The First Amendment is an indispensable part of our rights in society, and must not be casually limited. But regulating hate speech does not destroy the First Amendment any more than regulating pornography destroys sex. It is important to remove the potent weapon of hate speech from the hands of racists if America is ever to live up to its promise of equality for all its people. Only when racism is purged from the mainstream and the margins of American society will true democracy be created.

EVERYDAY RACISM AND THE CAMPAIGN OF HATRED

Robin D. Barnes

What happens when hate speech is protected by the First Amendment? Instead of expanding everyone's right to freedom of expression, Robin Barnes argues, such protection subverts the fundamental values of the Constitution it professes to support. Under the guise of neutrality, well-intentioned civil libertarians and others who adhere to an absolute view of the First Amendment inadvertently reinforce a status quo of racism, inequality, and second-class citizenship.

■

Tyranny is much more than a mere threat. It looms large in the daily lives of many students and professors, sometimes with the tacit consent of university officials.[1] I developed the following hypothetical event from actual incidents on university campuses across the nation as a classroom exercise for students at the University of Wisconsin.

Imagine that you are a black American female student, enrolled as a freshman at a well-known public university where you were admitted under an affirmative action program. Your college entrance exam scores placed you in the top twenty percent of your class, your grade point average was 3.1, and you are the first in your family to attend college. As you walk across campus to attend your first orientation session, a car full of white boys drives by. They yell out, "Hey baby, I bet you give good head." Immediately you survey the surrounding area only to discover no one is around but you. You arrive at the orientation session prepared to learn about the "greatest time of your life," and each time you attempt to take a seat, two or three students look at one another and the boldest of the bunch says, "It's taken." On the third try, someone unenthusiastically moves her coat, and you sit down. A member of the board of trustees approaches the podium and after many boring, although nonetheless encouraging, words about hard work, remarks that the black employees at her firm prefer selling drugs to working. Rightly offended, you are stunned when many students start to laugh. Later at the dorm, as you unpack your last bag in what is supposed to be home for the next year, you listen to the campus radio station and hear a student disc jockey say, "Hey, why is it that blacks always have sex on the brain? Answer: It's because their heads are covered with pubic hair." At the first meeting of the Black Students Association you mention these incidents. Someone remarks that last year, in your dorm, three white boys harassed and placed feces in the heating system of the apartment of two black women, and after a year of complaints the men were reassigned to another dorm. Someone else notes that just last semester the university responded to the spraying of "KKK" on a campus wall with red paint by merely repainting the wall, and another student recalls that while four students slept inside an anti-apartheid shanty someone doused it with gasoline and set it on fire. As a result, the black fraternity house was burned to the ground. The meeting ends, and, as you emerge from the building, you notice that a large sign had been posted at the entrance of the university that reads: White Male University. The sign displays four swastikas at the bottom. You cannot stand it any longer and take off running—you are getting out of there! Just as you turn the corner of the long driveway, sprinting toward freedom, a gang of white males catch and beat you senseless, all the while shouting, "The world is mine and nothing you do will ever change that." You lie there swearing revenge. All you really want to do, though, is go home.[2]

Each of these events occurred on a campus recently. The question I ask my students is, which of the events is speech and which action? Most of the time, they conclude that they constitute a coordinated campaign of harassment and that all should be treated as *action*.

Black Americans, inside and outside the walls of the university, experience racism as a group. Concerted treatment designed to inflict emotional distress must be classified as a campaign for exclusion. Those who support an absolutist position on free expression have argued that the university setting is a "separate sphere" and a distinct component of society with a special mission to educate future leaders and therefore should be exempt from any restrictions on the free flow of ideas. I agree that the university is unique, but understand it to have intersecting missions, the most important of which has nothing whatsoever to do with yielding to the free flow of harassment and intimidation. Education today is the linchpin of *equality*, just as it is the key determinant of meaningful social and economic opportunity in the United States. Therefore, the mission of the university must include the right, as well as the responsibility, to guarantee students and faculty of color unfettered and equitable access to the full educational and pedagogical enterprise. The purpose of hate speech in this context is not to expand discourse, but to deprive targeted group members of their civil and educational rights.[3] Tolerance of hate-speech activities in this setting contradicts our fundamental notions of justice and equality.

I am a strong proponent of the view that silencing is a bad thing when it is intentional. Yet I am equally convinced that it is important to recognize when it is not. I foresee danger in jurisprudential indifference toward the injury caused by hate-speech campaigns. We need to reconsider the First Amendment standard of "clear and present danger" of violence if we want to continue to place freedom of speech at the core of our national identity. Intentionally or not, it reinforces racism and hatred and produces a wholesale distortion of fundamental rights—a serious affront to this nation's proclamation of justice and equality for all. The most straightforward way for the judicial system to deal with the kind of racist speech in my hypothetical scenario is to view it as *action*, as my students did. Racist speech deprives people of their civil rights and should be punishable as such.

WHY THE FIRST AMENDMENT IS BEING USED TO PROTECT VIOLENCE AGAINST WOMEN

Twiss Butler

Twiss Butler argues that men's control of institutions of communication and education allows them to support speech that harms women and to suppress speech against that harm. She observes that the publishing industry funds legal, journalistic, and nonprofit organizations endorsing a First Amendment absolutist position. She contends that the industry's defense of pornography as protected speech serves the double purpose of dignifying misogyny and establishing the First Amendment as the publisher's product liability shield.

■

All unequal power relationships must, in the end, rely on the threat or reality of violence to protect themselves. *

Despite men's violence against women, the legal system continues to deny women's right to equal protection of the law. In addition, men still frame the public discourse so as to conceal this denial and to prevent our uniting in rebellion against it. As Sally Kempton wrote early in the women's movement, "It is hard to fight an enemy who has outposts in your head."[1] And, we might add, outposts in the schools, at newsstands, and on TV. If I seem to overstate the conflict, consider that every woman in this country is less free than every man to walk out of the house at night. What is it that so routinely restricts our freedom of movement? Abigail Adams identified it in a letter to Isaac Smith in 1771, saying that she longed to be "a rover," but citing as a deterrent "the many dangers we are subject to from your sex."[2]

If we admit that sex discrimination exists, it is not men-bashing, but ex-

---

* Lorenne M.G. Clark and Debra J. Lewis, *Rape: The Price of Coercive Sexuality* (Toronto: Canadian Women's Educational Press, 1977), p. 176.

planatory, to address the way that it advantages all men, just as racism advantages all whites. Where there is advantage, there is motivation to maintain it. Moreover, there is no point in discussing harm without identifying the beneficiaries of it.

Traditional First Amendment arguments for freedom of speech take for granted that we inhabit a civil society and meet on a level playing field to contest points on which we disagree. Such an egalitarian view of the Constitution, however, was hardly what the founding fathers had in mind. Writing in 1776, John Adams argued against permitting women—as well as men without property and "lads from twelve to twenty-one"—to have the vote because that would "destroy all distinctions and prostrate all ranks to one common level."[3] At the same time, he refused his wife Abigail's demand on behalf of women that the country's "new code of laws . . . put it out of the power of the vicious and the lawless to use us with cruelty and indignity with impunity." His chilling assurance to her was: "Depend upon it, we know better than to repeal our masculine systems."[4] Both her demand and his response were privately communicated, and her anger found its sole recorded outlet in a letter to her friend Mercy Otis Warren.[5] In contrast, his point of view was publicly enshrined in the United States Constitution.

A century and a half later, in 1920, masculine systems briefly appeared to be in some danger when women won recognition of the right to vote through the passage of the Nineteenth Amendment. Some men sensibly feared that women would use their vote, as Alice Paul urged, to amend the Constitution to secure their right to equal protection of the law. Those fears were unwarranted, however. The prolonged campaign for the vote had shown how hard it would be for women to get the information they needed to vote in their own interest so long as education and communication were dominated by men, and issues framed to men's advantage.

The civil rights movement of the 1960s, in a repeat of the post–Civil War campaigns for the Thirteenth, Fourteenth, and Fifteenth amendments, did not acknowledge women's virtual exclusion from the Constitution, in addition to that of African Americans. If society and the law treated women differently from men, in the post–civil rights era, that was presumably because women were different, not because men were keeping something of value from them- that is, their rights as citizens. If it were otherwise, surely our schoolbooks would have mentioned it. At public hearings in the 1970s, feminists who provided content analyses to document the trivialization and exclusion of women and girls from educational materials promptly learned that liberal patriarchs do not hesitate to use accusations of censorship to chill dissent and maintain a racist, sexist status quo.[6] Feminists expected resistance from the conservative patriarchy when we objected to sexist materials, but we were surprised by cries of censorship from the American Civil Liberties Union, People for the American Way, the American Library Association, and the National Council of Teachers of English—none of whom was providing leadership in the revision of educational materials that relegated girls and women to subordinate status. Their arguments against change equated criticism—that is, our bringing "more speech" into the vaunted marketplace of ideas—with censorship. At the same time, they acknowledged no de facto censorship in the minimal, stereotyped treatment of women and girls in materials in use.

In this fashion, from the beginning of this country, institutions of communication directed by men have blocked women's access to information and denied women the opportunity to shape public discourse in response to our experience. That is why it has been possible in this supposedly exemplary democracy not only to deny women their constitutional right to equal protection of the law, but also to keep them largely ignorant of that denial and how it affects their lives generation after generation. So ignorant that even the Equal Rights Amendment campaign could be fatally diverted from every issue that would have made it clear to men that advocates meant business, and clear to women that they could use their vote to establish their right to equality.

In the late 1980s, civil rights lobbyists worked together to get homophobic crime added to the Hate Crime Statistics Act, which already addressed crimes of racism and anti-Semitism. But when an advocate for battered women asked that rape be counted as a hate crime against women, coalition members balked, saying that rape was not a hate but a sex crime; that the legislation would never pass with rape included; that rape statistics would outnumber and overwhelm statistics on "real" hate crimes; and that if rape were included, Senator Helms would attach an anti-abortion amendment to the bill.

Did the women lobbyists walk out, refuse to help the men get their legislation passed, or go public with the issue to make it possible for women to support political action on their own behalf? No, they did not. So rape, men's quintessential hate crime against women, the one that defines all women as prey, is still invisible in federal hate crime statistics. Now we find ourselves endlessly repeating grim statistics about violence against women in every phase and circumstance of life from childhood to old age. Shouldn't we question why violence against women is treated as sexual chic or a natural occurrence, like bad weather, rather than repudiated as a behavior used by men to control women? Where is our resistance to this normalized subordination, this mundane terrorism? Is our only role to be practicing tactics of avoidance or cleaning up the damage? Why must we seek special legislation to go about our daily business? Where is our entitlement to the bodily integrity and equal protection that is men's constitutional birthright?

As John Adams conceded, violence is necessary to enforce subordination of an individual or group. Inevitably, the oppressor objectifies and dehumanizes the target group to justify violence against them. Men use pornography to objectify women, not only making subordination sexy, but effectively defining sexuality as dominance by men and the subordination of women. Calling subordination sex does not make it hurt any less, but in this area, as elsewhere, men's control over information is a critical element in maintaining their power.

When feminists criticize pornography as graphic misogyny, they are attacking not only the system of sexism itself, with its economic and social pay-offs for men, not only *Playboy*'s advertising rates, but also publishers' broad First Amendment shield against liability for any harm caused by the products that they produce and sell.

The publishing industry and the men in it therefore have a conflict of interest in reporting a critique of pornography as inimical to women's civil rights (unsecured as those rights are by the Constitution). We need to consider how that conflict of interest distorts the information we receive through journalistic coverage of public debate and action on this issue.

Publishers protect their liability shield either by silencing feminists while granting speech to those who vilify them, or by misrepresenting the feminist critique of pornography. Women are given credibility and access to speech to the extent that they say what men want them to say. Stray from the script and you will be attacked, misquoted, or simply go unheard. As power brokers in a large industry profiting from sexism, publishers disguise this censorship as selfless concern for the First Amendment and freedom of speech.

The Association of American Publishers, the American Booksellers Association, and other media trade groups have long promoted an aggressive First Amendment line, particularly since the publication in 1970 of the first report of the President's Commission on Obscenity and Pornography. Pressured by the lobbying of civil libertarian groups, the Commission abandoned its investigation as to whether pornography was harmful. Instead it came up with the fantasy of "pornography as catharsis," and a burgeoning industry was saved. *

The self-serving doctrine promoted by publishers and libertarians is summarized by law professor Frederick Schauer as follows: "[L]egal toleration of

---

* There are two main models scientists use to explain behavior: the *catharsis* model—which says the more you see the *less* you do, and the *imitative* model—which says the more you see the *more* you do. Most new research on pornography (and on violence) supports the validity of the imitative model.—Eds.

speech-related harm is the currency with which we as a society pay for First Amendment protection."[7] It is not enough to notice, as Schauer does, that this price is not borne equally when the reality remains unremedied so that license to wield harmful speech only profits the speaker and silences the victim.

In the news business as elsewhere, men have long relied on the weapon of pornography to avoid having to compete on their own merits.[8] The role pornography plays in keeping women journalists at a disadvantage is evident in the experience of Lynn Carrier, an editorial writer for the *San Diego Tribune* who sued the paper in 1990 for sex discrimination and harassment. Men coworkers attempted to intimidate and segregate Carrier by displaying pornography in the office, using sexual insults when talking with her, and asking her to run out and buy a copy of *Playboy* for her supervisor—who also wondered aloud what she would charge *Playboy* for posing nude for photographs. Carrier won her civil suit (refusing, incidentally, to accept a secret settlement), but the outcome was typical—she no longer works at the *Tribune*, but is employed instead at a smaller paper in the area.[9]

It becomes hard to tell where the news business ends and pornography begins when it is pornography that shapes standards for how women will be depicted. In addition, mainstream media legitimate pornography by touting the *Playboy* interview or the *Sports Illustrated* swimsuit issue. The hit-and-run intrusion of pornography into everyday journalism is epitomized by the tactic used by *Spy* magazine to attack Hillary Rodham Clinton on the cover of its February 1993 issue. In a skillfully doctored color photograph with Oval Office trappings in the background, her head is united with the body of a woman in scanty, black leather dominatrix attire, whip in hand. The studded collar around her neck neatly conceals the splice.

Given the value of pornography in supporting men's dominance, pornographers can count on help from publishers and the courts in defending their product from any meaningful legal restraint.[10] But, as I have mentioned, pornography has an even stronger claim on the resources of the publishing industry, because of their mutual interest in denying that published speech can be held accountable for harm.

An ad in an insurance trade periodical for a company whose slogan is "We insure free speech" warns: "Free speech can carry a high price for your media clients because publishers, broadcasters and advertising agencies are vulnerable to lawsuits in ways most companies are not."[11] An article in another insurance trade periodical explains: "Everything that is published, broadcast or advertised is protected by the First Amendment . . . [A] media liability policy is the only form of liability coverage that relies on constitutional law as a primary defense

. . . [W]hy is the coverage necessary? Because ongoing legal, political and social debate continues about how broad that constitutional protection should be."[12]

No industry is better situated to lobby the public on behalf of its commercial interests than one whose product consists of speech and images, whether categorized as news, education, entertainment, or advertising. The publishing industry is sparing no expense to control the debate on the breadth of constitutional protection of speech.

In February 1993, the Freedom Forum Foundation took a full-page advertisement in the *Washington Post* to announce that former Supreme Court justices William Brennan, Jr., and Thurgood Marshall would receive the organization's highest honor, the Free Spirit Award, along with cash awards of $100,000 "in recognition of their extraordinary achievement in promoting the values of free press, free speech, and free spirit."[13] The ad included pictures of the honorees and samples of their wise pronouncements on First Amendment protection of offensive speech and a man's right to read books or watch films of his own choosing in his own house. Not mentioned was that the Freedom Forum is funded by the Gannett Corporation, a media giant that publishes *USA Today*. Using corporate sponsorship to promote laissez-faire First Amendment platitudes from the highest of judicial sources typifies the publishing industry's increasingly bold exploitation of the First Amendment to sanctify its commercial self-interest.

Publishers also use grants to infiltrate academic institutions. As talking heads or op-ed writers, academics make classy mouthpieces for publishers' interests. They skillfully transform crass commercial concerns into lofty issues of public policy. Gannett set up Freedom Forum First Amendment centers at Columbia and Vanderbilt universities and gave a quarter of a million dollars to the University of Maryland to put its glossy Freedom Forum insert into the *American Journalism Review*. The Graduate School of Public Affairs at the University of Colorado at Denver is headquarters for the First Amendment Congress, with over forty contributing members, including "major print and broadcast news media associations," as well as schools of journalism and collegiate news associations.[14]

The list goes on: the University of Virginia has its Thomas Jefferson Center for the Protection of Free Expression, Penn State University has the Pennsylvania Center for the First Amendment, the College of William and Mary houses the Institute of Bill of Rights Law, and Harvard University's Kennedy School of Government has its Frank Stanton Professor of the First Amendment and fellow of the Joan Schorenstein Barone Center on the Press, Politics, and

Public Policy. That legal scholar serves, along with two ultraconservative colleagues, on a university committee appointed to help the Harvard community reflect on free speech questions "in a principled way."[15]

There are also the Theater of the First Amendment at George Mason University in Virginia; the First Amendment Lounge at the National Press Club in Washington, D.C.; and the annual Hugh M. Hefner First Amendment Award orchestrated for the Playboy Foundation by the American Civil Liberties Union. The television tabloid *Inside Edition* recently flashed pictures of women apparently sexually servicing men at a fund-raiser in Los Angeles for the Free Speech Legal Defense Fund to benefit the so-called adult video industry.

The self-righteousness produced by this institutional validation can be seen in *Chicago Tribune* columnist Clarence Page's commentary in November 1991 on the *Robinson v. Jacksonville Shipyard* case, about the use of pornography to harass women tradesworkers. Gazing at a newsroom colleague's poster-size, full-color photograph torn from the pages of the *Chicago Tribune*, featuring actress Heather Locklear in a swimsuit, Page cites the judge's finding in the shipyard case that there is no First Amendment right to harass. How long, he worries, can the press "remain free . . . once a court has determined that people can be damaged" by what he calls "non-libelous, non-obscene products of the press."[16]

As a multibillion-dollar business, pornography is an extremely popular product. Masquerading, however, as "the speech we hate, but must defend lest the Constitution be harmed," pornography plays a special role as a worst-case example calling for a heroic First Amendment defense. Any evidence of harm to women and children must be concealed or denied to safeguard the industry mantra, "If it's published, it's protected." That is why press reports on hearings held by the 1986 Attorney General's Commission on Pornography often put the word "victim" in quotation marks to suggest a dubious concept. (The National Coalition against Censorship continues to use this convention in its publications on pornography.) *Washington Post* reporter Howard Kurtz described commission witnesses as "a parade of self-described victims who tell their sad stories from behind an opaque screen. . . . Many experts on both sides of the question say such anecdotal tales of woe prove nothing about the effect of sexually explicit materials."[17]

To protect pornography, women's speech must be carefully controlled. When Linda Lovelace said she loved starring in pornographic films, she was treated as credible; when Linda Marchiano said that she had been beaten, raped, and coerced into making those films, her credibility was questioned.* No risk is

---

* Linda Lovelace was Linda Marchiano's stage name. —Eds.

overlooked. At a National Press Club speech by Christie Hefner in 1986, I addressed her "as a pornographer" in a written question about her lawsuit to censor testimony from a federal hearing that referred to *Playboy* as pornography; when my question was read aloud by the club's president, these three words were deleted.

Institutional protection of pornography is strikingly evident in reporting on the Andrea Dworkin/Catharine MacKinnon antipornography civil rights ordinance, which would have allowed women to seek damages under specific conditions from those responsible for harm proved attributable to pornography. While every media pundit was free to misrepresent the ordinance as a "ban" in the style of obscenity law, MacKinnon and Dworkin were never allowed an op-ed in any major newspaper to present it accurately or discuss it in their own words.

In 1991, the *New York Times* asked MacKinnon to write an op-ed column on the *Robinson* v. *Jacksonville Shipyard* decision, but insisted that she substitute ellipses for graphic language quoted from the trial record as examples of the sexual harassment endured by women shipyard workers. MacKinnon refused to do so and the op-ed was rejected.[18]*

In March 1993, a conference on speech, equality, and harm brought together distinguished theorists on pornography and hate speech at the University of Chicago Law School. The *New York Times*[19] report on the conference gave the lead and five of the first seven paragraphs to statements disparaging the conference and its participants. The lead exemplified the very tactics it purported to reject: "Treading close to what critics consider the land of the thought police, some legal scholars are joining together to fight against images they believe should never be produced and words they believe should never be spoken." Coming before the reader has any factual idea of the subject matter addressed, this statement is fear-mongering. Twenty paragraphs describe the conference or quote participants while thirteen paragraphs focus on critical views on it, a poor ratio of new ideas to status quo defense.

Identifying who gets speech when pornography is under attack demonstrates that the First Amendment does the best job of protecting those who need it least. When the Supreme Court agreed in 1986 to review routine obscenity and student speech cases but refused to hear arguments on the Indianapolis antipornography ordinance,[20] they showed by their choice that the speech they genuinely hate is that which lets women tell the truth about pornography.

---

* This is a common problem. When pornographers sell violent pornography as entertainment for men, it is protected by the First Amendment. But when feminists such as MacKinnon, Dworkin, or Nikki Craft use that same pornography—or the same pornographic technique—to expose pornographers, they are accused of being lewd and are censored by the media—or, in some instances, even arrested!—Eds.

In the case of the ordinance, the Supreme Court summarily affirmed an appeals court's opinion that women were harmed by pornography but that a civil rights remedy would hurt the First Amendment. Media reports praised the Court for preventing a First Amendment catastrophe. At the same time, the media praised the Court for decisions in other cases that rejected plaintiffs' arguments that their First Amendment rights were being abridged in favor of arguments affirming the importance of protecting commercial property values or upholding the authority of school officials. Justice Potter Stewart told us more than he intended about how power defines reality when he said of obscenity, "I know it when I see it."[21] Concerns about government censorship of publishers' speech seem irrelevant, however, compared to the nongovernmental ways in which women's speech is suppressed or devalued.

Most censorship, in fact, is carried out privately by those with editorial power. It is not called censorship, and it is subject to no public accountability whatever. There is no reason why women must tolerate this exercise of private rights against their right to equal protection of the law. The authoritative voice of the status quo speaks to us through a public television series characterizing the Constitution as "a delicate balance"—a warning to keep our hands off it. This is a warning that must be disregarded. The corollary to "If it ain't broke, don't fix it" is "If it's broke, fix it." If the First Amendment works for half the people to the detriment of the other half, then the First Amendment is broken and we need an Equal Rights Amendment to fix it. John Adams's conviction that masculine systems would be endangered if men could no longer abuse women with impunity holds true centuries later.

For feminists, the challenge remains how to think and communicate freely in a hostile environment that works to control our minds and silence our speech. If women's votes are to be marshaled to gain legal, social, and economic equality, we must find ways to overcome the enemy that has outposts in our heads.

COMMENTS OF AN OUTSIDER ON THE FIRST AMENDMENT

Kimberlé Crenshaw

Kimberlé Crenshaw attacks the logic and political underpinnings of the cross-burning case, *R.A.V.* v. *St. Paul*, pointing out that it demonstrates much of the perverse blindness of nineteenth century civil rights cases, including *Plessy* v. *Ferguson*'s "separate but equal." She shows that conservatives now wield concepts like "formal equality" in a way that disempowers African Americans and other people of color, and that this is especially true in the debate about hate speech.*

■

First Amendment defense of hate speech, and in particular, *R.A.V.* v. *St. Paul*, shares an ideological lineage with *City of Richmond* v. *J.A. Croson Co.* † and other anti-affirmative action cases. Their common ancestor is *Plessy* v. *Ferguson*. ‡ Indeed, the resemblance between *Plessy* and *R.A.V.* is so striking that those of us who have studied *Plessy* closely experienced *R.A.V.* as a reincarnation—*Plessy* raising from the dead. *Plessy* is the constitutional equivalent of the endless series of *Friday the Thirteenth/Halloween* movies—we just can't kill it. While it would certainly be possible to substantiate what some people will experience as a wild claim by making a point-by-point comparison, I want simply to consider in broad fashion the descriptive and normative worldview underlying *R.A.V.*, one that is common in other cases that have legitimized societal inequality. Ideologically, *R.A.V.* pays tribute to a social vision most frequently found in the "marketplace of ideas" metaphor. This

---

* "Formal equality" means equality without regard to history or cultural practices, as opposed to contextual or realist theory, which takes into account history, cultural practices, and other events that may affect how individuals or groups of people are positioned in society.—Eds.

† *Croson* is a key anti-affirmative action case. The City of Richmond required set-asides for minority contractors, who until then had received few city contracts. In 1989, the Supreme Court overturned that plan as constituting discrimination against white contractors.—Eds.

‡ *Plessy* v. *Ferguson* is the famous 1896 case that upheld a "separate but equal" regime in connection with railroad cars. At a later date, the Supreme Court interpreted *Plessy* as permitting boards of education to assign black children to all-black schools. It wasn't until *Brown* v. *Board of Education* in 1954 that the Supreme Court reversed its decision in *Plessy*.—Eds.

metaphor, paralleled in anti-affirmative action cases and in early twentieth century economic cases, invokes a particular descriptive and normative image of social relations that is thought to exist in the absence of state interference. It invokes an image of people who are formally equal with one another, who are interacting on a free plane, a space open to all, where any inequalities are the products of competition. It thus supports the notion that the state should refrain from disrupting this competition by attempting to prescribe outcomes in advance.

Plessy v. *Ferguson* is a historic testament to the ideological power of this metaphor: its ability to render segregation and discrimination consistent with the equality commands of the Fourteenth and Thirteenth Amendments, and more broadly, with a basic commitment to equality. *Plessy* teaches us how a system of segregation, central to the social subordination of blacks, could be constitutionalized through a rigid commitment to formalism, abstraction, dis-aggregation, and ahistoricism. All these features are paralleled in recent cases. In *Plessy*, we are told that segregation constitutes equal treatment because blacks and whites are treated similarly. Blacks cannot sit in white cars, whites cannot sit in black cars. Here formal equality functions as a plausible argument only through a wholesale denial of the social context of racial domination, a reality everyone knew. *Plessy* goes on to deny the significance of the social meaning of segregation by saying that the meaning of segregation is open, depending on the interpretation of the victims, and thus irrelevant.

Plessy is the beginning of what I call the "racial marketplace" idea—that if blacks are to be treated as equal, they will have to prove themselves in the social marketplace. *Plessy* is echoed in R.A.V. in particular, and in the broader discourse on hate speech. Racist speakers and antiracist speakers are rendered formally equal by the same analysis that rendered blacks and whites under segregation formally equal. Context, history, and social power relationships are denied. We are asked to assume that the purveyors of hate speech and the targets of hate speech are on the same plane: the black family is free under the First Amendment to burn a cross on a white family's lawn. Of course, a cross burning on the lawn of a white family is as different and ultimately as mean-ingless now as the practice of excluding whites from black cars was in the nineteenth century world of *Plessy*. The cross burning, just like segregation, takes on its meaning *precisely as a consequence of the asymmetrical position of the races*. Formal equality denies both of these realities, producing a result that essentially licenses one party to subordinate the other along racial lines.

Overtones of *Plessy* are apparent, as well, in the denial of the injury, both personal and societal, of racist speech. *Plessy*'s flip comment that "the meaning is only what blacks choose to place on it" is akin to comments that understand racial speech as a mere injury to feelings, one that thick skin can protect against. Indeed, the entire debate about racist speech denies the systemic injury that speech produces in much the same way that *Plessy* denied the injury of segregation, first, by disconnecting it in any way from the policy in question and, second, by making that injury irrelevant.

Finally, *Plessy*'s marketplace invocation—the answer to segregation is not forced integration, but blacks proving themselves—parallels the notion that the answer to racist speech is more speech in the marketplace of ideas. The *Plessy* rationale wholly denies the impact of the segregation, the reality of social disempowerment, and the fact that the very decision to segregate is both a product of and a contribution to the subordination of blacks. The entirety of the first Reconstruction was nullified by the force of this ideological vision; it helped render civil rights protections virtually meaningless, even in the presence of lynching and other terroristic practices meant wholly to suppress African Americans. One can only think of the Holfax massacre, when nearly one hundred blacks were killed by whites who forced them out of the courthouse where many of them were serving as elected public officials. Formal equality rendered the blacks who were lynched equal to the whites who were doing the lynching, as far as voting rights were concerned.

These notions of formal equality have not always reigned supreme. *Brown v. Board of Education* and a whole line of cases upholding the civil rights legislation of the sixties serve as counterweights, although of limited effectiveness. Significantly, all these cases were made possible by reconceiving social relations so that the reality of social power made invisible by formal equality was materialized and made relevant, to counter *Plessy*'s defense of segregation as symmetrical. In *Brown*, the Court cited Kenneth Clark's famous doll study, acknowledging that the effect of segregation was anything but symmetrical.* The doll study in *Brown* provided the counter to *Plessy*'s claim that the social meaning of segregation was simply a construction, irrelevant to the constitutional question, and that the injury was relevant. Indeed, part of the critical reaction to the use of the doll study as a grounding for *Brown* may have been recognition that contextualizing and historicizing constitutional jurisprudence might threaten the reign of an abstracted view of formal equality.

Similarly, the Court's decision upholding Title II against those charging that it was an unwarranted limitation of the freedom of innkeepers and restaurateurs was grounded, in part, on congressional hearings that effectively recharacterized

---

* In the study, Kenneth Clark, a Harvard psychologist and past president of the American Psychological Association, asked children of various races and ages which dolls seemed to them "nice" and which they wanted as a friend. The study showed that black children as young as age three associated their own skin color with ugliness, dirtiness, and meanness.—Eds.

discrimination as a massive social system of racial segregation.* Testimony about the pervasiveness of segregation and its social, cultural, and psychological costs provided support for the rejection of the view that the innkeeper stood on the same plane as the excluded African American. In this sense, race cases momentarily converged with the legal realist critique of freedom of contract.

These cases show not only the possibility and power of a competing, historicized vision, but the importance of understanding and recognizing the injury produced by a challenged activity. That injury is seldom invoked in constitutional discourse. The rare instance when it was has been lost to history. Consider *Beauharnais* v. *Illinois*, where the Court upheld a group libel statute aimed at racist speech. The statute in *Beauharnais* was adopted in the midst of increasing racial terror in the wake of two race riots where more than one hundred men, women, and children were killed. More than six thousand blacks left the area, finding it uninhabitable given the massive propaganda campaign that had whipped up an antiblack frenzy. The Court recognized the societal harm constituted by racist speech, particularly that dissenting speech in the face of disempowerment is not only inadequate, but frequently impossible. The absence of this understanding in discourse about racial violence—or, I should say, its wholesale rejection—is a central feature of the formalist view.

Plessy, R.A.V., and *Croson* depend, then, on a formalizing rhetoric that wholly abstracts race from the social context of power. This ideology has been increasingly challenged by legal realists. Racial power makes competition in the social marketplace useless. There is no space not already occupied by the dominant white culture. The notion that blacks can ultimately "prove themselves" within a society wholly constituted by racial power is as illusory as the notion that blacks are free to contest hate speech. That speech, like segregation, is an act of social power, one that the state, in *R.A.V.,* privileges individuals to make. The call for more speech is as hollow as *Plessy's* call for blacks to prove themselves.

Strains of this vision appear in other cases. Beginning with *Lochner* v. *New York* in 1937, a series of Supreme Court cases constructed labor legislation as the disruption of natural forces and discrimination against the employer. The Court based its decisions on what it called the "Freedom of Contract" doctrine, according to which any labor legislation that prohibited employers from imposing fourteen-hour work days or prohibited workers from unionizing violated the contract rights of both the employer and employee. Both were free to make a contract or to look elsewhere. The power differential—that employees frequently had no choice but to agree to the employer's terms—was irrelevant to

---

* Title II of the civil rights law provides for equal treatment in public accommodations: hotels, restaurants, and the like.—Eds.

the Court's definition of freedom. Legal realists asserted at the time that the power differential was significant, that it was not natural or prepolitical, and that states could regulate and redistribute employers' power in the public interest. Nevertheless, this era, often called the Lochner era, lasted for over twenty years. Finally, in another series of cases, the Court overturned *Lochner*. Labor legislation then limited the work day to eight hours, required overtime for additional work, outlawed child labor, and made many other adjustments to even out the power differential between employer and employee. Lochner-esque views of social relations are now rejected and frequently derided, but the case's narrow view of social power retains vitality in debates about affirmative action and free speech. One might wonder what accounts for this contradiction.

Any answer to this question can only be speculative, but I would like to suggest the following parallel. Although the purveyors of hate speech are often represented as ignorant, working-class extremists, hate speech may well occupy the same place in the consciousness of elites that affirmative action occupies in the consciousness of the masses. Each marks the spot where the values of antidomination meet the preestablished and apparently prepolitical prerogatives of those who are relatively empowered. Ironically, although the social vision that legitimizes hate speech, racial stratification, and even segregation, depends in large part upon a worldview dichotomized into public and private, that dichotomy is conveniently jettisoned by those seeking to defend their interests against antidomination politics, feminism, and antiracism.

Thus, as I shall show, while the ideological vision of free contract/free speech relies on an implicit rejection of the social power framework that I set forth here, it is apparent that those leading the anti-p.c.* movement understand the social power framework that they have formally rejected in other settings, and indeed rely on it to further their agenda. The First Amendment now functions as a retreat for those who fear the loss of certain prerogatives. Issues that in other settings they would defend as purely private, wholly unsuitable for regulation, they selectively choose to rearticulate as public. Contrary to the usual conservative position, when it comes to free speech the public sphere has been dramatically expanded.

In the 1960s, in response to antiracist, feminist, and antiestablishment critiques, conservatives, basing their arguments on academic freedom, argued that their freedom was being restrained by what they characterized as repressive, undemocratic, and uncivil critique. In that context, the answer to speech was not more speech, but disciplinary codes including the threat of expulsion for students, and firing for academics. But today, conservatives have sought the

---

* p.c. means "political correctness."—Eds.

sympathetic ear of the nation, characterizing themselves as the embattled troops defending the academy against irresponsible and unreasonable multiculturalists and feminists. One hears the tragic tales of accomplished academics who have forsworn the classroom, disheartened and silenced by the criticism of students and by the p.c. fervor of colleagues. Coming to their defense, anti-p.c. conservatives seek not more speech, but the suppression of these nefarious movements through defunding of departments and institutions, and, where necessary, by denying tenure. *Yet these same defenders reject as repressive campus codes that seek to create the space for civil discourse by prohibiting hate speech and sexual harassment.* Here, conservatives flip dramatically from defending the senior scholar, silenced by the dominance of p.c., to defending the rights of purveyors of racist and sexist dogma. Open discourse, it seems, can accommodate the incivility of the racist speaker, but will collapse under the weight of purveyors of political correctness.

Finally, conservatives flip on the issue of decentralization. Traditional defenders of localized, consensus-based decisionmaking, conservatives have bristled against federal intervention that would seek to impose certain norms. Relying on the First and Fourteenth amendments, they have vehemently defended the freedom of groups to organize themselves around common values. Yet when many private universities have undertaken the task of defining those values and have concluded that hate speech does not fall among them, conservatives turn to the state and federal government to limit and circumscribe the freedom of such institutions to do so. For example, Congress, at the behest of conservatives and civil libertarians, is now considering a proposal to deny federal funding to private institutions that have adopted hate speech codes. In California, the legislature has voted to extend the prohibitions of the First Amendment to private universities and secondary schools.* Supporters appear unfazed by the argument that is usually offered to defend private ordering— that at least one theory underlying the First Amendment is that state power is suspect, and that it should be restrained, where necessary, to protect and foster the private development of norms and social ordering.

The reaction of many recalls the innkeepers' claims that Title II violated their freedom to contract with whomever they pleased and that the new law constituted involuntary servitude under the Thirteenth Amendment. These claims are understood now as a product of fear and the desire to protect a certain way of life. Rejection of these views meant that whites could no longer exercise the right to marginalize and discriminate against blacks. People would

---

* E.g., Stanford cannot have a speech code. Any speech code that a private university adopts has to satisfy First Amendment requirements. Thus, there is no distinction between private and public institutions with regard to speech codes. —Eds.

have to act—therefore think—in different ways. The retreat to the Thirteenth Amendment then, like the retreat to the First now, can be understood as an attempt to protect those prerogatives through selective invocation of freedom.

I do not mean to suggest that fear motivates all of the discussion on the First Amendment. Much is merely the product of a commitment to values that are insufficiently attuned to social reality. What I mean to suggest, though, is that there are historical analogues to the debate we are having now and that, historically, many people felt strongly that personal freedoms were being threatened in a way that would lead to disastrous consequences. That those ideas seem foolish now is simply the consequence of one social vision having triumphed, however tentatively, over another.

We are similarly poised at this moment. We face anxious and worried claims that failing to protect hate speech will impair precious liberty. Whether these claims will eventually be seen, like those of the innkeepers, as historically specific or of enduring vitality depends on how this particular moment is resolved. While recognition of the historical contingency of this debate makes it all the more important, our having been here before is as much a reason for encouragement as it is a cause for worry.

THE TRIANGULAR POLITICS OF PORNOGRAPHY

John Stoltenberg

It was Susan Brownmiller who first noted that there are not two, but three sides to the pornography debate: the conservative perspective, which argues that pornography is bad, immoral, indecent; the liberal perspective, which argues that pornography is basically liberating—part of a sexual revolution that increases pleasure for all—and a radical feminist perspective, which identifies pornography as part of a larger, complex pattern of pro-rape, woman-hating images and depictions. And it was Andrea Dworkin who first observed that pornography is a practice that creates and perpetuates a climate of female subordination and threatens the safety and status of women in our society. Articulating what he calls "the triangular politics of pornography," John Stoltenberg notes that the policies of the left and right are both patriarchal and contends that the radical feminist perspective is the only one grounded in human rights.

■

A radical feminist critique of pornography has emerged that has, together with a radical human rights legal strategy, sharply challenged both the conservative right and the liberal left.

Since 1983 this legal strategy—conceived by Andrea Dworkin and Catharine A. MacKinnon—has been approved by the liberal city council of Minneapolis twice, by the conservative city council of Indianapolis once, and by community referendum in the progressive city of Bellingham, Washington, with 62 percent of the popular vote.[1] Dworkin's testimony before the Attorney General's Commission on Pornography in 1986[2] was acknowledged by several commissioners whose final report unanimously endorsed "legislation affording protection to those individuals whose civil rights have been violated by the production or distribution of pornography."[3] The innovative legal ideas in the civil rights approach to pornography have been considered in the governments of Sweden, the Philippines, New Zealand, Great Britain, Ireland, Germany, Australia, and other countries; portions have been incorporated into U.S. legislation;[4] and in 1991 a revised version of the complete Dworkin/MacKinnon anti-pornography civil rights ordinance was introduced into the Massachusetts State Legislature.[5]

The radical feminist human rights legal strategy is so distinct from the patriarchal policies of both right and left that neither side fully understands it. Here is why: conservatives wish to protect *private* sexual ownership of women's bodies, so they see pornography as "indecency" and attempt to prosecute it as "obscenity." The left extols *collectivized* sexual ownership—of virtually anything that moves—so they see in pornography the epitome of "sexual freedom." Radical feminists, meanwhile, believe that justice means nothing if not accountability to victims. Therefore radical feminists seek to empower the exploited: the people whose human rights have been violated.

Blinded by First Amendment fundamentalism—as dangerous and contemptuous as any fundamentalism can be—liberals defend a deregulated marketplace of sexual ownership in which manufacturers and brokers, pornographers and pimps, have state protection. Conservatives, loath to use civil rights law against *any* injustice, simply muddle along saying, "Blot out smut." Radical human rights feminists, meanwhile, seek to take the profit motive out of selling sex discrimination.

So long as the debate continues to ping-pong between liberals and conservatives, the pornography industry will be quite safe, and four human rights issues will remain ignored: the harm issue, the economic issue, the legal issue, and the conscience issue.

The Harm Issue

Pornography injures the women and children (and some men) who are used to manufacture it, who are sexually abused as a result of its consumption, and who are hurt by the civil inequality it engenders.

Liberals who say there is no proof of pornography's harms have simply decided to discount the credibility of real-life victims. In 1983, for the first time in history, people harmed by pornography testified directly before a governmental body, given a glimmer of hope by the antipornography civil rights ordinance that Dworkin and MacKinnon drafted for the Minneapolis City Council. These hearings, a landmark in human freedom, were published five years later in Great Britain[6] but have yet to be published in the United States. Meanwhile, the liberal media have helped pornographers spread the lie that pornography is harmless. For example, I once heard a woman member of the

Attorney General's Commission say at a press luncheon for magazine editors, "What's the harm of pornography—a paper cut?"—as if the male consumers of pornography, flipping pages, were the only ones affected; as if women and children who speak out about the harm are irrelevant. The line got a big laugh. The media generally obscure the reality of pornography's harms—most notoriously when victim testimony included in the 1986 final report of the Attorney General's Commission was completely ignored (thanks in part to a million-dollar disinformation campaign launched by the Media Coalition through Gray and Company,[7] a public relations firm that is now known as Hill & Knowlton). When victims of pornography testified in March 1992 before the Judiciary Committee of the Massachusetts State Legislature, and when victim-service providers (battered women's shelter representatives, rape crisis advocates, child trauma center directors) also testified that pornography is implicated in every form of violence against women, liberals, joined by the American Civil Liberties Union—defenders of the Klan, the Nazis, and other opponents of human freedom—once again rallied to defend the speech rights of exploiters and keep the exploited voiceless.

The Economic Issue

It would be difficult to think of another instance of the systematic violation of human rights today in which economic forces so entirely favor the power of the oppressors. Primarily through two influential trade organizations—the Center for Libel Defense Information and the Media Coalition (which financed its 1986 public relations smear of victim testimony largely with money from *Playboy*[8])—the pornography industry has formed a tacit protection pact with mainstream media, whose self-interest is blatant: they want to be shielded from liability for human harm done through *their* speech.[9]

Pornographers, with backing like that, have little to fear from any individual whose life was taken from her in the sex trade and used to manufacture a profitable product. Such victims are often so socially and economically marginalized (many work in prostitution) that hardly anyone believes them when they do speak out. They cannot strike or boycott. No lawyer will take their cases because under current interpretation of the Constitution, the harm done to them is protected. The law sees only disembodied "speech"; the lives damaged to produce pornography and those damaged by its sale and consumption are legally invisible. To add insult to injury, there is now a group of self-styled feminists defending the pornography industry's abuses of women's human rights in the corrupted name of "free speech." Both pornographers and the ACLU showcase them—they are patriarchy's new "chicks up front."[10] Once, male pornographers at least had to show their faces to defend themselves. Today they can hide behind a phalanx of opinionmakers and legal defenders, most of whom share an economic interest in suppressing the speech of pornography's victims.

The Legal Issue

Shall the real-life harms of pornography be exempt from the principle of "justice for all"? The question presents a constitutional crisis—a conflict between the First Amendment, which protects speech from government interference, and the principles underlying the Fourteenth Amendment, which guarantees the right to equality under the law.

In 1985, Judge Frank H. Easterbrook of the Seventh Circuit Court of Appeals ruled in *American Booksellers* v. *Hudnut* that speech takes precedence. Acknowledging that pornography does indeed "perpetuate subordination" of women and that "[t]he subordinate status of women in turn leads to affront and lower pay at work, insult and injury at home, battery and rape on the streets," Easterbrook dismissed these ills by arguing "this simply demonstrates the power of pornography as speech" and therefore, because this harm to women is done through speech, the Constitution protects it.

Pornographers—together with their allies both left and right—are trying to make sure that this pro-perpetrator viewpoint remains the law of the land. But a few beleaguered radical feminist antipornography activists are trying to create some justice for victims as well.

The Conscience Issue

Men of conscience must decide to act against human rights violations by pornographers. The decision is similar to the one white people from slave-holding families faced when they decided to work for abolition. It is similar to the one Germans of non-Jewish descent faced when they decided to resist fascism. The prevailing viewpoint in both cases—backed up legally and economically by the dominant power bloc—was that the oppression was not wrong because it was based on nature. Blacks by nature were unworthy of being more than slaves. Jews and other "non-Aryans" by nature were malevolent and had to be eradicated. The propaganda to reinforce these social policies was fierce, as was the ostracism and risk faced by anyone who stood up in dissent. Today, women's nature is being defined by the pornography industry as that which elicits and deserves men's sexual violence and domination. Men's sexual nature is being defined as well, as that which, by rights, eroticizes ownership.

From the testimony of women who are or have been sexually owned in marriage, raped, and/or sexually used for a fee in prostitution, it would appear that possession is a principal part of men's acculturated sexual behavior. In English—as in many other languages—the verb *to possess* means both "to own" and "to fuck," a semantic coincidence that is no accident. To have sex with someone and simultaneously to be "a real man" is to *have* that person, to *take* that person, to *possess* that person. To have sex and to have *a* sex requires a property relation of some sort: this explains all forms of commodified sex, including systems of prostitution and trafficking in pornography, for buying and selling ensures sexual ownership. The eroticization of owning is embedded in the law because that is what patriarchal law is *for*: to codify who gets to possess whom. The conflict between right and left, over whether sexual ownership should be private or collective, serves patriarchy's agenda no matter which side prevails. One way to stop this eroticization of ownership—a revolutionary human rights strategy—is to confront the state's one-sided collusion with sexual owners and to challenge the legal system to protect and redress the sexually owned. Dworkin and MacKinnon have shown us how to do that.

Today, throughout the world, a growing pornography industry produces propaganda for a variety of social policies in which rape, battery, incest, serial killing, femicide, and other forms of men's sexual violence will get only Band-Aid attention at best, because no one believes the eroticization of ownership can or will ever end—and because a powerful political bloc does not intend for it to end.

The right understands that there is something wrong with pornography, but the right is completely male-supremacist about what is wrong ("indecency")—and completely ineffectual about what to do about it (prosecute "obscenity," today an utterly empty concept). Meanwhile, the left doesn't understand that there's anything wrong at all—and, even if there might be, the left believes nothing can or should be done about it.

Human rights—women's rights—are being denied so that pornographers can sell "sex." And pornographers' liberal defenders stand dead in the way of human freedom, because they really don't give a damn.

PORNOGRAPHY HAPPENS TO WOMEN

Andrea Dworkin

African-American author Rosemary Bray and novelist Madison Smartt Bell
have called Andrea Dworkin the Malcolm X of the women's movement.
Certainly no one more powerfully presents the case against women's sexual
oppression through pornography. This article is a revised version of her
speech at the University of Chicago Law School, where she spoke to an
audience of about one thousand legal scholars, students, and community
leaders about the dehumanizing effects of pornography—the way in which
humiliation, cruelty, and insults are sexualized and sold for a profit by an
estimated $20-billion-a-year industry.

■

For twenty years, people that you know and people that you do not know inside
the women's movement, with its great grass-roots breadth and strength, have
been trying to communicate something very simple: pornography happens. It
happens. Lawyers, call it what you want—call it speech, call it act, call it
conduct. Catharine A. MacKinnon and I called it a practice when we described
it in the antipornography civil-rights ordinance that we drafted for the City of
Minneapolis in 1983; but the point is that it happens. It happens to women,
in real life. Women's lives are made two-dimensional and dead. We are flat-
tened on the page or on the screen. Our vaginal lips are painted purple for
the consumer to clue him in as to where to focus his attention such as it is.
Our rectums are highlighted so that he knows where to push. Our mouths are
used and our throats are used for deep penetration.

I am describing a process of dehumanization, a concrete means of changing
someone into something. We are not talking about violence yet; we are nowhere
near violence.

Dehumanization is real. It happens in real life; it happens to stigmatized
people. It has happened to us, to women. We say that women are objectified.

We hope that people will think that we are very smart when we use a long word. But being turned into an object is a real event; and the pornographic object is a particular kind of object. It is a target. You are turned into a target. And red or purple marks the spot where he's supposed to get you.

This object wants it. She is the only object with a will that says, hurt me. A car does not say, bang me up. But she, this nonhuman thing, says hurt me—and the more you hurt me, the more I will like it.

When we look at her, that purple painted thing, when we look at her vagina, when we look at her rectum, when we look at her mouth, when we look at her throat, those of us who know her and those of us who have been her still can barely remember that she is a human being.

In pornography we literally see the will of women as men want to experience it. This will is expressed through concrete scenarios, the ways in which women's bodies are positioned and used. We see, for instance, that the object wants to be penetrated; and so there is a motif in pornography of self-penetration. A woman takes some thing and she sticks it up herself. There is pornography in which pregnant women for some reason take hoses and stick the hoses up themselves. This is not a human being. One cannot look at such a photograph and say, There is a human being, she has rights, she has freedom, she has dignity, she is someone. One cannot. That is what pornography *does* to women.

We talk about fetishism in sex. * Psychologists have always made that mean, for example, a man who ejaculates to or on a shoe. The shoe can be posed as it were on a table far from the man. He is sexually excited; he masturbates, maybe rubs up against the shoe; he has sex "with" the shoe. In pornography, that is what happens to a woman's body: she is turned into a sexual fetish and the lover, the consumer, ejaculates on her. In the pornography itself, he does ejaculate *on* her. It is a convention of pornography that the sperm is on her,

---

* "The word *fetish* comes from the Portuguese *feitiço*, which means 'charm' or 'made thing.' A fetish is a magical, symbolic object. Its first meaning is religious: the magical object is regarded with irrational, extreme, extravagant trust or reverence (to paraphrase Merriam-Webster). In its sexual meaning, the magic of the fetish is in its power to cause and sustain penile erection. . . .

"No sense of her own purpose can supersede, finally, the male's sense of her purpose: to be that thing that enables him to experience raw phallic power. In pornography, his sense of purpose is fully realized. She is the pinup, the centerfold, the poster, the postcard, the dirty picture, naked, half-dressed, laid out, legs spread, breasts or ass protruding. She is the thing she is supposed to be: the thing that makes him erect. In literary and cinematic pornography, she is taught to be that thing: raped, beaten, bound, used, until she recognizes her true nature and purpose and complies—happily, greedily, begging for more. She is used until she knows only that she is a thing to be used. This knowledge is her authentic erotic sensibility: her erotic destiny. . . ."
Dworkin, *Pornography: Men Possessing Women* (New York: E. P. Dutton, 1989), pp. 123, 128.

See Andrea Dworkin, "Objects," in *Pornography: Men Possessing Women* (New York: E.P. Dutton, 1989), pp. 101–28.

not in her. It marks the spot, what he owns and how he owns it. The ejaculation on her is a way of saying (through showing) that she is contaminated with his dirt; that she is dirty. This is the pornographer's discourse, not mine; the Marquis de Sade always refers to ejaculate as pollution.

Pornographers use every attribute any woman has. They sexualize it. They find a way to dehumanize it. This is done in concrete ways so that, for instance, in pornography the skin of black women is taken to be a sexual organ, female of course, despised, needing punishment. The skin itself is the fetish, the charmed object; the skin is the place where the violation is acted out—through verbal insult (dirty words directed at the skin) and sexualized assault (hitting, whipping, cutting, spitting on, bondage including rope burns, biting, masturbating on, ejaculating on).

In pornography, this fetishizing of the female body, its sexualization and dehumanization, is always concrete and specific; it is never abstract and conceptual. That is why all these debates on the subject of pornography have such a bizarre quality to them. Those of us who know that pornography hurts women, and care, talk about women's real lives, insults and assaults that really happen to real women in real life—the women in the pornography and the women on whom the pornography is used. Those who argue for pornography, especially on the ground of freedom of speech, insist that pornography is a species of idea, thought, fantasy, situated inside the physical brain, the mind, of the consumer no less.

In fact we are told all the time that pornography is really about ideas. Well, a rectum doesn't have an idea, and a vagina doesn't have an idea, and the mouths of women in pornography do not express ideas; and when a woman has a penis thrust down to the bottom of her throat, as in the film *Deep Throat*, that throat is not part of a human being who is involved in discussing ideas. I am talking now about pornography without visible violence. I am talking about the cruelty of dehumanizing someone who has a right to more.

In pornography, everything means something. I have talked to you about the skin of black women. The skin of white women has a meaning in pornography. In a white-supremacist society, the skin of white women is supposed to indicate privilege. Being white is as good as it gets. What, then, does it mean that pornography is filled with white women? It means that when one takes a woman who is at the zenith of the hierarchy in racial terms and one asks her, What do you want?, she, who supposedly has some freedom and some choices, says, I want to be used. She says, use me, hurt me, exploit me, that is what I want. The society tells us that she is a standard, a standard of beauty, a standard of womanhood and femininity. But, in fact, she is a standard of compliance. She is a standard of submission. She is a standard *for* oppression, its emblem; she models oppression, she incarnates it; which is to say that she does what she needs to do in order to stay alive, the configuration of her conformity predetermined by the men who like to ejaculate on her white skin. She is for sale. And so what is her white skin worth? It makes her price a little higher.

When we talk about pornography that objectifies women, we are talking about the sexualization of insult, of humiliation; I insist that we are also talking about the sexualization of cruelty. And this is what I want to say to you—that there is cruelty that does not have in it overt violence.

There is cruelty that says to you, you are worth nothing in human terms. There is cruelty that says you exist in order for him to wipe his penis on you, that's who you are, that's what you are for. I say that dehumanizing someone is cruel; and that it does not have to be violent in order for it to be cruel.

Things are done to women day in and day out that would be construed to be violent if they were done in another context, not sexualized, to a man; women are pushed, shoved, felt up, called dirty names, have their passage physically blocked on the street or in the office; women simply move on, move through, unless the man escalates the violence to what the larger patriarchal world takes to be real violence: ax murder; sadistic stranger rape or gang rape; serial killing not of prostitutes. The touching, the pushing, the physical blockades—these same invasions done to men would be comprehended as attacks. Done to women, people seem to think it's bad but it's okay, it's bad but it's all right, it's bad but, hey, that's the way things are; *don't make a federal case out of it*. It occurs to me that we have to deal here—the heart of the double standard—with the impact of orgasm on our perception of what hatred is and is not.

Men use sex to hurt us. An argument can be made that men have to hurt us, diminish us, in order to be able to have sex with us—break down barriers to our bodies, aggress, be invasive, push a little, shove a little, express verbal or physical hostility or condescension. An argument can be made that in order for men to have sexual pleasure with women, we have to be inferior and dehumanized, which means controlled, which means less autonomous, less free, less real.

I am struck by how hate speech, racist hate speech, becomes more sexually explicit as it becomes more virulent—how its meaning becomes more sexualized, as if the sex is required to carry the hostility. In the history of anti-Semitism, by the time one gets to Hitler's ascendance to power in the Weimar Republic, one is looking at anti-Semitic hate speech that is indistinguishable from pornography*—and it is not only actively published and distributed, it is openly displayed. What does that orgasm do? That orgasm says, I am real and the lower creature, that thing, is not, and if the annihilation of that thing brings me pleasure, that is the way life should be; the racist hierarchy becomes a sexually charged ideal. There is a sense of biological inevitability that comes from the intensity of a sexual response derived from contempt; there is biological urgency, excitement, anger, irritation, a tension that is satisfied in humiliating and belittling the inferior one, in words, in acts. †

We wonder, with a tendentious ignorance, how it is that people believe bizarre and transparently false philosophies of biological superiority. One answer is that when racist ideologies are sexualized, turned into concrete scenarios of dominance and submission such that they give people sexual pleasure, the sexual feelings in themselves make the ideologies seem biologically true and inevitable. The feelings seem to be natural; no argument changes the feelings; and the ideologies, then, also seem to be based in nature. People defend the sexual feelings by defending the ideologies. They say: my feelings are natural so if I have an orgasm from hurting you, or feel excited just by thinking about it, you are my natural partner in these feelings and events—your natural role is whatever intensifies my sexual arousal, which I experience as self-importance, or potency; you are nothing but you are *my* nothing, which makes me someone; using you is my right because being someone means that I have the power— the social power, the economic power, the imperial sovereignty—to do to you or with you what I want.

---

* *Der Stürmer* is the outstanding example of anti-Semitic propaganda that reached the threshold of pornography while advocating race hate. Founded in 1923 by Julius Streicher, a rabid anti-Semite who joined forces with Hitler in 1921 after an independent run as a Jew-hating rabble-rouser, *Der Stürmer* had Hitler's strong support, from the years of struggle (as the Nazis called them) through Hitler's reign, the years of persecution and annihilation. As late as 1942, Joseph Goebbels, minister of propaganda, wrote in his diary: "The Führer sent word to me that he does not desire the circulation of the *Stürmer* to be reduced or that it stop publishing all together. . . . I, too, believe that our propaganda on the Jewish question must continue undiminished" (cited in Telford Taylor, *The Anatomy of the Nuremberg Trials* [New York: Alfred A. Knopf, 1992], p. 377).
† Tried at Nuremberg, Streicher was convicted of crimes against humanity and hanged on October 16, 1946. On his way to the hanging scaffolding he shouted "Heil Hitler!" and on it he shouted the bizarre—but in the circumstances clearly anti-Semitic—words, "Purim festival, 1946."
    In his fascinating recent account of the Nuremberg trials, Telford Taylor, who was one of the prosecutors for the United States, suggests that Streicher was wrongly sentenced to death because "there was no accusation that Streicher himself had participated in any violence against Jews, so the sole (and difficult) legal issue was whether or not 'incitement' was a sufficient basis for his conviction." (Taylor, p. 376.) This is a distinctly U.S.-based revisionism in keeping with the increasing fanaticism of First Amendment free-speech absolutism. In Nuremberg, a relationship between sexualized hate propaganda and genocide was demonstrated. Many western democracies responded by criminalizing the kind of hate speech, or incitement to genocide, in which Streicher engaged, indeed, at which he excelled. The United States has apparently, as a matter of law and public policy, decided to masturbate to it.

This phenomenon of feeling superior through a sexually reified racism is always sadistic; its purpose is always to hurt. Sadism is a dynamic in every expression of hate speech. In the use of a racial epithet directed at a person, for instance, there is a desire to hurt—to intimidate, to humiliate; there is an underlying dimension of pushing someone down, subordinating them, making them less. When that hate speech becomes fully sexualized—for instance, in the systematic reality of the pornography industry—and a whole class of people exists in order to provide sexual pleasure and a synonymous sense of superiority to another group, in this case men, when that happens, we dare not tolerate that being called freedom.

The problem for women is that being hurt is ordinary. It happens every day, all the time, somewhere to someone, in every neighborhood, on every street, in intimacy, in crowds; women are being hurt. We count ourselves lucky when we are only being humiliated and insulted. We count ourselves goddamn lucky when whatever happens falls short of rape. Those who have been beaten in marriage (a euphemism for torture) also have a sense of what luck is. We are always happy when something less bad happens than what we had thought possible or even likely, and we tell ourselves that if we do not settle for the less bad there is something wrong with us. It is time for us to stop that.

When one thinks about women's ordinary lives and the lives of children, especially female children, it is very hard not to think that one is looking at atrocity—if one's eyes are open. We have to accept that we are looking at ordinary life; the hurt is not exceptional; rather, it is systematic and it is real. Our culture accepts it, defends it, punishes us for resisting it. The hurt, the pushing down, the sexualized cruelty, are intended; they are not accidents or mistakes.

Pornography plays a big part in normalizing the ways in which we are demeaned and attacked, in how humiliating and insulting us is made to look natural and inevitable.

I would like you especially to think about these things. Number one: pornographers use our bodies as their language. Anything they say, they have to use us to say. They do not have that right. They must not have that right. Number two: constitutionally protecting pornography as if it were speech means that there is a new way in which we are legally chattel. If the Constitution protects pornography as speech, our bodies then belong to the pimps who need to use us to say something. They, the humans, have a human right of speech and the dignity of constitutional protection; we, chattel now, moveable property, are their ciphers, their semantic symbols, the pieces they arrange in order to communicate. We are recognized only as the discourse of a pimp. The Constitution is on the side it has always been on: the side of the profit-making property owner even when his property is a person defined as property because of the collusion between law and money, law and power. The Constitution is not ours unless it works for us, especially in providing refuge from exploiters and momentum toward human dignity. Number three: pornography uses those who in the United States were left out of the Constitution. Pornography uses white women, who were chattel. Pornography uses African-American women, who were slaves. Pornography uses stigmatized men; for instance, African-American men, who were slaves, are often sexualized by contemporary pornographers as animalistic rapists. Pornography is not made up of old white men. It isn't. Nobody comes on them. They are doing this to us; or protecting those who do this to us. They do benefit from it; and we do have to stop them.

Think about how marriage controlled women, how women were property under the law; this did not begin to change until the early years of the twentieth century. Think about the control the Church had over women. Think about what a resistance has been going on, and all the trouble you have made for these men who took for granted that you belonged to them. And think about pornography as a new institution of social control, a democratic use of terrorism against all women, a way of saying publicly to every woman who walks down the street: avert your eyes (a sign of second-class citizenship), look down, bitch, because when you look up you're going to see a picture of yourself being hung, you're going to see your legs spread open. That is what you are going to see.

Pornography tells us that the will of women is to be used. And I just want to say that the antipornography civil-rights ordinance that Catharine Mac-Kinnon and I developed in Minneapolis says that the will of women is *not* to be used; the Ordinance repudiates the premises of the pornography; its eventual use will show in the affirmative that women want equality.

Please note that the Ordinance was developed in Minneapolis, and that its twin city, St. Paul, passed a strong city ordinance against hate crimes; the courts struck down both. I want you to understand that there are some serious pornographers in Minneapolis and some serious racists in St. Paul and some serious citizens in both cities who want the pornography and the racism to stop. The Ordinance that Catharine and I drafted came out of that political culture, a grass-roots, participatory political culture that did not want to tolerate either kind of cruelty toward people.

In the fall of 1983, Catharine and I were asked by a group of neighborhood activists to testify at a local zoning committee meeting. The group represented an area of Minneapolis that was primarily African-American, with a small poor-white population. The City Council kept zoning pornography *into* their neighborhood. For seven years they had been fighting a host of zoning laws and zoning strategies that allowed pornography to destroy the quality of life around them. The city could write off their neighborhood and others like it because they mostly were not white and they mostly were poor; the pornography was purposefully put in such places and kept out of wealthier, whiter neighborhoods.

These activists came to us and said: we know now that the issue here is woman-hating. That is virtually a direct quote: we know now that the issue here is woman-hating. And we want to do something about it. What can we do?

They knew what to do. They organized MacKinnon and me, that's for sure; and they organized the City of Minneapolis. The whole city was organized on a grass-roots level to stand against the woman-hating in pornography. That was our mandate when we drafted the antipornography civil-rights law; and constituencies of poor people, people of color, were organized in behalf of the lives of women in those communities. A city in the United States was organized by an ever expanding feminist wave of political workers that brought in working-class women, current and former prostitutes, academics, out and visible lesbians, students, and, inter alia, a small army of sexual-abuse victims, to demand passage of an amendment to the municipal civil-rights law that recognized pornography as sex discrimination, as a violation of the civil rights of women. This amendment, which MacKinnon and I later redrafted to be a free-standing statute, is commonly called "the Ordinance."

The Ordinance got the massive, committed, excited support it did because it is fair, because it is honest, and because it is on the side of those who have been disenfranchised and oppressed. People mobilized—not from the top down but from the bottom up—to support the Ordinance because it does stand directly in the way of the woman-hating in pornography: the bigotry, the hostility, the aggression, that exploits and targets women. It does this by changing our perceptions of the will of women. It destroys the authority of the pornographers on that subject by putting a law, dignity, real power, meaningful citizenship, in the hands of the women they hurt. No matter how she is despised in the pornography or by the pornographers and their clients, she is respected by this law. Using the Ordinance, women get to say to the pimps and the johns: we are not your colony; you do not own us as if we are territory; my will as expressed through my use of this ordinance is, I don't want it, I don't like it, pain hurts, coercion isn't sexy, I resist being someone else's speech, I reject subordination, I speak, I speak for myself now, I am going into court to speak—to you; and you will listen.

We wanted a law that repudiates what happens to women when pornography happens to women. In general, the legal system's misogyny mimics the pornographers'; abstractly we can call it gender bias, but the legal system incorporates an almost visceral hatred of women's bodies, as if we exist to provoke assaults, like them, lie about them—and are not really injured by them. I have a character in *Mercy*—named Andrea—who says that you have to be clean to go before the law. * Now, no women are clean, or clean enough. That is what we find out every time we try to prosecute a rape; we're not clean.

But certainly the women who have been turned into pornography are not clean, and the women being sold on street corners are not clean, and the women who are being battered and pornographized in their homes are not clean. When a woman uses this Ordinance—if a woman ever gets a chance to use this Ordinance—she will not need to be clean to say, with dignity and authority, I am someone, therefore I resist.

When the Minneapolis City Council passed this Ordinance they said, women are someone, women matter, women want to fight back, we will give them what they want. The Minneapolis City Council had an idea of the will of women that contradicted the pornographers'; they got that different idea from the women who came to testify for the Ordinance, especially those who had grounds to use the Ordinance. The Ordinance's clarity and authority derive from the flesh-and-blood experiences of women who want to use it: women whose lives have been savaged by pornography. The Ordinance expresses their will to resist, and the enormous strength, translated into a legal right, of their capacity to endure, to survive.

The woman using the Ordinance will be saying, I am someone who has endured, I have survived, I matter, I know a lot, and what I know matters; it matters, and it is going to matter here in court, you pimp, because I am going to use what I know against you; and you Mr. Consumer, I know about you, and I am going to use what I know even about you, even when you are my teacher, even when you are my father, even when you are my lawyer, my doctor, my brother, my priest. I am going to use what I know.

It was not a surprise to Catharine MacKinnon and myself when, after the Ordinance was passed, the newspapers said—aha, it was a rightwing, fundamentalist achievement. They were saying to us, to MacKinnon and me, you are no one, you can't exist, it could not have been *your* idea. And it was not a surprise to us when people believed it. We did not like it, but it was not a surprise.

And when the court said to the injured women who wanted to use the

* ". . . and even if there's laws by the time they have hurt you you are too dirty for the law; the law needs clean ones but they dirty you up so the law won't take you; there's no crimes they committed that are crimes in the general perception because we don't count as to crimes as I have discovered time and time again as I try to think if what he did that hurt me so bad was a crime to anyone or was anything you could tell someone about so they would care; for you; about you; so you was human." (See Dworkin, *Mercy* [London: Secker & Warburg, 1990], pp. 303–4.)

Ordinance, you are no one, the pimp is someone, he matters, we are going to protect him, it was not a surprise. And when the court said, the consumer is someone, none of you women are anyone no matter how much you have been hurt but he is someone and we are here for him, that was not a surprise. And it was not a surprise when the court said to women: when you assert your right to equality you are expressing an opinion, a point of view, which we should be debating in the famous marketplace of ideas, not legislating; when you claim you were injured—that rape, that beating, that kidnapping—you have a viewpoint about it, but in and of itself the injury does not signify. And it was not a surprise when the court said that there was a direct relationship between pornography as defined in the Ordinance and injuries to women, including rape and battery, but that relationship does not matter because the court has a viewpoint, which happens to be the same as the pornographers': you women are not worth anything except what we pay for you in that famous free marketplace where we take your actual corporeal reality to be an idea.

None of this was a surprise. Every little tiny bit of it was an outrage.

We wrote the Ordinance for the women who had been raped and beaten and prostituted in and because of pornography. They wanted to use it to say, I am someone and I am going to win. We are part of them, we have lived lives as women, we are not exempt or separate from any of this. We wrote the Ordinance in behalf of our own lives, too.

I want to ask you to make certain that women will have a right and a chance to go into a U.S. court of law and say: this is what the pornographers did to me, this is what they took from me and I am taking it back, I am someone, I resist, I am in this court because I resist, I reject their power, their arrogance, their cold-blooded, cold-hearted malice, and I am going to win.

You here today have to make that possible. It has been ten years now. It has been ten years. Count the number of women who have been hurt in those ten years. Count how many of us have been lucky enough to be only insulted and humiliated. Count. We cannot wait another ten years; we need you, we need you now—please, organize.

PART II: THE REMEDIES

I do not weep at the world—I am too busy sharpening my oyster knife.

—Zora Neale Hurston

New times demand new measures and new men;
The world advances, and in time outgrows
The laws which in our father's day were best;
And doubtless, after us, some purer scheme
Will be shaped out by wiser men than we,
Made wiser by the steady growth of truth.

—James Russell Lowell,
"A Glance behind the Curtain"

CHAPTER FOUR

Formulating Strategies under Current Law

What should we do to control harmful speech and conduct? In this chapter, contributors argue that the most effective action can be taken within the current First Amendment framework. Tom Foley, the prosecutor in the cross-burning case of *R.A.V.* v. *St. Paul*, recounts how his office chose the legal strategy they did and the events that led him to argue the case in the Supreme Court. Eleanor Smeal and Helen Zia challenge attorneys and activists to explore new opportunities that are arising because of changes in the law and technology. Elena Kagan and Mary Becker take a sober look at the Supreme Court as it is currently constituted, warn that new laws could backfire, and urge that, rather than turning to the executive or judicial branches of government, we should use current obscenity and hate crimes legislation, as well as work to strengthen legislatures. Senator Ben Nighthorse Campbell discusses his work in opposition to the use of derogatory racial and ethnic stereotypes by professional sport teams. Finally, Dorchen Leidholdt and Marianne Wesson explore the use of Title VII and tort law to redress the harm of pornography.

One major stumbling block several of the authors grapple with is content neutrality, the current Supreme Court's insistence that any regulation of speech not discriminate based on what is said. Several of the authors address legal remedies that are content neutral and will not run afoul of the Supreme Court.

THE PROSECUTOR'S DILEMMA
An Interview with Tom Foley

Laura J. Lederer

In the predawn hours of June 21, 1990, Robert A. Viktora (R.A.V. in the now famous case *R.A.V. v. St. Paul*) and some friends taped together two broken chair legs to form a crude cross and then burned it inside the fenced yard of Russ and Laura Jones, a black family that lived in their neighborhood, Tom Foley, then Ramsey County prosecutor, charged Viktora under a St. Paul Hate Crimes Ordinance. While campaigning for the U.S. Senate, he agreed to this interview to give a sense of the legal strategies he used as the *R.A.V.* case wound its way up to the Supreme Court.

■

LJL: How did you come to argue R.A.V. in front of the Supreme Court?

TF: It is a bit complicated. You will remember that there were four individuals involved in the cross-burning. One was an adult, the other three, including R.A.V., were juveniles. The city handles adult violations of the law, so the city attorney charged the adult. He came in almost immediately and pled guilty to violating the Hate Crimes Ordinance. He didn't have a previous record so he was given probation. The juvenile division of my office charged R.A.V. with violating the St. Paul Hate Crimes Ordinance.

LJL: Some people have noted that there were other ordinances under which these three juveniles could have been charged. In fact, in the Supreme Court opinion, Justice Antonin Scalia suggests that there were several other laws already on the books that would have been better bets for charging them. He mentions trespass, vandalism, and arson and notes that violations of these laws carry much more stringent penalties than the Hate Crimes Ordinance, which was a misdemeanor.

TF: We looked at every possibility for charging the three juveniles. Justice Scalia is simply incorrect when he suggests that we could have used any of those laws. Trespass wouldn't have worked because under the law there has to be a warning, and none was given. Some of the elements of arson were missing, and the vandalism charge wouldn't have stuck because there was no real destruction of property. We couldn't even find a burned spot on the Joneses' grass. The only possible other charge we could have pressed was a state statute on terroristic threats, but, at the time, we were weighing other complicating factors in the case.

LJL: What kind of complicating factors?

TF: Well, the adult had already pleaded guilty to the Hate Crimes charge and received probation. It didn't seem fair at that point to charge the three juveniles with a felony when the adult had been charged with a misdemeanor and wasn't going to serve any time at all. We try to be evenhanded in our charging, especially with juveniles, and since none of the three had a record, the two young attorneys who did the work on this case didn't want to overcharge them. They felt that charging the juveniles with violation of the Hate Crimes Ordinance would be our best bet. We thought they would plead to the charge and it would give us a record on them, give them a warning, and send a message to the community that we wouldn't tolerate this kind of criminal activity. All in all, we felt we had made the best decision possible under the circumstances.

None of us in our wildest dreams thought that Robert Viktora would hire a First Amendment attorney, plead not guilty, and argue that the ordinance was unconstitutional. But that is exactly what he did. By then, it was too late to go back and rethink legal strategy. When the district court judge dismissed the charges prior to trial on the grounds that the ordinance was "overbroad" and censored expressive conduct in violation of the First Amendment, we decided to appeal. The case went directly to the Minnesota Supreme Court. There, the court reversed and remanded. It rejected the overbreadth claim, noting that the phrase in the ordinance which reads "arouses anger, alarm or resentment in others" could be construed to limit the ordinance's reach to "fighting words." Under a famous case in constitutional law, *Chaplinsky v. New Hampshire*, "fighting words" is a category of expression not protected by the First Amendment. The Minnesota Supreme Court found R.A.V.'s cross-burning a kind of "fighting words" that the city could regulate through its Bias-Motivated Crime Ordinance. I thought then, and still do now, that this interpretation of the ordinance was good law.

Then, R.A.V. applied to the U.S. Supreme Court for a writ of certiorari, which was granted. *

LJL: By then, this juvenile had some pretty powerful allies, didn't he?

TF: Yes. There is a pretty quick road from district court to the Supreme Court under Minnesota law, and along the way, he had a number of amicis briefs filed on his behalf, including ones by the ACLU and the American Jewish Congress. But then, the city of St. Paul had organizations which filed briefs on its behalf, too, including the Anti-Defamation League, the NAACP, and People for the American Way. They argued, along with us, that racist intimidation was not free speech and should not be protected by the First Amendment.

LJL: Did you feel comfortable arguing for the ordinance?

TF: The ordinance had an interesting history. The city generated the original ordinance in the early seventies when many of the synagogues in St. Paul were under attack. It was written specifically for that purpose and mentions swastikas and cross-burnings. In the early eighties gender was added to the ordinance, and in the late eighties race was added. So, in a sense, it was somewhat loosely developed. I felt comfortable arguing the Minnesota Supreme Court's interpretation of the ordinance, which narrows its construction. It essentially states that burning a cross falls within the category of "fighting words" and that as long as it is narrowly interpreted within the "fighting words" category, the Hate Crimes Ordinance is constitutional.

LJL: What was it like arguing before the Supreme Court?

TF: It was intense. You had to think on your feet, even with the months of preparation we all did. The justices each had their own concerns, and we had to address them as they came up. For example, Justice David Souter had a way of asking questions that sometimes made it difficult to see what he was after. He would talk what seemed like a good fifteen minutes and then say, "What do you think?" He was somewhat inscrutable, and we had to do our best to try to figure out what he was after. Of course, Justice Antonin Scalia dominated the discussion, and he was more direct. But he plays a lot of word games. In addition, he got all hung up on the language of the ordinance—the way it was originally written, not the way the Minnesota Supreme Court interpreted it. At least the questioning reflected that, if the opinion does not. I tended to agree with him and with the other justices that the original ordinance as drafted by the St. Paul City Council was overbroad. But I agree with

---

* A writ of certiorari is a written request that the Supreme Court review a lower court case. —Eds.

Justice John Stevens's opinion that "fighting words" are not protected by the First Amendment, and that a cross-burning inside the fence of a black family's yard could clearly be seen as "fighting words." Justice Scalia's opinion was mind-boggling: he basically said that while *Chaplinsky*—the "fighting words" case—is still good law, and "fighting words" are not protected speech under the First Amendment, the City of St. Paul could not have a "fighting words" ordinance that has any type of viewpoint discrimination. But, as Justice Stevens pointed out, if *all* fighting words are prohibited, why can't St. Paul, within that category of unprotected speech, further delineate what they will not tolerate?

LJL: Why do you think the Court took this convoluted route in its decision?

TF: I sometimes sensed there were some other agendas at work in the courtroom. At that time—and now for that matter—the whole issue of speech codes on college campuses was raging. They might have been attempting to skirt that issue with this case, but it was impossible to do because the facts of this case were so compelling, in my opinion.

LJL: Was the debate heated?

TF: Yes, particularly between Justice Scalia and Justice Sandra Day O'Connor. In fact, I heard a rumor that Scalia's majority opinion was written as a dissent, and, if you look at it, it does seem to be cast in dissent-type language. The rumor is that there was a shift by one of the justices, perhaps Anthony Kennedy or Souter, at the very last moment. If the rumor is true, it was a crucial shift, because it was a five–four decision, which means if it had gone the other way, the St. Paul ordinance might still be good law.

LJL: Still, there were some places you seemed to agree with the majority.

TF: My position was that most speech is protected, but that if speech reaches the criminal threshold it is not. For instance, if the skinheads in *R.A.V.* had decided to march down the street in a parade burning a cross, I would have, reluctantly, agreed with the majority that this was protected speech. I argued that if there is a threat to a particular individual, then it is not protected. For instance, I said that if someone threatens to kill the president, it is criminal speech and is not protected. In the same way, the cross-burning on the Joneses' lawn is criminal speech—it directly threatened them. But Justice Scalia distinguished the threat to a president's life by saying that the president was in a category all by himself—i.e., there is only one president and so threatening speech against him is not constitutionally protected!

LJL: Switching gears for a minute, had you encountered any incidents similar to this one in the area before the Jones's case came across your desk?

TF: Yes, we were aware of some skinhead activity, particularly in the area where the Joneses lived, but it was limited. Much of the activity was anti-Semitic. We also had a couple of kids defile a Jewish Hillel house around MacAlester campus, but that's about it.

LJL: If you had to do it over again, would you proceed in exactly the same way?

TF: In hindsight, knowing what I know now about how the juveniles decided to argue their case, I would most likely have charged them with terroristic threats as well, and forced them to plead guilty to one or another of the charges. I would still have charged them with violating the Hate Crimes Ordinance, though. I am glad that the Department of Justice came in after the Supreme Court case and charged R.A.V. again. He is now serving two years in a juvenile workhouse.

LJL: And what about the Supreme Court decision?

TF: Well, naturally, it was a great disappointment to lose. And, as I said, I still think the court made the wrong decision. I like Justice Stevens's opinion best. Essentially he argued that expressions that create special risks or cause special harms can be prohibited by special rules. He used as an example lighting a fire near an ammunition dump or a gasoline storage tank and said that this is especially dangerous and may be punished more severely than burning trash in a vacant lot. In the same way, he said, threatening someone because of her race or religious beliefs may cause particularly severe trauma or touch off a riot, and such threats should be able to be punished more severely than threats against someone based on, say, his support of a particular athletic team.

LJL: Right after the Supreme Court opinion, there was some talk in St. Paul of drafting a new law that would pass muster, or would challenge the current ruling. Do you think that is going to happen?

TF: No, I don't. There is a new city council now, and a new city attorney, and I don't think they are going to take it up again. However, the debate is still raging across the United States. I'm proud of the contribution I made to the issue and hope that in the long run it helps our country sort out some of the problems we have.

SPEECH AND VIOLENCE
Why Feminists Must Speak Out Against Pornography

Eleanor Smeal

Eleanor Smeal, former president of the National Organization for Women (NOW), considers new strategies for feminists and people of color who would like to eliminate media images of subordination and exploitation, and urges us to seize new technological opportunities for change.

■

What can women do about sexual exploitation in the media? What can we do about pornography? One of the reasons so many feminist activists are concerned about these issues is that everywhere we go audiences and individual women tell us over and over about the problems of violence against women, violence in the media, exploitation, sexual violence, date rape, domestic violence, marital rape, sexual assault, child assault, and sexual harassment. Many of us have heard for too long about the connections between media violence and real-life violence. We are desperate to figure out how to deal with the problem. Pornography is hate for women and no movement worth its salt would endure this assault of pornographic images without taking it on.

But the question of how to change our media—whether radio, television, video, newspapers, or magazines—is a difficult one. We know that we would like to see less exploitation and subordination of people based on their gender, race, or sexual orientation. But how shall we achieve this? Many of us have been slowed down by free speech arguments, but we are beginning to overcome this delay, focusing on creative ideas to improve women's status and safety, including new ideas about how to reshape the media.

The first step is to visualize how we would like the future to look. We need to envision it in order to decide what images we would like to produce and distribute—images that will encourage values such as equality, justice, and individual dignity; images that will improve the quality of our lives and the lives of our children. It is important to begin with this positive vision because we cannot merely eliminate what is wrong: we must also create what is right.

In the early seventies, the feminist movement took on media discrimination using Federal Communications Commission regulations. We employed the regulations to challenge TV and radio licenses—not only on the basis of sexism and racism in hiring, but also on the basis of sexism and racism in programming. The regulations were a lever: if station owners did not eliminate discriminatory behavior, or at least make an *effort* to eliminate it, we would question their right to a license.

Then, in the Reagan-Bush period, FCC regulations were gutted and that lever was no longer available. Since then, we have lost our direction. We do not have a strategy for how to improve media images of women. We have attempted to use direct action: taking on a television program here, a song there, a magazine over there. But as Barbara Mikulski once said, you can't free the slaves slave by slave, plantation by plantation. Likewise, direct action on a piece-by-piece, show-by-show basis is endless and exhausting. We can't possibly monitor every movie, book, magazine, song, and director—nor would we want to. We need new handles on how to attack the problem.

One new strategy is to focus on advertisers. The media industry is first and foremost a marketing game. It gathers an audience for the benefit of an advertiser. When advertisers think they are going to hear complaints from consumers, they will not buy advertising space from the magazine, newspaper, radio station, or television station. When advertisers do hear from consumers, they often quickly withdraw their support for a particular kind of programming.

A related strategy is to sue advertisers for discrimination. For example, in St. Paul, Minnesota, a feminist attorney brought a claim against Stroh's Brewery on behalf of a group of female employees who charged sexual harassment on the basis of an advertising campaign the brewery produced. The campaign featured scantily clad, big-bosomed blond women drinking beer. The employees charged that the ads encouraged sexual harassment inside the brewery. The suit has recently been settled for an undisclosed amount, but it was an exciting development for feminists because it hit sexual harassment, media advertising, and pornographic images all at the same time. It educated the employer, the employees, and the public in a dynamic way.

Another important strategy that women have not yet discussed is the creation of our own programming to combat the sexist and racist materials that are now so prevalent. We have an excellent opportunity ahead: fiber optics is radically altering electronic media. Soon there will be five hundred channels to choose from instead of fifty. Some of these channels should be reserved for women, for feminists, for progressives, and we must create the programming on these channels ourselves. We must encourage writers, artists, producers, and distributors to produce woman-friendly scripts. We need to keep in mind that a society that glorifies pornography and violence—in its movies, music, and entertainment—will perpetuate inequality. There can be no equality for women while discrimination is encouraged in this way. We need to answer this question: what do you think *should* be on—and what do you think *should not* be? If we do not determine this and act on it, the dream of equality will continue to elude us.

REGULATION OF HATE SPEECH AND PORNOGRAPHY AFTER *R.A.V.*

Elena Kagan

Much as many may dislike the Supreme Court's decision in *R.A.V.* v. *St. Paul*, it is now law. While some legal scholars and reformers are committed to drafting new legislation to redress the harm of pornography and hate speech, others argue that there is still much good law on the books that can be employed. Here, Elena Kagan revisits obscenity laws, the "fighting words" doctrine, the regulation of conduct as opposed to speech, and viewpoint-neutral restrictions on expression, and argues that current laws employing these concepts can be used to curb hate speech and pornography. This is an abridged version of an article with the same title that appeared in the Summer 1993 issue of *The University of Chicago Law Review.*

■

This essay addresses both practicalities and principles. I take it as a given that we live in a society marred by racial and gender inequality, that certain forms of speech perpetuate and promote this inequality, and that the uncoerced disappearance of such speech would be cause for great elation. But any attempt to regulate pornography or hate speech—or at least any attempt standing a chance of success—must take into account certain facts (the "is," not the "ought") of First Amendment doctrine. A law specifically disfavoring racist or sexist speech (or, to use another construction, a law distinguishing between depictions of group members as equal and depictions of group members as subordinate) runs headlong into the long-standing, and newly revivified, principle of viewpoint neutrality.* A purely pragmatic approach to regulating hate speech and pornography would seek to use laws not vulnerable to the viewpoint discrimination objection, while also seeking to justify—as exceptions—carefully crafted and limited departures from viewpoint neutrality. A focus on the

---

* Viewpoint neutrality is the legal principle that laws and other official actions may not regulate speech on the basis of the subject matter, attitude, or position of the speaker.—Eds.

feasible is arguably irresponsible if the feasible falls desperately short of the proper. But here, I think, that is not the case. If the current state of First Amendment doctrine counsels for certain proposals and not others, certain lines of argument and not others, so, too, do important values embodied in that doctrine. Specifically, the principle of viewpoint neutrality, which now stands as the primary barrier to certain modes of regulating pornography and hate speech, has at its core much good sense and reason. My view is that efforts to regulate pornography and hate speech not only will fail, but also should fail, to the extent that they trivialize or subvert this principle.

New Approaches

Instead, I would suggest three approaches that utilize current law: (1) the enactment of new bans on conduct, or stricter use of existing bans; (2) the enactment of certain kinds of viewpoint-neutral speech restrictions; and (3) enhanced use of the constitutionally unprotected category of obscenity.

CONDUCT The most obvious way to avoid changing First Amendment requirements is to regulate not speech, but conduct. The typical hate crimes law, as the Supreme Court unanimously ruled in 1993, presents no First Amendment problem.[1] Hate crimes laws, as usually written, provide for the enhancement of criminal penalties when a specified crime (say, assault) is committed because of the target's race, religion, or other listed status.[2] These laws are aimed not at speech, but at *acts*—because they apply regardless of whether the discriminatory conduct at issue expresses, or is meant to express, any sort of message. In this way, hate crimes laws function precisely as do other discrimination laws—for example, those in the sphere of employment.[3] When an employer fires an employee because she is black, the government may impose sanctions without constitutional qualm. This is so even when the discharge is accomplished (as almost all discharges are) through some form of expression, for whatever expression is involved is incidental both to the act accomplished and to the government's decision to prevent it.[4] Once again, the analysis ought not to change when a person assaults another because she is black, even if the conduct (assault on the basis of race) is accompanied by expression. A penalty enhancement constitutionally may follow because the penalty is pegged to an *act*—a racially based form of disadvantage—that the state wishes to prevent, and has an interest in preventing, irrespective of any expressive component.

In accord with this reasoning, communities should be able not only to impose enhanced criminal sanctions on the perpetrators of hate crimes, but also to provide special tort-based or other civil remedies for their victims. One of the accomplishments of the antipornography movement has been to highlight the benefits of using civil, as well as criminal, laws to deter and punish undesirable activity.[5] Civil actions offer fewer procedural safeguards for the defendant, including a much reduced standard of proof; as important, they may give greater control to the victim of the unlawful conduct than a criminal prosecution could ever do. Communities therefore should consider not merely the enactment of hate crimes laws, but also the provision of "hate tort" remedies. And in determining their scope, communities should consider the manner in which the laws apply to crimes or civil violations committed on the basis of sex, which now often fall outside the compass of hate crimes statutes.

Those favoring the direct regulation of pornography often charge that relying exclusively on bans on conduct—most notably, in this case, a ban on coerced performances—allows many abuses committed in the manufacture of pornography to continue.[6] This is true, but it must be measured against the reality that the most sweeping strategies also will be the ones most subject to constitutional challenge and most subversive of free speech principles. An increased emphasis on conduct, rather than speech, provides a realistic, principled, and perhaps surprisingly effective alternative.

VIEWPOINT-NEUTRAL RESTRICTIONS   The Supreme Court has often said that any speech restriction based on content, even if not based on viewpoint, presumptively violates the First Amendment.[7] But rhetoric on this issue is somewhat detached from reality: the Court has sometimes upheld regulations based on the subject matter of speech[8] and has, in several cases, approved restrictions on nonobscene, but sexually explicit or scatological speech.[9] Cases of this kind raise the possibility of eradicating the worst of hate speech and pornography through statutes that, although based on content, have no viewpoint bias on their face or as applied.

One could seek to enact legislation—or use existing laws—prohibiting carefully defined kinds of harassment, threats, or intimidation, including *but not limited to* those based on race and sex. For example, in considering the St. Paul ordinance, the Court in R.A.V. noted that the city could have achieved ". . . precisely the same beneficial effect . . ." through ". . . a[n] ordinance not limited to the favored topics . . ."—that is, through an ordinance prohibiting all fighting words, regardless of whether based on race, sex, or another specified category.[10] Such an ordinance would have presented no constitutional issue at all given the Court's prior holdings that fighting words are a form of unprotected expression.[11] A law prohibiting, in viewpoint-neutral terms, not merely fighting words, but other kinds of harassment and intimidation would and should face greater constitutional difficulties, relating most notably to overbreadth and vagueness; but a carefully drafted statute might well surmount these hurdles, and such a law would be unlikely to be subject to a challenge based on selectivity. Highly specific, viewpoint-neutral laws—whether framed in terms of fighting words or in some other manner—might be especially appropriate in communities, like educational institutions, whose very purpose requires the maintenance of a modicum of decency.[12]

Finally, the Constitution may well permit direct regulation of speech, if phrased in a viewpoint-neutral manner, when the regulation responds to a non-speech-related interest in controlling conduct involved in the material's manufacture. If the government has a strong interest in regulating the violence and coercion that often occur in the making of pornography, the Supreme Court's decision in *New York* v. *Ferber*[13] suggests that the government may punish the distribution of the product as well as the underlying unlawful conduct. In *Ferber*, the Court sustained a statute prohibiting the distribution of any material depicting a sexual performance by a child, primarily on the ground that the law arose from the government's interest in preventing the *conduct* (i.e., sexual exploitation of children) necessarily involved in producing the expression. Similarly, the government may prohibit directly the dissemination of any materials whose manufacture involves coercion of, or violence against, participants.

OBSCENITY   The government can also regulate sexually graphic materials harmful to women by using the long-established category of obscenity—an approach that has come to assume the aspect of heresy in the ranks of antipornography feminism. Those who have argued for regulating pornography have stressed the differences, in rationale and coverage, between bans on the pornographic and bans on the obscene. It is said that obscenity law focuses on morality, while pornography regulation focuses on power.[14] It is said that offensiveness and prurience (two of the requirements for finding a work obscene) bear no relation to sexual exploitation.[15] It is said that neither taking a work "as a whole," as obscenity law requires, nor exempting works of "serious value," as obscenity law does, are consistent with the goal of preventing harm to women.[16] I do not think any of this is flatly wrong, but I doubt whether these asserted points of difference—today, even if not in the past—point to the desirability of spurning the obscenity category.

My doubts began while I was first teaching a course on free expression. In keeping with the prevailing view, I rigidly separated the topics of obscenity and pornography. In discussing each, I reiterated the distinctions between them, in much the terms I have just described. I think I made the points clearly enough, but my students resisted; indeed, they could hardly talk about the one topic separately from the other. In discussing obscenity, they returned repeatedly to the exploitation of women; in discussing pornography, of course, they dwelt on the same. Those who favored regulation of pornography also favored regulation of obscenity—at least as a second-best alternative. Those who disapproved of regulation of pornography also disapproved of regulation of obscenity. Perhaps it was a dense class or I a bad teacher, but I think not; rather, I think the class understood—or, at least, unwittingly revealed—something important.

Even when initially formulated, the current standard for identifying obscenity was justified in part by reference to real-world harms. To be sure, the Supreme Court, in its fullest statement of the rationale for establishing the category of obscenity, spoke of the need ". . . to protect 'the social interest in . . . morality . . .' " and, what is perhaps the same thing, of the need ". . . 'to maintain a decent society.' . . ."[17] But the Court also spoke of—indeed, emphasized just as strongly—the "correlation between obscene material and crime" and, in particular, the correlation between obscene materials and "sex crimes."[18] And although some of the specific harms then perceived might now appear dated—the Court was thinking as much of unlawful acts involving "deviance" as of unlawful acts involving violence—still the Court understood the obscenity category as emerging not merely from a body of free-floating values, but from a set of tangible harms, perhaps including sexual violence.[19]

Much more important is the way conceptions of obscenity have evolved since then, in part because of the antipornography movement itself, and in part because of the deeper changes that movement reflects in public attitudes and morals. This shift in understanding, I think, accounts for my classroom experience. It is hard to test a proposition of this sort, but I will hazard it anyway: one of the great (if paradoxical) achievements of the antipornography movement has been to alter views on obscenity— to transform obscenity into a category of speech understood as intimately related, in part if not in whole, to harms against women.[20]

The key point here is that regulation of obscenity may accomplish some of the goals of the antipornography movement, and, partly because of the long-established nature of the category, such regulation may give rise to fewer concerns about compromising First Amendment principles. Even for those who think that the obscenity doctrine is in some sense a second-best alternative, it represents the first-best hope of achieving certain objectives. And the obscenity doctrine itself may be transformed, as antipornography efforts bring the doctrine into greater accord with the harm-based morality of today, rather than of the past.

THE LEGITIMACY OF JUDICIAL REVIEW IN SPEECH CASES

Mary Becker

During the 1960s and 1970s, civil rights and women's organizations consistently turned to the courts for help in achieving their equal rights goals. *Brown* v. *Board of Education* and *Roe* v. *Wade* are only two examples of major court battles that resulted in legal protection and redress. But now, Mary Becker argues, minorities and women cannot depend on judicial review. Especially in speech cases, which are difficult to win, a better bet may be to focus on other branches of government.

■

For those seeking legal redress for harms caused by hate speech and pornography, the major problem today is the free speech clause of the First Amendment. As a number of recent commentators have pointed out, the First Amendment has become conservative.[1] Early speech cases protected the speech of progressives and radicals: communists, labor organizers, draft resisters, and civil rights activists. Today, speech cases are often won by corporations, the media, and other powerful insiders. Free speech has become a negative right, a principle that protects the speech of those with the resources to speak, and that protects them only from regulation by government. Powerful private actors, such as pornographers and the media, are free to control, suppress, and distort the speech of others, and when they do, political processes cannot redress it.

I suggest that free speech is conservative in another sense: free speech claims are simply not visible when they are consistent with traditional norms and expectations. The implications for outsider groups are clear: speech claims are now less likely to be available to them when they are discriminated against because of the content of their speech, but are likely to bar attempts to protect them from harmful speech.

To make this point, I will examine judicial review of speech regulation in one specific setting: public universities. In many ways, this is an ideal setting in which to consider the extent to which binding judicial review in speech cases is conservative.*

In recent years, a number of universities, public and private, have adopted speech codes of various sorts designed to protect lesbians, gay men, racial minorities, and women targeted for harassment on their campuses. There is no Supreme Court case squarely on point, but dicta in a recent case suggest that the current justices would strike any such code in a public university.[2] In the lower federal courts, such codes have been struck because, like the anti-pornography ordinance, they regulate speech in terms of content and viewpoint.[3]

To many, it seems inescapable that lower federal courts strike speech codes at schools. The dominant image of universities in our culture is that they are places created for the exploration of all sorts of ideas in a free and open atmosphere. Of course, many of us who have lived within universities have not found them so free and open.

Indeed, there is nothing *important* that a university does that is not the regulation of speech. Universities are institutions that attempt to advance our understanding of the world around us and of ourselves by defining what counts as knowledge, what is important, true, and relevant to the world and the human condition. Inevitably, such assessments regulate speech in terms of content, viewpoint, and even ideology. For better or worse, American universities suppress countless viewpoints, beginning with the idea that the earth is flat and the universe revolves around it.

Often speech about issues important to lesbians, gay men, racial minorities, and women is suppressed because those who assess its value consider it trivial or not intellectually interesting or suspect its methodology. In classrooms, women students often raise issues only to have them dismissed by a teacher who considers them irrelevant. Women and minorities engaged in feminist or critical race research often lose hiring and promotion opportunities because of the content of their speech, their viewpoints, and their ideologies. Lesbians and gay men face similar problems—*if* they even feel safe enough to write scholarship that explicitly includes a queer perspective. Narrative approaches

---

* Binding judicial review is a finding by a court that legislation is valid or invalid. In general, courts have the authority to review the actions of most government institutions, including universities, for due process and other constitutional issues. Becker notes that universities are an ideal setting to examine judicial review because they are (1) manageable in size, so that firm conclusions are possible; (2) pervaded by state action so that analysis is not confounded by the public-private distinction, which seems so often to provide a "neutral" explanation for why constitutional law cannot reach oppression; and (3) readily understood by an academic who knows, from first-hand observation, how power operates and speech is regulated in this arena.—Eds.

to scholarship are considered of little value by many powerful academics, and thus go unsupported.*

Decisions on hiring and promotion of faculty are the most important and powerful ways in which universities regulate speech. Academic speech, particularly in classrooms, student papers, and exams, depends on who is hired and promoted. Speech at a law school without any critical race theorists will be different from speech at a law school with several. And these hiring and promotion decisions are based on assessments of the *content* of the applicant's speech; the quality of the applicant's arguments, research, methodology; and, inevitably—especially at the margins of academic discourse—viewpoints.

Obviously, no university offers every possible course. But many of the courses that are available routinely skip topics or methodologies many students, particularly lesbians, gays, women and minorities, consider important. We have all, for example, heard of criminal law courses that do not cover rape. At some universities, as at the University of Chicago, there may not even be a Women's Studies Department. And there may be strong arguments on both sides over whether to have a Women's Studies Department, but these arguments, and their resolution, are based on assessments of viewpoints and ideologies likely to be promoted by such a department.

Papers and written exams are graded in terms of the teacher's assessment of the content of the student's knowledge and quality of her or his reasoning and creative ideas. If a paper or exam contains the sorts of knowledge and insights the teacher considers valuable, even if he⁴ does not agree with them, it might seem that the grade is for quality irrespective of viewpoint or ideology. This is possible because the teacher's beliefs include a range of approaches he considers valid, without having to agree with them all. But if a student's paper or exam is based on an ideology the teacher considers truly stupid or irrational, the importance of his viewpoint in evaluating the content would be obvious. Imagine, for example, that you are grading an essay question on gradations of punishment for various forms of rape. You read an exam that argues that rape should be legal, even rewarded, because women enjoy the experience. Indeed, the more violent the rape, the greater should be the reward. You would and should be affected by the exam's viewpoint in assigning a grade to it.

Thus, the boundaries of every academic conversation, as well as many assessments of academic quality, turn on questions of content, viewpoint, and ideology. More pointedly, unspoken rules and understandings about what speech is high quality permeate university life—and these turn on content and

---

* The narrative approach has been championed by Derrick Bell, Patricia Williams, Richard Delgado, and others who include personal experiences and storytelling in their legal analyses and theory. —Eds.

viewpoint. These assessments, grounded as they inevitably are in traditional notions of what a discipline is about, what counts as "truth," and what methods are valuable, hurt many newcomers to university communities because these new entrants look at things differently, value things differently, and see different methods as appropriate and necessary. Indeed, that the value of their speech could lie precisely in its divergence from university standards is not an idea with which many powerful people with more traditional perspectives would agree. Yet no court would entertain a constitutional challenge under the free speech clause grounded in the allegation that a public university's consideration of the *content* of speech in any of these ways—in setting courses, syllabi, or the canon; in evaluating the work of a lesbian or gay scholar, a critical race scholar, or a feminist for hiring or promotion—was unconstitutional.[5]

What is different about speech codes? Perhaps it is that they are *explicit*. But many of these other content-based judgments are also explicit. Course listings and syllabi are explicit; students are given explicit feedback on exams and papers. Indeed, *explicit* critique is essential for effective education.

Perhaps it is the *disciplinary* nature of proceedings under the speech codes that makes them different. But low grades can lead to precisely the same sorts of negative events disciplinary proceedings can lead to: probation, suspension, or expulsion. In fact, disciplinary proceedings often lead to less serious events than do low grades: the requirement to issue an apology, or view a video on racism, or move from one dorm to another.

Or perhaps the difference is that speech codes are policies set at *too high a level*. But many of the routine regulations of speech are also set at high levels: what will be included in the common core requirements for all undergraduates; what will be in the canon for various departments; what courses will be offered; whether there will be a women's studies department.

The idea that routine university assessments of speech are different in that they regulate speech only in terms of *quality*, not viewpoint, I have already suggested cannot withstand scrutiny. But—equally important—university speech codes are also based on assessments of quality: that the intellectual quality of proscribed racist and sexist speech is low; that the proscribed speech hurts, more than it promotes, high-quality intellectual debate in a university community.

What is patently different about speech codes is that they protect new entrants to academic communities in *nontraditional* ways. Therefore the regulation in terms of content is unusually *visible* as such, making the courts willing to consider constitutional challenges based on content discrimination, and making the speech codes seem *inappropriate* and *inconsistent* with the idea of a university.

In fact, free speech arguments can be advanced on both sides in the speech code cases. For example, one could regard university faculty, especially public university faculty, as protected from judicial review by a notion of academic freedom and university autonomy grounded in the free speech clause of the First Amendment. One could regard assessments of the academic quality of speech as within the peculiar competence of these faculty, and beyond the competence of federal judges. Under this approach, concerns for free speech would cut against judicial review of speech codes, leaving academic communities free to define quality speech in their area, just like other communities that are independent of federal judicial oversight.

This approach has been taken in Title VII challenges to academic hiring and promotion decisions, making Title VII, which bans discrimination in employment on the basis of sex and race, ineffective in a university environment. Women and minorities who have attempted to bring Title VII challenges to university evaluations of the content of their speech at hiring and promotion have found the federal courts *less* willing to review content-based university assessments of speech than they are in the context of similar decisions by other kinds of employers.[6]

Thus far, I have shown that federal judicial review of public university speech codes is conservative. It tends to support the status quo because judges seem unable to see viewpoint discrimination if it looks like tradition, and likely to see it when action is *nontraditional*. Given the need for new approaches if we are to end the systemic subordination of lesbians and gay men, racial minorities, and women, limitations on viewpoint regulation by government will inevitably support the status quo.

If binding judicial review in speech cases is conservative, then progressives and radicals should reexamine their commitment to using constitutional law (and binding judicial review) as an instrument of change. Under binding judicial review, a constitutional decision reached by the Supreme Court of the United States binds and limits subsequent legislative action. And such decisions may well support the power of those most like the federal judiciary: a minority group of apparently straight, white men. The majority of Americans might be better off operating in a political system without the limitations set by this group. It would, for example, be easier to put in place laws compensating those harmed by pornography and hate speech were there no binding judicial review in speech cases.* The best route to change may be instead to focus on the

---

* In other words, if communities were free to make their own laws, the St. Paul ordinance banning cross-burnings would still be good law, and the antipornography civil rights ordinance, which passed in Minneapolis, Indianapolis, and Bellingham, Washington, would also still be in force. —Eds.

law-making bodies—federal and state legislatures, city councils, and boards of education.

There are, of course, many problems inherent in seeking change through legislatures. These bodies are themselves old boys' networks and hardly the most open-minded or progressive organizations in America today. Yet legislators are subject to direct pressure from constituents, most of whom are *not* straight, white men, and legislators do not operate within a system formally bounded by precedent.* As the political power of lesbians, gay men, racial minorities, and women continues to grow, this difference is likely to become increasingly important. Binding judicial review insulates decisions harmful to these groups—such as limits on the regulation of hate speech—from correction through constituents' participation and pressure, even if they have majority status.

The case for binding judicial review in a democracy has always been tenuous. Why should a small elite group of lawyers, who are not politically accountable, be able to block legislation desired by a majority of the citizens? Perhaps we should begin to undermine the legitimacy of this approach, particularly in speech cases. Supreme Court justices are quite concerned with their own legitimacy, and might be more hesitant to strike regulations of speech helpful to outsider groups if their decisions were perceived as illegitimate. As Mari Matsuda has pointed out, hate speech and pornography are antidemocratic; they contribute to the political subordination of a majority of the population —women and racial minorities. Women and racial minorities were excluded from key constitutional moments when the free speech clauses of the First Amendment were framed. They were excluded from the processes that pro-duced the Constitution, the Bill of Rights, and binding judicial review, though they were and are a majority of the polity. Moreover, a system of precedent —i.e., tradition—broadly speaking, is a problem from the perspective of Af-rican Americans and women.

Federal judicial review of university speech regulation provides a concrete illustration of the problems with this standard in a democracy. First, it is antidemocratic: (a) it is countermajoritarian, in that it is inconsistent with the desires of a large number of people, seeking to enact policies through non-judicial governmental institutions; and (b) it frustrates the efforts of outsiders to attain equality throughout society, including in the political arena, thus preserving the political dominance of a minority group (straight, white men). Racist and sexist language and harassment make it harder for outsiders to

---

* Here the author refers to "precedent" as a term of art. In the law, stare decisis, which means "let the decision stand," binds courts, except in unusual cases, to follow earlier decisions. Legislators are not so bound. —Eds.

succeed in academic life, and such success—including the internal confidence a supportive environment can give—is an important credential for a successful political life.

Second, it is not pragmatic: we may need experimentation to figure out how best in a free society to deal with complex issues like university speech codes, hate speech, and pornography. If this experimentation is impossible, we may never find a *democratic* solution.

In light of the problems with binding judicial review in the narrow area of university speech codes, radicals and progressives should reassess their commitment to using constitutional law as a means of redistributing power more equitably along lines of class, race, sex, or sexual orientation. It may be easier to achieve effective change through the political system and nonjudicial governmental organizations than through judicial decisions. Supreme Court judges are an elite, mostly male, mostly white, straight group operating within a system that gives a great deal of weight to precedents—i.e., tradition—established by earlier and even less diverse courts. As a decisionmaking body, they are likely to preserve the power of those who have traditionally held power rather than to reach decisions that will threaten seriously the status quo. Limits on legislative action imposed by such a body may impede, rather than advance, the interests of those who have today less than their share of political power.

If it is the case that these problems only arise in the context of free speech, the Supreme Court should stop striking legislation on speech grounds, even if binding judicial review under other clauses continues. We do not, after all, have the same level of judicial review for all clauses of the constitution.

In truth, the federal judiciary has only limited institutional power. It cannot make women and men equal. It can only address the narrow issues that arise in the cases that make their way to federal court. In no area outside constitutional law are feminists or blacks as likely to look to straight, white men for needed change, rather than to their own creation of pressure. To the extent that judicial decisions limit the ability of outsiders working through the political system to make the changes they see as necessary—perhaps a custody standard at divorce favoring mothers[7]—binding judicial review is inconsistent with real social equality.

I suspect that the probability of change would be larger in legislative bodies without such judicial review. It would make them more likely to institute both worse laws and more excellent laws (from the perspective of women) than those that would be enacted and survive in a world *with* binding judicial review. The enactment of awful laws would, however, goad us to greater direct political participation; such laws might be unlikely to survive for long given outsiders' majority status. In recent years we have seen at least two instances in which women's political action increased as the result of decisions that made them angry: when it looked like the *Webster*[8] decision was about to destroy *Roe* v. *Wade*[9] and when Clarence Thomas was appointed to the Supreme Court despite Anita Hill's testimony of harassment and his apparently undisputed record as a consumer of pornography. But I doubt we will ever see equality without substantial possibilities for positive change.

The greatest cost of the "good" Supreme Court decisions has been their inevitable tendency to encourage litigants to rely on the courts, rather than on their own political power. The cases encourage disenfranchised people to look to the federal judiciary for protection of their interests, rather than focusing on electoral politics and organizing at the grass-roots level. In the end, legislative reform is needed if outsiders are to achieve equality through the courts, and any "good" decisions in the past have been, at best, a mixed blessing.[10] The race-equality cases are a perfect example:[11] they made a very conservative notion of equality into constitutional doctrine, and have thus helped to legitimate the remaining inequities and lower the pressure for further social change. Even *Brown* v. *Board of Education*[12] did not produce much social change in itself; significant desegregation in Southern schools came only with executive and legislative action in the sixties.[13] Perhaps the civil rights movement would have achieved more had it focused entirely and only on change through legislative and executive action, rather than through constitutional decisionmaking, since today, constitutional decisions often bar needed racial remedies.[14]

For meaningful change, power must be exercised through ordinary politics, so that rules and practices serve the needs of disempowered groups.[15] Judicial decisions that limit what legislatures can do because of constitutional constraints may actually entrench the power of the dominant minority group in this country: white males. Free speech is a case in point, given the current conservative understanding of the meaning of this constitutional right and the barrier it forms to the redress of speech-related harms to lesbians, gay men, minorities, and women. But the problem may be much broader, and our reassessment should include all fundamental and individual rights.

PORNOGRAPHY IN THE WORKPLACE
Sexual Harrassment Litigation under Title VII

Dorchen Leidholdt

Pornography in the workplace is not a new phenomenon, either for women workers who must endure it as a condition of their employment, or for litigators seeking redress for sexual harassment. Dorchen Leidholdt reviews cases in which the Court held that the use of pornography was a form of sexual harassment and a violation of the civil rights of women workers under Title VII of the Civil Rights Act.

■

Among the 249 women who used the crisis intervention service of Working Women's Institute in 1980, 76 percent reported working in environments that promoted sexual harassment. Prominent among the illustrations they provided were such experiences as confronting nude photographs of women in the mailroom and pornographic slogans on the walls.[1] In *Kyriatzi* v. *Western Electric*, an influential 1978 federal district court decision, the plaintiff, Cleo Kyriatzi, prevailed not only on her claim that her employer had systematically discriminated against women in hiring and promotion, but also on her charge that her male coworkers' act of circulating a pornographic cartoon caricaturing her body was part of a pattern of sexual harassment.[2] A ground-breaking decision just two years later was the first to hold an employer liable under Title VII for a sexually hostile work environment. In this case, the court focused on violent sexual slurs that had been directed against the plaintiff (for example, "any man in his right mind would want to rape you"), but pornography loomed large in the background: among the "sexually stereotyped insults and demeaning propositions" that the court said "illegally poisoned" plaintiff Sandra Bundy's work environment were repeated requests from her supervisor that she let him show her books and pictures that, he contended, bore out his claim that women like Bundy who rode horses did so for sexual release.[3]

In recent years, women workers increasingly have argued under Title VII that they have been injured by pornography. Some have brought tort claims —usually for intentional infliction of emotional distress—in lieu of or in addition to sex discrimination charges. The growing number of legal actions against pornography by women workers can be attributed to a variety of factors: the continued movement of women into employment areas that have traditionally been men-only,[4] the steady growth of the pornography industry and the resulting proliferation of pornographic materials throughout the culture,[5] and feminist criticism of pornography as a practice of sexual exploitation that threatens women's safety and lowers women's status.[6]

Workplace Sexual Harassment through Pornography

PRACTICE AND EFFECTS   Women workers who have challenged the presence of pornographic materials in their workplaces have reported a range of experiences. For some, like Cleo Kyriatzi, pornography has been used to single out and humiliate them as individual women, often by identifying them with a particularly stigmatizing sexual stereotype. The cartoon circulated of Kyriatzi showed a heavy naked woman who had maimed a scrawny little man by sitting on him, an attack not only on Cleo Kyriatzi's physical proportions, but also on her assertive personality.[7] There are other examples, too. Carol Zabkowicz's male coworkers subjected her to dozens of drawings depicting a naked woman with exaggerated sexual characteristics and bearing her initials, all of which reflected her harassers' perception of her as a "sexy bitch" who was "hot and horny."[8] An athletic and independent female police officer in a large Southern city filed suit under Title VII after enduring the public display, throughout the precinct headquarters, of pornographic pictures of two women fondling each other, inscribed with her name and that of another female police officer.[9] The stereotypes evoked by the pornography in the working environments of each of these women—castrator, whore, and dyke—referred to and reinforced specific misogynistic perceptions of the victim's sexuality.

Such individually directed pornographic assaults on a woman worker's sexuality usually succeed, as intended, in humiliating her. They often also succeed, as intended, in driving her out of her job. Kyriatzi was terminated by her employer in retaliation for her filing a sex discrimination complaint; the harassment directed at Zabkowicz so traumatized her that she was forced to take an extended medical leave. The use of pornography in a prolonged campaign of sexual harassment can cause psychological damage and create a climate so hostile that it becomes impossible for the targeted woman to work there.

The reaction of women exposed to pornography generally in their work environment does not appear to differ qualitatively from that of the women who are targeted as individuals. Moreover, when women protest the presence of pornographic displays, they often end up being individual targets. The men responsible invariably defend the spectacle of women in public displays of sexual access and submission as an homage to female beauty or as merely the expression of lusty interest in sex.

Lois Robinson, a welder at Jacksonville Shipyards in Florida who successfully sued her employer for violating her rights under Title VII,[10] described working with male coworkers (who outnumbered her and the other women craftsworkers by more than one hundred to one) around such publicly displayed calendar illustrations as a photograph of a woman bending over a bed, pulling down her underwear, and presenting her exposed buttocks to the viewer, and one of a woman in a crouching position clad only in a harness made of leather and chains. Pornographic calendars were delivered to the shipyard by its major suppliers, and the company, by its own admission, then distributed them among its male employees. In deposition testimony, Robinson vividly described the impact on her of this management-sanctioned pornography: "I felt very distressed, frustrated, embarrassed, ashamed. I didn't feel like I was viewed as an equal in this place."[11]

Robinson's complaint to her supervisors about the display of pornography in the shipyard sparked an onslaught of sexual harassment in which workers used pornography to target her as an individual. One of her female coworkers recalled that "[a] group from the pipe shop came and put some photographs on our gang box . . . so she would see them when she put her tools away in the evening."[12] The pictures were explicit pornographic shots of women posed spread-eagle, in full labial display. Shortly thereafter, a "Men Only" sign was posted on the door of a workroom papered with pornographic pictures of women, and Robinson began to receive materials from a pornographic mailing house addressed to her at home.

Though the sexual harassment of women workers through pornography stems from motivations that range from resentment of an individual woman or of women workers as a group, to a desire for sexual entertainment on the job or for a sexual encounter with a particular woman, its impact on women workers is remarkably similar: emotional distress, sometimes reaching the proportions of psychic trauma. The ultimate outcome is to undermine a woman worker's peace of mind, to disable her job performance, and—sometimes—to push her out of her job entirely. Intentionally or inadvertently, pornography in the workplace is a barrier to equal employment opportunities for women.

SEX HARASSMENT CASES   Prior to the decision of the D.C. Court of Appeals in *Bundy* v. *Jackson*, a woman employee did not have an actionable claim under Title VII for sexual harassment unless her rejection of her superior's sexual advances caused her to lose a tangible employment benefit of an economic nature, such as a promotion, a desired work assignment, or the job itself.[13] Aptly termed "quid pro quo" by Catharine MacKinnon in *The Sexual Harassment of Working Women*,[14] this form of harassment was understood as threatening to turn a woman's employment into a form of prostitution in which she was required to sexually service her employer or supervisor in order to get or retain a job or an advancement. *Bundy* expanded this legal understanding of workplace sexual harassment by holding that the phrase "terms, conditions, or privileges of employment" in Title VII encompasses not only the tangible economic benefits of a job, but its psychological and social environment, as well.

The decision of the Eleventh Circuit in *Henson* v. *City of Dundee*, decided just a year after *Bundy*, reiterated *Bundy*'s holding that sexually hostile work environments are actionable under Title VII and specified the requirements for prevailing on such a claim.[15] The *Henson* court attempted to spell out the degree of workplace hostility necessary for a successful sexual harassment claim. To be actionable under Title VII, the harassment "must be sufficiently pervasive so as to alter the conditions of employment and create an abusive working environment." In determining whether a working environment is "abusive," that is, whether it "affect[s] seriously the psychological well-being of the employees," the trier of fact must assess "the totality of the circumstances."[16]

The question of whether sexually hostile work environments are actionable under Title VII was answered affirmatively and definitively by the Supreme Court in *Meritor* v. *Vinson*.[17] Although the sexual harassment alleged by plaintiff Mechelle Vinson included criminal conduct, including a series of rapes, the Supreme Court made it clear that Title VII protects female employees not only from physical abuse, but from "discriminatory intimidation, ridicule, and insult." Emphasizing the breadth of its holding, the Supreme Court asserted that Title VII "evinces a congressional intent to strike at the entire spectrum of disparate treatment of men and women."[18]

HOSTILE ENVIRONMENT   *Bundy* and *Henson* provided a strong foundation for a pre-*Vinson* court decision in which pornography was found to be part of a pattern and practice of hostile-environment sexual harassment prohibited by Title VII. In this case, sexual harassment through pornography was central to plaintiff Ramona Arnold's claims, although she also alleged other, related practices of sexually discriminatory conduct. Like her predecessor Cleo Kyriatzi, Arnold was employed in a line of work that had previously been exclusively male. She was subjected to harassment that in degree and duration far exceeded *Henson*'s threshold for pervasiveness.

Without a doubt, Arnold was a superb and dedicated police officer.[19] When one of her colleagues radioed for help after he ran into trouble trying to break up a fight at a neighborhood bar, Arnold appeared on the scene, removed a woman who was struggling with him, and brought a hostile crowd of onlookers under control. She spent a lunch break counseling a new mother, whom she had previously taken off a bus so that the woman could deliver her baby. She had received high scores for her marksmanship. Becoming a police officer was her life's ambition, one she had no doubt gotten from her father, who had served as chief of police for Oklahoma City and commissioner of public safety for the State of Oklahoma. Arnold seemed destined to achieve success on the police force.

In 1977, Arnold became the first woman police officer in the City of Seminole. Lieutenant Herdlitchka, a male officer who preceded her there by two years, had met her while working under her father and disliked her ambition. He was determined to bring Arnold down to what he viewed as her proper place, and to enlist the help of the other men on the police force in doing so. He succeeded on both accounts. The vehicle for his destruction of Arnold and her career was pornography.

Herdlitchka's harassment of Arnold began shortly after she was assigned to his unit in 1977. He made derogatory comments about her; pornographic cartoons appeared on the walls of the officers' quarters; and within two months pornographic pictures with Arnold's name on them were posted in areas of the police station open to the public. As time passed, the pornography became increasingly explicit and demeaning: one picture with Arnold's name written on it showed a naked man and woman engaged in a sex act; another showed a man having intercourse with a goat, with Arnold's name written on the goat; a third showed a naked woman with her legs spread and Arnold's name written on her genitals. The clear message of the displays was that Arnold was not the competent police officer that she appeared to be, but instead was merely an object for sexual use.

Not only did the pictures humiliate and upset Arnold, but, accompanied by Herdlitchka's constant derogatory comments about her and women police officers in general, they turned her into an object of hatred and a target of abuse for the other men in the department. First she was excluded from squad meetings. Then someone underlined references in the police manual to "he" and "his." Soon many of Arnold's fellow officers refused to speak to her or even to recognize her existence. One year after the campaign began, the chief of police himself posted a pornographic picture with Arnold's name on it.

Arnold complained repeatedly to her superiors and eventually went to the city manager, members of the city council, and finally to a state senator. When

Arnold complained to a new chief of police, he informed her that she would have to endure the harassment because it long preceded his tenure at the Seminole department. He refused to order Herdlitchka and the other officers to remove the pornographic displays from their lockers and accused Arnold of being "picky" for wanting them down. When Arnold's husband approached him with pornographic pictures in hand and threatened to show them to city officials, the police chief finally became concerned, met with Arnold, and asked her what she wanted him to do about the situation. To her reply that she wanted him to get the pornography out of the male officers' lockers, he replied, "I'll handle this in my own way." Arnold's superiors regarded the harassment either as a personal feud between Arnold and Herdlitchka with which they had no business interfering, or as a risk Arnold had assumed by being female and presuming to work as a police officer.

By January 1984, the harassment had taken its toll. Arnold took an extended leave of absence, citing mental and physical problems she and her physician attributed to the harassment. The court described them in its findings of fact:

83. Plaintiff suffers from post-traumatic stress syndrome, that is, a severe reaction to very unusual stress conditions. It is a condition which is characterized by an inability to let go of the trauma. The circumstances of the stress keep coming back to plaintiff. She continues to relive the circumstances which cause and continue to cause the stress. Her sleep patterns have been and continue to be disturbed. She had and continues to have extremely high blood pressure; in fact, her blood pressure has been nearly at stroke level.

84. The massive anxiety and depression from which plaintiff has suffered and continues to suffer is of the same kind and intensity as that resulting from sexual assault.

85. Plaintiff also suffers from the rejection and lack of support of her peers, and from the constant threat of losing her job. Her sense of identity was entirely anchored to her role as a police officer. The overt rejection, harassment, and discrimination by her peers was perceived by plaintiff as a rejection of self, resulting in great damage to her personality structure. Her sense of selfhood, her view of the world, of justice, and of the police as guardians of justice were severely assaulted. . . . One psychiatrist witness for the defendant testified that she could not say that the plaintiff would ever recover.[20]

Ramona Arnold brought Title VII claims for disparate treatment, sexual harassment, and retaliation against the City of Seminole, its mayor, its city manager, its police chief, and Herdlitchka, prevailing on all three claims. The harassment carried out through pornography was central to the court's conclusions of law on all three of Arnold's claims. The court perceived that the use of pornography was integral to the entire pattern of illegal sex discrimination.

QUID PRO QUO   Ramona Arnold's Title VII sexual harassment claim was litigated under the hostile-environment theory. Because the creation of a hostile, offensive, or intimidating work environment is the primary injury to women workers resulting from pornography in their workplace, this theory will usually be the most appropriate method of analysis under Title VII. Moreover, unless the pornography-based harassment is linked to the loss of a concrete economic benefit, it would seem to be the only approach available to many plaintiffs. The 1987 decision of a federal district court in Tennessee, however, demonstrates that some women workers who are harassed on the job through pornography may be able to win under Title VII using the theory of quid pro quo.

Unlike Arnold, Rose Boyd held a job that could be characterized as traditionally female: she processed claims for a health care agency.[21] Like most women in such jobs, her supervisor was a man. Although Boyd's job was hardly on the cutting edge of progress for women, to Boyd it represented an important advance over her previous job as a clerk in an insurance claims office.

Boyd's difficulties with her supervisor, McLaughlin, began on a business trip to a conference in Nashville, Tennessee. He had insisted that she accompany him to the event, even though the seminar topics were directed at managerial employees, not clerical workers like Boyd. During the evening of the first day of the trip, McLaughlin insisted that Boyd come to his hotel room to discuss a work-related matter, and she reluctantly agreed. Once she was there, he turned on a pornographic movie. Boyd immediately became upset and told him that she was not interested in watching the film. When she got up to leave, McLaughlin put his hand on her shoulder and tried to persuade her to stay. She refused and walked out of his room. McLaughlin slammed the door behind her.

After the trip, McLaughlin's attitude toward Boyd changed. He stopped speaking to her, became extremely critical of her productivity, and informed one of her coworkers that she would soon be gone. Several months later McLaughlin fired Boyd, prompting her to file suit under Title VII for sexual harassment.

Whereas a hostile environment theory is available whenever sexual harassment invades a plaintiff's work environment, establishing sexual harassment under a quid pro quo theory necessitates proof that the plaintiff's refusal to submit to sexual advances caused a concrete and measurable job detriment, such as the loss of a promotion or of the job itself. At issue in Boyd's sexual harassment case were two questions: whether McLaughlin's showing her pornography constituted sexual advances and, if so, whether it was her rejection of these advances that eventually led McLaughlin to fire her. Although McLaughlin did not dispute Boyd's testimony that he showed her pornography during the trip, he insisted that the incidents were not sexual advances.

The court analyzed the totality of the circumstances—including McLaughlin's insistence that Boyd come to his hotel room, his attempt to restrain her when she tried to leave, and the content of the film he showed her—and concluded that together these factors established a sexual advance. It answered the second question in the affirmative, as well, pointing to the credibility of Boyd's testimony, the corroborating testimony of her coworkers about the change in McLaughlin's attitude and behavior toward her after the Nashville trip, and an assessment that her work performance was competent and her termination unjustified.

The Backlash: Rabidue

Most federal court decisions since *Bundy* have recognized pornography in the workplace as a significant factor in the creation of a sexually hostile work environment. However, one important case, involving a hostile environment claim with allegations of sexual harassment through pornography, represents a backlash to this trend. *Rabidue* v. *Osceola Refining Co.*, a Sixth Circuit decision, is a disturbing precedent.[22] This decision was not unanimous: the influential and widely quoted dissent of Judge Keith has come to overshadow the opinion of the majority. A recent blow to *Rabidue* was the Supreme Court's rejection in *Harris* v. *Forklift Systems, Inc.* of the majority's requirement that a plaintiff prove that her psychological well-being was seriously affected by the harassment.[23] Nevertheless, the *Rabidue* majority has articulated arguments that have proved popular with sexual harassment defendants and judges sympathetic to them and must be addressed.[24]

The pictures of plaintiff Vivienne Rabidue's working conditions at the Osceola Refining Company painted by the majority and the dissent differ almost as much as the legal conclusions they reached. The majority described a clash between two colorful, strong-willed individuals—between an "abrasive, rude, antagonistic" woman and her coworker, Douglas Henry, a "vulgar and crude" man.[25] The court's description of the gender-related aspects of the conflict and of the working conditions at Osceola, a petrochemical plant, is muted.

In the dissent, another scenario emerges. Far from being the ostensible equals portrayed by the majority, Vivienne Rabidue and Douglas Henry were in very different positions. Despite numerous complaints about his belligerent behavior, Henry, the Computer Division Supervisor, was protected and indulged by management and given helpful pointers on how to become "an executive-type person." Rabidue, the only woman in management, was systematically excluded from managerial social activities and denied standard managerial privileges. One of her supervisors remarked characteristically, "Vivienne is doing a good job as credit manager, but we really need a man on that job."

Rabidue's second-class status at Osceola was vividly dramatized by the comments Henry made about her. To Henry, she was a "fat ass" and "a bitch" who needed "a good lay." Rabidue was not the only object of Henry's abuse. He routinely referred to the other women there as "whores," "cunts," and "pussy." Upset by Henry's language, and afraid for their jobs if they complained, these women commissioned Rabidue to file written complaints on their behalf. Management's response was to give Henry "a little fatherly advice," and then ignore the complaints.[26]

Henry's language was only part of the problem. Pornographic pictures of women were daily fare in common work areas and private offices. One poster, displayed for seven years, showed a woman on her back with a golf ball balanced on one of her breasts as a man stood over her, swinging a club."[27]

That of the only woman in an upper-level position previously occupied solely by men, Rabidue's situation bore a strong resemblance to Cleo Kyriatzi's almost a decade earlier. Yet where the court in *Kyriatzi* found sexual harassment on the basis of fewer if not milder incidents, the Sixth Circuit affirmed the trial court's finding that Osceola's actions toward Rabidue failed to evince "an anti-female animus."[28]

In part, this conclusion can be explained by the selective perception employed by the majority: the *Rabidue* court interpreted a woman employee's efforts to stop a male employee from sexually harassing her as a dispute between individuals, demanding neutrality. In part, the holding emerged from subtle but important modifications the Sixth Circuit effected in proof requirements.[29]

A central factor was the vantage point from which the majority surveyed the Osceola workplace—that of the "reasonable person."[30] Although a virtual stranger to the law of employment discrimination, the "reasonable person" has had a long history in the law of torts, first appearing as "the man of ordinary prudence" in an 1837 negligence case.[31] Prosser explained that the reasonable person is "the personification of a community ideal of reasonable behavior," the exemplar of the status quo.[32] Thus the perspective of the reasonable person is the prevailing point of view, that of the group with the social power to impose its point of view on others. Judge Keith explained the consequences of the majority's adoption of this standard: ". . . the defendants as well as the courts are permitted to sustain ingrained notions of reasonable behavior fashioned by the offenders, in this case, men."[33]

Also imported from tort law is the legal theory bolstering the majority's implicit conclusion: a woman assumes the risk of working in an anti-female environment.[34] Although assumption of risk was once used by employers defending themselves in actions brought by employees injured on the job, a statute passed by Congress in 1939 abolished this use of the defense, largely because it left workers seeking recovery for workplace injuries hopelessly disadvantaged.[35] Its introduction by the *Rabidue* majority into the law of employment discrimination was a throwback to an era in which employees were denied legal protection. Simply put, it gave employers whose workplaces have traditionally been hostile to women license to keep them that way.

The *Rabidue* majority reached even farther afield—to criminal obscenity law—for the doctrinal basis of its argument that pornographic portrayals of women are lawful in the workplace when they are acceptable to community standards. This is the essence of the "contemporary community standards" provision of the famous *Miller* test for obscenity.[36] The illogic of this approach becomes apparent when one tries to imagine a court invalidating a sexual harassment claim because it is not uncommon for men in a particular community to grab at the bodies of women who venture outside unescorted. The fact that sexual harassment is inflicted on women outside the workplace does not diminish the harm to women subjected to it within. Nor should it shield employers who tolerate it from liability.

In *Rabidue*, the majority reached an extraordinary conclusion: sexual denigration in society justifies sexual denigration at work. The court cited no caselaw for this proposition, perhaps because it would have been hard pressed to find any within the last few decades. But the notion that traditional patterns of prejudice can justify prejudice in the present is not entirely foreign to our legal system. In upholding a Louisiana statute requiring segregated railroad cars, the Supreme Court concluded in 1896 that the law was reasonable because the practice it mandated conformed to "the established usages, customs, and traditions of the people.[37] The decision of the Sixth Circuit in *Rabidue* has precedent, but the legal tradition in which it stands runs counter to over thirty years of civil rights advances.

The First Amendment and Sexual Harassment through Pornography

Although the Supreme Court has never directly addressed the question of whether the First Amendment shields an employer from liability for "expressive" workplace conduct that sexually harasses female employees, the Court's analysis in *Meritor* v. *Vinson* suggests that it does not.[38] There the Court approvingly quotes Equal Employment Opportunity Commission guidelines describing conduct actionable under Title VII: it includes "*requests* for sexual favors, and *verbal conduct* of a sexual nature*,*" i.e., speech (emphasis added).[39] The Court goes on to cite and discuss numerous judicial decisions holding that "discriminatory intimidation, ridicule, and insult" carried out through words, pictures, or other forms of expressive conduct are actionable under Title VII.[40] In particular, the Court points to *Compston* v. *Borden*, in which a federal district court held that repeated anti-Semitic verbal slurs constituted illegal discrimination on the basis of religion;[41] *Katz* v. *Dole,* in which the Fourth Circuit held that sexual slurs and insults violated a female air traffic controller's rights under Title VII;[42] and *Zabkowicz* v. *West Bend*, the case mentioned above in which a federal district court held that pornographic drawings of the plaintiff, slurs, and sexually insulting gestures were illegal sexual harassment within the meaning of Title VII.[43]

The balancing of First Amendment interests against sex equality implicit in *Meritor* v. *Vinson* is explicit in two earlier Supreme Court decisions—*Roberts* v. *United States Jaycees* and *Pittsburgh Press Company* v. *Pittsburgh Commission on Human Relations.*[44] Both cases involved First Amendment challenges to state or local statutes prohibiting sex discrimination, and in both the government's interest in sex equality tipped the scales.

In *Roberts*, the Court weighed the right of the Jaycees to associate for expressive purposes in an organization that enfranchised only males against Minnesota's interest in eradicating sex discrimination against its female citizens. It concluded that sex equality was a compelling state interest that outweighed the First Amendment rights of the Jaycees.

The Court performed a similar balancing test in *Pittsburgh Press*, where it upheld as constitutional a city human rights ordinance that prohibited classified employment ads categorized according to sex. While acknowledging that the press is entitled to vigorous First Amendment protection, the Court concluded that even the special status the press enjoys does not immunize it from restrictions on commercial speech that facilitates sex discrimination in employment. In effect, the Court in *Pittsburgh Press* upheld a content-based restriction that not only prohibited employers from placing employment ads classified according to gender, but banned newspapers from using phrases like "Jobs—Male Interest" and "Jobs—Female Interest." Central to its determination were the facts that the speech at issue was low-value—"commercial speech"—and that the ordinance forbidding sex-based classified advertising was passed to further the goal of eliminating sex discrimination in employment, not for the purpose of muzzling or curbing the press.[45]

Pittsburgh Press suggests how the Court would balance speech and equality interests in a Title VII sexual harassment action against workplace pornography. Like classified ads, pornographic materials are likely to be considered low-value speech, falling within one or more categories of expression the Court has determined to have a lesser degree of constitutional protection. Much pornographic material is sexually explicit, a category accorded reduced First Amendment protection in *Young* v. *American Mini-Theaters*,[46] and some pornography meets the definition of obscenity set out by the Court in *Miller* v. *California*, making it entitled to no First Amendment protection at all.[47] Workplace pornographic displays are often commercial advertisements—calendars or posters in which scantily clad or nude models are used to promote products used in the workplace or in subcontractors' businesses. In *Central Hudson Gas* v. *Public Service Commission*, the Court held that restrictions on commercial speech are constitutional if they directly advance a substantial government interest and are "no more extensive than necessary" to serve that interest.[48] The state's interest in sex equality is not merely a substantial, but a compelling interest, according to *Roberts*, and prohibitions on pornographic workplace displays are likely to be interpreted as directly advancing that interest.

Offensive speech foisted on unwilling recipients has also been held to be low-value expression, unworthy of full First Amendment protection. In *FCC* v. *Pacifica*, the Court upheld the constitutionality of a letter of sanction sent by the Federal Communications Commission to WBAI radio for airing a comedy routine entitled "Seven Dirty Words."[49] The FCC was acting on a complaint made by a man who had been driving in his automobile with his young son when the routine was broadcast over his car radio. The Court held that because the WBAI broadcast could be assaultive to an unwarned and captive audience, it was subject to the regulatory powers of the state. The Court explicitly rejected the notion that the radio listener's option to turn off the program was adequate protection from offensive broadcasts: "To say that one may avoid further offense by turning off the radio . . . is like saying that the remedy for an assault is to run away after the first blow."[50]

Even more than the listeners of a radio station, women who work for employers who condone pornography in the workplace are an unwarned and captive audience, never knowing when or where they will encounter sexually denigrating materials, forced to endure sporadic visual assaults by the necessity of earning a living. If being subjected to offensive language in radio broadcasts is an invasion of the privacy of a driver in his car, surely being required to work in an environment with pictures of women stripped and put on sexual display is an invasion of the privacy of a woman worker.

In *Pittsburgh Press* the Court did not merely hold that the gender-based classified ads were entitled to reduced protection under the First Amendment because they were low-value commercial speech; they were not entitled to *any* First Amendment protection because they facilitated an activity illegal under Pittsburgh's Human Rights Act—sex discrimination in employment. Classified ads specifying that some jobs are suitable to men while other lower paying, less prestigious jobs are appropriate to women do not simply advocate sex discrimination—they effectuate it by actively discouraging women from pursuing job opportunities available to men.

The parallels between sex-based employment ads and sex-based workplace displays are striking. Pornography in the workplace does not simply advocate the sexual subordination of the women who work there; it intensifies the existing inequality between them and their male coworkers by graphically demonstrating who women are in the eyes of their male bosses and coworkers.[51] Pornography in the workplace does not simply encourage sexual assaults of women workers, although considerable research suggests that it does; it assaults women as actively as hostile verbal slurs or contemptuous, obscene gestures do.[52] Under this analysis, visible pornography in the workplace *is* the sexual harassment of the women who work there, and, when it is sufficiently pervasive or assaultive to meet the legal requirements for sexual harassment prohibited by Title VII, the use of pornography *is* illegal sex discrimination in the workplace, no more entitled to First Amendment protection than the discriminatory ads in *Pittsburgh Press*.

Pornography, Stereotyping, and Workplace Segregation

Employees may once have been able to engage with impunity in the type of conduct that unquestioningly allowed women to be treated as sex objects. But this is no longer the case.
                                                                —*Sage* v. *EEOC*

Pornography stereotypes women. Whether it is a calendar that shows a smiling topless model in a cheesecake pose, a page from a "men's entertainment" magazine that depicts a spread-eagled model inviting penetration, or a film of sexualized scenes of women being tortured and raped, the underlying message is the same: women are not self-determining human beings, the equals of men, but instead are sexual objects who are, by their very nature, unconditionally available for any sexual treatment men choose to impose on them. While most stereotypes of women in popular culture are demeaning, pornographic stereotypes are particularly damaging to women's status because they elicit a response that is not only hostile to women, but sexually pleasurable to men. Pornography eroticizes women's inequality. The result is that many men have simultaneously a superiority stake in pornographic stereotypes of women and a sexual stake as well. This combination exerts considerable influence over many men's perceptions of and thus, inevitably, treatment of women.

Like other forms of sexual harassment, pornographic stereotypes "convey the message that a woman is a sexual object before she is a contributing worker."[53] They shake the woman's confidence in her ability to perform her job, as they diminish her in the eyes of her male superiors and coworkers. They attack a fundamental principle underlying well over a decade of sex-discrimination litigation under Title VII: women workers are individuals entitled to equality on the job. If women are just sexual playthings for men—the premise of pornography—then equal employment for women is a sham; the only role for women in the workplace is to sexually service the men who work there. Nadine Taub contends that sexual demands and allusions—especially the presentation of women as sexually available—"functions to keep women in their place":

> That allusions to sexual availability have an especially pejorative meaning for women is . . . apparent from our language. An examination of epithets relating to females indicates that they are primarily references to women in solely sexual terms, i.e., as the objects of sexual desire. . . . it is clear that references to sexuality—[even] without explicit demands attached—are part of an arsenal of weapons that serves to exclude women from a male domain.[54]

When heightened job visibility—which comes with a woman worker's promotion or her movement into a traditionally male labor force—exacts a toll of sexual humiliation and abuse, a woman may decide that the increase in salary and status outside the workplace is not worth the psychological and physical price she pays for denigration within it.

For the moment, however, many women workers—especially those in the forefront of employment advances for women—seem determined to stand and fight. Most claims of sexual harassment through pornography have been brought by women in nontraditional jobs, a high percentage of whom have been the first or among the first women hired for jobs previously held only by men. Ramona Arnold was the first woman police officer hired by the Seminole, Oklahoma Police Department. Lois Robinson was one of half-a-dozen female skilled craftsworkers working among hundreds of men.

Why are claims for sexual harassment through pornography brought most often by women in jobs once held exclusively by men? Perhaps women who enter traditionally male-only fields are especially independent and assertive, imbued with the confidence and courage necessary to defy sex-role stereotypes. It is also probable that women assume nontraditional jobs not with the expectation of humiliation and abuse as the *Rabidue* majority suggests, but in the hope of achieving social and economic equality. When the very stereotypes they rejected in seeking their jobs are inflicted on them in the workplace, they may react with exceptional dismay—and outrage. Women who pursue jobs once open exclusively to men may be less likely than other women to passively submit to inequality once they achieve their employment goal.

Another explanation is that women in nontraditional jobs are more likely to be exposed to pornography in the workplace. This would account for Suzanne Carothers and Peggy Crull's observation that, whereas women in traditional jobs are usually subjected to quid pro quo sexual harassment, women in nontraditional jobs are most often harassed by "sexually demeaning work environment[s] manifested by slurs and public displays of derogatory images of women."[55] Carothers and Crull see sexual harassment in traditionally female jobs partly as an extension of long-established sex roles and partly as a function of the power differential between men and women in these job environments. By contrast, they argue, sexual harassment directed against women in nontraditional jobs "appears to be a form of retaliation against the women for invading a male sphere and threatening male economic and social status."[56] This difference should not obscure that pornography is used to harass women in both settings.

When pornography does appear in sex-role traditional workplaces, it is likely to mirror its use in sex-role traditional domestic relationships, where it is often enjoyed by the man in secret and made known to the woman only when he decides to initiate a sexual relationship with her—at which point it becomes part of the initiation process.[57] The sexual harassment of Mechelle Vinson, whose harasser kept a stack of pornographic magazines hidden in his office and used them as a prelude to his assaults on her, fits this pattern.[58] Sandra Bundy's harasser worked in the same way, except that he kept the pornographic books he enjoyed describing to her at home.[59] It is perhaps significant that one of the few sexual harassment cases involving pornography without a companion hostile environment claim—*Boyd* v. *Hayes Living Center*—was brought by a woman worker in a sex-role traditional job.[60] When pornography is used to sexually harass women in traditionally female jobs, it seems to serve more as a blueprint for the harassment than as a vehicle for it. Accordingly, it may never surface in the litigation, and, when it does, it is likely to appear as a background fact, a seemingly insignificant part of the pattern of abuse.

If, as Carothers and Crull suggest, the sexual harassment of women in sex-role traditional jobs is modeled after male sexual prerogative in the home,[61] the sexual harassment of women in nontraditional jobs may also be founded on an equally time-honored, equally sexist model: male sexual prerogative in the brothel. Harassment on the brothel model would be largely created out of sexist perceptions of women as sexual chattels, developed partly through interaction with prostitutes and partly through exposure to pornographic stereotypes—possibly the sole representations of women in the workplace before Title VII and the advent of flesh-and-blood women at male-only worksites.

If there is any arena in which contemporary women have invested their dreams of social and political equality, it is the workplace. Rightly or wrongly, many have given up on the domestic front, steeped as it is in centuries of male domination and walled protectively against any challenges to that dominance by the legal doctrine of privacy. The workplace outside the home beckoned as a promising arena for social change. It was new territory for women and offered not only social and material rewards, but the economic independence that would enable women, for the first time, to enter into intimate relationships not out of the necessity for economic survival, but by choice. It offered an end to the socially sanctioned prostitution that has long been women's condition. It made autonomy for women a real-life possibility instead of a hollow feminist slogan.

Pornography destroys the possibilities of the workplace as a means to women's self-determination and social equality by transporting into it the valuation of women as inferior creatures that exist to sexually serve men. Fortunately, decisional law that would force women to endure pornographic stereotypes as a condition of employment and immunize employers that condone pornography from liability is as yet a minority trend.

For women, Title VII may not be the ultimate solution to social and political equality, but it is still a rare and valuable legal wedge. Empowering women to fight pornographic stereotypes as sex discrimination in employment under Title VII increases the pressure on recalcitrant employers and brings closer the day when women's dreams of workplace equality will be realized.

WHERE RACE AND GENDER MEET
Racism, Hate Crimes, and Pornography

Helen Zia

In February 1984, a seven-months'-pregnant Asian-American woman was pushed under a New York subway train by a man who "had a phobia of Asian women." Why was this crime investigated as a murder and not, in addition, as a hate crime? Helen Zia contends that patterns of racism in rape, battery, assault, and other crimes against women are virtually ignored by law enforcement officials and argues that they should be encouraged to prosecute these as hate crimes at the federal, state, and local levels.

■

There is a specific area where racism, hate crimes, and pornography intersect, and where current civil rights law fails: racially motivated, gender-based crimes against women of color. This area of bias-motivated sexual assault has been called "ethnorape"; I refer to it as "hate rape."

I started looking into this issue after years of organizing against hate killings of Asian Americans. After a while, I noticed that all the cases I could name concerned male victims. I wondered why. Perhaps it was because Asian-American men came into contact with perpetrator types more often or because they are more hated and therefore more often attacked by racists. But the subordination and vulnerability of Asian-American women, who are thought to be sexually exotic, subservient, and passive, argued against that interpretation. So where were the Asian-American women hate-crime victims?

Once I began looking, I found them, in random news clippings, in footnotes in books, through word of mouth. Let me share with you some examples I unearthed of bias-motivated attacks and sexual assaults:

• In February 1984, Ly Yung Cheung, a nineteen-year-old Chinese woman who was seven months pregnant, was pushed in front of a New York City subway train and decapitated. Her attacker, a white male high school teacher, claimed he suffered from "a phobia of Asian people" and was overcome with the urge to kill this woman. He successfully pleaded insanity. If this case had been investigated as a hate crime, there might have been more information about his so-called phobia and whether it was part of a pattern of racism. But it was not.

• On December 7, 1984, fifty-two-year-old Japanese-American Helen Fukui disappeared in Denver, Colorado. Her decomposed body was found weeks later. Her disappearance on Pearl Harbor Day, when anti-Asian speech and incidents increase dramatically, was considered significant in the community. But the case was not investigated as a hate crime and no suspects were ever apprehended.

• In 1985 an eight-year-old Chinese girl named Jean Har-Kaw Fewel was found raped and lynched in Chapel Hill, North Carolina—two months after *Penthouse* featured pictures of Asian women in various poses of bondage and torture, including hanging bound from trees. Were epithets or pornography used during the attack? No one knows—her rape and killing were not investigated as a possible hate crime.

• Recently a serial rapist was convicted of kidnapping and raping a Japanese exchange student in Oregon. He had also assaulted a Japanese woman in Arizona, and another in San Francisco. He was sentenced to jail for these crimes, but they were never pursued as hate crimes, even though California has a hate statute. Was hate speech or race-specific pornography used? No one knows.

• At Ohio State University, two Asian women were gang raped by fraternity brothers in two separate incidents. One of the rapes was part of a racially targeted game called the "Ethnic Sex Challenge," in which the fraternity men followed an ethnic checklist indicating what kind of women to gang rape. Because the women feared humiliation and ostracism by their communities, neither reported the rapes. However, campus officials found out about the attacks, but did not take them up as hate crimes, or as anything else.

All of these incidents could have been investigated and prosecuted either as state hate crimes or as federal civil rights cases. But they were not. To have done so would have required one of two things: awareness and interest on the part of police investigators and prosecutors—who generally have a poor track record on race and gender issues—or awareness and support for civil rights charges by the Asian-American community—which is generally lacking on issues surrounding women, gender, sex, and sexual assault. The result is a double-silencing effect on the assaults and deaths of these women, who become invisible because of their gender and their race.

Although my research centers on hate crimes and Asian women, this silence and this failure to provide equal protection have parallels in all of the other classes protected by federal civil rights and hate statutes. That is, all other communities of color have a similar prosecution rate for hate crimes against the women in their communities—namely, zero. This dismal record is almost as bad in lesbian and gay antiviolence projects: the vast preponderance of hate crimes reported, tracked, and prosecuted concern gay men—very few concern lesbians. So where are all the women?

The answer to this question lies in the way our justice system was designed, and the way women are mere shadows in the existing civil rights framework. But in spite of this history, federal and state law do offer legal avenues for women to be heard. Federal civil rights prosecutions, for example, can be excellent platforms for high-visibility community education on the harmful impact of hate speech and behavior. When on June 19, 1982, two white auto workers in Detroit screamed racial epithets at Chinese-American Vincent Chin and said, "It's because of you motherfuckers that we're out of work," a public furor followed, raising the level of national discourse on what constitutes racism toward Asian Americans. Constitutional law professors, and members of the American Civil Liberties Union and the National Lawyers Guild had acted as if Asian Americans were not covered by civil rights law. Asian Americans emphatically corrected that misconception.

Hate crimes remedies can be used to force the criminal justice bureaucracy to adopt new attitudes. Patrick Purdy went to an elementary school in Stockton, California, in which 85 percent of the students came from Southeast Asia. When he selected that school as the place to open fire with his automatic weapon and killed five eight-year-olds and wounded thirty other children, the police and the media did not think it was a bias-motivated crime. Their denial reminds me of the response by the Montreal officials to the anti-feminist killings of fourteen women students there. But an outraged Asian-American community forced a state investigation into the Purdy incident and uncovered hate literature in the killer's effects. As a result, the community was validated, and, in addition, the criminal justice system and the media acquired a new level of understanding.

Imagine if a federal civil rights investigation had been launched in the case of the African-American student at St. John's University who was raped and sodomized by white members of the school lacrosse team, who were later acquitted. Investigators could have raised issues of those white men's attitudes toward the victim as a black woman, found out whether hate speech or race-specific pornography was present, investigated the overall racial climate on campus, and brought all of the silenced aspects of the incident to the public eye. Community discourse could have been raised to a higher level.

Making these investigations happen will not be an easy road. Hate crimes efforts are generally expended on blatant cases, with high community consensus, not ones that bring up hard issues like gender-based violence. Yet these intersections of race and gender hatred are the very issues we must give voice to.

There is a serious difficulty with pushing for use of federal and state hate remedies. Some state statutes have been used against men of color: specifically, on behalf of white rape victims against African-American men. We know that the system, if left unchecked, will try to use antihate laws to enforce unequal justice. On the other hand, state hate statutes could be used to prosecute men of color who are believed to have assaulted women of color of another race—interminority assaults are increasing. Also, if violence against women generally were made into a hate crime, women of color could seek prosecutions against men in their own community for their gender-based violence—even if this would make it harder to win the support of men in communities of color, and of women in those communities who would not want to be accused of dividing the community.

But at least within the Asian-American antiviolence community, this discourse is taking place now. Asian-American feminists in San Francisco have prepared a critique of the Asian movement against hate crimes and the men of that movement are listening. Other communities of color should also examine the nexus between race and gender for women of color, and by extension, for all women.

The legal system must expand the boundaries of existing law to include the most invisible women. There are hundreds of cases involving women of color waiting to be filed. Activists in the violence-against-women movement must reexamine current views on gender-based violence. Not all sexual assaults are the same. Racism in a sexual assault adds another dimension to the pain and harm inflicted. By taking women of color out of the legal shadows, out of invisibility, all women make gains toward full human dignity and human rights.

HOMAGE TO HERITAGE
Native Americans Say No to Racial Stereotyping

Ben Nighthorse Campbell

In July 1993, Senator Ben Nighthorse Campbell introduced a bill to amend the District of Columbia Stadium Act of 1957, which authorized the construction, maintenance, and operation of a stadium in the District of Columbia. The bill would have prohibited the use of the new stadium by any person or organization exploiting any racial or ethnic group or using nomenclature that included a reference to real or alleged physical characteristics of Native Americans or any other group of human beings. The bill caused quite a stir and called attention to the continuing use of degrading depictions and descriptions of Native Americans in this country. Here Campbell explains why he introduced his bill.

■

From my Indian elders, I learned the stories of our difficult Native American history—how our way of life was uprooted, our culture and religion almost completely destroyed. I learned about our defeats in battle over land and about how our numbers dwindled drastically through disease brought to our native land by European settlers. Five hundred years ago, the Native American population numbered in the millions; now we consist of less than 1 percent of the U.S. population. Banished to small, scattered reservations of hardened wasteland, American Indians are fighting to save the last vestiges of our pride and heritage.

Even today, it is not easy growing up Indian. Young American Indians have to fight battles against alcoholism, chronic unemployment, suicide, and poverty. In the midst of lives of hardship, they must also contend with the feeling among too many people that they are uneducated and uneducable savages.

To survive and prosper, young American Indians need respect and self-esteem. I tell them that they should look to our proud heritage for strength and inspiration, as I have. But I can't tell those same boys and girls to look with pride on the name of Washington's professional football team—despite what team officials say.

With the football season upon us, Redskins owner Jack Kent Cooke and his supporters will again be heard insisting that the use of the name "Redskins" is a tribute to the strength and courage of American Indians. But I've never heard of Cooke or his supporters making such a statement to an Indian in a face-to-face meeting. Indeed, Cooke has not yet accepted offers from Native American communities to discuss how the recipients of his intended compliment feel about it.

To me and, I think, to most other people with Native American ancestors, "redskins" is a term that purports to describe the color of American Indian skin, but says nothing about character or courage. It certainly does not feel like an homage to my heritage.

That's why I recently introduced a bill in the U.S. Senate about the federally owned land in Northeast Washington where Cooke hopes to build a new football stadium. The bill would prohibit leasing of the land to any person or organization that uses derogatory or offensive ethnic or racial stereotypes in their names or slogans. I could support the construction of the new stadium on one condition—that the federal contract turning over use of the land contain provisions urging the name change. The site north of Robert F. Kennedy Stadium that has been set aside for the proposed stadium is owned by all Americans. If the Redskins organization chooses not to respect that fact, then it cannot expect to be granted the privilege of using federally owned land.

There is good precedent for sticking to this principle. In 1961, the federal government, in the person of Secretary of the Interior Stewart Udall and several members of Congress, threatened to prohibit the use of federal land as the site of a new stadium unless the owner, George Preston Marshall, hired black players. Marshall was the last owner in the National Football League to do so. Only the threat of imminent federal action persuaded Marshall to abandon his bigoted hiring practices. I'm not alone in thinking that pressure on the Washington football organization must be increased. Washington, D.C., mayor Sharon Pratt Kelly recently said in response to a caller's question on WPFW-FM, "As an African-American, I know how I'd feel if I heard something equivalent [to redskins]. And I think that we, as people who have been traditionally disrespected, have an obligation to be up there in the front lines to support others who have been disrespected."

In endorsing my legislation, D.C. city councilman Bill Lightfoot noted, "The District of Columbia is not only a multicultural community, but it is the nation's capital and, as such, we should set the example by not being passive participants in perpetuating racial or cultural stereotypes."

As a Coloradan and a Denver Broncos fan, I can understand how important the Washington team is to its fans and to the community. To say that the name "Redskins" is an anachronism that should be changed is no slight to the players or the fans. Neither those players nor those fans would approve of team names such as Spics, Niggers, Greasers, Spearchuckers, Wops, Kikes, Nips, Krauts, or Pollacks. Just as the use of those terms makes many Americans feel exploited and degraded, so the use of the name "Redskins" is offensive and uncivil to Native Americans.

My intent is not to change every single team name that refers to Indian culture. Many Native Americans, myself included, do not have a problem with the use of specific Indian tribal names, if the affected tribe agrees. There is a world of difference between calling a team the "Seminoles" and calling a team the "Redskins" (though there are teams that use appropriate Indian names but employ offensive logos or caricatures). The team logo of the Washington football team is not offensive, but the name is. Our guide should be common decency.

The debate over this issue reminds us that there is still much racial insensitivity in our country. More than a few of my constituents have questioned my decision to spend time on this issue. My response is old-fashioned: just as cutting the budget deficit, creating jobs, and reforming our health care system are important to our country's well-being, so is fighting mindless bigotry and racism.

GIRLS SHOULD BRING LAWSUITS EVERYWHERE . . . NOTHING WILL BE CORRUPTED
Pornography as Speech and Product

Marianne Wesson

Legislative solutions to hate speech and pornography—including Andrea Dworkin and Catharine MacKinnon's famous 1984 ordinance—have faced a rough road. The model antipornography ordinance has been proposed in a half dozen cities and occasionally approved by voters. But it has not been adopted anywhere because of mayors' vetoes or court injunctions. Thus, while MacKinnon and Dworkin have succeeded in reframing the issue of pornography and calling attention to its harm, they have not been able to secure a remedy for it. Marianne Wesson argues that even without enacting new legislation, women harmed by pornography can use tort law to bring civil actions against the producers and distributors of pornography.

■

At the beginning of his recent anticensorship memoir, *Girls Lean Back Everywhere: The Law of Obscenity and the Assault on Genius*, obscenity lawyer Edward de Grazia quotes Jane Heap* as saying, "Girls lean back everywhere, showing lace and silk stockings; wear low-cut sleeveless blouses, breathless bathing suits; men think thoughts and have emotions about these things everywhere and no one is corrupted."[1] He then proceeds to castigate—among others—those whom he calls "anti-porn feminists."[2] The Heap quotation is singularly infuriating, for it suggests that the romantic pictures conjured up— girls reclining in lacy underwear, beautiful women exposing their bare arms

---

* Jane Heap was a feminist and lesbian who ran the Washington Square Bookstore and coedited the literary magazine *The Little Review*, beginning in 1916. She was arrested along with her lover in 1920 and convicted of publishing obscenity after printing an excerpt from James Joyce's *Ulysses.*—Eds.

to the sun—are characteristic of the materials that antipornography feminists seek to suppress. Furthermore, it hints that those who fight against pornography are paranoid in their belief that such sights will "corrupt" the viewer. I suggest that this ascription of paranoia to the antipornography activist may be a bit of projection: it is, after all, persons in de Grazia's camp who often suggest that any discouragement of the pornography industry will lead to book-burning, empty libraries, and thought control. I offer here a practical proposal for antipornography activists, to wit: girls should bring lawsuits everywhere. I will argue that if my proposal is pursued, nothing that a civil libertarian holds dear will be harmed.

Proposals to permit victims of pornography to recover damages from those who create or distribute it are among the most defensible and conservative items on the agenda of antipornography activism, yet they are still controversial. The reasons why these proposals still stir opposition lie partly in history, partly in the politics of the women's movement, partly in the Supreme Court's confused and confusing treatment of First Amendment issues, and partly in the efforts of the pornography industry to protect its privileges and profits. The intersection of these factors has hindered serious feminist consideration of strategies that might accomplish many of the goals of the antipornography movement. The measure I propose to fill this gap is quite simple. It requires no debate, no lobbying, no legislation. All it requires is the right client and the right lawyer. The right client will be a person (most likely a woman) who has been harmed by an identifiable work of pornography. The right lawyer will be a person (again, most likely a woman) with the resources to bring a lawsuit against the maker or distributors of the material and the skill to prove the harm, show its foreseeability, identify its causal link to the pornography, and overcome the First Amendment objections that are certain to arise.

A brief rehearsal of familiar events may provide some context for this proposal. Pioneering efforts to create remedies for victims of pornography defined both "pornography" and "victim" in an expansive way. In particular, the MacKinnon-Dworkin antipornography civil rights ordinance and its progeny included in their definition of pornography "women . . . presented in scenarios of degradation, humiliation, injury, torture, shown as filthy or inferior, bleeding, bruised, or hurt in a context that makes these conditions sexual . . . presented dehumanized as sexual objects, things, or commodities . . . [or] presented in postures or positions of sexual submission, servility, or display," if these depictions constitute the "graphic sexually explicit subordination of women."[3] The ordinances also provided for enforcement actions to be brought by "[a]ny woman . . . acting against the subordination of women." If a woman could prove that certain material met the ordinance's definition of pornography, an injunction against the further sale or dissemination of the material could be obtained.

I admire and salute the efforts of MacKinnon, Dworkin, and others who worked tirelessly on the campaign for the ordinances, but their success came indirectly, more through reframing the issue of pornography, creating a convincing language for talking about it, and calling attention to its harm, than by securing a remedy. Indeed, the MacKinnon-Dworkin ordinance was held to be unconstitutional under the First Amendment.[4]

Moreover, even some self-described feminists opposed the ordinances, arguing that they could be used to censor such mainstream speech as the Lina Wertmuller film *Swept Away* and many images of women used in common advertising. Canadian novelist Margaret Atwood published *The Handmaid's Tale*, a bleak dystopian novel in which a movement aimed at suppressing pornography and violence against women led eventually to the governmental appropriation of the bodies of women for reproductive purposes and the enforcement of a harshly puritanical code of sexual conduct, a code shaped and enforced by women, but serving the needs of a totalitarian patriarchy. It was difficult not to read this powerful book as, among other things, a critique of the antipornography movement.

Some proponents of the ordinances berated their opponents for disloyalty to their gender. Scientists on whose work many had relied to support the claim that pornography's existence harms women complained that they had been misrepresented; at best, they argued, their work shows a link between exposure to "violent" pornography and attitudinal changes that might lead to violent behavior toward women.[5] In general, the atmosphere in which the pornography question was discussed became threatening and divisive. I suspect that many women who consider themselves feminists were relieved when the Supreme Court chilled discussion of the MacKinnon-Dworkin approach by summarily affirming the Seventh Circuit's ruling that the Indianapolis version of their ordinance was unconstitutional.

Throughout all of this history, those who make and profit from pornography maintained a campaign to preserve their privilege to publish and sell materials without legal interference. The industry, a shadowy and daunting network, relied on "moderate" organizations like the ACLU and the Playboy Foundation to continue to portray antipornography feminism as a threat to everyone's freedom of speech. Feminists who dedicated themselves to contesting pornography's freedom to harm were labeled puritanical, moralistic, antisex, antilove, fascist reactionaries. When a well-known constitutional law scholar expressed the view that the model ordinance was "not obviously unconstitutional," an equally well-known columnist suggested that the scholar's highly regarded mind had "turn[ed] to mush." Authors of such feminist classics as *Our Bodies, Ourselves* opposed the passage of antipornography ordinances because they feared the laws would be used to censor their work. Mainstream booksellers and authors were persuaded to denounce any efforts to control either the magnitude of pornography production or its increasingly violent content.[6] Divided, exhausted, and confused, many feminists decided they would rather move on to other issues, of which there are, after all, many.

But others began considering and debating possible revisions to or variations on the MacKinnon-Dworkin ordinance, with an eye to finding a less sweeping alternative. One result of these discussions was the Pornography Victims Compensation Act, designed to "allow victims of sexual assault to sue distributors of obscene material or child pornography."[7] Introduced in 1991 by Senator Mitch McConnell of Kentucky, the bill was approved, in slightly different form, by the Judiciary Committee in 1992.[8] The bill has some virtues, and also some serious defects; nevertheless, most of its critics ignored both and based their opposition on likening the proposal to the MacKinnon-Dworkin ordinance. They took note of the vast differences between the two only to minimize them, and characterized the new law as a warmed-over version of a measure already declared unconstitutional. It was argued in editorial pages across the nation that the bill was dangerous; and with equal conviction that if passed, it would be completely ineffective. It was given the nickname "the Bundy Bill," and various critics seized on the suggestion conveyed by the nickname to argue that it would allow murderers and rapists to evade responsibility for their crimes by placing the blame on producers and distributors of pornography.

A Perhaps Excessively Modest Proposal

It is difficult to go far in discussing pornography without defining it. I define "pornography" as material that links the viewer's or reader's sexual gratification to the infliction of violence. Pornography is a depiction, in any medium, of violence directed against, or pain inflicted on, an unconsenting person or a child, for the purpose of anyone's real or apparent sexual arousal or gratification, of a kind that suggests endorsement or approval of such behavior and that is likely to promote or encourage similar behavior in those exposed to the depiction. I do not intend to suggest this definition as legislative language, as I do not believe that legislation is necessary to enable the litigation of victim-harm suits against pornographers. My definition is only a description of material that I think is vulnerable to civil sanctions; I do not mean for it to preclude the use of other definitions in other contexts.[9]

Having offered this definition, I propose that persons claiming to have been "proximately" harmed by a particular piece of pornography bring civil actions against the originators and distributors of the material. New legislation should not be necessary to enable such suits, as they are unexceptionable instances of personal liability litigation. It would be best if there were many such suits pending at any given time, if there were a virtual campaign of litigation that could spawn class actions, plaintiff's committees, the invocation of "complex rules," and other court-created management techniques. Techniques employed in other sorts of mass-tort litigation, such as epidemiological evidence and market-share liability, should be explored. First Amendment objections undoubtedly will be made to any such suit as soon as it is filed, but these objections can be answered. The following section suggests the form that the answer might take.

The R.A.V. Objection to Suits against Pornographers

Proponents of measures to deter and punish "hate speech" have often made common cause with proponents of measures to restrict pornography; some even see pornography as a subset of hate speech. The Supreme Court's recent decision in R.A.V. v. City of St. Paul was thus disquieting to both groups— in its particular disapproval of the St. Paul measure to be sure, but also in its suggestion that even speech "unprotected" by the First Amendment may not be penalized if it is sanctioned because of its "viewpoint," rather than its other features.

Since many of the measures proposed to penalize the creation and distribution of pornography are criticized for discriminating against pornography because of the "viewpoint" it espouses, it is important to understand certain nuances of the R.A.V. opinions. According to the majority, the St. Paul ordinance could not stand, even if it were successfully "narrowed" to encompass only the unprotected category of "fighting words." Its flaw was that, even so narrowed, it would punish only a subcategory of "fighting words": those that had their effect "on the basis of race, color, creed, religion, or gender." This aspect of the ordinance rendered it "unconstitutional in that it prohibits otherwise permitted speech solely on the basis of the subject the speech addresses."*

The concurring opinions in R.A.V. exposed many gaps in the majority's

---

* See Charles R. Lawrence III and Elena Kagan in this volume, pp. 114 and 202, for full discussions of the R.A.V. decision. —Eds.

reasoning—especially Justice Byron White's concurrence, which observed that the majority acknowledged the existence of an exception to the general prohibition of discrimination among subcategories of unprotected speech, an exception so large as to swallow completely the rule it announced. Justices Harry Blackmun and John Stevens, also concurring, suggested that the Court had announced a rule that had no application beyond the case before it. It may be, therefore, that antipornography efforts have nothing to fear from R.A.V. because its purported rule was dead on arrival—fashioned to have no effect beyond its accompanying judgment. But it would be dangerous to assume so, since, as others have pointed out, the recent tradition on the Court, especially among some of the justices concurring in R.A.V., is one of respect for stare decisis.[10]

There are other reasons—beyond those provided by the concurring justices—why the decision in R.A.V. poses no constitutional threat to civil actions for damages. R.A.V. concerned the imposition of a criminal sanction. By contrast, the most similar civil cases to have faced a First Amendment challenge are defamation actions by private plaintiffs (that is, people who are not public figures). In such cases, the First Amendment requires that the plaintiff prove some degree of fault in the media defendant, and some actual damage—but that is all.[11]

In connection with the implications of R.A.V., however, the most important feature of civil suits against pornographers is that they are just one of the many sorts of personal injury actions that can be brought under a jurisdiction's laws, requiring no specific statutory authorization. There is nothing "underinclusive," in the sense condemned by R.A.V., in the instituting or maintenance of such actions: they are not exclusive or limiting except in the trivial sense that any lawsuit is exclusive by claiming only what it claims and seeking only what it seeks.

Of course, the definition of pornography that I offer is exclusive, in the sense that it does not include all sorts of speech or even all sorts of harmful speech. But the definition is offered to satisfy, rather than to offend, First Amendment constraints: the requirement that there be a showing of fault on the part of the maker or distributor, and the requirement to define the type of damage that could foreseeably have been expected to flow from the pornographic material by its very nature. It excludes nothing. If another lawyer wishes to bring a different suit charging that his client has been proximately harmed by a violent but nonsexual film, a nonviolent advertisement for a weight-control program, or a classified ad soliciting the commission of a crime, nothing in what I propose prevents such suits. If there is something in the First Amendment to hinder them, that is the other lawyer's problem and not mine.

A First Amendment Defense of My Proposal

Apart from any complications posed by R.A.V., recognition and encouragement of victim actions against pornographers is consistent with the premises and aspirations of the First Amendment. Pornography is both speech and product. This double character has confounded the debate about the constitutionality of laws that would penalize the creation or dissemination of pornography. Those who emphasize the speech aspect point to the First Amendment and its prohibition against any law "abridging the freedom of speech." Those who find the product aspect more important have proposed that protection of the public justifies a ban on the production or distribution of dangerous products—of which, they argue, pornography is one. They argue that, in the absence of a ban, those who sell pornography, like those who profit from other commercial products, should be liable for the harms their product causes. Sometimes there seems to be little ground for compromise between these two views, but in fact they share a commitment to free speech.

Free-speech advocates often defend and elaborate the Constitution's protection of speech by reference to a concept borrowed from the world of products: the "marketplace of ideas."[12] According to this theory, the world of thought, analysis, emotion, and contemplation that is expressed by speech is best protected by fostering a "marketplace" in which all speech (and hence all expressible ideas, emotions, opinions, and the like) may be offered to the would-be recipient, who is free to listen or not, and to believe or not. Thus the discriminating listener will make choices based on the quality and persuasiveness of the marketplace's offerings, and in the end the better, truer, and more beautiful speech will survive. One who accepts this model will also accept another First Amendment cliché: that the cure for bad speech is more speech.[13] Law and economics analysts and public choice theorists employ the same metaphor, setting up the marketplace for speech as similar to the marketplace for other products.

There are, of course, many things wrong with this metaphor, most of which are obvious even from reading the rendition above. As feminists and others have pointed out, there are numerous ways in which the so-called "marketplace of ideas" does not at all resemble a marketplace, or resembles, at best, a very flawed one. One obstacle to the freedom of this marketplace is what economists call "barriers to entry": not everyone who would like her ideas to be heard can afford to buy time on network television. A.J. Liebling, speaking for an earlier era, observed that "[f]reedom of the press is guaranteed only to those who own one." Ross Perot is sufficient evidence, in this electronic age, of this remark's lasting relevance. The "marketplace" vision of governmental censorship as an interference with universal access to the channels of communication may be apt, but it ignores the censoring effect of illiteracy or poverty (or, to a lesser degree, anything less than affluence). Another related shortcoming of the marketplace model is that it does not account for the "silencing" effect of some speech: the speaker with the loudest amplifier may make it impossible for listeners to sample the words or sounds of alternative speakers, or one speaker may capture the market by discouraging his listeners from listening to others. Some feminists have maintained that pornography has this silencing effect on the voices of women, especially when they wish to speak of sexuality and equality.

But even if the "marketplace of ideas" is a flawed concept, its flaws will be magnified if pornography is insulated from the discipline the marketplace imposes on other products. For example: if an automobile is poorly designed, and catches fire on impact, as did the Pinto, accident victims clearly have the right to sue the producers of the car for damages. In the same way, acceptance of the civil libertarian and utilitarian view of speech as a market entails not only tolerating, but affirmatively insisting on, the right of pornography's victims to sue its creators for damages when a causal link between the pornography and the damage is established. This proposition may be surprising, since civil libertarian groups and speakers have consistently opposed not only bans on producing or distributing pornography, but also the creation of any tort remedies for those who are harmed by it. They seem not to notice that the necessity of such remedies is implicit in the free marketplace theory of the First Amendment.

It is a fundamental feature of an efficient marketplace that it be free of externalities, where an externality is the imposition of some cost to a transaction on someone other than the parties. Air pollution is an externality to the transaction of producing, purchasing, and using an automobile, and a perfect market would require that the cost of preventing or cleaning up the pollution generated by an automobile be built into the transaction—whether by requiring that all vehicles have expensive antipollution equipment, imposing a tax on the sale of each car, or some other stratagem (such as taxing each gallon of gasoline sold or collecting tolls for the use of roads). In the absence of some accounting for the cost of pollution, the cost is borne by all who breathe (if no mitigating measures are taken) or all who pay general taxes (if measures are undertaken by the government); in addition, in the absence of their shouldering of pollution costs, manufacturers and sellers of vehicles have no economic incentive to minimize pollution, nor have purchasers any economic incentive to favor (or, certainly, to pay more for) vehicles that pollute less. Economic analysts agree virtually unanimously that a rational market must force producers of polluting vehicles to internalize the cost of the pollution their vehicles will produce—otherwise, air pollution and its harms will increase to the detriment of all, including those who have no interest in and derive no benefit from the transaction. Economic injustice will certainly result, and perhaps overall economic inefficiency, since it is possible that the overall cost of air pollution exceeds the marginal economic benefit gained from manufacturing and driving vehicles that create it (rather than vehicles that do not).

Thus, if the transaction that encompasses the creation, distribution, and consumption of pornography is one that creates a serious external harm, the logic of the marketplace dictates that the pornography industry should internalize the harm. A tax on pornography is neither feasible nor efficient, since arguments are certain to arise about whether or not particular items are "pornography" and different pornographic materials almost certainly differ in the harm they cause. But if outsiders to the transaction (that is, women and others who can show they have been harmed by pornography) can recover compensation for the harm the transaction imposes on them, those who profit from the transaction will bear the cost, and the harm will be internalized. Pornography will become more expensive to produce as those who traffic in it must set aside funds to pay for anticipated damage awards, or to purchase insurance. Those who do not take these precautions may be forced to go out of business if a large award consumes their operating capital. The price of pornography will rise, and it may consequently attract fewer customers. Its remaining creators may decide to stop disseminating it. This is not censorship—it is the market at work.

The Market at Work

Some readers may doubt that courts will ever be persuaded to treat speech like a product and subject it to the discipline of the market. But consider the recent case *Soldier of Fortune* v. *Braun*.[14] *Soldier of Fortune* is a magazine published in my hometown of Boulder, Colorado, and devoted to the cult of manly mercenary violence. In addition to articles about survivalism, weapons, and adventures in various world hot spots, the magazine at one time published classified advertising. In one of these ads Michael Savage advertised his willingness to accept work requiring "[b]odyguard, courier, and other special skills" (although he promised "[a]ll jobs considered"); in listing his qualifications he described himself as a "37 year old professional mercenary," a "Vietnam Veteran," and "[d]iscreet and very private."[15] Among those responding to the ad were Bruce Gastwirth and Horton Moore, who had failed in three previous attempts to murder Gastwirth's business partner Richard Braun and apparently had decided they needed professional assistance. Gastwirth and Moore enlisted Savage's help, and within three months of the day the ad first appeared in *Soldier of Fortune*, Braun was dead—murdered by a man named Doutre, apparently assisted by Savage. The attack also injured Braun's teenage son Michael.

Michael Braun and his brother filed a civil action against *Soldier of Fortune* seeking damages for the death of their father (under Georgia's wrongful death statute) and for the injuries inflicted on Michael. A federal jury awarded the Brauns two million dollars in compensatory damages on their wrongful death claim, and $375,000 in compensatory and ten million dollars in punitive damages for Michael Braun's personal injury claim.[16] On appeal, *Soldier of Fortune* argued that the First Amendment prohibits the imposition of damages (particularly such "crushing" damages) on publishers, but the Court of Appeals for the Eleventh Circuit rejected this argument, and the Supreme Court denied review. Distinguishing this case from an earlier one in which the Fifth Circuit had overturned a jury verdict on similar facts, the Court of Appeals noted that the Braun jury had found that the "ad in question contained a clearly identified unreasonable risk, that the offer in the ad is one to commit a serious violent crime." The court also rejected *Soldier of Fortune*'s argument that it could not be held responsible for independent acts of a third party. The court observed that Georgia law, like that in most American jurisdictions, allows for such liability if the acts were foreseeable: if the magazine could have foreseen that an ad for a mercenary could result in a death, then the magazine would be liable. The Supreme Court's refusal to review the outcome of *Soldier of Fortune* v. *Braun* suggests that violent pornography, too—to the extent that it implicitly but unmistakably advocates directing sexual violence at women—can be the subject of a civil suit for damages without violating the First Amendment.

It may be objected that the Braun suit is different from the sort of civil action advocated by antipornography feminists, because advertisements are "commercial speech" and hence deserve less First Amendment protection than speech that constitutes the product itself. And it is true that the Court of Appeals treated the *Soldier of Fortune* ad as "commercial speech" and noted that such speech has diminished First Amendment protection. But other courts have upheld damage awards for injuries caused by speech that was more in the nature of "the thing itself" than of an advertisement. Defamation of a private individual, for example, is actionable if it is false and the publisher is negligent about that fact.[17]

Or consider *Weirum* v. *RKO General, Inc.*, brought by the survivors of a man killed when his automobile was forced off a highway by a pair of cars.

The teenage drivers were listening to a radio broadcast that intermittently gave clues to the location of a disc jockey who was driving around the region, and they were attempting to locate the deejay in order to win a prize offered by the radio station. A jury found the radio station liable for the death of the deceased, and the California Supreme Court rejected the station's First Amendment argument as "clearly without merit," commenting that "[t]he First Amendment does not sanction the infliction of physical injury merely because achieved by word, rather than act." The broadcast was not an advertisement, yet those responsible were made to bear their share of liability for the harm caused as surely as those responsible for *Soldier of Fortune*'s ad.

Of course, in neither *Braun* nor *Weirum* were the defendants' words the immediate cause of the plaintiffs' injuries. The words did not fly out and strike the victims, killing or injuring them. Rather, they encouraged or enabled others to inflict the death or injury, whether intentionally or accidentally. This pattern is common in product liability and negligence suits, where other necessary factors may come into play between the creation of the risk and the victims' injuries: a person is attacked by an individual under the influence of a dangerous prescription drug; a driver is injured when a dump truck with defectively designed brakes, driven carelessly, collides with her car. It has never been the rule that the acts of a third party will inevitably cut off the liability of the person who created the risk (although the other actors may share the liability and may have to pay part of the judgment). To impose liability on the original source of the risk, a court must simply find that she or he should have foreseen the likelihood of that risk.

Notice that no special legislation concerning liability for classified advertising or radio promotional contests was necessary for the results in *Braun* or *Weirum*. The outcomes of these cases merely represented the application of principles governing other product liability or negligence lawsuits. These suits are approved by most economic analysts of the law, because they contribute to the formation or maintenance of efficient markets by making producers internalize the costs of their products' harm. Those who persist in committing harmful speech acts may eventually find it difficult to stay in business, but they are not compelled by any governmental agent to stop running classified ads placed by ambitious thugs or broadcasting invitations to drive like maniacs.[18] While the First Amendment does not permit that kind of regulation, it has much less to say about tort law.

It is true that there are cases in which the First Amendment has shielded the creators or publishers of speech that would have generated tort liability, but for that shield. In *Olivia N. v. National Broadcasting Company*, for example, the plaintiff was deprived of any recovery when the defendant's broadcast of the rape of a girl with a "plumber's helper" was found to have induced a group of boys to rape the plaintiff using the same method. The California Court of Appeals found that the First Amendment required this result, and the Supreme Court denied review. In *Herceg v. Hustler Magazine, Inc.*, no recovery was allowed when a teenage boy hanged himself, apparently while seeking to achieve an autoerotic experience described in detail (together with the method of achieving it and a "warning" that the reader should not attempt the practice) in the defendant's publication. The Court of Appeals reversed a judgment of $169,000 in favor of the boy's mother on First Amendment grounds, and the Supreme Court again denied review. In *Eimann v. Soldier of Fortune*, the Fifth Circuit overturned a multimillion-dollar verdict in favor of survivors of a murder victim whose husband had hired an assassin from the classified ads of *Soldier of Fortune* magazine, and the Supreme Court refused review. The lawyer who would represent the pornography victim must contend with these precedents, but they do not pose insuperable obstacles.

The *Olivia N.* court suggested the outcome might have been different if the program's depiction of the assault were an "incitement" to commit a similar crime. Although the court hinted that proof of "incitement" would require a showing that the defendant intended to encourage the behavior, an alternative interpretation of that term would encompass any implication that the broadcaster, writer, or filmmaker approves of the conduct depicted. Under this interpretation, the sort of suit I have suggested would be consistent with the First Amendment, since my definition of pornography includes only those materials that depict sexualized violence in a way that implies approval of it and is likely to encourage others to engage in it.

In *Herceg*, the plaintiff's attorneys premised their arguments on appeal entirely on the theory that *Hustler* had incited Herceg's experiment with autoerotic asphyxiation, abandoning their other claims. The court did not find enough evidence of "incitement" as it understood the term, in part because *Hustler* had included a "warning" that its readers should not attempt the practice it described, and in part because there was no proof that the article's encouragement created an "imminent" danger. Although the dissenting opinion is certainly right in criticizing the majority's fanatically wooden application of the categories generated by the Supreme Court's First Amendment cases, *Herceg* can be distinguished as a case in which the plaintiff did not attempt to articulate a theory of liability beyond that of "imminent incitement to lawless action." In *Eimann*, the plaintiff's verdict was overturned because the advertisement was held to be ambiguous as a matter of law, and because the jury instructions—the trial judge's statement of the applicable law—suggested that *Soldier of Fortune* had a duty to investigate the "context" of the ad. The court did not rest its holding on the defendant's First Amendment arguments, and the eventual outcome of *Braun* v. *Soldier of Fortune* confirms *Eimann's* limited reach by permitting recovery on similar facts.

Complexities of Causation and Harm

In any suit of the sort I suggest, the plaintiff's attorney must address two different types of causation. One is a general causal relation between pornography (defined as I have suggested) and violent harm to persons, and the other is the particular causal relation between the particular pornographic material produced or distributed by the defendant and the harm suffered by the plaintiff. The second of these tasks is, of course, one that must be undertaken by any plaintiff's attorney in any personal injury lawsuit. The congeries of doctrines known collectively as the law of proximate cause is both complex and uncertain, but no more so in this sort of case than in many others.[19] The intervening agency of a third party (the rapist, the assailant, the one who forces pornography on the victim) does not defeat proof of a causal relationship between the pornographic material and the harm, if such harm was foreseeable by the pornographer-defendant. As more and more research seems to affirm that exposure of men to violent sexual material leads to harm to women, and as this research and its conclusions are publicized and discussed, it will become more and more difficult for creators of and dealers in pornography to maintain they did not foresee that their activities would lead to harm. It will become correspondingly more likely that juries and judges will accept the arguments of victims that the risk of their sorts of injuries could reasonably have been known to the defendants.

Establishing general causation reassures the judge who, in its absence, would harbor a solicitude for the defendant's conduct generated by the First Amendment. In civil suits seeking damages for injuries caused by speech, courts have traditionally assuaged their concerns about the speech-inhibiting character of a plaintiff's recovery by observing that the defendant's speech was known to have been likely to cause harm. Whether phrased as negligence or causation, evidence of a reasonable defendant's knowledge that his speech act risked harm to another is an integral ingredient of the plaintiff's case. This is why my definition of pornography has a built-in foreseeability element: "Pornography is a depiction . . . likely to promote or encourage similar behavior in those exposed to the depiction."

I do not think that many plaintiff's attorneys will fail to produce evidence of a general link between exposure to violent pornography and harm to women.

Although a few researchers have been reluctant to affirm such a link, those who have done the most work in this area acknowledge that exposure to materials that depict the infliction of pain or rape does have a damaging effect. After a series of disputes about what they did and did not find, and whether their work had or had not been misused by antipornography forces,[20] researchers Daniel Linz and Edward Donnerstein clarified their views as follows:

> Researchers have documented that men who view sexually violent materials in controlled situations may demonstrate increased callousness toward women. The men undergo several attitudinal and perceptual changes, tending to see a rape victim presented to them later as less injured and more responsible for her assault. The men are also more likely to endorse myths such as the idea that women secretly enjoy sexual assault.[21]

Linz and Donnerstein emphasize, however, that these findings do not suggest a relationship between exposure to nonviolent sexually explicit material and any such attitudinal changes; indeed, they insist that it is the violence of the material rather than the explicitness of its sexual content that makes it dangerous. Slasher films, they say, are more likely to have harmful effects than some X-rated materials. I believe that my definition of pornography, "a depiction . . . of violence directed against, or pain inflicted on, an unconsenting person or a child, for the purpose of anyone's real or apparent sexual arousal or gratification," captures the essence of the materials that have been documented as likely to lead to harm. The definition certainly does not exclude materials that depict the unconsenting victim as later grateful for being hurt or raped. Such depictions are among the most infuriating to feminists, and for a good reason: research suggests that such "positive outcome" depictions of sexualized violence are among those most likely to induce dangerous attitudinal or behavioral changes in people exposed to them.[22]

Many have argued that pornography is harmful to women in more subtle and important ways than the narrow inducement of harm that would generate a successful lawsuit under my proposal. I do not disagree with the claims of those who argue that pornography, in the broad sense, harms women in ways that the clumsy drama of a lawsuit cannot reach. As MacKinnon says,

> Instead of [a] more complex causality . . . the view became that pornography must cause harm the way negligence causes car accidents or its effects are not cognizable as harm. The trouble with this individuated, atomistic, linear, isolated, tort-like—in a word, posi-

tivistic—conception of injury is that the way pornography targets and defines women for abuse and discrimination does not work like this.

I also do not disagree with the claims of MacKinnon and others who argue that pornography (again, in the broad sense) does not just cause harm to women, it *is* harm to women.[23] I do not doubt the power of speech and ideas to force identities onto women that we have not chosen, yet find impossible to contest. However, I do doubt whether a legal system that protects hate speech that causes harm *of a similar sort* will be persuaded to uphold a prohibition on pornography because of the reality that it constructs. Even so, I do not propose a limit on what should count as a cognizable legal harm.

The real source of disagreement here is less about causation than about what counts as harm in the legal system. It is true that many of the harms women encounter in their daily lives are never codified in lawsuits or criminal codes because they are invisible, incomprehensible, or just uninteresting to those whose interests constructed the law.[24] It is also true that inspired lawyering can sometimes make those harms visible and illegal—it can both "out" and "outlaw" them.[25] Although I doubt the success of lawsuits predicated on a woman's emotional distress at being perceived or constructed as less than fully human, the law of personal injury does sometimes recognize harms to the psyche. From the obvious case of the woman who is raped by a man to the accompaniment of a pornographic videocassette, to the far more challenging case of a woman who feels imprisoned in her home after dark because of the clientele of the adults-only bookstore on the corner, it must be left to the ingenuity, resourcefulness, and eloquence of the attorneys in such cases to convince the judges and juries that there has been real, legally compensable injury.

Happily, one need not prove "causation" in these cases to the satisfaction of a philosopher,[26] for the law is more amenable to manipulation. From the standpoint of a critical legal theorist this is a bad thing, but for the proposal I make here it is a blessing. I understand that there is a constant "background" exposure to sexualized violence against women in print, on television, in advertising, and in movies. I also appreciate the difficulty in separating the causal contribution of this background effect from that of any particular piece or pieces of pornography. Nevertheless, I believe most jurors would be horrified and disgusted by the sort of violent pornography that this proposal targets. I believe further that their reaction would lead them, where there is any evidence of a causal contribution, to resolve doubt in favor of finding a causal connection between a particular piece of pornography and any harm to a victim they find believable and appealing. In the same way, jurors are often willing to find that exposure to a particular carcinogen caused a worker's cancer, even against a background of toxic exposure experienced by all and despite defense arguments about the confounding of causality that it occasions.

Other Objections Considered

I anticipate other objections to the campaign of personal injury litigation that I suggest. Some will argue that placing liability for the injuries of raped or assaulted women on pornographers will create a psychological escape from responsibility, or even a legal defense, for the criminal who immediately commits the crime. I cannot say I understand the psychology of violent criminals well enough to address the first possibility, but Diana Scully's work suggests that the opposite may be true—that it is in fact the availability and prevalence of pornography, in the absence of any public suggestion that the scenes it depicts are wrong or objectionable, that assuages whatever qualms the would-be sexual criminal might otherwise experience. In any event, the second concern is not necessary. The law of solicitation allows for the guilt, the complicity, of both the encourager and the actor. Both negligence and product liability law recognize that two or more parties may be liable to an individual for harm caused by the *joint operation* of their conduct. To the extent that a sexual criminal wishes to identify a particular piece or pieces of pornography as having inspired his crimes, he will find himself no less guilty.

The next objection is the opposite of "If you build it, they will come."[27] That is, people will say that even if the lawsuits I describe would be heard by courts, and could overcome First Amendment obstacles, no one will bring them—due to the poverty of the likely plaintiffs, the uncertainty of recovery, and the difficulty of identifying the source of the pornography. I concede these difficulties, especially the last. Unless there is some "signature" or other circumstance to suggest a sex criminal's inspiration by a particular work of pornography, there may be insuperable proof difficulties. However, the criminal himself may disclose the identity of his despicable muse, and I would expect resourceful plaintiffs' attorneys to find ways to establish these connections, as did resourceful plaintiffs' attorneys in the asbestos litigation, where most of the stricken plaintiffs had no idea who had manufactured the particular asbestos product to which they were exposed.

Another objection—one that has been raised to almost every proposal designed to discourage pornography—is that we need education, not litigation. But the two do not exclude one another and may converge in important respects.

Litigation has played an enormous educational role in this country's history, around issues from desegregation to sexual harassment to rape to employment discrimination. Moreover, entire research industries emerge once issues become legal issues. When a woman's entitlement to certain legal benefits depends on whether she suffers from a learning disability, learning disability experts begin to appear. When lawsuits begin to claim that exposure to high-intensity electromagnetic fields may cause cancer or miscarriages, studies are done. When DNA evidence begins to be admitted in criminal cases, labs begin to tool up to do that kind of work. There has been some research on the causes of sexual violence (both in general and in particular cases), but there needs to be more; recognizing lawsuits against pornographers will encourage research into the effects of pornography.

A further objection is that a proposal such as mine will inevitably be turned against feminist speech. Such a fear animated the writers of the FACT brief, and was expressed by many in the debate over the model ordinance.[28]* Audre Lorde's observation that "the Master's tools will never dismantle the Master's house" captures the reservations of many feminists toward strategies that would award a male-dominated legal system a role in controlling violence against women.[29] But I do not believe that Lorde meant to caution against using any male-originated power against continuing male dominance and violence; such a universal caution would have discouraged enforcement of the Civil Rights Act of 1964 (including those provisions later held to prohibit sexual harassment), the reform of rape laws, and the prosecution of domestic violence. I cannot conceive, moreover, of any speech that I would call "feminist" that would fit within the definition of pornography used here—the depiction of unconsented sexual violence in a context implying approval of the same and likely to encourage the observer to do the same, that is, to inflict unconsented violence. I have read the arguments of lesbians and others who value sadomasochistic sexual practice and I do not understand them to argue for the value of speech that encourages nonconsensual violence.

Finally, I expect this proposal to be criticized because it offers too little. Catharine MacKinnon has said that individual lawsuits by victims of pornography can never amount to more than a mopping-up operation. This may be true, metaphorically speaking. But others criticized MacKinnon and Dworkin's model ordinance on the ground that in a world full of male violence, combating pornography was a task with very small potential for good—in other words, a mopping-up operation. What I propose will not save women from the use of

---

* The FACT brief was a brief amici curiae of The Feminist Anti-Censorship Task Force (FACT), filed in *The American Booksellers Association* v. *Hudnut* case on April 8, 1985. It argued that the Indianapolis antipornography ordinance was unconstitutional and would hurt women.—Eds.

rape as a political weapon in Bosnia, will not heal the wounds of incest victims in Illinois or Colorado, and probably will not eliminate pornography, even violent pornography. It's mopping up, but women are good at that. When I visualize the master's tools, mops are not among them. If we wield them well, we may well dismantle a part of his house.

CHAPTER FIVE

New Legal Paradigms

In this chapter, scholars move beyond the current legal framework and into the future. They contend that we stand at a crossroads now, with nineteenth century concepts of freedom of expression behind us—formulations that worked for the white male dominant society of the past, but which are failing us in the present and will stand in the way of any real democracy in the future. They argue that a commitment to civil liberties, while a good start, is only a beginning for a society that seeks genuine liberty and genuine equality. In order to create that society, they say, we will have to take into account the historic exclusion that many have suffered, and the continuing harm of racist speech, hate propaganda, and pornography. They believe that nothing less than a rethinking of our legal framework can adequately address these problems, and in their articles, they critique tired shibboleths, attack sacred cows, and excoriate apologists. Finally, they present new paradigms that take into account the real harm and suffering caused by damaging speech and offer new visions for reconciling freedom of speech and equality.

UNCOUPLING FREE SPEECH

Frederick Schauer

Most legal scholars assume that if speech is to be free it must be *free*, that is, beyond court-imposed pecuniary sanction. In this excerpt from his path-breaking article in the *Columbia Law Review*, Frederick Schauer points out that this approach assures that the costs of a system of free speech are borne unevenly and unfairly. He suggests that this need not be so and proposes that we "uncouple" the notion of liberty and that of compensation, leading to the possibility that the price of free speech protection be borne other than by the victims of harmful speech.

■

Sticks and stones may break your bones, but names will never hurt you. Or so our parents admonished us when we were young. Later, we realized that our parents were wrong, and that a host of communicative acts could indeed hurt us.

This capacity of speech to injure conflicts in many ways with the goal of strong free speech protection. Indeed, it is a commonplace that robust free speech systems protect speech not because it is harmless, but despite the harm it may cause. Given that existing First Amendment doctrine protects those who negligently and erroneously charge public officials and public figures with criminal behavior,[1] immunizes from tort liability publications causing bodily injury or death,[2] and shields from prosecution those who successfully abet violent criminal acts,[3] it can scarcely be denied that a major consequence of a highly protective approach to freedom of speech and freedom of the press is to shelter from legal reach a set of behaviors that could otherwise be punished and a set of harms that could otherwise be compensated. In short, existing understandings of the First Amendment presuppose that legal toleration of speech-related harm is the currency with which we as a society pay for First Amendment protection. Although people disagree about the amount of free speech protection they wish to have and, consequently, the extent of harm they wish to have their legal system tolerate, they agree about the necessary connection between speeches protected and harms tolerated.

I propose to call into question this very relationship, suggesting that the coupling of harm toleration and speech protection is by no means inevitable. It ought to be troubling whenever the cost of a general societal benefit must be borne exclusively or disproportionately by a small subset of the beneficiaries. And when in some situations those who bear the cost are those who are least able to afford it, there is even greater cause for concern. If free speech benefits us all, then ideally we all ought to pay for it, not only those who are the victims of harmful speech.

Let me start with a concrete example. In *Ocala Star-Banner Co.* v. *Damron*,[4] the Supreme Court demonstrated with stunning clarity the costs commonly associated with *New York Times Co.* v. *Sullivan*,[5] and its near-absolute protection of the press from libel suits. The facts of *Ocala Star-Banner* are straightforward: Leonard Damron was the mayor of the town of Crystal River, Florida, and a candidate for County Tax Assessor of Citrus County. On April 17, 1966, a reporter telephoned the *Star-Banner* with a story that James Damron (who happened to be the brother of Leonard Damron) had been arrested and charged with perjury in the United States District Court in Gainesville, with the trial to take place in the following term of that court. The area editor, who had been working at the paper for just more than a month, wrote up the story for publication, changing the name from James Damron to Leonard Damron, quite possibly on the assumption either that the two were one and the same or that the reporter on the scene had misstated Leonard Damron's name. As it appeared in the next day's paper, under the headline "Damron Case Passed Over to Next U.S. Court Term," the story commenced with: "A case charging local garage owner Leonard Damron with perjury was passed over for the present term of Federal Court after Damron entered a not guilty plea before Federal Judge Harrold Carswell in Gainesville."

Although the *Star-Banner* printed two retractions before the election took place, Leonard Damron lost. He sued the *Star-Banner* for libel and succeeded in establishing falsity, negligence, and a relationship between the falsity and both general damage to his reputation and specific damage to his electoral prospects. Damron ultimately won a jury award of compensatory damages in the amount of $22,000.

The $22,000 award was upheld in the Florida courts[6] but was overturned by a unanimous United States Supreme Court. Justice Potter Stewart's brief opinion made clear that the case presented little more than a mechanical application of an earlier ruling in *New York Times Co.* v. *Sullivan*, which protected the press from libel suits, since no plausible case for the existence of actual malice on the part of the *Star-Banner* could be maintained.[7] Thus, not only is *Ocala Star-Banner* an easy case under the *New York Times* rule, but it also enables us to identify with some precision the cost of the *New York Times* rule—$22,000—since that is what Damron would have received had that rule not been in place. Consequently, in order to prevent the *Ocala Star-Banner* from being excessively chilled in its pursuit of truth, Leonard Damron is compelled to forgo an award of $22,000, which is the economic equivalent of compelling him to pay $22,000.

But why Leonard Damron? He is certainly not the primary beneficiary of liberating the *Star-Banner* and every other American newspaper and magazine from the fear, or chill, of libel suits. On the contrary, as Justice Byron White's concurrence makes so clear, Leonard Damron is the unfortunate victim of the social benefit coming from the relaxed rule of liability that *New York Times* established.[8]

My thesis is that there are alternatives at least worth considering, ones that do not entail Leonard Damron's forgoing $22,000, yet that do not encourage the self-censorship of the *Ocala Star-Banner*. My working postulate is that any rule of liability more stringent than that of *New York Times* would produce too much self-censorship by the *Star-Banner* and other publications, and my whole point would be lost were I to relax that assumption. But if the goal is to liberate editors and reporters from fear of liability, then it is important to recognize that the $22,000 would be paid not by the editorial department but by the publisher of the newspaper, and it is hardly necessary that the publisher would require that the editorial department change its practices in order to minimize publisher liability. If the rule of liability were negligence rather than (as required by *New York Times*) actual malice, Damron would recover his $22,000. But if the publisher were to pay the award and at the same time make clear to the editorial staff that the publisher expected the editorial staff to operate *as if* the *New York Times* rule were in place, Damron would be compensated and the editorial staff would be no more chilled than it is now.

New York Times, and indeed the entire constitutionalization of American defamation law, is based on the assumption that if the publisher is at financial risk, then this risk will filter down to the editorial department, with a consequent inhibiting effect on the content of the newspaper.[9] And certainly this seems a plausible assumption, not only because the law generally assumes that businesses are undifferentiated economic units, but also because the trickling (or pouring) down of trouble from above resonates so easily with what we know about how institutions operate.

Yet however plausible the assumption of trickle-down chilling appears, it turns out to be at odds with one of the pervasive tenets of the press itself—the separation of the advertising and editorial functions.[10] Thus, although it is frequently the case that advertisers refrain from advertising in newspapers because of some aspect of the content of the paper, it is a central credo of American "elite" journalism that an advertiser's threat to do so, or act of doing so, will have no effect on editorial content. If an article critical of Mobil Oil or Chase Manhattan, or of oil companies or banks in general, will prompt Mobil or Chase to withdraw its ads, that is the price to be paid for the editorial independence that defines a high-quality newspaper, magazine, or news broadcast. Thus, to put a number on all of this, if publishing an article critical of Mobil Oil were to lead Mobil to withdraw advertising for which it would have paid $22,000, then many American publishers would say that paying $22,000 for editorial freedom was well worth the price. The loss would be absorbed outside of the editorial function, and the editorial staff would be under no pressure to change their behavior toward Mobil or other advertisers. Similarly, therefore, it is at least possible that publishers rather than victims might pay the costs of a free speech system. And we can also imagine ways in which these costs might be passed on to consumers or to the public at large, as with publicly subsidized libel insurance. Any of these proposals could produce no reduction in the amount of editorial freedom, but would just shift the locus of the payment for that freedom from victims to someone else.

My ideas are only in a narrow sense about defamation and about speech causally related to otherwise compensable physical harms. The advantage of commencing with these two areas is that they are ones in which alternative compensation schemes seem most practically plausible, in large part because they deal with areas in which existing law, but for the First Amendment, would allow recovery.[11] But expanding the circle outward from these two instances indicates further applications. One example, as pressing as it is timely, is the general topic of hate speech, within which I include, first, utterances intended to and likely to have the effect of inducing others to commit acts of violence or acts of unlawful discrimination based on the race, religion, gender, or sexual orientation of the victim; and, second, utterances addressed to and intended to harm the listener (or viewer) because of her race, religion, gender, or sexual orientation.[12]

I offer this definition because these two varieties of hate speech are relevantly different. Suppose that a member of the audience at a speech being given by Frank Brandenburg,* call him Lester, becomes enraged, feels that the time for "revengeance," in Brandenburg's words,[13] is now, and then proceeds to use an ax handle to commit an act of revengeance against the first African

---

* The reference is to *Brandenburg* v. *Ohio*, a U.S. Supreme Court decision providing validation for provocative public speech. —Eds.

American he sees. The victim then proceeds to sue both Lester and Brandenburg for battery and seeks damages for medical costs and pain and suffering. Although she knows that the action against Lester is legally easy, she knows that Lester's pockets are particularly shallow, so she also joins the substantially deeper but one-step-removed pockets of Brandenburg.

Now we know from *Brandenburg* v. *Ohio* itself that Brandenburg is likely to be found immune from liability. Yet we know as well that there are circumstances under which Brandenburg would be held responsible as a matter of tort law even though he is currently immunized by the First Amendment.

But even were Brandenburg not liable as a matter of tort law, his utterances, when combined with those of many others, are still likely to have some effect on the level of racial violence. To put it more broadly, assume that a wide range of constitutionally protected utterances, including but not limited to those of members of the Ku Klux Klan and related groups, have some effect on the level of racial violence and race discrimination in this country. Some of this effect may take the form of provoking those previously inclined toward racism, some the form of reinforcing existing attitudes that might otherwise be more susceptible to change, some through coordinating the behavior of those who act only when they are confident that others will join in their actions, and some the form of assisting in the creation of attitudes that in turn shape behavior. Assume as well that the existence of the First Amendment prevents the United States from having laws (such as ones prohibiting the incitement to racial hatred) that would make unlawful some of these utterances, laws of the kind that are common in many democratic societies.[14] And, finally, assume that the absence of such laws has an effect on the degree of proliferation of statements promoting racial violence or race discrimination, which in turn has an effect on the degree of racial violence and race discrimination.

Each of these assumptions incorporates empirical propositions that could be otherwise. My aim is not to test these assumptions, however, but to explore their implications. If the assumptions are sound, then the implication is that there is more race discrimination and racial violence than there would be if everything else about the First Amendment were the same except for its permission of advocacy of racial violence or race discrimination.[15]

If there is accordingly more racial violence and more race discrimination than there would have been under different understandings of the First Amendment, then the understandings that we do have carry prices that the victims of the violence and discrimination pay disproportionately. Increases in the amount of violence and discrimination are the marginal costs of increased First Amendment protection, costs not borne proportionately by all those who benefit from that increased protection.

So, too, in a number of other areas. If one believes that constitutionally protected endorsements of sexual violence or sex discrimination have an effect on the level of sexual violence and sex discrimination,[16] then again the price of the First Amendment is hardly being borne equally by the entire citizenry. Rather, it is disproportionately borne in this respect by those likely to be the victims of sexual violence or sex discrimination, a class that consists overwhelmingly of women.[17] Indeed, if one accepts the proposition that the domain of materials explicitly or implicitly endorsing sexual violence is much larger than the domain of materials explicitly or even implicitly endorsing racial violence, then the First Amendment may have this particular consequence even more in the area of gender than of race.

With respect to all of these examples, providing compensation in a literal sense to those who pay for everyone's First Amendment is difficult, and in most instances impossible. Nevertheless, means exist for compensating victims that are not strictly monetary. As we think about social responses to racism or sexual violence on campus, or anywhere else, or as we think about social responses to many other phenomena that are likely to be increased as a result of existing understandings of the First Amendment, should we consider more seriously whether compensatory responses are merely a way of recognizing that some may bear the costs of our constitutional rights more than others?

Indeed, the issue of distribution arises not only in the context of constitutionally protected communications causally related to the incidence of a social harm. It arises as well in the context of the second part of the definition of "hate speech" that I offered above—communications that are themselves harmful[18] to some involuntary perceivers, as in the case of racial epithets, the proposed Nazi march in Skokie,[19] sexually violent or degrading images that women cannot avoid,[20] flag desecration,[21] targeted picketing,[22] or the word "fuck" on a dissident's jacket.[23] Especially where there is intent to injure, as when the Nazis selected Skokie rather than some other community precisely because the likelihood of injury would be greater there than in other locations, many of these cases are ones in which the intentional infliction of emotional distress would otherwise be compensable as a matter of tort law, but in which the First Amendment prevents recovery.[24]

In some of these instances, the likely targets of the speech may disproportionately be those who can least afford to bear the cost, if for no other reason than that they have to bear it more often than others.[25] When the costs of the First Amendment are not, even over time, evenly distributed, the arguments for taking those costs seriously become even stronger. If we understand that some people are more likely to be the targets of racial epithets than others; if we understand that the display of images of sexual violence hurts women more often, more severely, and more immediately than it hurts men, then thinking about reactions to hate speech could be quite different. But even if the speech must remain protected, keeping in mind the identities of those who pay the costs of that protection is important. All too often, those who defend the existing approach by saying "this is the price we pay for a free society" are not the ones that pay very much of the price.[26] By recognizing that it is not inevitable that the victims of harmful speech be the ones who are to pay for all of society's free speech protections, we may be on a path toward a more equitable distribution of the costs of free speech.

WORDS, CONDUCT, CASTE

Cass R. Sunstein

The general principle in interpreting the First Amendment is that speech cannot be regulated, while conduct can. But how do we categorize pornography, racist speech, and hate propaganda? Some say that pornography is not speech at all, but a practice and therefore not protected by the First Amendment. Others believe it is entirely speech and falls squarely within First Amendment protections. And what of hate speech? Civil libertarians argue that hate speech expresses an idea, although one repugnant to most people, and ideas, under current First Amendment law, are protected. If we continue to judge these difficult cases in a vacuum, without examining the history of racial and sexual caste in this country, we will never solve these problems. In this chapter, Cass Sunstein sets out some new guidelines for interpreting pornography and hate speech and applying an "anti-caste" principle.

■

The Anti-Caste Principle—And Free Speech

CASTE   I am concerned here with the relationship between equality and free speech. To discuss that relationship, we must first identify the appropriate conception of equality. At the origin, the central target of the Fourteenth Amendment was not irrational distinctions based on race, but rather the system of racial caste in American society. For those who ratified the post–Civil War Amendments, the problem was that the law had contributed to a system of caste based on race, thought to be a morally irrelevant characteristic.

The motivating idea behind an anticaste principle is that without very good reasons, social and legal structures ought not to turn morally irrelevant differences into social disadvantages, and certainly not if the disadvantage is systemic. A difference is morally irrelevant if it has no relationship to individual entitlement or desert. Race and sex are certainly morally irrelevant characteristics in this sense; the bare fact of skin color or gender does not entitle one to social superiority.

A systemic disadvantage is one that operates along standard and predictable lines in multiple-important spheres of life, and applies in realms that relate to basic participation as a citizen in a democracy. These realms include education, health care, freedom from private and public violence, wealth, political representation, and political influence. A particular concern is that self-respect and its social bases ought not to be distributed along the lines of race and gender. The social practices in a system of caste produce a range of obstacles to the development of self-respect, largely because of the presence of the morally irrelevant characteristic that gives rise to caste-like status.

In the areas of race and sex discrimination, the problem is precisely this sort of systemic disadvantage. A social or biological difference systematically subordinates the relevant group—not because of "nature," but because of social and legal practices. The resulting inequality occurs in multiple spheres and along multiple indices of social welfare: poverty, education, health, political power, employment, susceptibility to violence and crime, and so forth. That is the caste system to which the legal system should respond. This point does not deny the fact of biological difference or even biological disadvantage. I do not claim that there would be equality in the state of nature, a question that is irrelevant for our purposes. The point is that social and legal practices make biological diffferences count or matter, and this point is not falsified by showing what would happen in "nature." What is at issue is whether the social and legal practices are justified.

SPEECH Very provisionally, I propose that the free speech principle attempts to protect all symbols, whether or not words, that contribute to the exchange of ideas. Thus understood, the free speech principle can march hand-in-hand with the anticaste principle, and there is usually no tension between them. When tension does arise, courts ought to minimize infringements on either principle. But it is certainly imaginable that unrestricted speech can contribute to gender and racial caste. For example, a principal feature of a caste system consi:`~ of disproportionate subjection to public and private violence. Acts that are symbolic and expressive in character—like some lynchings and some rapes—are important features of a constitutionally unacceptable caste system. But the problem is not limited to expressive acts. It is plausible that in their production and use, some forms of pornography are associated with violence against women. It is also plausible that both pornography and racial hate speech have corrosive consequences on the self-respect of women and blacks. In these circumstances, unrestricted speech may contribute to the maintenance of a system with caste-like features.

The constitutional task then is to interpret the free speech and anticaste principles in such a way as to accommodate both aspirations. We might perform this task in two ways. First the definition of protected speech could seek to exclude the most damaging forms of expression, on the theory that those forms do not belong in the "top tier" of constitutional protection and can be regulated because they cause sufficient harms. Second, the government might be permitted to justify certain narrow restrictions on speech by reference to the Civil War Amendments, by claiming that the interest in equality is sufficiently neutral and weighty to support those restrictions. I will invoke both of these strategies below.

Pornography

Pornographic material causes sufficient harms to justify regulation under the more lenient standards applied to speech that does not fit within the free speech core. Of course it is possible to question the extent of the relevant harms; the empirical debates are complex, and I will only summarize some of the evidence here.

The harms fall in three categories. First the existence of the pornography market produces a number of harms to models and actresses. Many women, usually very young, are coerced into pornography. Others are abused and mistreated, often in grotesque ways, once they enter the pornography "market." To be sure, most women who participate are not so abused. It is therefore tempting to respond that government should adopt a less restrictive alternative. Rather than regulating the speech, government should ban the coercion or mistreatment, as indeed current state law does. Usually the strategy is indeed better and even constitutionally required. But in this peculiar setting, such an alternative would be a recipe for disaster, because it would simply allow existing practices to continue. The enforcement problems are so difficult that restrictions on the material are necessary to supplement the criminal ban.

Second, it is reasonable to think that there is a causal connection between pornography and violence against women. No one suggests that sexual violence would disappear if pornography were eliminated or that most consumers of violent pornography act out what they see or read. But a review of the literature suggests a reasonable legislature could conclude that pornography does increase the incidence of sexual violence against women.

These first two arguments—harm to participants and a causal connection with violent acts—suggest that antipornography legislation should be addressed only to movies and pictures and not the written word. Of course it is only in movies and pictures that abuse of participants will occur. (One might similarly support a law against child pornography in movies and print while allowing written essays that amount to child pornography.) Moreover, the evidence on pornography as a stimulus to violence deals mostly with the movies and pictures and the immediacy and vividness of these media suggest a possible distinction from written texts. I do not discuss the exact breadth of an antipornography statute here. But the possibility of exempting written texts, no matter what they contain, suggests the weakness of the objection from neutrality: a statute that exempts written texts is very plausibly treated as harm based rather than viewpoint based.

The third and most general point is that pornography promotes degrading and dehumanizing behavior toward women. Significantly, this behavior includes a variety of forms of illegal conduct, prominent among them sexual harassment. The pornography industry operates as a conditioning factor for some men and women, a factor that has consequences for equality between men and women. These conditioning effects are associated with harmful consequences for self-respect. Of course, pornography is more symptom than cause; but it is cause as well. One need not believe that the elimination of pornography would bring about sexual equality, eliminate sexual violence, or change social attitudes in any fundamental way in order to agree that a regulatory effort could reduce violence and diminish views that contribute to existing inequalities.

Taken as a whole, these considerations suggest a quite conventional argument for regulation of pornography, one that fits well with the rest of free speech law. For example, misleading commercial speech is regulable because it is not entitled to the highest form of protection and because the harms produced by such speech are sufficient to allow for regulation. The same is true of libel of private persons, criminal solicitation, unlicensed legal or medical advice, and conspiracy. Certain forms of pornography should be approached similarly. Indeed, the argument for regulation—in view of the nature of the material and the evidence of harm—seems more powerful than the corresponding argument for many forms of speech now subject to government control. Thus far, then, the hard issues have to do with the appropriate breadth and clarity of any prohibition, not with the basic approach.

Hate Speech

Hate speech raises quite different issues from pornography. Hate speech is often part and parcel of public debate on certain questions; pornography is not. Many forms of pornography are far from the center of constitutional concern; nothing of this sort can be said for the many kinds of hate speech that are designed and received as judgments about certain social questions. If restrictions on hate speech cover not merely epithets but also speech that is part of social deliberation, they appear overbroad and unconstitutional for that very reason. Speech that is intended and received as a contribution to social deliberation is constitutionally protected even if it amounts to hate speech—even if it is racist and sexist.

A good deal of public debate involves racial or religious bigotry or even hatred, implicit or explicit. If we were to excise all such speech from political debate, we would severely curtail our discussion of such important matters as civil rights, foreign policy, crime, conscription, abortion, and social welfare policy. Even if a form of hate speech is involved, it might well be thought a legitimate part of the deliberate process—it bears directly on politics. Foreclosure of such speech would probably accomplish little good, and by stopping people from hearing certain ideas, it could bring about a great deal of harm.

These general propositions do not resolve all of the questions raised by restrictions on hate speech, but they do suggest that distinctions must be drawn between different forms of speech that fall within the category. It seems to follow that many imaginable restrictions on hate speech cut too broadly. Consider, for example, the University of Michigan's judicially invalidated ban on "[a]ny behavior, verbal or physical, that stigmatizes or victimizes an individual on the basis of race, ethnicity, religion, sex, sexual orientation, creed, national origin, ancestry, age, marital status, handicap or Vietnam-era veteran status, and that . . . [c]reates an intimidating, hostile, or demeaning environment for educational pursuits. . . ." This sort of broad ban forbids a wide range of statements that are part of the exchange of ideas. It also fails to give people sufficient notice of what statements are allowed. For both reasons, it should be invalidated.

But some restrictions on hate speech do not run afoul of these principles. For example, Stanford now forbids speech that amounts to "harassment by personal vilification." (Stanford is a private university, free from constitutional restraint; but it has chosen to comply with its understanding of what the First Amendment means as applied to public universities.) Under the Stanford rule, speech qualifies as regulable "harassment" if it:

(a) is intended to insult or stigmatize an individual or a small number of individuals on the basis of their sex, race, color, handicap, religion, sexual orientation, or national and ethnic origin; (b) is addressed directly to the individual or individuals whom it insults or stigmatizes; and (c) makes use of insulting or "fighting" words or nonverbal symbols.

To qualify under (c) the speech must by its "very utterance inflict injury or tend to incite to an immediate breach of the peace," and must be "commonly understood to convey direct and visceral hatred or contempt for human beings on the basis of" grounds enumerated in (b).

The Stanford regulation should not be faulted for excessive breadth. It is quite narrowly defined. Unlike the Michigan rule, it does not reach far beyond epithets to forbid the expression of views on public issues. On an analogy to the obscene telephone call, which is without constitutional protection, official restrictions of the sort represented by the Stanford regulations should not be invalidated under the First Amendment. If this general approach is correct, the problem of hate speech should turn on whether the speech at issue plausibly qualifies as a contribution to the exchange of ideas. If it does not, it can be regulated on the basis of the relevant showing of harm.

Conclusion

Certain narrowly defined categories of pornography and hate speech can be regulated consistent with the First Amendment. They count as "low value" speech, and they cause sufficient harms to be regulable under existing standards. Broadly speaking, the argument for regulating pornography is stronger than the corresponding argument for regulating hate speech, on both the value and the harm sides; but some well-defined categories of hate speech might be subject to legal controls.

A more general lesson follows from these claims. The concerns about pornography and hate speech are in one sense new, but in another sense very old; they recall the original goal of the Civil War Amendments: the elimination of caste systems. As I have emphasized, the caste-like features of current practices are not as severe as those of traditional caste systems, but they are nonetheless conspicuous. An important element of those practices consists of the disproportionate subjection of women and blacks to public and private violence and to frequent intrusions on their self-respect—the time-honored constitutional notion of stigma. Many imaginable limits on sexually explicit materials and on racist speech would indeed violate the First Amendment. I suggest, however, that narrow and well-defined legal controls on pornography and hate speech are simply a part of the attack on systems of racial and gender caste. If they are understood in this light, and if they are appropriately narrow and clear, they can operate without making significant intrusions into a well-functioning system of free expression.

CIVIL LIBERTIES, SILENCING, AND SUBORDINATION

Frank I. Michelman

Harvard law professor Frank Michelman takes issue with the view that silencing and subordination can be excluded from consideration in deciding whether and how far to regulate pornography and hate speech. Responding to concerns that these effects are all in the victim's head, or are boundless in their reach, he argues that conscientious civil libertarians not only may but should take them into account.

■

Harm matters. This idea is already contained in what we mean by *harm*, and that is why it is so hard to see how the mattering can stop just because the harm is set into relation with a question about the legal proprieties of restrictions of liberty—even liberty of expression. Perhaps not everyone accepts this point, but I would guess that all lawyers do—and this certainly includes Cass Sunstein. In his book, *Democracy and the Problem of Free Speech*, Sunstein urges that not all harms are equal in fitness for First Amendment analysis. Specifically, Sunstein would keep "silencing" and "subordination" off the First Amendment radar. He does not exclude these categories from the field of harms that speech can cause, nor does he minimize their gravity, but still he would screen them out of consideration when it comes to a legal appraisal of restrictions on speech. I wonder whether this position is tenable.

Sunstein's argument is one of rule-utilitarian prudence, a kind of categorical balancing. The silencing effect, Sunstein says, "is produced by social attitudes resulting from the speech itself, and one cannot find that to be a reason for regulation without making excessive inroads on a system of free expression."[1] In a like vein, Sunstein finds that "the category of subordination is . . . too difficult to use when we are dealing with free speech."[2] Sunstein is concerned about the indefinition and potential breadth of these two categories—silencing and subordination—as excuses for censorship.

Without a doubt, the concern is valid. What I question is whether conscientious civil libertarians can let it be conclusive for constitutional law in this country now. I think, rather, that it leaves us with a truly disturbing and unresolved dilemma, and that a main reason for this dilemma is the persistent social fact of subordination, or caste, to use Sunstein's term. I am saying little here with which I understand Sunstein to disagree.

Let us try to speak as conscientious civil libertarians, as committed defenders of the values of expressive freedom in human life, and therefore of a legally established *system* of freedom of expression *for all*. What are we to make of the idea of the silencing of some people by the speech of others? Once we let ourselves entertain it seriously, that idea has a uniquely disquieting force for the friends of expressive freedom. The point of raising the issue of silencing is to justify restrictions on freedom of expression in the name of the one value that we cannot conceivably rank below freedom of expression, namely, freedom of expression. It is certainly true that keeping appeals to silencing out of the picture (I will come to subordination later) makes First Amendment appraisal of some laws much more manageable and less vexing than it otherwise would be. It also makes the world safer than it otherwise would be for some freedom of expression, even a great deal of it. Unfortunately, however, a great deal does not mean all and these benefits, therefore, cannot justify conscientious civil libertarians in turning a deaf ear to claims of silencing. If harm counts, then so must its distribution.

For those like Sunstein who would locate civic deliberation and participation as one of the most valuable sites of freedom of expression, loss or weakening of voices in public exchange must register as a harm of the first order.[3] And this would seem to hold especially when the voices weakened or lost belong to those who may, by reason of social-group identification, already stand at a disadvantage in social and political contention. Of course, not everyone accepts this civic view of the value of freedom of expression. In fact, some people have found the civic view objectionable, even ominous, for the very reason that it leaves the door open to the sort of restriction-justifying argument I just sketched.

Perhaps they think they can bolt the door shut by locating the core value of freedom of expression in individual autonomy or self-actualization. But how can this possibly work? A main premise would have to be that being able to speak one's mind to others is crucial to autonomy. From this it would follow that for a person to be stopped by another's actions from speaking his or her mind to others is the infliction of a loss of autonomy. That loss is not erased, it is not shrunk, just because the actions that inflict it are an exercise of someone else's autonomy. This is an absolutely crucial point. It means that we have autonomy values on both sides, a truth that ought to make conscientious civil libertarians squirm. This, of course, is exactly why the constitutional appraisal grows so much more manageable if we treat silencing harms as categorically inadmissible to First Amendment inquiry.

In many settings, we may feel completely at ease about bolstering the law's manageability by restricting its view of reality in ways that we know to be artificial. We are less likely (let us hope) to feel so easy when we see that what we are placing beyond legal concern are human interests that our system professes to count as fundamental. But that is just what we would do by framing silencing effects right out of the law's conception of freedom of expression. It would be more comfortable, then, if we had some substantive reason of *principle*—beyond a concern for management—for this exclusion of silencing harms.

There are reasons of that kind in circulation, but I have yet to see one that withstands scrutiny. The ones I know of invite confusions that conscientious civil libertarians should be at pains to dispel. People sometimes talk as if they detect some peculiarity in the way speech produces silencing effects, and find in this peculiarity a substantive reason of principle why such effects cannot count in First Amendment inquiry. Sunstein remarks, as noted earlier, that "silencing is produced by attitudes resulting from speech itself."[4] Judge Easterbrook writes in his *Hudnut* opinion that "all of [pornography's] unhappy effects depend on mental intermediation."[5] Charles Fried points out that "the purported silencing of which MacKinnon complains" comes about only if people "are convinced that women are not worth listening to"[6] (adding, without sufficient reason that I can see, that it happens only if the women themselves get the message of their lack of worth and are swayed by it). These observations all seem more or less true. What they do not do, however, is explain how they render the silencing effect any less real, any less existent, any less harmful, than if the causal chain resulting in the silencing had not issued from speech and passed through processes of mental intermediation.

If any category is too boundless for use in First Amendment analysis, "mental intermediation" is that category. Someone falsely and maliciously yells "fire" in a crowded theater, and as a consequence people end up maimed. But we know that yelling "fire" in a crowded theater produces all its unhappy effects through a chain of causes that runs through mental intermediation. Come to think of it, what is a chilling effect if not a product of mental intermediation?*

Perhaps what people are really meaning to say here is that any silencing effect produced by speech is itself a purely "mental" effect—*it's all in the mind*, as someone might say; or *it is intangible*, as Sunstein might[7]—and that there are reasons why a harm that is all in the mind should not ever be allowed

---

* "Chilling effect" refers to the notion that a law forbidding clearly harmful speech may "chill" —or deter—other forms of speech that are vital and good.—Eds.

to tell against freedom of speech. Perhaps there are such reasons, but, if so, they do not apply here because it is obviously false that silencing effects are only in people's minds. The effects are right out here, in the world we share. They are no more exclusively mental than a misprized investment, a ruined reputation, a loss of trade and profits, and a chilling effect are exclusively mental. Silencings are social and transactional events consisting of needs not being articulated, visions not being voiced, ideas and information not being conveyed—selves not being actualized—all suffered by people who do in fact have selves, needs, visions, ideas, and information that in other circumstances they would be actualizing, articulating, voicing, and conveying.

Now I certainly have never heard my friend Cass Sunstein disagree with what I have just been saying. For him, what is important about the way in which silencing effects are "produced by social attitudes resulting from speech itself" is just that "one cannot find that to be a reason for regulation without making excessive inroads on a system of free expression." Sunstein here is calling attention to the ways in which silencings—shuttings up—can occur by force of eloquence, by force of wit or satire, by force of charisma, or by force of a speaker's reputation as an authority in the field. Silencings thus produced—often surely with specific intent to produce them—doubtless both impair autonomy and keep potentially valuable voices and visions from being taken seriously in public discourse, but we know in our bones that we cannot on that account go around justifying restrictions of speech by showing that the speech in question causes such effects whether designedly or accidentally. The very thought will be repugnant, I feel sure, to everyone reading this. It is a thought we cannot make consistent with our notions of liberty and freedom of action. This, then, is the point where we have to take into consideration the problem of subordination—or caste. I have not heard anyone call happy the prospect of having legal judgment pivot on so controversial a category. Still, the issue is fairly raised whether our law and our selves and our form of life *can* perhaps manage—if not happily—with a restricted category of silencing effects, namely, those resulting from speech that evidently both exploits and inflames existing cultures of caste and subordination so as to induce prejudgment; speech by which some speakers degrade the speech of others by summoning castelike perceptions of the others as unworthy to be heard; and speech that by such off-the-merits means discredits in advance whatever those others say and in the process reinforces caste.

I am supposing, as I believe Sunstein does,[8] that there really can be speech that produces silencing effects in that caste-dependent, caste-reproductive way. Supposing it to exist, is not such speech egregiously harmful in a normative public order that aspires not only to freedom of expression for all but also to the overcoming of castelike entrenched hierarchies? How in all consistency can that society read its Constitution to forbid absolutely restrictions of speech when those restrictions appear aptly and sincerely to be aimed against the evils of caste and subordination, as those evils are reasonably perceived to invade and inhabit and corrupt the system of freedom of expression itself?

Granting that much speech does contribute to social subordination, Sunstein goes on to argue that because the same speech "is also part of political discussion," it probably cannot be regulated without "unacceptable risks" to democratic deliberation. The argument seems incomplete. Whether a risk is acceptable or not depends on the alternatives, and so it remains to say something about the converse risk: that absolute and blanket refusal to accept prevention or reduction of caste-based silencings as a reason for restricting any speech, ever, in any way or degree, may itself, in current American circumstances, raise a severe danger to democratic deliberation—not to mention the severe danger it may raise to autonomy, self-actualization, and a conscientiously defensible ideal of a system of freedom of expression for all.

I am by no means proposing judicial abdication from rigorous questioning of "hate speech" regulations. I assume the courts will still retain the last word on questions of constitutionality. In a case of regulation of speech for which prevention of silencing and subordination are said to be the reasons, courts may legitimately demand solid showings on a number of fronts: that the harms are real and substantial and are substantially caused by the targeted speech; that the targeting is narrowly drawn; that effective and feasible but less restrictive remedies cannot be found; in short, that the regulation is a product, so far as the court can tell, of conscientious effort by lawmakers to minimize the sum of constitutionally cognizable harms.

Is this messy? Yes. Is it risky? Yes. Does the Constitution countenance the risk? I do not see how to deny it. We have on our hands a constitutional dilemma rooted in the persistence of the social fact of caste. The post-Reconstruction Constitution, committing us both to have done with caste and to leave speech free, may not have reckoned with that persistence. That oversight cannot excuse us from the reckoning.

RECOGNIZING THE CONSTITUTIONAL SIGNIFICANCE OF HARMFUL SPEECH
The Canadian View of Pornography and Hate Propaganda

Kathleen E. Mahoney

In *R. v. Butler* (1992), an internationally noted decision, the Canadian Supreme Court changed the definition of obscenity to "harm to women," thereby changing the focus from morality to the effects of pornography on women and children. A few years earlier, in *R. v. Keegstra* (1990), the same Court had criminalized hate speech. In effect, this catapulted Canada into a leadership position in cases of harmful speech and conduct. Here, Kathleen Mahoney, prime architect of the Canadian campaign that led to the Supreme Court decisions in *Keegstra* and *Butler*, explores the significance of these landmark decisions.

■

We are at the crossroads, in both the U.S. and Canada, of ground-breaking legal developments concerning freedom of expression, harm, and equality. New alliances are forming around these issues among feminists, people of color, ethnic and religious minorities, gays and lesbians, and a variety of human rights activists working against sexism, racism, and ethnic and religious hatreds. In addition, international alliances are forming as we realize that what happens somewhere in this interdependent world, happens everywhere. People are beginning to realize that hate propaganda and pornography are international issues that transcend boundaries of sex, race, culture, geography, and nation-state.

The *Keegstra* trilogy of decisions on hate propaganda and the *Butler* decision on pornography are not really surprising in the overall context of constitutional interpretation in Canada. A paradigm shift, under way since 1985, has dramatically altered the way in which we understand equality, inequality, and discrimination in our country. The Canadian Supreme Court decisions in *Keegstra* and in *Butler* balanced freedom of expression guarantees against the competing right to equality in the Canadian Charter of Rights and Freedoms, finding in favor of equality. In this essay I describe this process. I also address some of the arguments and criticisms put forward by the dissenting judges, some members of the lesbian and gay community, and civil libertarians. I conclude with some comments about obligations of nation-states to come to grips with the problem of hate propaganda and pornography on an international scale. Unless the problem is acknowledged globally and acted upon locally, women and disadvantaged groups stand little chance of ever achieving equality anywhere. The United States in particular has a crucial role to play.

The Equality Context

When the decisions were announced in both the *Keegstra* trilogy and in *Butler* to uphold legislation limiting freedom of expression, many Americans gasped in disbelief. Politically, Americans have seen our conservatism as liberal, our liberalism as socialist, and our socialism as beyond the pale. But when, constitutionally, our Supreme Court decided to interpret our guarantees of freedom of expression contrary to First Amendment values, many in your country seemed to think we had lost our grip completely. Supposedly objective members of the American press found it difficult to disguise their incredulousness at this assault on such crucial aspects of Western culture as rugged individualism and capitalism. "Why would Canadian judges suddenly launch such an attack on our shared cultural realities?" they asked.

Justice Bertha Wilson, one of our greatest judges, provided a partial explanation when she recently spoke of the role of government in Canadian society. Comparing Canadian to American attitudes she said:

> Canadians recognize that government has traditionally had and continues to have an important role to play in the preservation of a just Canadian society. . . . It is, in my view, untenable to suggest that freedom is co-extensive with the absence of government. Experience shows the contrary, that freedom has often required the intervention and protection of government against private action.[1]

But a basic trust and reliance on government fails to explain adequately the truly radical doctrinal metamorphosis these judgments represent. The recognition by the Court that hate propaganda and pornography harm equality rights was startling enough. But favoring equality in the balance against freedom of expression was truly radical.

A more complete explanation begins with Canada's adoption, in 1982, of a new Charter of Rights and Freedoms.[2] This was a turning point. With the advent of the Charter, Canada became a different kind of society from the one it had been. Our social as well as our legal culture changed. We are no longer just a democratic federation whose constitutional players are federal and provincial governments, fighting over powers. In 1982, the *people* of Canada received much enhanced roles. Equality proponents, in particular, by virtue of the most massive lobbying effort in Canada's history, achieved an amazingly comprehensive set of equality rights.[3] An affirmative action clause was enacted,[4] as well as a blanket guarantee of gender equality in the exercise of Charter rights[5] and a multiculturalism clause, mandating that the Charter be interpreted in a manner consistent with preservation and enhancement of the multicultural heritage of Canadians.[6] These changes brought about a significant reordering of the political balance of power in the country. The Charter provided a clean constitutional slate, an opportunity to correct embarrassing mistakes made under the Bill of Rights[7] and to develop the law in a principled manner consistent with an evolving society that likes to think of itself as tolerant and understanding. In addition, the majority of the judges sitting on our highest Court were prepared to accept the challenge for change that the new Charter presented, in a creative, uniquely Canadian way. This was important since the Court would have the task of interpreting and implementing the new Charter.

The desire to forge a uniquely Canadian constitutional jurisprudence had been clear in judicial comments from the early days of Charter interpretation. Former Chief Justice Brian Dickson and others urged that Canadians avoid mechanical application of concepts developed in different cultural and constitutional settings, ages, and circumstances.[8] American jurisprudence in particular was targeted both substantively and procedurally.[9] Justice Bertha Wilson quite pointedly criticized the American "framers' intent"* approach to constitutional interpretation:

> Why should a group of men (and I stress men) long since deceased
> be allowed to constrain the progressive development of the American
> constitution? Why should they put it into an Eighteenth Century
> straight jacket?
> My point here can be underlined by a simple thought experiment.
> Let us ask ourselves what the United States framers' intent was on

---

* Framers' intent is the notion that laws should be interpreted in light of what we know about the intended meaning and purpose of their drafters. —Eds.

the issue of rights of women. We must keep in mind that we are talking about a period long before women had the right to vote; a period when married women had no legal existence separate from their husbands. . . . Surely women's rights were not high on the agenda of the framers of the American constitution.

Well, haven't times changed? Today's approach to women's rights is informed by an overall societal commitment to sexual equality. And yet, if we took the framers' intent school seriously, we would be forced to admit that [today's societal commitment does not reflect] an original constitutional truth. . . .

Thus, we can see that in certain cases it would be unthinkable to allow the framers' intent to govern constitutional interpretation.[10]

So instead of adopting the "framers' intent" approach, the Canadian Supreme Court came down firmly on the side of a *purposive approach* to constitutional interpretation.[11] Justice Wilson describes this approach as based on the premise that the Charter's purpose is to protect from an overbearing collectivity those typically shut out of the political process—the poor, the oppressed, the powerless, and racial minorities.[12] In other words, it is antimajoritarian. She said judges must ask themselves how to create a climate in which the quality of life of all Canadians can be enhanced and their aspirations for self-fulfillment fully realized. Ultimately, the true test of rights will be how well they serve the less privileged and least popular segments of society.[13]

Another theme developed early on in Charter jurisprudence was the principle that the interpretive exercise must be dynamic, not static. The "living tree" metaphor adopted for constitutional interpretation was tied to the community's normative framework with the view that if community norms nourish constitutional principles, the Constitution will evolve in a way that is sensitive to change.[14] Justice Rosalie Abella of the Ontario Court of Appeal reflects this theme in her description of equality:

Equality is evolutionary, in process as well as in substance. It is cumulative, it is contextual and it is persistent. Equality is, at the very least, freedom from adverse discrimination. But what constitutes adverse discrimination changes with time, with information, with experience and with insight. What we tolerated as a society 100, 50 or even 10 years ago is no longer necessarily tolerable. Equality is thus a process, a process of constant and flexible examination, of vigilant introspection, and of aggressive open-mindedness.[15]

Translated into practice, the purposive approach requires that the focus of constitutional analysis be result-oriented. In one of the earlier Charter cases the Court said that a law would violate the Charter if either its purpose or effects were contrary to the freedoms guaranteed by the Charter.[16] But that was not the last word: the analysis has grown deeper as Charter history has unfolded.

The most profound effects of the purposive approach can be seen in cases that directly or indirectly engaged equality rights. In their first opportunity to define discrimination and to address the scope of the equality guarantees, the Court made clear that it saw the role of the Charter not as neutral on inequality, but rather as having a commitment to ending it. The monumental decision to reject the old Aristotelian test for discrimination, saying that it was so un-principled it could have justified Hitler's Nuremberg laws, was the clearest indication that a paradigm shift was under way.[17] Sweeping away centuries of accepted law, the new test measures discrimination in terms of social, political, and economic disadvantage. If a claimant is a member of a group that has experienced persistent disadvantage on the basis of characteristics such as sex or race, and if the measure the claimant is challenging continues or worsens that disadvantage, that measure violates the equality guarantee. Intention to discriminate is not relevant, and only those who fall into persistently disad-vantaged groups may claim protection of the equality guarantee.

Procedurally, the test provides an escape from the abstract rules of the past and the doctrinal straitjackets they created. Instead of operating from univer-salistic principles, it situates constitutional law right in the middle of the messy reality of life. That is to say, women and disadvantaged minorities can now tell judges their stories—tell the Court how they have been persistently at a disadvantage because of sexual violence, pregnancy, racism, homophobia, un-equal pay, lack of reproductive self-determination, or any other systemic barrier. In each case, the Court looks at the law, policy, or government action in question and determines whether or not it perpetuates or increases the disad-vantage in question. If it does, it is discriminatory. This approach paves the way for many new constitutional claims, particularly gender-specific ones. For example, in a pregnancy discrimination case in which a policy excluding pregnant women from disability insurance plans was challenged, the Court found discrimination.[18] The Court explained its decision in terms of the historic disadvantage pregnant women have endured. In another case, the law of self-defense was found to be flawed when the Court discovered it was based on a barroom brawl model that anticipates only male combatants of similar size and strengths. When a battered woman killed to save her own life, a contextualized approach revealed that she should have access to the defense even though she defended herself differently from the way a male combatant might. Gender was found to be germane to the defense. Although a constitutional equality claim was not made in the case, it is easy to see how the equality analysis could justify the result. Clearly, the traditional use of self-defense claims increases the persistent disadvantage of battered women.[19]

These cases illustrate how the disadvantage test can affect legal outcomes. When the analysis is context-based, it makes our previous failings so obvious that it forces prejudices concerning disadvantaged groups out in the open and, sometimes, out of the law. This, really, is the key to understanding the decisions in the hate propaganda and pornography cases. Once the courts adopted the purposive and contextual analysis, the door opened for women and minority groups to make their case for constitutionally supportable regulations of hate propaganda and pornography.

The Decisions

REGINA V. KEEGSTRA   The Supreme Court of Canada heard *Regina* v. *Keegstra* with two other appeals.[20] They raised similar issues: the constitutional validity of criminal code provisions prohibiting the willful promotion of hatred, other than in private conversation, toward any section of the public distinguished by color, race, religion, or ethnic origin; and the constitutional validity of human rights legislation prohibiting the communication of similar messages over the telephone.[21] In the main case, a teacher had made disparaging remarks to his students about Jews and insisted that the Holocaust had not happened. As a first step, the Court was required to decide whether the hate propaganda laws in the criminal code violated the guarantee of freedom of expression in the new Charter. If the answer was yes, the second step would be to determine whether the violation could be justified under section 1 of the Charter, which permits limitations on rights if those limits are consistent with the free and democratic society of Canada.[22]

At the first stage of inquiry, both pieces of legislation were found to violate the freedom of expression guarantee because they were directed at the content of expression rather than its form. This moved the analysis to section 1, where the violations of freedom of expression were found to be justified by four members of the Court.[23] Three judges dissented.

First, the Court rejected the American "clear and present danger" test* and the categorical approach to balancing speech rights. They found the test prob-

---

* The frequently applied principle that speech should ordinarily not be restricted unless a clear and present danger requires it. —Eds.

lematic because it cannot address the psychological trauma hate propaganda causes, nor the subtle and incremental way that hate propaganda works. The Court was also not eager to embrace the various categorizations of speech generated by American law because they do not allow a contextual analysis.

The Court then embarked on an analysis of American case law suggesting that First Amendment jurisprudence does not necessarily preclude content-based antihate laws, concluding that *Beauharnais* v. *Illinois* (a U.S. decision upholding an Illinois group libel law) was correctly decided and more in keeping with Canadian values than U.S. decisions that subsequently undermined it.[24] Moreover, the Court declared that First Amendment jurisprudence could constitutionally accommodate hate propaganda statutes if the courts were to consider their constitutionality from the perspective of the undermining effects of hate propaganda on free speech values. In particular, it found that First Amendment aversion to content-based regulation is often exaggerated. The Chief Justice pointed to a number of precedents for content-based categorizations in American law and concluded that content-based regulation of hate propaganda could be constitutionally valid under the First Amendment.[25]

After this rather unusual detour into American law, the Court turned back to the section 1 analysis required under the Canadian Charter.[26] First, in order to show that an infringement of a right is justified, the Charter requires the government to show that the challenged law relates to a *pressing* and *substantial concern*. Second, *proportionality* between Parliament's objective and the law must be demonstrated. What this means is that the law must be carefully designed to meet its objective; it cannot be arbitrary, unfair, or based on irrational considerations; it must impair the Charter right as little as possible; and there must be proportionality between its effects and the state's objective in limiting the right.

THE PRESSING AND SUBSTANTIAL CONCERN TEST   The Court had no difficulty finding that the hate propaganda laws in question met the pressing and substantial concern test. Their analysis focused on the harm hate propaganda inflicts both on members of the target group and on the fundamental democratic value of equality that underlies all of the Charter guarantees. The Court held that reducing or preventing these harms was of utmost importance, justifying limits on other constitutionally protected rights and freedoms. The entire Court was in agreement on this point.

The harms of hate propaganda to group members included humiliation, degradation, self-hate, isolation, and hostility, all of which were considered to be gravely serious, beyond mere offensiveness. The harms to society included the discrimination and potential violence that might be perpetrated by those persuaded to act.

Although the finding of harm to specific groups was important, the further finding that hate propaganda harmed the democratic value of equality by having a role in discrimination against the target groups was much more legally significant. Equating public, willful promotion of group hatred with discrimination allowed the Court to consider the constitutional significance of equality-promoting legislation. In other words, the Court established that the Charter can be used as a shield as well as a sword, that equality rights are relevant in determining the scope and content of freedom of expression, regardless of whether or not there is a law or state action that puts the guarantee of equality into question. Here private individuals, not the state, were violating equality principles, but the government action against group hate received special constitutional consideration because it promoted social equality.[27] The Court said that when laws prohibit messages that certain members of Canadian society should not enjoy equality, concern, respect, or consideration, it is *promoting* values central to a free and democratic society. This is very important: it tells us that no rights in the Charter can be assessed in isolation from other Charter rights. For the Canadian Supreme Court the Charter is a seamless web of interdependent rights.

The Court also linked the principle of nondiscrimination with the multi-cultural section of the Charter, declaring that the need to prevent attacks on an individual's connection with his or her culture underlies the purpose of this section.[28] If free rein is given to the promotion of hatred, multiculturalism cannot be preserved, let alone enhanced.[29]

I think it is fair to say that in pre-Charter doctrine, Canadian Courts regarded free speech as the cornerstone of all other democratic freedoms.[30] Since the *Keegstra* decision, equality and freedom of expression appear to be equally fundamental to our system of democracy.

PROPORTIONALITY   Earlier cases had already established that, for purposes of Charter interpretation, not all expression is equally worthy of protection nor are all infringements of expression equally serious. The assessment depends on the factual and social context of the case.[31] For example, regulation of commercial advertising or of the public revelation of details of a matrimonial dispute are considered less serious infringements than limitations on expression affecting participation in the political process or on achieving spiritual or artistic self-fulfillment. So when the Court moved to this part of the analysis, it balanced the purpose of the freedom of expression guarantee against the value of what the hate mongers were saying. By carefully considering the circumstances surrounding the use of both the freedom and the legislative limit, the majority found that the hate propagandists' expression was of limited importance. They said it not only fails to promote freedom of expression values; it works against them. Neither human flourishing nor the quest for the truth nor self-development is enhanced. The fostering of a vibrant democracy is subverted because the attack on target groups limits their ability to participate equally in the political process. The Court admitted that the muzzling of the hate promoters undeniably detracts from free expression values and that they must attach the highest importance to political speech, but found that in this case the degree of harm to those values was minimal.[32] Any "political" value hate speech has is weakened when it compromises the very democratic values used to sustain it.

The dissenting judges agreed that the objectives of avoiding discrimination and racial violence and promoting multiculturalism can justify limits on expression, but they did not agree that anti-hate speech laws were appropriate limits. One of the problems, they said, was that hate propaganda laws fail effectively to address the problem they seek to cure. They argued that such laws actually promote the cause of hate mongers by giving them media attention, creating martyrs of their leaders, and generating sympathy in the community for "underdogs" engaged in battle with the mighty power of the state. In addition, the public might assume that the government is trying to suppress something important and seek out the material. Finally, they argued that hate propaganda laws are ineffective because similar antihate laws existing in Nazi Germany in the 1920s and '30s did not stop the dissemination and implementation of the Nazi racist philosophy.

The majority addressed the first two arguments by saying that while the media attention is extreme whenever hate propaganda is prosecuted, the process of a criminal trial itself is a form of expression. The legislation and trials are a means through which both the values beneficial to a free and democratic society and the harms of hate propaganda are publicized.[33] More important, the criminal prosecution of hate mongers reassures members of the target groups that their equality is affirmed and the ideas of the hate mongers are rejected.

The Court found the argument regarding the ineffectiveness of hate laws in pre-Nazi Germany to be irrelevant. The rise of Nazism was possible, it said, because of conditions peculiar to Germany in the pre–World War II years. While hate propaganda laws cannot prevent a Holocaust, their worth as part of a free and democratic society's bid to prevent the spread of racism has been affirmed by the passage, since World War II, of more comprehensive hate laws in Germany and other Western European democracies.

REGINA V. BUTLER In 1987 Donald Victor Butler and an employee were charged with some 250 violations of the obscenity provisions of the criminal code.[34] Butler responded by challenging the legal definition of obscenity as a violation of his freedom of expression guaranteed by the Charter. The definition reads as follows:

> any publication a dominant characteristic of which is the undue exploitation of sex, or of sex and any one or more of . . . crime, horror, cruelty and violence, shall be deemed to be obscene.

By the time the case reached the Supreme Court of Canada, the *Keegstra* case had been decided. Even though it was a close 4–3 decision, its break-through idea that expression could be more than speech—that it could amount to discrimination—established a legal foundation for arguing in *Butler* that pornography could be constitutionally regulated on a harms-based equality analysis.

The basic issue was the same as in the hate propaganda cases—did the obscenity law violate the freedom of expression provision? If so, could it be justified under section 1 of the Charter as a reasonable limit in a free and democratic society? The answers to both questions were the same, but this time the decision was unanimous. Not only did all three dissenting judges join the majority, but one of the dissenters in *Keegstra*, Justice Sopinka, wrote the decision for the Court in *Butler*.

THE PRESSING AND SUBSTANTIAL CONCERN TEST   The analysis in *Butler* was similar to that in the *Keegstra* case, but there were major differences over the initial question of whether the obscenity law addressed pressing and sub-stantial concerns such as freedom of speech.

For more than 300 years, obscenity law was thought to enforce sexual mo-rality. In *Butler*, the Court rejected this rationale as no longer defensible under the Charter. This was a critically important finding: the focus on morality and prurient interest has obscured pornography's discriminating effects on women for a long time. When courts are governed by a morality standard, they start from the following assumptions: that sexual displays are immodest and un-chaste, women's naked bodies are indecent, homosexuality is repulsive, and sex outside traditional marriage is a sin. Women usually fall through the cracks in this kind of legal analysis of obscene materials, and their exploitation is often legitimized by liberal judges unable to abide such a morality standard.

Instead of striking down the obscenity law, which it could easily have done on the basis of an impermissible purpose, the Court upheld it. It did this by reinterpreting its purpose in terms of the Charter, contemporary community values, and harm to society, and asserting that avoidance of such harm justifies some restriction on freedom of speech.[35]

The Court's contextual analysis revealed that pornography is commonplace, socially accepted, and widely distributed across Canadian society; and that in this society, women are not only socially, economically, and politically subordinate to men, but rape, battery, prostitution, incest, and sexual harassment are everyday realities millions of women endure. While admitting that direct harm was not susceptible of exact proof, the Court said it was "reasonable to conclude that there is an appreciable risk of harm to society in portrayal of such materials." Discrimination, violence, the abject and servile victimization of women and children, and the legitimation of detrimental male-female stereotypes were all cited as examples of the harms of obscenity that seriously offend fundamental Canadian values, and which Parliament is constitutionally entitled to prohibit.

Further support for the Court's ruling was found in international human rights agreements that Canada has signed and therefore is obliged to respect, [36] and in the rapid growth of the pornography industry.

THE PROPORTIONALITY TEST   Turning to the issue of proportionality, the Court said the values that underlie the protection of freedom of expression— the search for the truth, full political participation, and individual self-fulfillment—are minimally present in the type of pornography the legislation prohibits. Like hate propaganda, pornography lies far from the core of freedom of expression values. Furthermore, when, as in the overwhelming majority of cases, the expression is motivated by economic profit, the Court said infringements are easier to justify. [37]

Civil liberties intervenors argued that pornography is political discourse that engages core values underlying the freedom of expression guarantee. In support of their argument, they cited some familiar American feminist sources including the Feminist Anti-Censorship Task Force (FACT) brief in the *American Booksellers Association* v. *Hudnut* case. [38]* The Court had no difficulty agreeing that explicit sexual materials that celebrate female nature and validate female sexuality are of value and cannot be proscribed, but they disagreed with the rather rosy picture of pornography painted by the British Columbia Civil Liberties Association.

Civil liberties groups and Butler further argued that no causal link with direct harm had been proven, and, therefore, the law could not be said to be rationally connected to its purpose. After canvassing the social scientific research and acknowledging some of the divergencies of opinion on the question of causality, the Court said proof of a direct causal link is not necessary to justify the legislation. In a situation in which there is conflicting social science evidence,

---

* FACT is an organization devoted to preserving pornography on the ground that regulating it would violate free-speech principles and backfire against women.

the question is whether the government has a reasonable basis for concluding that materials that depict violence, cruelty, and dehumanization in sexual relations cause harm. The Court found that they did.

Civil libertarians argued that the law was too vague or overbroad. The Court disagreed, citing four reasons. First, it was designed only for the prosecution of material that creates a risk of harm. Second, explicitly sexual erotica was not forbidden, nor were materials having scientific, artistic, or literary merit. Third, even though the standard of "undue exploitation" may have been somewhat abstract, if properly interpreted in a contextually sensitive manner, responsive to progress in knowledge and understanding and linked to Charter values, it would be appropriate. Fourth, the law did not reach the private consumption or use of obscene materials.

Civil libertarians also argued that the objectives of preventing harm to women could be met by less intrusive alternatives. They suggested that "time, place, and manner" restrictions would be preferable to outright prohibition. They maintained that if pornography encourages violence against women, activities that discourage it such as counseling rape victims to charge their assailants, providing shelter for battered women, campaigning for law reform, and educating law enforcement agencies should be taken up instead of antipornography laws.

The Court said in response that once they had established that the objective of the law was *avoidance* of harm, it was untenable and hypocritical to argue that these harms could be avoided by access restrictions. Merely making harmful material more difficult to obtain defeats the law's purpose, as the harm remains the same regardless of conditions of use. Regarding the argument that better shelters be provided for battered women and support be provided to rape victims to charge their assailants, the Court said that these are responses to harm caused by negative attitudes toward women engendered by the pornography the legislation seeks to limit. These suggested actions do nothing to *prevent* the harm. The Court agreed that alternative measures should be employed to control the dissemination of pornography, but said that because of the gravity of the harm and threat to values at stake, they should be used *in addition to* rather than *in place of* criminal restrictions. The Court said serious social problems such as violence against women require multipronged approaches.

CONCLUSION   I began with a brief overview of the Canadian constitutional approach to the interpretation of rights, explaining that it was the key to understanding the *Keegstra* and *Butler* decisions because this contextual, purposive, harms-based, equality approach exposes previously hidden issues. This exposure affects how the issues are framed and how legal principles are applied. The Canadian approach challenges the assumption that human behavior can be generalized into natural, universal laws. It challenges the civil liberties tradition centered on the individual's relationship to the state by emphasizing the importance of the relationship of individuals to one another. It recognizes that not all Canadians suffer historic, generic exclusion because of their group membership, and it recognizes that intellectual pluralism does not, and cannot, mean that racism or sexism will be given the same deference as tolerance. Finally, it recognizes that equality is an emerging right. Establishing it requires reciprocity of respect and parity of regard for physical dignity and personal integrity. It recognizes that legal interpretation must be guided by these values if equality is to be preserved.

The goal of a more humane and egalitarian society requires a new conversation, with new ways of talking about freedom of expression and its limits. That conversation began in an official way in the Supreme Court of Canada. It will continue in the United States just as it is continuing at meetings, conferences, and government caucuses in England, Spain, Australia, Chile, Switzerland, and France, where hate speech and obscenity laws are being rethought. The momentum against legalized violence and hatred is small, but growing.

PRESSURE VALVES AND BLOODIED CHICKENS
An Assessment of Four Paternalistic Arguments for Resisting Hate-Speech Regulation

Richard Delgado and David Yun

At Macalester College in St. Paul, Minnesota, the dorm room of Asian-American women was broken into and vandalized; the letters KKK were painted on the walls. At the University of Michigan, racist jokes were aired on a campus radio station. A series of anti-Semitic cartoons ran in the Syracuse University newspaper. These are but a few of the thousands of hate speech incidents that have been documented in the last ten years on college campuses. In response, some scholars and students have drafted campus antiracism codes that include prohibitions against hate speech. Civil libertarians have objected, arguing that these codes are unconstitutional, and, further, that they will harm the very people they are meant to protect. Here David Yun and Richard Delgado take on what they term "paternalistic" objections to campus regulation of hate speech.

■

In the late 1980s a number of campuses responded to a wave of racial incidents by enacting student conduct codes penalizing certain types of racist acts or expressions. Then federal courts struck down codes like these at the universities of Michigan and Wisconsin. Within a short time, the Supreme Court invalidated a St. Paul, Minnesota, ordinance under which a white youth had been convicted of burning a cross on the lawn of a black family. Most institutions that had been considering hate-speech rules put them on hold.

But the recent Supreme Court decision of *Wisconsin* v. *Mitchell*, upholding sentence enhancement for individuals convicted of racially motivated crimes, coupled with recent scholarship on tort-based regulation[1] have spurred renewed interest. Today, many writers—including even some detractors of hate speech rules—believe that properly drafted prohibitions would be held constitutional.[2]

But will they be? And, if so, would they be wise? Many university administrators and scholars of color answer yes on both counts. The ACLU, free-speech absolutists, and some First Amendment scholars have their doubts.[3]

This article examines a group of objections deployed against hate speech rules that we term *paternalistic*.[4] Each urges that such rules would harm their intended beneficiaries: i.e., if minorities knew their own self-interest, they would oppose them. Some make the argument that there is no conflict between equality and liberty, since protecting speech also protects minorities—again, even though they may not realize it.[5] Our decision to focus on this group of objections is sparked by more than theoretical interest: these arguments are put forward by respected commentators, including the national president of the ACLU.[6]

We begin by reviewing the development and current state of the hate speech controversy. Then, we critique four paternalistic objections that free-speech absolutists have put forward. We close with a discussion of *hubris*, a concept rooted in early Greek thought, which we believe explains many of the blind spots and resistances one sees in the debate over campus antiracism rules.

The Campus Antiracism Debate

Beginning around 1979, many campuses began noticing a rise in the number of incidents of hate-ridden speech directed at minorities, gays, lesbians, and others. At the University of California at Berkeley, for example, a fraternity member shouted obscenities and racial slurs at a group of black students as they passed his house; later, a disc jockey told black students to "go back to Oakland" when they asked the campus station to play rap music. At Stanford, when black students insisted that Beethoven was a mulatto, some white students denied it and publicly defaced a poster of the composer by scribbling stereotypically black facial features on it. At the University of Massachusetts, postgame racial tensions exploded in a brawl that left a number of students injured. According to the *Chronicle of Higher Education*, nearly 200 institutions of higher learning have experienced racial unrest serious enough to be reported in the news.[7] The National Institute Against Prejudice and Violence estimates that at least 20 percent of minority students are victimized at least once during their college years.[8]

Experts are divided on both the causes and the believability of this apparent upsurge in campus racism. A few argue that there is no such increase—that the numbers are the result of better reporting or heightened social sensitivities. Most, however, believe the change is real, noting that it is a part of a steady rise in attacks on foreigners, immigrants, and ethnic minorities under way in many Western industrialized nations.[9] These events may reflect deteriorating economies and increasing competition for jobs, growth in populations of color stemming from immigration patterns and a high birthrate, the ending of the cold war, or all of these.

Whatever its cause, campus racism is a major concern for educators and university officials. At the University of Wisconsin, for example, black enrollment dropped sharply in the wake of highly publicized incidents of campus racism. Finding themselves faced with this kind of negative publicity and declining minority numbers, many institutions established campus programs aimed at racial awareness. Others broadened their curriculum to include more multicultural offerings and events. Still others enacted hate speech codes that prohibit slurs and disparaging remarks directed against persons on account of their ethnicity, religion, or sexual orientation. Sometimes these are patterned after existing torts or the "fighting words" exception to the First Amendment. One, at the University of Texas, bars personalized insults that amount to intentional infliction of emotional distress.[10] Another, at the University of California at Berkeley, prohibits "those personally abusive epithets which directly addressed to any ordinary person, are likely to provoke a violent reaction whether or not they actually do so."[11]

It was not long before campus speech codes were challenged. In *Doe v. University of Michigan* (1989), the university unsuccessfully sought to defend a student conduct code that prohibited verbal or physical behavior that "stigmatizes or victimizes" any individual on the basis of various immutable and cultural characteristics, and that "creates an intimidating, hostile or demeaning" environment.[12] Citing earlier cases, a United States district court found Michigan's code fatally vague and overbroad. Two years later, in *U.M.W. Post v. Board of Regents, University of Wisconsin* (1991), a different federal district court considered a campus rule that prohibited epithets directed against an individual because of his or her race, religion, or sexual orientation.[13] Finding the measure overbroad and ambiguous, and refusing to apply either a balancing test that would weigh the social value of the speech with its harmful character, or Title VII by analogy, the district court invalidated the rule.

Finally, in the famous cross-burning case *R.A.V. v. City of St. Paul*, the Supreme Court struck down a city ordinance that selectively prohibited certain forms of racist expression.[14] Even after adopting the Minnesota Supreme Court's interpretation of the ordinance as aimed only at fighting words, the Supreme Court found it unconstitutional. It held that fighting words are not entirely devoid of First Amendment protection and, in particular, may not be prohibited based on the content of the message. Not only did the ordinance do this, it also discriminated based on viewpoint by punishing only fighting words that expressed an opinion with which the city disagreed.

More recent decisions have proven more supportive of some authorities' efforts to take a stand against racism. In *Wisconsin* v. *Mitchell*, a black man was convicted of aggravated battery for beating a white youth.[15] Because the battery was motivated by racial hatred, the defendant's sentence was increased by an additional two years under Wisconsin's penalty-enhancement statute. The Supreme Court affirmed the statute's constitutionality. It held that motive, such as racial hatred, can be considered in determining a sentence's severity. While "abstract beliefs, however obnoxious" are protected under the First Amendment, they are not protected once they express themselves in the commission of a crime.

In Canada, two recent decisions also upheld the state's power to prohibit certain types of offensive expression. In *Regina* v. *Keegstra*, a teacher had disparaged Jews to his pupils and declared that the Holocaust did not take place.[16] In upholding a portion of the national criminal code under which the defendant had been charged, Canada's Supreme Court emphasized that this type of hate speech harms its victims and society, sufficiently so as to render criminalizing it constitutional. In *Regina* v. *Butler*, the same court again used societal harm-based reasoning in reversing a trial court dismissal of criminal pornography charges.[17]

A final development suggesting the feasibility of regulating hate speech is the recent interest in torts-based approaches. Several scholars have been urging the torts of intentional infliction of emotional distress or group defamation as avenues for regulating hate speech.[18] These writers believe that the law of tort might be tapped to supply models for harm-based codes that would meet constitutional standards. They emphasize that tort law's historic policy of redressing personal wrongs, its neutrality, and its relative freedom from constitutional restraints are powerful advantages for rules aimed at curbing hate speech.

At present then, case law and commentary suggest a number of avenues for enacting hate speech restrictions that will comply with the First Amendment. Given the feasibility of enacting anti-hate speech codes coupled with the continued rise of racism on college campuses, the future seems to lie squarely in the hands of the policymakers. Defenders of the old absolutist paradigm must now, for the first time, defend their choice of approach.

Paternalistic Justifications

As we have seen, much of the debate over hate speech rules has moved from issues of constitutionality to ones of policy. Central to this debate are four paternalistic arguments made by opponents of antiracism rules; each invokes the interest of the group seeking protection.[19] The four arguments are:

1. Permitting racists to utter racist remarks and insults allows them to blow off steam harmlessly. As a consequence, minorities are safer than they would be under a regime of antiracism rules. We will refer to this as the "pressure valve" argument.

2. Enacting antiracism rules will end up hurting minorities because authorities will apply the rules against them, rather than against members of the majority group. This we will call the reverse-enforcement argument.

3. Free speech has been minorities' best friend. It is a principal instrument of social reform, so, as persons interested in achieving reform, minorities should resist placing any fetters on freedom of expression. This we term the "best friend" objection.

4. More speech—talking back to the aggressor—is the solution to racist speech. Talking back is more empowering than regulation. It strengthens one's identity, reduces victimization, and instills pride in one's heritage. This we term the "talk back" argument.

We believe each of these arguments to be seriously flawed; indeed, the situation is often the opposite of what its proponents understand it to be. Racist speech, far from serving as a pressure valve, deepens minorities' predicament. Except in authoritarian countries like South Africa, authorities generally do not apply antiracism rules against minorities. Free speech has not generally proven a trusty friend of racial reformers. And talking back is rarely a realistic possibility for the victim of hate speech.

The Pressure Valve Argument

The pressure valve argument holds that rules prohibiting hate speech are unwise because they increase minorities' vulnerability.[20] Forcing racists to bottle up their dislike of minority group members means that they will be likely to say or do something more hurtful later. Free speech functions like a pressure valve, allowing tension to dissipate before it reaches a dangerous level. The argument is paternalistic in that it says, we need to deny you what you say you want, for your own good; antiracism rules will really make matters worse; if you understood this, you would join us in opposing them.

Hate speech may make the speaker feel better, at least momentarily, but it does not make the victim safer. Quite the contrary. Social science evidence shows that permitting one person to say or do hateful things to another *increases*, rather than decreases, the likelihood that he or she will do so in the future.[21] Moreover, this permission will lead others to believe that they may follow suit.[22] Human beings are not mechanical objects; our behavior is more complex than the laws of physics that describe pressure valves, tanks, or the behavior of a gas in a tube. In particular, we use symbols to construct our social world, one that contains categories and expectations for "black," "woman," "child," "criminal," "wartime enemy," and so on.[23] The roles we create for each other, once in place, govern the way we speak of and act toward each other in the future.

Even simple barnyard animals act on the basis of categories. Poultry farmers know a chicken with a speck of blood will be pecked to death by the others. With chickens, of course, the categories are neural and innate, functioning at a level more basic than language. But social science experiments demonstrate that the way we categorize others changes our treatment of them almost as dramatically. At Yale, Stanley Milgram showed that most members of a university community could be induced to violate their conscience if an authority figure urged them to do so and assured them that this was permissible and safe.[24] At Stanford, Phillip Zimbardo assigned students to play the parts of prisoner and prison guard, but was forced to discontinue the study when the guards began to take their assignment too seriously.[25] An Iowa teacher's "blue eyes/brown eyes" experiment showed that even a one-day assignment of stigma could change behavior and school performance.[26] And Diane Sculley's interviews with male sexual offenders showed that many did not see themselves as offenders at all; images and scripts internalized from hard-core pornography had taught them their victims actually welcomed their advances.[27]

Allowing individuals to revile others, then, does not render the others safer, but more at risk. Once the speaker identifies someone as being in the category of deserved victim, his or her behavior toward that person is likely to escalate from reviling to bullying and physical violence. Further, social science literature shows that stereotypical treatment tends to generalize: what we do teaches others that they may do likewise. Pressure valves may make steam pipes safer; they don't work that way with human beings.

The "Reverse Enforcement" Argument

A reverse enforcement argument asserts that enacting antiracism rules is sure to hurt minorities because the new rules will eventually be applied against *them*.[28] A vicious insult hurled by a white to a black will go unpunished, but even a mild expression of irritation by a black motorist to a police officer or a student to a professor will bring harsh sanctions. The argument gains plausibility because certain authorities are, indeed, racist and dislike blacks who speak out of turn, and because a few incidents of blacks charged with hate speech for innocuous behavior have occurred.

But the evidence does not suggest that this is the pattern, much less the rule. Police reports and FBI compilations show that hate crimes are committed much more frequently by whites against blacks than the reverse;[29] statistics published by the National Institute Against Violence and Prejudice show the same patterns for hate speech.[30] And the distribution of enforcement seems to be in keeping with that of the offenses. Although an occasional minority group member may, indeed, be charged with a hate crime or with violating a campus hate-speech code, such prosecutions are relatively rare.[31] Racism, of course, is not a one-way street; some blacks, Latinos, and other minorities have harassed and badgered whites or one another. Still, the reverse-enforcement objection seems to have little validity in the U.S. While a recent study of the international aspects of hate speech regulation showed that in repressive societies, such as South Africa and the former Soviet Union, laws against hate speech indeed have been applied to stifle dissenters and members of minority groups, this has not happened in more progressive countries.[32] The likelihood that officials here would turn hate-speech laws into weapons against minorities seems remote.

Free Speech as Minorities' Best Friend

Many First Amendment absolutists argue that this amendment historically has been a great friend and ally of reformers. Nadine Strossen, for example, argues that without free speech, Martin Luther King could not have moved the American public as he did.[33] Other reform movements also are said to have relied heavily on speeches, exhortation, and appeals to conscience. This argument, like the two earlier ones, is paternalistic because it is based on a presumed best interest of the protected group: if that group understood where its welfare truly lay, the argument goes, it would not demand to bridle speech.

This argument rests on questionable historical premises; moreover, it misconceives the situation that exists today. Historically, minorities have made the greatest progress when they acted in *defiance* of the First Amendment.[34] The original Constitution protected slavery in several of its provisions; for nearly one hundred years the First Amendment existed side by side with slavery.[35] Free speech for slaves, women, and the propertyless was not a serious concern for the drafters of the amendment, who appear to have conceived it mainly as a protection for the type of refined political, scientific, and artistic discourse they and their class held dear.

Later, of course, abolitionism and civil rights activism broke out. But examination of the role of speech in these movements shows that the relationship of the First Amendment to social advance is not so simple as free-speech absolutists maintain. In the civil rights era, for example, Martin Luther King and others did use speech and other symbolic acts to appeal to America's conscience, but, as often as not, they found the First Amendment, as then understood, deployed *against* them. They rallied, but were arrested and convicted; sat in, but were arrested and convicted; marched, sang, and spoke— but were arrested and convicted. Their speech struck lawgivers as too forceful, too disruptive. Some years later, to be sure, some of their convictions would be reversed on appeal—at the cost of thousands of dollars and much gallant lawyering. But the First Amendment, as then understood, served more as an obstacle than a friend.

Why does this happen? Narrative theory shows that we interpret new stories in terms of old ones we have internalized and now use to judge reality, new stories that would recharacterize that reality not excepted.[36] Stories that deviate too drastically from those that constitute our current understanding we denounce as false and dangerous. The free market of ideas is useful mainly for solving small, clearly bounded disputes. History shows it has proven much less useful for redressing deeply inscribed systemic evils, such as racism. Language requires an interpretive paradigm, a set of meanings that a group agrees to attach to words and terms. But if racism is a central paradigm—woven into a thousand scripts, stories, and roles—one cannot speak out against it without seeming incoherent or irresponsible.

An examination of the current landscape of First Amendment doctrine reveals a similar pattern. Our system has carved out and now tolerates dozens of "exceptions" to the free speech principle—words of threat, conspiracy, or libel; copyrighted terms; misleading advertising; disrespectful words uttered to a judge, teacher, or other authority figure; plagiarism; and official secrets, to name a few.[37] These exceptions (each responding to some interest of a powerful group) seem familiar and acceptable, as indeed perhaps they are. But the suggestion that we recognize a new one to protect some of the most defenseless members of society—for example, eighteen-year-old black undergraduates at predominantly white campuses—immediately produces consternation. Suddenly the First Amendment must be a seamless web.

This language is ironic, however, for it is we who are caught in a web, the web of the familiar. An instrument that seems to us valuable—that reflects our interests and sense of the world, that makes certain distinctions, that tolerates certain exceptions, that functions in a particular way—we assume will be equally valuable for others. But the First Amendment's history, as well as the current landscape of exceptions and special doctrines, shows it is far more valuable to the majority than to the minority; far more useful for maintaining the status quo than facilitating change.

"More Speech": Talking Back as a Means of Combating Hate Speech

Some defenders of the First Amendment argue that minorities should simply talk back to their aggressors. Nat Hentoff writes that antiracism rules teach black people to depend on whites for protection, while talking back clears the air and strengthens one's self-image as an active agent in charge of one's own destiny.[38] Talking back draws force from the First Amendment doctrine of "more speech," according to which additional dialogue is always a preferred response to speech that some find troubling. Proponents of this approach oppose antiracism rules not so much because the rules limit speech, but because they believe that it is good for minorities to learn to speak out. A few also argue that a minority who speaks out will be able to educate a speaker who has uttered a hurtful remark, to alter that speaker's perception by explaining matters, so that the speaker will no longer say such things in the future.[39]

How valid is this argument? Like many paternalistic arguments, it is offered blandly, virtually as an article of faith. Those who make it are in a position of power (that is the nature of paternalism) and so believe themselves able to make things so merely by stating them. They rarely offer empirical proof of their claims because none is needed. The social world is as they say, because it is the world they created.[40]

The "speak up" argument is similar to the "more speech" argument, and as weak. Those who hurl racial epithets do so because they feel empowered to utter them. One who talks back is seen as issuing a direct challenge to that power. Many racist remarks are delivered by a crowd to an individual, a situation in which responding in kind would be foolhardy.[41] Many highly publicized cases of racial assault began in just this fashion: a group began badgering a black person; the victim talked back, and paid with his or her life. Other racist remarks are delivered in a cowardly fashion, by means of graffiti scrawled on a campus wall late at night or a leaflet placed under a student's dormitory door. In these situations, talking back, of course, is impossible.

Racist speech is rarely a mistake, rarely something that could be corrected or countered by discussion. What would be the answer to "Nigger, go back to Africa. You don't belong here"? "Sir, you misconceive the situation. Prevailing ethics and constitutional interpretation hold that I, an African American, am an individual of equal dignity and entitled to attend this university in the same manner as others. Now that you understand this, I am sure you will modify your remarks in the future"? The idea that talking back is safe for the black person or potentially educative for the white person is a dangerous fiction. It ignores the power dimension to racist remarks, encourages minorities to run very real risks, and treats as an invitation to dialogue that which has the opposite intent—the banishment of the victim from the human community. Even when successful, talking back is a burden. Why should minority undergraduates, already charged with their own education, be responsible for educating others?

Hubris

In summary, the four paternalistic arguments do not bear close analysis. Powerful and well-connected whites who resist hate-speech rules must realize that the reasons for that resistance lie on *their* side of the ledger. Censorship and governmental nest-feathering are not concerns when speech is private. Nor does targeted racial vilification promote any of the theoretical rationales for protecting free speech, such as facilitation of political discourse or self-fulfillment of the speaker. Much less does toleration of racist name-calling benefit the victim, as the ACLU and others have argued. Far from acting as a pressure valve that enables rage to dissipate harmlessly, epithets increase their victims' vulnerability. Demeaning images create a world in which some are one down, and others come to see them as legitimate victims. Like farmyard chickens with a speck of blood, they are targeted for mistreatment. This mistreatment ranges from slights and derision to denial of jobs and even beatings.

The Greeks had another term for this paternalism: *hubris*, the crime of believing that one may "treat other people just as one pleases, with the arrogant confidence that one will escape any penalty for violating their rights."[42] Those who tell ethnic jokes and hurl epithets are guilty of this kind of arrogance. But those who defend these practices, including some backers of First Amendment absolutism, are guilty as well. Insisting on free speech above all, as though *no* countervailing interests were at stake; putting forward transparently paternalistic justifications for a regime in which hate speech is as protected as political discourse—these are also *hubris*, the insistence of someone powerful that what he or she values must also be what you want. Unilateral power is prone to this kind of arrogance, this insistence that one person's worldview, interests, way of framing an issue, is the only one.

Unfettered speech, a free market in which only some prevail, becomes an exercise in power. Insistence that this current regime is necessary and virtuous, that minorities acquiesce in a definition of virtue that condemns them to second-class status, and that their refusal to do so is evidence of their childlike simplicity and incomprehension of their own condition—this may well be the greatest hubris of all.[43]

SPEECH, EQUALITY, AND HARM
The Case Against Pornography

Catharine A. MacKinnon

What stops society from adopting effective antipornography measures? In this chapter, writer and law professor Catharine MacKinnon, coauthor with Andrea Dworkin of the civil rights ordinances against pornography, analyzes a constellation of lies, misconceptions, and rationalizations that powerful groups and the law use to maintain sexual and racial inequality.

■

In the civil rights tradition, Andrea Dworkin and I have always understood race and sex as together and interrelated in our equality approach to speech. This work has analyzed the hate in pornography, often tellingly mistaken for love, as well as in hate speech. We have found racial animus to have a more deeply sexual dynamic than is usually acknowledged, and we have seen racism as sexual in and through pornography in which women of color and men of color are distinctively brutalized.

In this light, the harms of racist propaganda and pornography sometimes overlap and are sometimes distinct. Both lie, both defame groups, but individuals do not have to be used directly to make racist propaganda as they do to make visual pornography. All the harms of both—including stereotyping, objectification, deprivation of human dignity, targeting for violence, and terrorization of target groups—are harms of social inequality. The United States makes these harms into rights through protecting what it calls speech.

The problems of pornography and racist hate propaganda have therefore been misnamed and misconceived in American law, with the result that neither is effectively addressed by it. Both practices are located in the legal system as potential exceptions to the guarantee of free speech for their perpetrators, rather than as rights to equality for their victims. Pornography is called obscenity; hate speech is called group libel. Both are really human rights violations. So we reframed them, shifted them from the doctrine of offensive utterances to the doctrine of civil subordination, from the criminal law of morals regulation to the civil law of discrimination, from law that empowers the state to law that empowers the people. These changes recognize group-based harm and redistribute power to citizens.

The civil rights law on pornography that most distinctively embodies this approach is ten years old. It has been highly productive in its first decade of life. It has freed volumes of speech about atrocities that women have long endured in silence and has helped create legitimacy for speaking about its wrongs. It has stimulated academic theorizing on two legal issues that were dead or nearly comatose. It has inspired the introduction of several truncated or hybridized derivatives in Congress. One is Senator Mitch McConnell's Pornography Victims Compensation Act, which would allow victims of sexual assault and murder caused by pornography to sue pornographers. The obscenity definition it ultimately adopted made the bill almost worthless to victims seeking relief. If the materials could be proven obscene, they would not be there to cause rape and murder. Yet the bill was viciously attacked as looming censorship because it held pornographers responsible for violence they could be proven to have caused and reached up the food chain to the profiteers. Another congressional attempt was Senator Arlen Specter's Pornography Victims Protection Act, which would have permitted all children and coerced women in pornography to sue. This act was not the subject of a concerted campaign of public abuse. But it was not passed either.

The civil rights ordinance has also been productive for law and policy development worldwide. It has been recommended for legislative consideration by national commissions in the U.S., Canada, and New Zealand. It has been introduced in various forms in Sweden, Germany, and the Philippines. Canada adopted its harm approach as a guide for interpreting both its preexisting hate propaganda and obscenity provisions. Unlike the United States, Canada's constitution has a serious equality guarantee, which provides a counterbalance to its equally serious guarantee of freedom of expression. However, this did not place the power to address pornography in women's hands. Canada is still not stopping the pornography, which proliferates in increasingly open contempt of the Supreme Court's stand for women's rights.

The ordinance, we are continually reassured, has transformed "the debate." Discussion of pornography has been reoriented from moralizing about the good or evil of women and sex to exposing the concrete injuries it accomplishes, beginning with those who make the movies and magazines. Focus on the concrete injuries to victims of hate propaganda has been spurred as well. The death of the ordinance, which may have been prematurely declared, is said to be redeemed by this reinvigorated discourse.

But what about the harm it was written to address? What about the women coerced into pornography who remain without remedy? What is done for those who have pornography forced on them? Those who are assaulted through pornography or defamed in it, trafficked in and civilly subordinated as a consequence of that traffic? Has anything changed for them? What about the ordinance itself?

Whatever else has happened, the ordinance has not been passed again anywhere. It is not now actively under consideration anywhere. Low on the list of explanations for this is sincere ignorance. High is the power of the pornographers and their front people, including press, lawyers, and academics. Their arsenal includes a rather effective parade of lies purchased by the Media Coalition arguing that the academic research on the harm of pornography does not support the conclusion that it does any. This simple big lie, repeated loudly and often, has created a long-running climate of disbelief in that harm, undermining the necessity to address it at all. Then there is the cowardice of most politicians. If the ordinance is introduced and passed, the press will never forgive them; if it is introduced and not passed, the people will never forgive them. The solution is not to introduce it, and if that fails, ensure that it never comes to a vote.

A further ideological barrier to the ordinance becoming law is, in a word, *Hudnut*. This Seventh Circuit decision on the version of the ordinance passed by Indianapolis has given rise to the belief that the equality approach is unconstitutional, a violation of the First Amendment. This continues to be believed in spite of increasingly clear and pointed critiques that show that decision to be simply wrong as a matter of law. It is accepted as authoritative in spite of some extraordinary departures, such as ruling, in effect, that sex-discriminatory child pornography is protected speech, when all child pornography is already constitutionally criminal. In other words, under this ruling, a child may not sue civilly for damages for the same acts and materials for which the perpetrator can be thrown in jail. *Hudnut* also holds that no amount of the harm of sex discrimination is enough to outweigh a speech interest. Presumably, no amount of harm of statutorily recognized racist propaganda would be enough either. This is the fundamental holding of *Hudnut*, and it is astounding: the more harm the materials do, the more they are protected. Indeed, the harm shows their power, and hence their value, as speech.

The fact is, barely a First Amendment area exists that does not give support to the constitutionality of the ordinance. And no First Amendment doctrine, correctly applied, invalidates it. Under the First Amendment, harm counts—against the materials, not for them.

Pornography's harm lies in what it does. There are many ways to say what pornography says, in the sense of its content, but nothing else does what it does. The question becomes: do the pornographers, saying that they are only saying what pornography says, have a speech right to do what only it does?

Similarly, on the consumption end, it is not the ideas in pornography that assault women. It is the men who are constructed and changed and impelled by pornography who assault women. Pornography doesn't leap off the shelf and assault women. It is what it takes to make it and what happens through its use that are the problem.

Empirically, of all two-dimensional forms of sex, only pornography, not its ideas as such, gives men erections that support aggression against women in particular. An erection is neither a thought nor a feeling. It is a behavior. It is only pornography that rapists use sexually to prepare for their rapes and to select whom to rape. This is not because they are persuaded by its ideas or even inflamed by its emotions, certainly not because it is so conceptually compelling. It is because they are sexually habituated to its kick, a process that is largely not conscious and works as primitive conditioning, the words and pictures as stimuli. Pornography's consumers are not consuming an idea any more than eating a loaf of bread is consuming the ideas on its wrapper or the ideas in its recipe.

This is not to object to primitiveness or sensuality or subtlety or habituation in communication as such. Speech conveys a lot more than its literal meaning, and its undertones and nuances are part of what is protected about it. It is to question the extent to which the First Amendment protects unconscious mental intrusion and physical manipulation even by pictures and words, particularly when the results are further acted out through aggression and other forms of discrimination against a protected group. It is also to observe that pornography does not engage the conscious mind in the chosen way that the model of content, in terms of which it is endlessly defended, envisions and requires. In the words of Judge Frank Easterbrook in *Hudnut*, who so effectively described our theory even as he rejected it, pornography "does not persuade people so much as change them."

Pornography is masturbation material. It is used as sex; therefore it is sex. Men know this. It feels stupid to have to keep saying it. This is not a critique of masturbation or a definition of pornography, but a description of how pornography works and a descriptive critique of what men are masturbating to. In pornography, men masturbate to women being exposed, humiliated, violated, degraded, mutilated, dismembered, bound, gagged, tortured, and killed. In the visual materials, men experience this being done by watching it being done. As Meg Baldwin said, "I don't see the pictures anymore; neither do they." Sexually speaking, they are not seeing pictures of it being done, they are seeing it being done. The women are in two dimensions. The men have sex with them in their own three-dimensional bodies, not in their minds alone. Men come doing this. This too is a behavior. It is not a thought. It is not an argument. If you think it is, try arguing with an orgasm sometime. It is not the ideas they are ejaculating over. It is the experience of sexual access and power that the materials provide.

One consumer of rape pornography and snuff films recently made this point as only an honest perpetrator can: "I can remember when I get horny from looking at girlie books and watching girlie shows that I would want to go rape somebody. Every time I would jack off before I would come, I would be thinking of rape and the women I had raped and remembering how exciting it was: the pain on their faces, the thrill, the excitement." This, presumably, is what the *Hudnut* court meant when it protected pornography as speech on the grounds that its effects depended upon "mental intermediation." He was watching, wanting, thinking, remembering, feeling. This particular individual was also receiving the death penalty for murdering a young woman after raping her, having vaginal and anal intercourse with her corpse, and chewing on several parts of her body.

Sooner or later, in one way or another, the consumers want to live out the pornography further in three dimensions instead of two; the rest of women are that third dimension. And sooner or later, in one way or another, they do. *It* makes them want to. When *they* believe they can, when *they* feel they can get away with it, *they* do. Once more: *it* makes them want to; *they* do it. Depending on their chosen sphere of operation, they may use whatever power they have to keep the world a pornographic place so they can continue to get hard from everyday life. Teachers who consume pornography may become epistemically incapable of seeing their women students as their potential equals. They may teach about rape, unconsciously adopting the viewpoint of the accused. Doctors may molest anesthetized women, enjoy watching and inflicting pain during childbirth, and use pornography to teach sex education to young doctors. Some consumers write on bathroom walls. Some undoubtedly write judicial opinions. Some pornography consumers presumably serve on juries. One said he sits on the Senate Judiciary Committee. Some must answer police reports for domestic violence, edit media accounts of child sexual abuse, and produce mainstream films. Some make their wives or daughters or clients or students or prostitutes—we know this because we are all of them—look at it and do what is in it. Some sexually harass their employees and clients, molest their daughters, batter their wives, and use prostitutes with pornography directly present and integral to their acts. Some gang rape women in fraternities and at rest stops on highways, holding up the pornography and reading it aloud and mimicking it. Some become serial rapists and murderers, using and making pornography as part of doing that, either free-lancing or in sex packs, known variously as sex rings, organized crime, religious cults, and white supremacist organizations. Some make pornography for their own use and as a sex act in itself, or to make money to support the group's habit.

The message of these materials, and there is one, as there is to all conscious activity, is: get her. Pointing at all women, for a profit of ten million dollars a year and counting. This message is addressed directly to the penis, delivered through an erection, and taken out on women in the real world.

None of the evidence just mentioned has been dignified as "the data" on pornography's effects. Everything that women have said about what happens in life, in the pornography where we can see what is being done, in the social studies that ask women what has happened to them or men what they have done—none of this counts as "the data." "The data" are produced mostly by men in laboratories looking at men looking at women. In any case, all this evidence supports the same conclusions. The testimony of victims and perpetrators—which is called evidence in court and has the benefit of being real—together with the social studies that attempt to capture social reality in all its messiness, support the same conclusions as the laboratory studies, in which variables are controlled and predisposed men can be eliminated or studied separately. All show that these materials change attitudes and impel behaviors in ways that are unique in their extent and devastating for women in their consequences.

In human society, where no one does not live, the physical response to pornography appears to be nearly a universal if conditioned male reaction. This tends to hold whether the consumers like or agree with the materials or not. There is a lot wider variation in men's conscious attitudes toward pornography than in their sexual response to it.

There is no evidence that pornography does no harm; not even courts equivocate over its carnage anymore. Even the *Hudnut* court conceded the harm. Its new insult was that the potency of pornography as an idea, therefore its protection as speech, is proved by the harm it does in the world. Having made real harm into the idea of harm, this court then tells us in essence that to the extent that materials also contain these ideas—if they express the idea of discrimination by discriminating, for example—they are protected speech, even as they actually discriminate against women from objectification to murder.

In response to this approach, we are told that ours is a metaphorical or magical analysis, rhetorical or unreal, literary hyperbole or propaganda device. The assumption here is that words have only a referential relation to reality, which is an insult to any serious writer. Pornography is defended as only words. This is done even when it is pictures, even when it is pictures women had to be directly used to make, even when the means of writing are women's bodies, even when a woman is destroyed in order to say it or show it, or because it was said or shown.

The theory of protected speech that is applied to invalidate our ordinance begins here. Words express, hence are presumed speech in the protected sense; pictures partake of the same level of presumptive expressive protection. But social life is full of words that are legally treated as the acts they constitute, without so much as a whisper from the First Amendment. What is interesting is when the First Amendment frame is invoked, and when it is not. Saying "kill" to a trained attack dog is only words. Yet it is not seen as expressing the viewpoint "I want you dead," which it usually, in fact, does express. It is seen as performing an act tantamount to someone's destruction, like saying "Ready, aim, fire" to a firing squad. Under bribery statutes, saying the word "aye" in a legislative vote triggers a crime that consists almost entirely of what people say.

Then there is price fixing under antitrust laws. "Raise your goddamn fares twenty percent and I'll raise mine the next morning" is not protected speech. It is attempted joint monopolization, "a verbal crime." In this particular case, conviction for saying this nicely disproved the defendant's view that "we can talk about any goddamn thing we want to talk about." Along with other mere words like "not guilty" and "I do," such words are uniformly treated as the institutions and practices that they constitute, rather than as expressions of the ideas they embody or further. They are not seen as saying anything—although they do—but as doing something. Nobody confuses discussing them with doing them, such as discussing a verdict of "guilty" with a jury passing a verdict of "guilty." Such words are not considered speech at all. They are what linguists call "performatives."

Social inequality is substantially created and enforced, that is, *done*, through words and images. Social hierarchy cannot and does not exist without being embodied in meanings and expressed in communications. A sign saying "White only" is only words, but it is not legally seen as expressing the viewpoint that we do not want black people in this store or as dissenting from the policy view that both blacks and whites must be served, or even as hate speech, the restriction of which would need to be debated endlessly in First Amendment terms. It is seen as the act of segregation that it is, like *"Juden nicht erwunscht"*—Jews not wanted. Segregation cannot happen without someone *saying* "get out" or "you don't belong here" at some point. Elevation and denigration are all accomplished through meaningful symbols and communicative acts, in which saying it is doing it.

Words unproblematically treated as acts in the inequality context include those that constitute sexual and racial harassment. They also include "You're fired"; "Help wanted—male"; "Sleep with me and I'll give you an A"; "Walk more femininely, talk more femininely, dress more femininely, wear makeup, have your hair styled, and wear jewelry"; and "It was essential that the understudy to my administrative assistant be a man." All of these are taken from successful discrimination suits. They either constitute actionable discrimination in themselves, or they transform otherwise nonsuspect acts into bias-motivated, hence discriminatory, ones.

Whatever damage is done through such words is done not only through their context, but through their content, in the sense that if they did not contain what they contain and convey the meanings and feelings and thoughts that they convey, they would not be the discrimination they are, or actualize the discrimination they do. On the basis of this reality of pornography, and this analysis of the law of discrimination, the speech of inequality is not constitutionally protected activity.

Andrea Dworkin and I have accordingly defined pornography as a discriminatory practice, as graphic sexually explicit subordination of women through pictures or words. This definition encompasses both what is in the pornography and what must be there for the materials to work as sex and to promote sexual abuse across a broad spectrum of consumers. The definition includes what pornography says but defines its harm in terms of its role as subordination, as sex discrimination. It would include much of the content of magazines like *Playboy*, in which women are objectified and presented dehumanized as sexual objects or things for use; films that display the torture of women and the sexualization of racism and the fetishization of women's body parts; and snuff films in which actual murder is the ultimate sex act, making the silence of women literal and complete. Such material combines the graphic sexual explicit—graphically and explicitly showing sex—with hurting, degrading, violating, humiliating, actively subordinating on the basis of sex, and trafficking in it. Pornography is not restricted because of what it says, but through what it does.

It is not new to observe that while the doctrinal distinction between speech and action is obvious on one level, on closer scrutiny it makes little sense. On issues of social inequality, it makes almost no sense. If you read the First Amendment through an equality lens, discrimination does not divide into acts on one side and speech on the other. Speech acts. It also makes no sense from the action side. Acts speak. In the context of social inequality, so-called speech can be an exercise of power that constructs the reality in which people live, all the way from objectification to genocide. Words and images are either then direct acts of inequality—as is making pornography or requiring Jews to wear yellow stars—or they are connected to acts of inequality, either immediately, linearly, and directly or in more complicated, indirect, and extended ways. Together with all the material supports for inequality, authoritatively *saying* someone is inferior is largely how structures of status and differential treatment are demarcated and actualized. Words and images are how people are placed in hierarchies, in castes. They are the way social stratification is made to seem inevitable and right, how feelings of inferiority and superiority are engendered, how indifference to violence against those on the bottom of these hierarchies is rationalized and made to seem normal. Social supremacy is made inside and between people through making meanings, and words and images make these meanings. They can be unmade only if these meanings and their technologies are unmade.

A recent example of the inextricability of expression with action in what is still an unrecognized context of sex inequality is provided by a Supreme Court decision on nude dancing. Chief Justice William Rehnquist wrote for the Court that nude dancing can be regulated without violating the First Amendment because one can say the same thing by dancing in pasties and G-string. No issues of women's inequality to men were raised in pondering the deep issues of the First Amendment, although the dancers who were the parties in the case could not have been clearer that they were not expressing anything. In previous cases like this, no one has ever explained exactly what behavior like customers shoving dollar bills up women's vaginas expresses. The fact that the accessibility and exploitation of women through their use as sex is, in nude dancing, at once being said and done through presenting women dancing nude, is not confronted at all. That women's inequality is simultaneously being expressed and exploited is never mentioned. Given the role of access to women's genitals in gender inequality, dancing in a G-string neither says the same speech nor does the same harm as dancing nude.

Justice David Souter, in a separate concurrence, came a lot closer to reality when he said that nude dancing could be regulated because of the harm of rape and prostitution attendant to it. These harms are arguably worse when dancing with no protection than when dancing partly clothed. Yet he did not see that those particular harms are inextricable from and occur exactly through what nude dancing expresses. Dancing in a G-string does not, he said, express eroticism in the same way that nude dancing does. In other words, men are measurably more turned on by seeing women entirely expose their sexual parts to public view than almost entirely. Nobody said that to express eroticism is to engage in eroticism, to perform a public sex act. To say it is to do it and to do it is to say it—as well as to do the harm of doing it and to exacerbate the attendant harm surrounding it. Legally unrecognized is the fact that to participate in this performance is to practice inequality on the basis of sex as well as to express it.

The legal treatment of cross-burning provides another example of the incoherence of distinguishing speech and conduct in the equality context. Cross-burning is nothing but action; yet it is pure expression. It does the harm it does solely through the message it conveys. Nobody weeps for the charred wood. By symbolically invoking the entire violent history of the Ku Klux Klan, it says blacks (and sometimes Jews) get out, thus engaging in terrorism and enforcing segregation. It carries the historic message of white indifference both to this message and to the imminent torture and murder for which it stands. By the same token, segregating transportation communicated that African-Americans were not worthy of riding in the same car as whites. It was not seen to raise thorny issues of symbolic expression. Ads for segregated housing are also only words, yet are widely prohibited outright as acts of segregation.

Like pornography, cross-burning is seen to raise crucial expressive issues. Its function as an enforcer of segregation, an instigator of lynch mobs, an instiller of terror, and an emblem of official impunity to all of this is transmuted by the Supreme Court decision in *R.A.V.* v. *St. Paul* into a discussion of "disfavored subjects." The burning cross is the discussion. The topic is race and religion. The bland indifference to reality in this decision is underlined by the lack of a single mention by anyone of the Ku Klux Klan. Recognizing that the cross-burning communicated content, Justice Harry Blackmun aptly characterized the cross-burning as "nothing more than a crude form of physical intimidation." Now separate the speech from the conduct.

In this country, nothing has at once expressed racial hatred and effectuated racial subordination more effectively than the murder and hanging of a mutilated body. Usually it has been of a black man. I guess that makes black male bodies the topic of the discussion. Lynching expresses a clear point of view. Photographs were sometimes taken of the body and sold to extend the message and pleasure of viewing it to those unable to see it firsthand. More discussion. Are those acts inexpressive and contentless? Are the pictures protected speech? Is a black man's death made unreal by the photographs in the same way women's subordination is? Suppose lynching were done to make pictures of lynchings. Should their racial content protect them as political speech since they do their harm by conveying a political ideology? Is bigoted incitement to murder closer to protected speech than plain old everyday incitement to murder? Does the lynching itself raise speech issues since it is animated by a racist ideology? A categorical no will not do here. Why, consistent with existing speech theories, are rape and lynching not expressive? And as such why not protected?

Now consider snuff pornography, in which women and children are killed to make sex films. These are films of sexual murders in the process of being committed. Doing the murders is sex for those who do it. The sexual climax is the moment of death. The consumer has a sexual experience watching it. Those who kill as and for sex are having sex through doing the murders. A snuff film is not a discussion of the idea of sexual murder any more than the act being filmed is a discussion of the idea of sexual murder. A snuff film is not about sexual murder. It sexualizes murder. Is your first concern about a snuff film what it says about women and sex? Or is it what it does? Now, why is a film of an actual rape different?

Child pornography is exclusively pictures and words. The Supreme Court may consider it "pure speech." Civil libertarians and publishers argued to protect it on the same grounds they now argue to protect pornography of adult women. Child pornography conveys very effectively the idea that children enjoy having sex with adults and the feeling that this is liberating for the child. Yet child pornography is prohibited as child abuse based on the use of children to make it. A recent case extended this recognition of harm to other children downstream who are later made to see and imitate the pictures by adults who consume them. Possessing and distributing such pictures is punishable by imprisonment. This has been held consistent with the First Amendment even though private reading is thereby restricted. Harm like this may be what the Supreme Court left open to be recognized when, in guaranteeing free access to obscenity in private, it stated, "compelling reasons may exist for overriding the right of the individual to possess the prohibited material."

The point here is that, based on what is in fact the inequality between children and adults, sex pictures are legally considered sex acts. For seeing the pictures as tantamount to acts, how, other than by the fact that sexuality is what socially defines women, is inequality among adults different? Now compare the lynching photographs and the snuff films with the *Penthouse* spread of December 1984 in which Asian women are trussed and hung. One, bound between her legs with a thick rope, appears to be a child. These photos all express ideology, all had to be done to someone to be made, all presumably convey something as well as provide entertainment. If used at work, this *Penthouse* series would create a hostile working environment actionable under federal discrimination law as sexual harassment. It is racism and sexism combined. But there is no law against a hostile living environment, so everywhere else it is protected speech. Not long after this issue of *Penthouse* appeared, a little Asian girl was found strung up and sexually molested, dead, in North Carolina. Suppose, hypothetically, the murderer consumed the *Penthouse* and then went and killed the little girl. He did say he spent much of the day on which it was proven he did the murder at an adult bookstore. This kind of potential causality, an obsession of pornography defenders, is not all that rare or difficult to prove. It is only one effect of pornography. But when one has that effect, is restricting those pictures "thought control"? This is the judicial epithet used to invalidate the law that Andrea Dworkin and I wrote to make such situations actionable. Under these circumstances, would that little girl's death be what *Penthouse* said?

In this country, the state protects pornography. This protection centrally relies on putting it into the context of the silence of violated women, the context that takes it as an idea or a viewpoint. This totally derealizes the subordination of women and makes a technologically sophisticated traffic in women into a consumer choice of expressive content. It turns abused women into a pornographer's thought or feeling. In this approach, pornography falls presumptively into the category of speech, which then has to be negated before one can do anything about it. It comes to be treated essentially as a form of defamation, in terms of negative content about a group, rather than as a form of discrimination, in terms of bigoted actions toward that group. Pornography is not seen in terms of what it does, but in terms of what it says alone. Again, this is not to say that pornography says nothing. It is rather that if there is anything only pornography can say, that is exactly the measure of the harm that only pornography can do.

Now reconsider the definition of pornography that Andrea Dworkin and I wrote: the graphic sexually explicit subordination of women. This is exactly what only pornography does. This definition embodies the function of pornography as defamation or hate speech, but defines it in terms of the way it subordinates on the basis of sex and as a practice of sex discrimination. It is not that pornography is conduct and therefore not speech, or that it does things and therefore says nothing and is without meaning, or that all its harms are noncontent harms. Rather, what is at stake in constructing pornography as speech in opposition to conduct is gaining constitutional protection for doing what pornography does. Subordinating women through sex, which is what it does, is not its content alone. Nor is it wholly other than its content. It is its function. The proper concern of law is with this function—not with what speech says, but with what it does. The meaning of pornography in the sense of its content may be an interesting problem, but it is not our problem. Our problem is what it does to our lives.

The concerns most commonly raised to this approach are essentially political rather than narrowly legal. The one Andrea Dworkin early called the "what can I still have" question is: Do you make all sexually explicit material actionable? Under our definition, if the materials cannot be proven to subordinate anyone, you can still have it. Our ordinance gives victims access to court to prove that they are hurt by pornography. Its passage does not in itself prove that harm. It only accepts that somebody might be able to prove it, and if they can, it is a form of sex discrimination for which they can get relief. That materials are sexually explicit does not, in itself, mean that they subordinate. The definition is not redundant. The only real question is whether sexually explicit materials that do not hurt anyone are sexually arousing like the ones that hurt people are. This is not a problem our law has to solve.

A second common question is: "Doesn't women's subordination happen without pornography?" Second-class status for women is sexualized in many ways worldwide. That women's inferiority is sexualized where there is little or no pornography as we know it does not mean that, where there *is* pornography, women's inferiority is not being sexualized through it. Racists do not wear white sheets in South Africa, so far as I know. That does not make the Klan wearing white sheets nonracist in America. Inequality takes socially specific forms. They need to be addressed in whatever form they exist.

We are also usually asked whether, under our ordinance, gay and lesbian materials will be the first to go. The United States already has an obscenity law that is moralistic, antisex, homophobic, criminal, in the hands of the police, and, for over a decade now, in the hands of the right. It is the perfect tool to eliminate any gay and lesbian material that they want to eliminate. During this time, such materials have only proliferated. The myth that repressive right-wing forces want to destroy pornography is a myth that keeps pornography defined as a form of freedom. They do not want to destroy it, or they would have. It is time to face that the forces of repression may be using it.

Our ordinance recognizes a sex equality right of gay men and lesbians not to be sexually abused. This establishes a human right to be free of sexual abuse for the first time in the same-sex context by legislating against it as discrimination on the basis of sex. Not to cover gay and lesbian materials would exempt harm to gays and lesbians. This would be an abomination.

Finally, there is the question of women's choice to be in these materials. The women who are in the materials are the women who have the fewest choices. If this is a choice, why does it take sexual abuse, poverty, homelessness, and pimps to get a woman to make it? The concept of choice for women here is this: first preclude 99 percent of her options; then, when she spreads her legs for a camera, it is her choice. Finally, although this is more complicated, choosing your chains does not make them not chains.

If a woman in the materials was not coerced into them, she will not use this ordinance. If this hypothetically free woman is used to make materials that hurt other women, they will be able to use it. No matter how a woman got into the materials, those materials can be used to violate other women. The woman in the materials as such is never a target of our law. But when other women can show they are hurt by materials covered by the definition, it will be bad for business.

PORNOGRAPHY AND GLOBAL SEXUAL EXPLOITATION
A New Agenda for Feminist Human Rights

Kathleen Barry

Neither prostitution nor pornography is inevitable, says Kathleen Barry. That is the basic assumption of the proposed Convention Against Sexual Exploitation, a new international human rights instrument based on Barry's work and developed in collaboration with women in countries around the world. In this article, she discusses the global marketing of women's sexuality, and critiques how "liberal individualism" promotes the sexual exploitation of women.

■

Pornography, traditionally defined as the visual representation of prostitutes in the sex trade, is both the practice of sexual exploitation and the ideology that promotes it. As a practice of sexual exploitation, pornography shapes personal relationships and the everyday experience of sexuality, leading to a normalization of prostituted sexuality in everyday life. But pornography is also a set of ideas, an "ideology of cultural sadism" that justifies, legitimizes, and normalizes the power relations that produce women's oppression. It culturally fosters asymmetrical gender relations, promoting sadistic sexual use of women. Through the ideology of cultural sadism, pornography becomes the cornerstone of women's oppression, particularly in Western, economically developed, power-wielding countries.

I am not speaking of pornography only as violence against women. The foundation of all pornography is the objectification of sex. To place pornography only in the framework of violence obscures its larger impact, especially in women's lives. Pornography may be more or less violent, but it is always sexual objectification, an act of power by which women are reduced to the status of things, no longer human. It reduces sex from a human experience to a thing to be gotten, had, taken. Pornography promotes the idea that a woman is sex, a thing, to be purchased for sex, married for sex, dated for sex, used for sex, seized for sex.

Feminist action against pornography is confrontation against sexual oppression in which sex and sexuality are used to subjugate women to an inferior class. It operates through power structures of gender hierarchies to sustain women's inferior status in economic, political, and social life. Exploitation is not only sexual; it maintains reproductive control over women and promotes their economic marginalization in the labor force.

The International Marketplace in Sex

Massive global industries market sex, and women are the sex that is portrayed and *enacted*, bought and sold, in pornography and in prostitution. This sexual exploitation of women in pornography and in prostitution, increasingly accepted as "sex between consenting adults," is both a condition of women's oppression in the West and an instrument of Western hegemony in the developing or "third" world. Sex is marketed and traded in world economies for Western consumers such as businessmen and military men. In industrializing economies, sex industries are financed by Western-based corporations and individuals until they become self-sustaining. In *Prostitution of Sexuality* (New York University Press, 1995) I have identified four general types of sexual exploitation that prevail in different stages of economic and social development:

1. *Trafficking in women.* This exploitation predominates in the least economically developed, poorest countries of the world, where women have almost no place in the public sector. When women are excluded from the public sector, their labor is marginalized in the informal economy, and sexual exploitation is used to service men in marriage or in prostitution. But considering the privatization of women in marriage and the family, prostitution most frequently is the result of brutal force and kidnapping by traffickers.

2. *Military prostitution.* This type of sexual exploitation is organized where there is the massive deployment of military troops in war-ravaged regions. Both trafficking and sex industries are organized to meet male market demand from the military presence, usually by procuring women and girls who are displaced during war.

3. *Sex industrialization in newly developing countries.* In the developing world, with the intensification of economic development comes a population shift from rural to urban and from domestic-oriented production to export-oriented production. Women migrate to cities as they are displaced from their traditional (informal sector) labor in rural areas. Sex industries appropriate

them, marginalizing them from the developing labor force. In the first phases of sex industrialization, Western prostitution and pornography industries establish markets and business operations in the newly developing economies. This, like military prostitution, is an acute phase in which Western control of world markets facilitates deployment and growth of new sex industries. It is the transitional phase in sexual oppression, as women's privatized sexual exploitation in the home, marriage, and the family is made public, institutional, and economic in ways that it had not been when social life was private and primarily rural, and women's lives were confined within the household and the informal economic sector.

4. *Prostitution of sexuality.* In advanced economically developed countries—where the private sector of marriage and family is no longer the primary or only domain of women—sexual oppression configures around women as a public fact. Public sexual exploitation takes place particularly through the normalization of prostitution and pornography, which produces what I have called "the prostitution of sexuality." When, because of economic development, women cannot be contained and confined by the private oppression in the family and in marriage, then potential economic and emotional independence from patriarchal domination is thwarted by public sexual exploitation. Pornography becomes a central tool for the subordination of women. Liberalized laws and attitudes facilitate its widespread dissemination through public reduction of women to sex. Sexual exploitation follows women to work and down the street as sexual harassment. It follows women in dating and at parties, in personal relationships increasingly influenced by the pornographic sexualization of society.

Not only does sexual exploitation as a marketed fact of women's oppression vary according to stages of economic development and the public and private conditions of women that I have identified here, but it is an instrument of Western hegemony over the developing world. The production of sex industries in the West is not the problem only of U.S. or European or Australian women. When those industries are marketed to the developing world, Western women become part of the apparatus of Western control. For example, the pornography and prostitution demanded by Western military men stationed in developing countries leads to massive sexual exploitation of women in those regions. This appetite for prostitution is an extension of the men's access to pornography at home. Their sexual contempt for American women is extended to and against women of the region to which they are assigned, where race or culture as well as gender are invoked by customers to reduce women to whores, to be used for sex.

The Hegemony of Liberal Individualism

In the United States, the social institutions of pornography and prostitution are imbedded in the liberal state, the state that elevates individualism for the sake of promoting market exchange above all other values. I am not speaking of the superficial, relatively meaningless political party distinctions between liberal and conservative. Rather, I am referring to liberalism as a state ideology of capitalist market economies in advanced economically developed countries. Central to the perpetuation of those market economies is the ideology of liberal individualism, which reifies the individual as separate, disconnected from others, autonomous in society. That formulation of individualism is the foundation needed to promote market exchange and a competitive labor market.

The 1990s "debates" over pornography, particularly in the U.S., reflect reactive responses that come from the capitalist market economy and its supporting ideology of liberal individualism—"debate" being a construct that suggests freedom of expression and acceptance of varying points of view. But in liberal individualism, *anything* that is produced is marketable. To insure that market force, the market defines and controls the debates.

By contrast, in liberation struggles, oppression is not debatable. There are not two or many pluralist viewpoints from the standpoint of the oppressed. By elevating choice and speech above all other human actions and socio-political conditions, Western liberal ideology renders oppression invisible. Consequently, the years of censorship that those of us who have confronted sexual oppression have been subjected to are excluded from the liberal, market-driven discussions of freedom, speech, and choice as that discourse excludes oppression as a fact and as a thought.

In the liberal and patriarchal state's production of pornography, speech has been made into the defining feature of freedom because liberal individualism (in its promotion of market economies) reduces freedom to that which services markets. The liberal ideology creates a public psychology that serves individuals and individual rights. Analysis of and debates over whether pornography is speech, whether that speech is harmful and hateful, are founded in a discourse of liberal individualism that is intended to obscure the fundamental power relations inherent in both liberal market economies and patriarchies.

As liberalism attempts to colonize feminist action against sexual exploitation by reducing it to its terms, we witness the return of blaming the victim. Right-wing spokesmen such as Rush Limbaugh and writers such as Katie Roiphe and Naomi Wolfe promote the idea that women are obsessed with being victims. In denying oppression, they obscure male agency in the sexual exploitation of women. In the same way officials now treat drug abuse as the fault of the abuser, diverting attention from the traffickers, the harm to women from sexual exploitation is said to be their own fault.

Inevitably, feminist action must confront sexual oppression within the ideological and material conditions of its society. In the United States and the West in general, radical feminist legal action that confronts pornography must struggle both within and against liberal individualism. Invariably, the dominant patriarchal discourse imposes the terms of the debate, and in the case of feminist anti-pornography action, those terms are increasingly framed within the context of "speech." This is not the appropriate framework for a struggle for liberation from sexual exploitation. Hence debates about speech, about whether speech is speech or speech is an act, are meant to constrain the movement and deflect attention from the fact that, from a sociological standpoint, all speech is human action—and it is the *acts* of sexual exploitation that oppress women, acts sustained and promoted by the ideology of cultural sadism.

Consequently feminist struggle for liberation from sexual oppression must fight both within the dominant discourse, against its definition of speech, and outside that discourse, beyond the limits of national ideology and state interest in market relations. That means addressing the global condition of women not only in particular challenges to any of the ideologies but from global norms that transcend all state ideologies. Beyond liberal or socialist or any other state ideology, global feminist consciousness develops from the common dimensions of women's oppression.

Yet at the same time, pornography and sex industries are the core of normalized sexual exploitation in the U.S. and in the West. Because the U.S. still controls the dominant interests in the global economy, its culture is exported to the developing and underdeveloped and war-ravaged parts of the world and is implicated in women's oppression everywhere.

The New Feminist Agenda: Internationalizing the Problem

To cast sexual oppression in a global setting, I have drawn from United Nations human rights principles that protect both the rights of individual human beings and the collective rights of peoples to self-determination. I have analyzed the material conditions of sexual exploitation as they vary from developing to developed world regions. There are no international or national laws that are not patriarchal, and certainly international human rights law, as codified in United Nations conventions, bears the stamp of liberal individualism with its focus on individual rights. But international human rights law protects economic, social, and cultural rights. It recognizes the right of self-determination of peoples, thus recognizing conditions of group oppression.

The Coalition Against Trafficking in Women, working internationally with UNESCO, as well as through feminist networks in each world region, has developed a new international human rights law against sexual exploitation. The Convention Against Sexual Exploitation defines "sexual exploitation" as:

> a practice by which person(s) achieve sexual gratification or financial gain or advancement through the abuse of a person's sexuality by abrogating that person's human right to dignity, equality autonomy, and physical and mental well-being.

By casting the widest possible net, this definition encompasses the range of conditions of sexual oppression. Accordingly, following from the universal principles of human rights, the Convention Against Sexual Exploitation declares that "it is a fundamental human right to be free from sexual exploitation in all of its forms." Its forms include battering, pornography, prostitution, genital mutilation, female seclusion, dowry and bride price, forced sterilization and child-bearing, sexual harassment, rape, incest, sexual abuse, and trafficking in women.

In transcending the liberal individualistic discourse of advanced or developed states, the Convention identifies sexual exploitation as oppression, specifically rejecting a distinction some have made between so-called "free" prostitution and "forced" prostitution. In the act of sexual exploitation—where exploiters gain and those who are exploited are harmed—the issue of consent is not the primary defining characteristic of human rights violation. The main issue is that in prostitution a woman's body is bought and sold as a commodity, exchanged, not always for money, but for some gain on the part of the purchase. Therefore, in the Convention, states are called upon to reject any policy or law that legitimizes prostitution of any person, male or female, adult or child, so-called "first" or "third" world, that distinguishes between free and forced prostitution, or that legalizes or regulates prostitution in any way as a profession or occupation. Instead, states are called upon to adopt appropriate legislation that recognizes prostitution as an acute form of sexual exploitation, and therefore to penalize customers while rejecting any form of penalization of the prostitute.

In addition, the Convention calls upon states to enact regulations that hold pornographers liable for violation of women's human rights through sexual exploitation. And it calls upon developing states to reject policies and practices of economic development that channel women into conditions of sexual exploitation, eroding their traditional economic base where it has existed and denying them the economic advantages of development.

The Convention introduces the human right of women to full integration into economic development with dignified paid labor at a decent standard of living following the already existing United Nations human rights protection of each person's right to meaningful and dignified labor at a decent standard of living. It requires prohibiting sex tourism and mail-order bride arrangements that have already been prohibited in the Philippines. Furthermore, this Convention recognizes the need for women in the migrating process to be protected from sexual exploitation; this is especially true for women engaged in domestic labor. As women migrate from rural to urban settings or from one country to another for domestic labor, they are particularly vulnerable to rape and to being trafficked into prostitution. The Convention establishes that employers who sexually exploit women in the migrating process be held criminally liable.

The Convention recognizes sexual exploitation as a political condition of oppression and requires that states recognize escaped victims of sexual exploitation as politically persecuted and provide them with asylum, as well as accord them refugee status. Protection from fraudulent contracts and the right to retain one's own passport are required.

Notably, this Convention establishes the groundwork for national legislation appropriate to the condition of sexual exploitation that prevails in that region. It goes beyond sanctions initiated by victims. Daringly, it recognizes sexual exploitation as a human rights violation and requires sanctions to alleviate it. No new law will end oppression. However, in the struggle for liberation from sexual exploitation, law is a force that can generate new norms and standards. Feminist activism that introduces new legal norms and standards opens the way for supportive programming and policy changes. Developed in conjunction with feminist and human rights projects, the Convention has also helped to spur their work. This is among the potential effects of the new Convention.

A widely based network of individuals and women's organizations in each world region discussed, analyzed, and commented on the developing draft of the Convention to be introduced to the United Nations. It is thus an international grassroots feminist action modified and reformulated to fit the particular needs of women in different world regions, cultures, and conditions. But resistance to it is strong. The new United Nations Declaration to Eliminate All Forms of Violence Against Women *excludes both pornography and prostitution* from its list of forms of violence. With the adoption of this Declaration in 1994, the U.N. is now convinced it has addressed the issue of violence against women. Thus, securing the adoption of the Convention Against Sexual Exploitation becomes even more urgent to women's human rights.

The terms of the global feminist struggle for human rights have been established. It is a struggle that must engage feminists around the world. Ultimately law, neither civil nor criminal, neither national nor international, can replace the struggle against sexual exploitation. Feminist consciousness is the foundation of the struggle, and it must continually be expanding into the range of conditions of sexual exploitation that both confine and connect women globally. It begins and is sustained in the conviction that a world without sexual exploitation is possible.

THE CASES FOR REGULATION OF HATE SPEECH AND PORNOGRAPHY
Are They the Same or Different?

Devona Futch

Until recently, women's organizations and communities of color had made parallel, but independent, progress in analyzing the impact of pornography and hate speech on their respective communities, but there was little intellectual and informational exchange among the various groups working on these issues. However, a few significant events, including the decisions by the Canadian Supreme Court that criminalized hate speech and redefined obscenity as "harm to women," foreshadowed new alliances between feminist scholars and critical race theorists. But how much do the anti–hate speech activists and the antipornography activists have in common? Devona Futch compares the cases for regulation of hate speech and pornography.

■

The March 1993 conference from which this volume grew was the first time that antipornography feminists and anti–hate speech activists joined forces in their battles against hate speech and pornography. Because some have criticized this coalition as unworkable, a brief examination of the commonalities as well as the differences between the two groups is in order.

Both groups begin with a focus on the harm of the protected speech and its silencing effect on the victim—two features with obvious First Amendment implications, and both weighing in favor of regulation. Both groups also emphasize that speech has already been limited in other, similar, areas, but that the doctrines and case laws developed in these areas are inadequate to deal with the full magnitude of the current problem. Despite these similarities, the interests of the two groups are not identical.

Some may suggest that a key difference between the two lies in the fact that conservatives in America will help the antipornography movement but will be indifferent or hostile to hate-speech activism. But this is a shallow reading.

While a greater desire to fight "moral" battles does come in times of increased conservatism, antipornography feminists continue to fight pornography as an issue of domination and discrimination, and not as a moral issue. Although the result sought at both ends of the political spectrum is some limitation of pornography, conservatives want to limit pornography because it is sexually explicit, while feminists want to limit it because it subordinates women. But feminists realize that a politics of inhibiting sexual expression, while possibly contributing to the mainstream acceptance of pornography regulation, would harm the women's movement as a whole. For example, a "morality" rationale would support the regulation of sexually explicit feminist works which involve no subordination of women. Therefore, though at first glance the conservative "morality" movement may seem to be a positive force for antipornography feminists, women in this movement have continued to assert their own theoretical basis for redress from the harm of pornography, and the two groups have continued to operate independently.

The standard argument of "more speech" as the appropriate way to deal with offensive speech presents more of an obstacle for hate-speech activists than for antipornography feminists.* More speech, or talking back, is arguably a more effective counter to the spoken words of hate speech (whether against minorities, gays, women, or whomever) than to the pictures of pornography. It is difficult to imagine the speech that would effectively diffuse the harm of a snuff film. But words of hatred, it seems, may sometimes be effectively countered by words of reason. This distinction, however, is more true in theory than in reality. Although it may be easier to formulate a response to a verbal assault than to a photograph, actually articulating the response can be highly dangerous for a person of color who is the victim of hate speech. A closer look at real life shows that more speech is neither an effective nor a safe way of dealing with *either* form of harmful and discriminatory speech; still, a problem persists in that the legal theory of more speech is likely to cut more harshly against hate-speech regulation than it will against pornography regulation.

Another difference comes from the seemingly distinct risks of violence created by hate speech and pornography. In the case of racist speech, the victim is usually within a few feet of the speaker, and the threat of harm seems more immediate and more closely related to the speech; pornography may look like the mere distribution of an inert product, disconnected from a palpable threat. As with the last point, this distinction disappears under closer scrutiny—for three reasons. First, the apparent difference is based on a mistaken assumption

---

* "More speech" is the requirement in First Amendment jurisprudence that laws regulating speech not be put in place if a countering message could just as easily control the evil of the offensive speech. —Eds.

that no women are raped, assaulted, or murdered in the production of pornography. Second, both speech acts can incite others to commit violent acts
against women and minorities. Observers may hear racist slurs and be incited
to act immediately and violently against a person of color, and the consumer
of pornography is no less susceptible to being influenced to imitate the violence
that he has seen, for example, in an "adult" movie theater. Third, pornography
and hate speech are both instruments of subordination and, as such, work
similarly to reinforce in the dominant group the belief that the lives of women
and minorities are less valuable than their own. This belief leads in both cases
to greater toleration of violence against women and minorities.

Because the First Amendment was primarily intended to protect political
speech, it is easier to regulate speech that is not political. This, too, sets up a
disequilibrium. Pornography is the product of an industry driven by the profit
motive, and as such, is less political than hate speech, which is arguably the
expression of a viewpoint about the society we live in. It is difficult to describe
a photograph of a woman who is gagged, chained, and covered with her own
blood as an expression of a political viewpoint. The relative ease of defining
"niggers should go back to Africa" as political expression may make a court
more willing to accept a narrow regulation of pornography than an equally
well-defined regulation of racist hate speech. (Though some pornographers mix
it up, i.e., use political articles and text to help them make the case that they
publish material with socially redeeming value.) Even if one tried to define
certain pornography materials as the expression of a political viewpoint, the
primary objective of most pornographers is still to make money. They will only
sell what the consumers will buy, and thus will not usually express an unpopular
viewpoint at the expense of their revenue.

The degree of regulation that is ultimately allowed—of either hate speech
or pornography—may also be affected by such factors as who wins first, and
the basis of that victory. For example, if feminists succeed in regulating pornography on the basis that it is not speech, the Court may be reluctant to
permit inroads into the First Amendment to protect victims of hate speech.
Hate-speech regulations cannot as easily be justified on the basis that the acts
they prohibit are not speech, so the Court may succumb to a "slippery slope"
argument. Although Charles Lawrence's argument about *Brown*—that it was
actually a case of prohibiting speech—would provide an analysis not inconsistent with an "it isn't speech" victory for the feminists, the Court would
undoubtedly be hesitant to allow two new exceptions to the First Amendment. *
If, on the other hand, the hate-speech activists were to win first, especially if

---

* For a further discussion of Lawrence's contention that *Brown* v. *Board of Education* was in
reality a case about symbolic expression, see john powell, this volume, p. 332.—Eds.

they won on the basis of the silencing of the victim, it would be easier for feminists to benefit from this success.

Although some of the distinctions I have discussed recede upon further analysis, some remain. Those that persist, however, do not seem to be so pervasive as to preclude coalition between anti–hate speech activists and antipornography feminists. Critical race theory begins with the basic idea that racism is endemic to American society; feminists seeking to eliminate pornography start with the notion that patriarchy is a defining element of American society. Ultimately, however, both critical race theorists and feminists are fighting the same enemy: the protection that the law has given to the most effective weapon against them—the power to alienate, disenfranchise, silence, and subordinate by words and pictures.

FIRST AMENDMENT FORMALISM IS GIVING WAY TO FIRST AMENDMENT LEGAL REALISM

Richard Delgado

Several prominent writers, civil libertarians, and journalists have argued that the alliance between antipornography feminists and hate-speech opponents is a dangerous one, gathering what one termed "speech repressive momentum." But is this accurate? In this article, Richard Delgado argues that this concern only rings true from the perspective of the old paradigm of First Amendment thinking, which is rapidly slipping away into history.

■

First Amendment Legal Realism Arrives
on the Scene, Seventy Years Later

In a recent article and series of op-ed columns, Nadine Strossen, who is president of the ACLU, sets out to explain some of the controversies currently flaring, both inside and outside that organization, over its First Amendment advocacy.[1] In response to critics who charge that the organization has been balancing its commitment to free speech against its commitment to other values, she responds that this is nothing new. The ACLU has always championed these other values, including civil rights and equality. Yet the group is not flagging in defense of free speech, either—in fact, it is near absolutist in this defense. Is there a conflict between promoting equality and the rights of hate speakers and pornographers? No, she says, but if there ever should be one, we could accommodate both by choosing the least speech-restrictive method that will offer the victimized group a degree of protection.

Her tone is reassuring and conciliatory. She presents a picture of the ACLU as a happy family, its internal struggles as healthy disagreement. She also presents a picture in which affiliates that have broken with the national position and endorsed campus speech codes, for example, have in reality not strayed so far from the national position; in which the organization is merely adjusting its ground slightly, arranging its position a few degrees this way or that along the continuum of First Amendment vigilance.

What she says may be true, even laudable, in an organizational sense.[2] But there is another much more intellectually intriguing explanation for the rifts and tugs-of-war taking place inside the ACLU over issues such as pornography and hate speech that test the limits of First Amendment orthodoxy. In this other vision, the skirmishes are not so much questions of standing one's ground, as some of the old-timers see it, or even refining that ground slightly, as Strossen wants to make it appear. Rather, they are skirmishes that arise because the ground itself is shifting. The prevailing First Amendment paradigm is undergoing a slow, inexorable shift. We are seeing the arrival here, nearly seventy years after its appearance in other areas of law, of First Amendment legal realism.[3]* The old, formalist view of speech as a near-perfect instrument for testing ideas and promoting social progress is passing into history. Replacing it is a much more nuanced, skeptical, and realistic view of what speech can do, one that looks to self-interest, class interest, linguistic science, politics, and other tools of the realist approach to understand how expression functions in our system of politics. We are losing our innocence about the First Amendment, but we will all be wiser, not to mention more humane, when that process is complete.

Early in our history, we thought of the First Amendment as the crowning jewel of our jurisprudence.[4] As recently as 1960, prominent scholars were describing our system of free expression in sweeping, exalted terms.[5] But around fifteen years ago, some writers began expressing doubts about whether First Amendment doctrine was capable of delivering on its promises;[6] in the last few years, under the impetus of challenges from critical groups and feminism, the doubts have turned from a trickle into a flood.[7] In what follows, I make no claim to be comprehensive; I am sure my catalogue of new First Amendment conceptions is personal to me. Moreover, the transition to the new paradigm is far from complete; those who write from it still expend much energy defending themselves from charges that they are Satanic, forgetful of history, wrong-headed, or in league with fascism.[8] It is impossible to predict what the new understanding will look like when it is fully mature, just as the early realists could scarcely have predicted how their movement would lead the way to clinical legal education, perspectivism, critical legal studies, or elite law reviews.

---

* Legal realism is the view that judges decide cases based on a host of "realist" factors, including self- and class-interest, preference, and concern over their own reelection, rather than strictly on the basis of legal principles. —Eds.

With those cautions, here are some themes I see forming the outlines of the new conception of the First Amendment.

One is a sense of that amendment's limitations. As mentioned, early in our history, we made grandiose claims for what the system of free expression can do.[9] But recently scholars have shown that our much-vaunted marketplace of ideas works best in connection with questions that are narrowly limited in scope and bounded.[10] Is this parking space safer to leave the car in than another? Does a heavy object fall faster than a light one in a vacuum? Would a voucher school-finance scheme adversely affect the poor? With such clearly bounded disputes, free speech—that is, discussion, debate, reading—can indeed often help us avoid error and arrive at a consensus. But with systemic social ills like racism and sexism, the marketplace of ideas is much less effective. These broad-scale ills are embedded in the reigning paradigms, the sets of meanings and conventions by which we construct and interpret reality. Someone who speaks out against the racism of his or her day is seen as extreme, political, or incoherent. It turns out that speech is least effective where we need it most.[11]

A second theme is the notion of free expression as a legitimating tool.[12] If we have a perfect marketplace of ideas, then the current distribution of social power and resources must be roughly what fairness and justice would dictate. Our more energetic, Western ideas (for example) competed with those other more easygoing ones and won—it was a fair competition. But of course, it was not: communication is expensive, so the poor are often excluded; the dominant paradigm renders certain ideas unsayable or incomprehensible; and our system of ideas and images constructs certain people so that they have little credibility to potential listeners.[13]

This leads to a third component of the new First Amendment legal realism; namely, the idea that language and expression can sometimes serve as instruments of positive harm. Incessant depiction of a group as lazy, stupid, and hypersexual—or as ornamental, for that matter—alters social reality so that members of that group are always one down, that is to say, disadvantaged, the bearers of stigma and lowered expectations.[14] Once this process is complete, even the most scrupulously neutral laws and rules will not save them from falling further and further behind. Affirmative action will become necessary, which will in turn reinforce the view that they are naturally inferior (because they are now in need of special help). Pornography and hate speech are the two most visible fronts on which these battles are currently waged; the struggles around them are also the most likely to come under attack. Naturally, when powerful groups find a particular type of speech offensive and likely to render them one down, they pass a law to curtail it. We rarely notice these "exceptions" and special doctrines, however, because they are time-honored and have become second nature to us. Of course there would be an exception for state secrets, plagiarism, false advertising, and dozens of other types of speech, we say. But one to protect impressionable, young black undergraduates at predominantly white institutions? Oh no, we say—that would be free-speech heresy.[15]

We are beginning to notice how even the labeling of something as a First Amendment problem channels and predetermines the analysis. But why, feminists and civil rights activists ask, should I be a mere compelling state interest in your First Amendment jurisprudence, and not you a compelling state interest in my equality-based analysis?[16] We are belatedly realizing that treating hate speech as a First Amendment problem may make as little sense as treating murder under the commerce clause.

We are beginning to scrutinize such sweeping generalizations as: speech is the best friend of minorities; suppressing racism simply causes it to explode in more virulent forms later; talking back is the best solution to bigotry and sexism; and tolerating face-to-face insults is necessary to an institution of higher learning's status as a center of free speech and inquiry.[17] We are beginning to ask about free speech: Who benefits? And we are beginning to raise the possibility that scoundrels and bigots are hiding under its mantle.[18] We are questioning whether the much-discussed continuum of high-value (viz., normal) and low-value speech may not be all there is. Could there be no-value speech, or speech that has negative value?[19]

We are beginning to flip stock arguments. For example, it is often said that free speech is the best protector of equality. But, perhaps equality is a precondition of effective speech, at least in the grand, dialogic sense.[20] Or, it is said that the campus ought to be a bastion of free speech, which might just as well be rendered: the campus ought to be a bastion of equal, respectful treatment.[21] Or finally, why couldn't the old saw "The cure is more speech" become "The cure is more equality"?

Until now, we have thought that the following argument was decisive: the First Amendment condemns that; therefore it is wrong. Now, we are raising the possibility that the correct argument may sometimes be: the First Amendment condemns that; therefore the First Amendment (or the way we understand it) is wrong.[22] We are beginning to realize that even judges who set out to be scrupulously fair may not be able to balance values in cases such as those concerning hate speech, where free speech and another value (say community) come into conflict, since speech and community are in reality a dyad, not two separate things that a judge could balance, like Jones's right to build a fence and Smith's right to have more sun in his living room.[23]

On the level of ideas, then, the ground is inexorably shifting; First Amendment formalism is giving way to First Amendment realism. Virtually every scholar who keeps up with the field knows this is so. The ACLU's own internal struggles reveal the anxiety and ferment that presage a paradigm shift. It is all there—the ad hominem arguments,[24] the effort to have it both ways, accusations of straying from a holy truth,[25] a sense of beleaguerment,[26] an increase of the decibel level, the resort to paternalistic arguments ("if those minorities knew their own best interest, they would not be clamoring for . . ."),[27] and the strategic retreat ("how about the narrowest possible speech code?").[28]

What will the new paradigm mean for civil rights and civil liberties activism and scholarship? Will we not lose a valuable tool for convincing judges to do equity (that is to say, act fairly and responsibly) and protect human values? Imagine that the same question were asked of any of the early legal realist scholars seventy years ago. They might have replied that misplaced faith in law as a science could not possibly benefit minorities and the oppressed. They might have replied that understanding how law really works is a first step to marshaling that discipline in the service of causes one holds dear. They might have replied that safety does not lie in pleasant fictions. Much the same would seem to hold true today. And in any event, it is too late to turn back. First Amendment realism has arrived. The last fortress of formalist thought and faith has fallen. Unless the ACLU adjusts its thinking to take account of the more nuanced, skeptical view now emerging, its program, counsels, and pronouncements will seem more and more the futile products of a backwater of legal thought.

WORLDS APART
Reconciling Freedom of Speech and Equality

john a. powell

There is a pressing need for dialogue between free speech advocates—who believe that the First Amendment forbids most forms of legal action to redress the harms of hate speech and pornography—and equality advocates—who believe that new approaches to racist and sexist speech and conduct must be considered if we are serious about our commitment to genuine equality and freedom of expression in this country. What prevents this discourse? john a. powell explores the problems the two sides have had coming to terms with one another and makes suggestions for creating a "common bridge" between them.

■

We and the world in which we live are constituted through language.[1] When we tell different stories, we are also inhabiting different worlds that our language constructs. Of course, our stories and worlds are open to revision and change; we are not hermetically sealed off from each other. But these changes do not come about through appealing to a common metalanguage; they come about through our real participation in the world we inhabit and wish to inhabit.

Free speech and equality are two narratives that in large measure describe two different worlds. In a recent article, Richard Delgado captures some of the significance of these differences. He describes reactions to racial incidents on college campuses, first using the voice of a traditional free speech advocate and then using the voice of a traditional advocate of equal opportunity. It is worth recounting his description in detail:

> Persons tend to react to the problem of racial insults in one of two ways. On hearing that a university has enacted rules forbidding certain forms of speech, some will say: "I recognize that; it's a First Amendment problem. The rules limit speech, and the Constitution forbids official regulation of speech without a very good reason." If one takes

that starting point, several consequences follow. First, one shifts the burden to the other side to show that the interest in protecting members of the campus community from insults and name-calling is compelling enough to overcome our usual presumption in favor of free speech. Further, there must be no less onerous way of accomplishing that objective. Moreover, one [who takes this position] will worry about who will enforce the regulation and the risk that he or she will turn into a censor, imposing narrow-minded restraints on campus discussion. One will also be concerned about slippery slopes and [other such] problems. . . . [F]or others "the issue" is the scope of an educational institution's power to promote values of equal personhood on campus. . . . Now, the defenders of racially scathing speech are required to show that the interest in permitting it is compelling enough to overcome our usual preference for equal personhood. We will now want to make sure that this interest is advanced in the way least damaging to equality.[2]

One tradition tells the story of people asserting their autonomy through participation, free thought, and self-expression in the polity. This tradition is wary of any government or community constraint.[3] Indeed, there is the suggestion that such restraint is the great evil to be avoided in society. The other tradition tells the story of a people whom communities and government conspired to exclude from any meaningful participation in the polity or public institution. It tells the story of a government that until very recently actively engaged in efforts to exclude, and now passively stands by while private actors and powerful social forces continue to shut the door to persons seeking full membership in society. This tradition also tells of a long struggle for status, not just as members of the polity, but as complete and respected human beings.[4] Indeed, the great evil to be avoided, as seen from this framework, is discrimination that undermines or destroys someone's humanity.

It is not helpful to ask which of these descriptions is more correct. The assumption that there is some metanarrative we can use to decide which is the better narrative has added to the confusion and lack of dialogue in the current debate.[5] If one inhabits a world in which restraint on self-expression has been one's major concern, then the free speech narrative is more compelling; if one inhabits a world in which inequality has been one's primary concern, then the narrative that privileges equality rings more true. But these are not just stories people tell; they are the great normative values of our Constitution. The question, then, is not simply *which does one choose?*, but *how may these issues be addressed without privileging one over the other?*

It is the way these two paradigms often produce different results in the area of racist speech that creates these difficulties. When two systems are incommensurable, there is no easy way to make a point-by-point comparison. One must be careful that any commonalities are real and not illusory. There is no neutral vantage point from which to work, so one must begin by teasing out from the stories themselves the bases for mediating the two views. Accomplishing this requires giving up the false goal of finding that objective standpoint from which to measure their competing claims. There have been many attempts to find this perspectiveless place. All have failed. Instead, what is required is a reconstitution of the narrative through a dialogical process that both discovers and creates difference and commonality.

Years ago, when the issue of hate speech and equality was first being discussed, I argued that there was no real conflict between the values of free speech and equality. I did this in part because I believe strongly in both sets of values and could see early on that there was a threat of privileging one set over the other. I also argued that there was no principled way of choosing one over the other. Now it is clear that I was wrong in my assertion that there was no conflict. But I was correct that there is no principled way of choosing one over the other. Although it may not be possible, my goal is to suggest a framework in which to give force to both sets of values, since I continue to believe strongly in both.[6]

The most common response to the dilemma of the incommensurability of the free speech and equality narratives is simply to favor one over the other.[7] The only way for someone to make a claim in this way is to tell his or her story and deny that of others.[8] A particular form of this privileging is simply to assert that one set of values is more important than the other, by saying either that this is self-evidently so,[9] or that one narrative is "essential" or normal, while the other is "nonessential" or marginal. For example, many in the ACLU have held that free speech is a constitutional concern, while equality is only a statutory matter in the hate speech context.[10] Another form of this privileging is to characterize the disfavored narrative as derivative of the favored one, and thus of lesser value.[11] A final approach is to redefine the concerns of the disfavored narrative in the terms of the favored one.[12] One takes what could easily be viewed as an equality issue and simply declares it to be a speech issue, or the reverse: "We can talk about your issue, but it must be my story."

In our legal history, and even today, we often assume that the First Amendment is the essential amendment and the Fourteenth the unessential or epiphenomenal one. This position leads to three types of favoritism. The first is the burden of proof: it is the Fourteenth Amendment claimant who must prove that his or her concern is important or necessary, *and that it will not affect* *the favored position in a significant way.* The second calls upon those making equality claims to draw bright lines* in an acceptable way that will leave all of the First Amendment framework undisturbed. Any failure to do this suggests that the Fourteenth Amendment position must give way to the essential free speech narrative. The third is the slippery slope, which calls for even greater assurances. It suggests that even if one can draw acceptable lines in this case, the equality-based narrative must be able to show that the lines will hold in the future and will not be the start of an unacceptable descent.[13] Fred Schauer has suggested that the slippery slope is not a logical argument, but a metaphor to stop real analysis.[14]

Many of the discussions about the relationship between the claims of equality and free speech use some such form of privileging. In most instances, those who use these techniques are not even aware of it. Nor is it always clear to the person advocating the equality paradigm that he or she has been put on the defensive not by the force of an argument, but by the force of a favored narrative.[15] Indeed, the invisibility of privileging often accounts for its power.

The insistence that there is one complete narrative that accurately reflects the world is more than a philosophical error; it can rob people of their own narrative—and therefore their own world. They are forced to live through someone else's story. The struggle in law and in the larger society over the proper language or narrative to use is a struggle for legitimacy, law, and power. The law is replete with examples of how people have been coerced through the silencing of their narratives. For example, consider the Senate Judiciary Committee's Clarence Thomas–Anita Hill hearing: the men insisted that for Professor Hill to have credibility she had to explain herself through a male narrative, one that tells the story that normal people, if harassed at work, will leave.[16] On these terms, since Hill did not leave, she would now have to come forward with a good explanation or be deemed abnormal. She never overcame the burden of this negative assumption.

Another example of how a totalizing narrative can effectively destroy the voice of others is in the *Mashpee Tribe* v. *Town of Mashpee* case.[17] The Court was to decide if land had been expropriated from a tribe in conflict with American law. The main issue was whether the people were a tribe. There were a number of legal categorical slots that the Mashpee were required to meet to qualify as a tribe. One requirement was that all its members be of one race. Another was that the tribe have a leader. Even though the Mashpee considered themselves a tribe, they could not fit into the necessary categories set up by the American legal system.[18] The tribe failed to prove that it was

---

* "Bright lines" means outright legal rules that are susceptible to no other interpretation, that contain no possible ambiguity. —Eds.

made up of one race. The Court never acknowledged that the tribe did not use racial categories to divide the world in the same way that the law does. Not fitting into the "natural categories" that the Court used, or experiencing the world in the terms the law required, caused the Mashpee to lose their voice and their land.

Even when privileging by totalizing does not deny a people the ability to speak,[19] it can deny them a voice that makes sense, and the chance to constitute and maintain their world.[20]

Privileging and the Free Speech/Equality Debate

Let us now consider how privileging manifests itself through the work of Charles Lawrence and Nadine Strossen. I have selected their addresses at a recent ACLU conference (published in the *Duke Law Journal*) as examples because these two writers clearly value both free speech and equality. Each attempts to avoid favoring one set of values over the other. Yet, despite their efforts, each ends up reflecting the bias of his or her dominant narrative on a number of critical points and undermining an opportunity for dialogue.

Strossen and Lawrence begin by making clear that each values both free speech and equality,[21] and that they would like to avoid the conflict between these two narratives. But each finds the other's way of avoiding the conflict unacceptable. Lawrence argues that the most famous equality case should be read as a free speech case: "*Brown* [v. *Board of Education*] held that segregated schools were unconstitutional primarily because of the *message* segregation conveys—the message that black children are an untouchable caste, unfit to be educated with white children."[22] He makes this point to challenge the often cited free speech position that there is a clear line between speech and conduct, and to argue that racist speech is often 100 percent conduct.[23]

Lawrence's argument is subtle and powerful. It gains strength from his re-formulation of *Brown*, in which he focuses on both the positive goal of *Brown* of equal citizenship and the negative one of eliminating a certain type of harm or injury. He argues with elegance and force that racist speech can injure both equality and free speech, and to do this he reappropriates existing language from the narratives of each:

> The second reason that racial insults should not fall under protected speech relates to the purpose underlying the First Amendment. If the purpose of the First Amendment is to foster the greatest amount of speech, then racial insults disserve that purpose. Assaultive racist

speech functions as a preemptive strike. The racial invective is experienced as a blow, not a proffered idea, and once the blow is struck, it is unlikely that dialogue will follow. Racial insults are undeserving of First Amendment protection because the perpetrator's intention is not to discover truth or initiate dialogue but to injure the victim.[24]

The discussion of injury caused by racist speech is one of the most powerful parts of Lawrence's analysis. Here, again, he tries to situate his objection to racist speech within the free speech narrative. It is when he discusses the injury that regulation may cause to free speech that he slips into privileging the equality narrative: "Our experience is that the American system of justice has never been symmetrical where race is concerned. No wonder we see equality as a precondition to free speech, and we place more weight on that side of the balance aimed at the removal of the badges and incidents of slavery."[25] Whether one agrees with this statement or not, it is clear that it speaks from outside the narrative of free speech. Although Lawrence at first reformulates *Brown* as a speech case, he then subtly moves to have equality trump speech. He argues not only that it is appropriate to balance free speech and equality, but that equality must prevail.[26] Indeed, he suggests that this position was the point of *Brown*.

Strossen is no less concerned with avoiding a sharp conflict between free speech and equality. She begins by considering that campuses have an obligation both to equal opportunity and to free speech.[27] She also acknowledges that some of the injuries to which Lawrence refers could be reduced by hate-speech rules. But she ducks the hard issues by asserting that much of the speech activity about which he is concerned is not protected under the First Amendment, assuming in the process that if it were speech under First Amendment protection, it could not be regulated even if it did cause the injuries Lawrence chronicles. Strossen argues generally that we all have an obligation to fight racism and that this has been a priority for the ACLU.[28]

Once she addresses the specific concerns raised by Lawrence, she writes from a strong First Amendment position. Within that position, her arguments are persuasive, but the balance she wishes to maintain between a concern for speech and equality is quickly lost. While Lawrence writes about the injury racist speech can cause, Strossen reduces most of these injuries to mere offense.[29]

Those who emphasize the free speech narrative, like Strossen, are extremely reluctant to concede that racist speech is ever any more than offensive, while those speaking from an equality narrative are more likely to speak of racist speech as an injury or wound.[30] Strossen is not entirely unaware of this problem and repeatedly tries to avoid these sharp extremes in labeling. In her analysis, however, she frequently slips back into trivialization: "The essentials of a *Skokie*-type setting are that the offensive speech occurs in a public place. . . . Hence the offensive speech can be either avoided or countered. . . ."[31]

Strossen's principal argument against Lawrence's position is that his proposal would change, cut back, and chill free speech.* She seems unaware that her approach would limit, if not undermine, equality. This oversight is easily made once she chooses to argue from the existing narrative of free speech, with its only slight acknowledgment of the value of equality, at least where it conflicts with free speech. For example, while Strossen acknowledges that injury can result from hate speech, she assumes that if the injury runs up against free speech, we have to accept the injury: "[S]tatements that defame groups convey opinions or ideas on matters of public concern, and therefore should be protected even if those statements also injure reputations or feelings."[32] She further states, "[T]here is an inescapable risk that any hate speech regulation, no matter how narrowly drawn, will chill speech beyond its intended scope."[33] She does not seem to be aware that such a description of what can be regulated can have a harsh impact on equality.

In sum, even in talking about constitutional goals and constraints, Lawrence and Strossen split at points of conflict, and prioritize the Fourteenth Amendment and the First Amendment, respectively. They, like most commentators, want to avoid the most difficult aspect of the problem: how do we resolve the tension when First Amendment–protected speech conflicts with the constitutional value of equality? Strossen simply denies that such a conflict exists— though if forced to acknowledge it, she would privilege speech. Lawrence, on the other hand, defines protected speech so that harmful speech either falls outside First Amendment protection, or is made to give way to equality concerns.

While Strossen argues that Lawrence's proposal would injure our current understanding of free speech, Lawrence would argue that Strossen's approach would restrict our understanding of the Thirteenth and Fourteenth amendments and retard racial equality. Who, in court, has the burden to draw the line in the "appropriate" place and prove that it will hold? Whoever has the burden loses.

Lawrence and Strossen are not the only ones who lapse into privileging in the ways I have described. Courts do so as well. There have not been many cases where the Court has had to address the tension between equality and free

---

* Chilling refers to the way in which rules aimed at preventing bad speech may deter good speech as well. —Eds.

speech, but where the tension has arisen, the Court has reproduced the problem of privilege exhibited in the Strossen/Lawrence debate, but without their sensitivity. These cases reveal more about how the judges privilege one framework over the other than about how, in a principled way, to select the "correct" framework or to mediate between the two. In *Doe v. University of Michigan*[34] and *UWM Post Inc. v. Regents, University of Wisconsin*[35] each court unreflectively and with little sense of the ambiguities at stake adopted the free speech perspective. In *Hazelwood School District v. Kuhlmeier*,[36] the Court submerged the First Amendment interests of the students to those of the school administration. And in *Robinson v. Jacksonville Shipyards*,[37] the Supreme Court embraced the equality paradigm in a workplace harassment case, even though the case contained a substantial free-expression component.

Participation and membership in critical institutions are essential to the development of both social values and the autonomous self. This participation must be free of domination and subjugation for the norms and values a society produces to be legitimate:[38] the slave and master can apparently participate in dialogue, but they cannot together generate valid collective norms. In other words, the conception of what harms must be blocked to preserve participation must be broader than what was allowed by the formalism of *Plessy v. Ferguson*: it upheld the principle of "separate but equal" even where substantive equality was undermined. Yet it must not be so broad as to consume free speech, which would also undermine the values central to equality of autonomy and the production of intersubjective norms and values.

Although traditional proponents of free speech often disagree on which values underlie the First Amendment, there is virtual consensus on two central values: participation in the democratic process and self-actualization through expression.[39] Much of the debate among free speech proponents focuses on whether speech is primarily a social value—enabling participation in the cultural and political structures—or a liberty value—promoting self-actualization and self-expression to achieve and maintain autonomy. I suggest that participation is central to both.

Recently, the debate about the underlying values of free speech has been informed by the work of Jürgen Habermas and others who urge an antiobjectivist, antifoundationalist stance toward truth and value. According to these writers, the individual's needs, wants, and identity have meaning only because of the social or cultural context,[40] something that early proponents of free speech maintained as well when they characterized truth-finding and law-making as essential parts of the social value of free speech.[41] This is crucial: seeing truth as created instead of discovered[42] places greater emphasis on the value of participation.

The value of this approach is often muted by failure to consider seriously what distorts and invalidates the communicative process that generates truths. Habermas recognizes that domination and unequal power undermine the validity of truth claims that are produced through their presence. He calls for a move toward an ideal speech situation where participation is not distorted by such power or domination. It should be emphasized that this is a call not for a new language theory, but for a clear view of what is necessary for successful dialogue: meaningful participation. His ideal requires equality and mutuality among the speakers, requirements that are closely tied to what is necessary for full participation and membership in society.

In our liberal society, we recognize the normative foundation of the equal right to participate. If value and truth claims are to have any legitimacy, participation must be both uncoerced and open to all as equals. As S. Benhabib has written, "[There is] no universalizability without participation."[43] The only universal then that we can recognize is the right to universal participation. Participation is not something we simply use; it is through participation that we obtain and maintain our autonomy. Conversely, if someone is denied participation and membership, it is doubtful that he or she can even develop an autonomous self. As Habermas makes clear, our autonomy is communicative. Participation, therefore, has both a social and an individual role.

Equality proponents are increasingly noting the central role of participation. Although some commentators have argued that equality is formal and requires no particular normative content, they confuse equality as a philosophical concept with equality as a historical, constitutional value. The question, then, is crystallized as: what is the substantive content of equality? I believe there are many components—antisubordination, dignity, and citizenship, to name a few. But most central to our notion of what constitutional equality means is the ideal of participation. Kenneth Karst argues that the historical and judicial concept for the meaning of the Fourteenth Amendment is grounded in the right to belong, participate, and be a full member. He asserts that this is what animated not only the enactment of the amendment, but also a number of the great decisions by the Court, including *Brown*. One of the evils of segregation was that it denied blacks the right to participate as equal citizens. The refusal to recognize slaves as full members of society was closely tied to their legal status as nonpersons devoid of autonomy, a status reaffirmed by the Court in the *Dred Scott* decision. In each case, the harm was not only to the social participation of blacks, but also to their development of self.

Michael Walzer supports the primacy of the value of participation. He states that the primary good that a society distributes is not liberty or equality, but membership. It is from membership and the right to participation that all other goods are produced and take on meaning.[44] It is the basic premise of our constitutional democracy that all citizens should have an equal right to participate in both political and cultural life. While the exact, and even the functional, meaning of equality and free speech may remain seriously contested, the centrality of participation to both sets of values is itself not controversial, especially in what I call "critical institutions."

Work and school are two such places. The relationships that occur in these places enhance individual identity and the capacity for autonomy; they are sites for the construction and development of social values and truths. Participation in particular kinds of work allows one to take part in the social construction of the expectations of one's community. Being paid for work, and thus having access to financial resources, also serves to develop self-worth and social worth—since our society seriously calls into question the value of someone without financial resources. Employment helps to define us and give our life meaning. The plaintiff in the *Jacksonville Shipyards* case,*[45] through her employment in a nontraditional trade, is able to participate in an ongoing social dialogue about the meaning of gender.

The university is similarly important, in that it provides access to future employment and fosters the development of individual and social meaning. To deny an individual or group the right to participate in campus decisions shuts out a potential voice in the academic discourse, and thus distorts and delegitimizes the values that result from this process.[46] This suggests another way the Court might look at racist speech. The Court could first determine how critical the institution or location is for generating individual and social participation values, what the particular participation interests are, and whether they could be adequately exercised in a different context without substantial burden. The Court could then consider the nature of the speech activity and how strongly it is tied to the particular setting. The alternatives open to the different parties would also be considered. Then the Court could make a judgment on these grounds. If the speech activity injured participation by excluding others, this would weigh toward proscribing it, or would at least weaken the Court's protection.

We speak from different narratives that describe different worlds. And yet, since language is open, sometimes two worlds touch. To do justice to each of these worlds, we need to develop approaches that describe and transform; we

* An important decision establishing the cause of action for workplace harassment.—Eds.

must avoid the assumption that there is an objective foundation that relieves one from engaging with the other. We must refrain from premature surrender, from declaring that there is no way of communicating with the other, no possibility of finding or creating a common and shared language. We must avoid the complementary illusions of believing that we are either radically the same or radically different. We must be suspicious of domination that hides behind radical relativism or radical objectivism.

It is because we are both the same and different that dialogue is necessary and possible.

EPILOGUE
Unfreeze the Discussion

This collection's first-person accounts, empirical studies, and analyses of a legal system under strain all converge on a single, ineluctable truth: our society is in the middle of a major sea change in the way it thinks about pornography and hate speech.

Despite resistance from free speech traditionalists and proponents of conventional categorical thinking, we are seeing the emergence of a new approach to the First Amendment, one we might call a "theory of problematic speech," or "First Amendment legal realism." Just as other Realist scholars have done since the early years of this century, these First Amendment Realists are showing how current social practice favors particular groups or industries. They are demonstrating that the way we frame a problem influences the answer. They are analyzing how science and pseudoscience contribute to the construction of social reality through their authoritative statements: *"This* is harm, and not that"; *"This* chilling effect we will agree to be serious, and not that one." This unlocking and broadening of the range of topics under discussion is already under way, and it is wholly salutary. It is helping us define and redefine ourselves as a people.

Rigid rules that always deem only certain matters relevant—that say certain interests will forever trump others—interfere with the kind of broad discussion we need to have before we can arrive at decisions on the troubling issues this book raises. The lower federal courts are a perfect laboratory for consideration of these issues. The Supreme Court should free them to do so. During times of change, bright line rules laid down in times when we were not in flux —when everyone knew what men could say about women, whites about minorities—may no longer serve us well. At a minimum, they could foreclose prematurely discussion of important matters that are now being seriously debated. Carrying these rules forward now inhibits the type of wide-ranging debate our society relies on for redefining itself, for deciding when or how it should change.

In previous eras, the Supreme Court drew criticism for getting too far out in front of society. Today, with hate speech and pornography, it risks getting too far behind; it risks becoming an impediment to serious social dialogue; it risks depriving the nation of the benefit it could reap from further discussion. To be sure, the Court has allies in academia, certain industries, even in some impeccably liberal organizations, who affirm that its approach is the right one. But before too long, we predict, their view will be swept aside by history. Then, looking back, an irony will stand out starkly. And that irony is that the most stubborn resistance to the national town meeting we propose stems from those who wear, most solemnly and unself-consciously, the mantle of the First Amendment.

NOTES AND REFERENCES

Chapter Two

HOWARD I. EHRLICH, BARBARA E.K. LARCOM, AND ROBERT D. PURVIS

Kevin T. Berrill. "Anti-Gay Violence and Victimization in the United States: An Overview," in Gregory M. Herek and Kevin T. Berrill, eds., *Hate Crimes: Confronting Violence Against Lesbians and Gay Men.* Newberry Park, Calif.: Sage Publications, 1992.

Howard J. Ehrlich. "Studying Workplace Ethnoviolence." *International Journal of Group Tensions* 19: 69–80, 1989.

Howard J. Ehrlich. *Campus Ethnoviolence: A Research Review.* Baltimore, Md.: National Institute Against Prejudice and Violence, Institute Report no. 5, 1992.

Howard J. Ehrlich, Fred L. Pincus, and Cornel Morton. *Ethnoviolence on Campus: The UMBC Study.* Baltimore, Md.: National Institute Against Prejudice and Violence, 1987.

Federal Bureau of Investigation. *Hate Crime Data Collection Guidelines.* Washington, D.C.: FBI, 1990.

National Gay and Lesbian Task Force Policy Institute. *Making Injustice Visible: Documenting Bias-Motivated Incidents.* Washington, D.C.: NGLTF, 1992.

National Institute Against Prejudice and Violence. *Community Response to Bias-Crimes and Ethnoviolent Incidents.* Baltimore, Md.: NIAPV, 1993.

Donald R. Peterson. *Students Speak on Prejudice.* Rutgers, N.J.: [The University] Committee to Advance Our Common Purposes, 1990.

Anthony Taylor. *Campus Discrimination and Prejudice.* Taylor: SUNY College at Cortland, 1990.

Joan C. Weiss, Howard J. Ehrlich, and Barbara E.K. Larcom. "Ethnoviolence at Work." *Journal of Intergroup Relations* 18 (4): 21–33, 1991–92.

The complete report of the National Victimization Survey appears as a report to the Ford Foundation under grant 880-0507, *The Ethnoviolence Project: Final Narrative Report of the First National Survey of Prejudice and Violence in the United States (October 1992).*

The complete report on the corporate workplace study appears as a report to the National Institute of Justice under grant 90-IJ-CX-0056, *Prejudice and Violence in the Workplace (August 1993).*

Both reports are available from their sponsors or from the Prejudice Institute/Center for the Applied Study of Ethnoviolence, Stephens Hall Annex, TSU, Towson, Md. 21204.

WENDY STOCK

Buchman, J. "Effects of Repeated Exposure to Nonviolent Erotica on Attitudes about Sexual Child Abuse," in D. Zillmann and J. Bryant, eds., *Pornography: Research Advances and Policy Considerations.* Hillsdale, NJ: Erlbaum, 1989.

Campbell, B. "A Portrait of an Angel: The Life of a Porn Star." In D. Russell, ed., *Making Violence Sexy.* New York: Teachers College Press, 1993.

Check, J., B. Elias, and S. Barton. "Hostility toward Men and Sexual Victimization." In G. W. Russell, ed., *Violence in Intimate Adult Relationships.* New York: Spectrum, 1987.

Check, J. and T. Guloien. "Reported Proclivity for Coercive Sex Following Repeated Exposure to Sexually Violent Pornography, Nonviolent Dehumanizing Pornography, and Erotica." In D. Zillmann and J. Bryant, eds., *Pornography: Research Advances and Policy Considerations.* Hillsdale, NJ: Erlbaum, 1989.

Cowan, G. "Degrading Pornography: Not Just in the Beholder's Eye." *Journal of Sex Research,* accepted 1993; forthcoming.

Cowan, G., C. Lee, D. Levy, and D. Snyder. "Dominance and Inequality in X-Rated Video-cassettes." *Psychology of Women Quarterly*, 12, 299–311, 1988.

Donnerstein, E. and G. Barrett. "Effects of Erotic Stimuli on Male Aggression toward Females." *Journal of Personality and Social Psychology*, 36 (2), 180–188, 1978.

Donnerstein, E. and J. Hallam. "Facilitating Effects of Erotica on Aggression against Women." *Journal of Personality and Social Psychology*, 36 (11), 1270–1277, 1978.

Dworkin, A. Address at the Symposium on Media Violence and Pornography, February 5, 1984, Toronto, Ontario, Canada.

Dworkin, A. "Against the Male Flood: Censorship, Pornography, and Equality." *Harvard Women's Law Journal*, 8, 1–29, 1985.

French, M. *The War against Women*. New York: Random House, 1992.

Giobbe, E. "Surviving Commercial Sexual Exploitation." In D. Russell, ed., *Making Violence Sexy*. New York: Teachers College Press, 1993.

Hariton, B. and J. Singer. "Women's Fantasies during Sexual Intercourse." *Journal of Consulting and Clinical Psychology*, 42 (3), 313–322, 1974.

Harmon, P. and J. Check. *The Role of Pornography in Woman Abuse* (report no. 33). Toronto: LaMarsh Research Programme on Violence and Conflict Resolution, York University, 1989.

Heiman, J. "A Psychophysiological Exploration of Sexual Arousal Patterns in Females and Males." *Psychophysiology*, 14 (3), 266–274, 1975.

Koss, M. and T. Dinero. "Predictors of Sexual Aggression among a Sample of Male College Students." In V. Quinsey and R. Prentky, eds., *Human Sexual Aggression: Current Perspectives*. Annals of the New York Academy of Sciences, 528, 133–147, 1989.

Krafka, C. *Sexually Explicit, Sexually Violent, and Violent Media: Effects of Multiple Naturalistic Exposures and Debriefing on Female Viewers*. Unpublished doctoral dissertation, University of Wisconsin, Madison, 1985.

Leidholdt, D. "Commentary: The *Hustler* Connection." Opening remarks, debate on pornography sponsored by Campbell University School of Law, Raleigh, North Carolina, April 5, 1983.

Linz, D., E. Donnerstein, and S. Penrod. "The Effects of Multiple Exposures to Filmed Violence against Women." *Journal of Communication*, 34 (3), 130–147, 1984.

Malamuth, N. "Aggression against Women: Cultural and Individual Causes." In N. Malamuth and E. Donnerstein, eds., *Pornography and Sexual Aggression*. New York: Academic Press, 1984.

Malamuth, N. and J. Check. "The Effects of Mass Media Exposure on Acceptance of Violence against Women: A Field Experiment." *Journal of Research in Personality*, 15, 436–446, 1981.

Malamuth, N. and J. Check. "Penile Tumescence and Perceptual Responses to Rape as a Function of Victim's Perceived Reactions." *Journal of Applied Social Psychology*, 10, 528–547, 1980.

Malamuth, N., M. Heim, and S. Feshbach. "The Sexual Responsiveness of College Students to Rape Depictions: Inhibitory and Disinhibitory Effects." *Journal of Personality and Social Psychology*, 38, 399–408, 1980.

Mosher, D. "Sex Differences, Sex Experience, Sex Guilt, and Explicitly Sexual Films." *Journal of Social Issues*, 29 (5), 95–112, 1973.

Mosher, D. and I. Greenberg. "Females' Affective Reactions to Reading Erotic Literature." *Journal of Consulting and Clinical Psychology*, 33, 472–477, 1969.

Russell, D. "Pornography and Violence: What Does the New Research Say?" in L. Lederer, ed., *Take Back the Night: Women on Pornography*. New York: William Morrow, 1980.

Russell, D. "From Witches to Bitches: Sexual Terrorism Begets *Thelma and Louise*." In D. Russell, ed., *Making Violence Sexy*. New York: Teachers College Press, 1993.

Russell, D. "The Experts Cop Out." In D. Russell, ed., *Making Violence Sexy*. New York: Teachers College Press, 1993.

Senn, C., and H. Radtke. "Women's Evaluations of and Affective Reactions to Mainstream Violent Pornography, Nonviolent Pornography, and Erotica." *Violence and Victims*, 5 (3), 143–155, 1990.

Silbert, M., and A. Pines. "Pornography and Sexual Abuse of Women." *Sex Roles*, 10 (11–12), 857–868, 1984.

Smith, D. "The Social Content of Pornography." *Journal of Communication*, 26, 16–33, 1977.

Sommers, E., and J. Check. "An Empirical Investigation of the Role of Pornography in the Verbal and Physical Abuse of Women." *Violence and Victims*, 2 (3), 189–209, 1987.

Spence, J., and R. Helmreich. *Masculinity and Femininity: Their Psychological Dimensions, Correlates, and Antecedents.* Austin: University of Texas Press, 1978.

Steinem, G. "Erotica and Pornography: A Clear and Present Difference." *Ms.*, 7 (5), 53–54, 75–78. Also in L. Lederer, ed., *Take Back the Night: Women on Pornography.* New York: William Morrow, 1980.

Steinem, G., and C. Steiner. "The Real Linda Lovelace." In D. Russell, ed., *Making Violence Sexy.* New York: Teachers College Press, 1993.

Steiner, C. "Radical Psychiatry: Principles." In C. Steiner, ed., *Readings in Radical Psychiatry.* New York: Grove Press, 1975.

Stock, W. *The Effects of Violent Pornography on the Sexual Responsiveness and the Attitudes of Women.* Unpublished doctoral dissertation, State University of New York at Stony Brook, 1983.

Stock, W. "Differential Responses of Women and Men to Pornography and Erotica." Symposium on the effects of film stimuli on sexual attitudes, Division of Media Psychology (46), American Psychological Association, San Francisco, CA, August 18, 1991.

Stock, W. "Female Genital and Subjective Responses to Pornography." Symposium on research issues in female sexuality. International Academy of Sex Research, Eighteenth Annual Meeting, Prague, Czechoslovakia, July 7, 1992.

Stock, W. "The Effects of Pornography on Women." Symposium on new research on pornography. Annual meeting of the Society for the Scientific Study of Sex, November 5, 1993, Chicago, IL.

Stoller, R. "Sexual excitement." *Archives of General Psychiatry*, 33, 899–909, 1976.

Strachan, B. "Pornographic Content of Popular Adult Home Video Cassettes in Kitchener-Waterloo." Undergraduate thesis, Department of Recreation, Human Kinetics and Leisure Studies, University of Waterloo, 1985.

Weaver, J. *Effects of Portrayals of Female Sexuality and Violence against Women on Perceptions of Women.* Doctoral dissertation, Indiana University, Bloomington, 1987.

Zillmann, D., and J. Bryant. "Effects of Massive Exposure to Pornography." In N. Malamuth and E. Donnerstein, eds., *Pornography and Sexual Aggression.* New York: Academic Press, 1984.

Zillmann, D., and J. Bryant. "Effects of Prolonged Consumption of Pornography." In D. Zillmann and J. Bryant, eds., *Pornography: Research Advances and Policy Considerations.* Hillsdale, NJ: Erlbaum, 1989.

GLORIA COWAN

Bell, L., ed. *Good Girls/Bad Girls: Feminists and Sex Trade Workers Face to Face.* Toronto: Seal, 1987.

Collins, P. H. "The Sexual Politics of Black Womanhood." In P. B. Bart and E. G. Moran, eds., *Violence against Women: The Bloody Footprints.* Newbury Park, CA: Sage, 1993.

Cowan, G., and R. R. Campbell. "Racism and Sexism in Interracial Pornography." *Psychology of Women Quarterly*, forthcoming.

Cowan, G., C. Lee, D. Levy, and D. Snyder. "Dominance and Inequality in X-Rated Videocassettes." *Psychology of Women Quarterly*, 12, 299–312, 1988.

Cowan, G., and G. Stahly. "Attitudes toward Pornography Control." In J. C. Chrisler and D. Howard, eds., *New Directions in Feminist Psychology: Practice, Theory, and Research.* New York: Springer Publishing Company, 1992.

Forna, A. "Pornography and Racism: Sexualizing Oppression and Inciting Hatred." In C. Itzen, ed., *Pornography: Women, Violence, and Civil Liberties: A Radical New View.* New York: Oxford University Press, 1992.

Johnson, J. D. *The Differential Racial Effects of Exposure to Erotica.* Unpublished doctoral dissertation, Indiana University, Bloomington, 1984.

Muehlenhard, C. L. " 'Nice Women' Don't Say Yes and 'Real Men' Don't Say No: How Miscommunication and the Double Standard Can Cause Sexual Problems." *Women and Therapy: A Feminist Quarterly*, 7, 95–108, 1988.

Roper Center for Public Opinion Research. *General Social Survey*, 1972–1986: Cumulative Codebook, July 1985. Storrs, CT: University of Connecticut Press, 1986.

Russo, A. "Conflicts and Contradictions among Feminists over Issues of Pornography and Sexual Freedom." *Women's Studies International Forum*, 10, 103–112, 1987.

Staples, R. "Blacks and Pornography: A Different Response." In M. Kimmel, ed., *Men Confront Pornography*. New York: Meridian, 1991.

Zillmann, D. "Effects of Prolonged Exposure to Pornography." In D. Zillmann and J. Bryant, eds., *Pornography: Research Advances and Policy Consideration*. Hillsdale, NJ: Erlbaum, 1989.

GLORIA COWAN AND WENDY STOCK

Baron, L. "Pornography and Gender Inequality: An Empirical Analysis." *Journal of Sex Research*, 27, 363–380, 1990.

Baron, L. "Immoral, Inviolate, or Inconclusive?" *Society*, 6–12, July/August, 1987.

Berkowitz, L., and E. Donnerstein. "External Validity Is More than Skin Deep: Some Answers to Criticisms of Laboratory Experiments." *American Psychologist*, 37, 245–257, 1982.

Brosius, H., J. B. Weaver III, and J. F. Staab. "Exploring the Social and Sexual 'Reality' of Contemporary Pornography." *Journal of Sex Research*, 30, 161–170, 1993.

Check, J. V. P., and T. H. Guloien. "Rape Proclivity for Coercive Sex Following Repeated Exposure to Sexually Violent Pornography, Nonviolent Dehumanizing Pornography, and Erotica." In D. Zillmann and J. Bryant, eds., *Pornography: Research Advances and Policy Considerations*. Hillsdale, NJ: Erlbaum, 1989.

Check, J. V. P., and D. K. Maxwell. "Pornography Consumption and Pro-Rape Attitudes in Children." Paper presented at the 25th International Congress of Psychology, Brussels, July 1992.

Cowan, G., and R. R. Campbell. "Racism and Sexism in Interracial Pornography." *Psychology of Women Quarterly*, forthcoming.

Cowan, G., and K. F. Dunn. "What Is Degrading to Women in Pornography?" *Journal of Sex Research*, forthcoming.

Cowan, G., C. Lee, D. Levy, and D. Snyder. "Dominance and Inequality in X-Rated Video-cassettes." *Psychology of Women Quarterly*, 12, 299–311, 1988.

Donnerstein, E., D. Linz, and S. Penrod. *The Question of Pornography: Research Findings and Policy Implications*. New York: The Free Press, 1987.

Hamburger, M. E., and L. J. Dawson. "Pornography and Aggression: A Meta-Analytic Review." Paper presented at the annual meeting of the Society for the Scientific Study of Sex, Chicago, 1993.

Jaffee, D., and M. A. Straus. "Sexual Climate and Reported Rape: A State-Level Analysis." *Archives of Sex Research*, 16, 107–123, 1987.

Linz, D., and E. Donnerstein. "The Role of Social Scientists in Policy Decision Making about Pornography: A Reply to Page." *Canadian Psychology*, 31, 368–370, 1990.

Linz, D., E. Donnerstein, and S. Penrod. "The Findings and Recommendations of the Attorney General's Commission on Pornography: Do the Psychological 'Facts' Fit the Political Fury?" *American Psychologist*, 42, 946–953, 1987.

Linz, D., E. Donnerstein, and S. Penrod. "Effects of Long-Term Exposure to Violent and Sexually Degrading Depictions of Women." *Journal of Personality and Social Psychology*, 55, 758–768, 1988.

MacKinnon, C. A. "To Quash a Lie." *Smith Alumnae Quarterly*, 11–14, Summer 1991.

Page, S. "The Turnaround on Pornography Research: Some Implications for Psychology and Women." *Canadian Psychology*, 31, 259–267, 1990.

Page, S. "On Linz and Donnerstein's View of Pornography Research." *Canadian Psychology*, 31, 371–373, 1990.

Russell, D. E. H. "The Experts Cop Out." In D. E. H. Russell, ed., *Making Violence Sexy: Feminist Views on Pornography*. New York: Teachers College Press, 1993.

Sabini, J. *Social Psychology*. New York: W. W. Norton, 1992.

Zillmann, D. "Effects of Prolonged Consumption of Pornography." 1989.

Zillmann, D. "Pornography Research and Public Policy." In D. Zillmann and J. Bryant, eds.,

Pornography: Research Advances and Policy Considerations. Hillsdale, NJ: Erlbaum, 1989.
Zillmann, D., and J. Bryant. "Pornography, Sexual Callousness, and the Trivialization of Rape." *Journal of Communication*, 32 (4), 10–21, 1982.
Zillmann, D., and J. Bryant. "Effects of Massive Exposure to Pornography." In N. Malamuth and E. Donnerstein, eds., *Pornography and Sexual Aggression.* Orlando, FL: Academic Press, 1984.

Chapter Three

CHARLES R. LAWRENCE III

1. Existing equality law has long recognized that practices similar to cross-burning constitute violations of their victims' civil rights. Title 42 U.S.C. sec. 1971(b) provides that "no person shall intimidate, threaten, coerce, or attempt to intimidate, threaten, or coerce any other person for the purpose of interfering with the right of such other person to vote or to vote as he may choose. . . ." 42 U.S.C. sec. 1971(b) (1988). This provision has been invoked where sharecropper-tenants in possession of real estate under contract are threatened, intimidated, or coerced by landlords for the purposes of interfering with their rights of franchise. *United States* v. *Bruce*, 353 F. 2d 474 (5th Cir. 1965); *United States* v. *Beaty*, 288 F. 2d 653 (6th Cir. 1961). Similarly, 42 U.S.C. sec. 2000(b) provides for an action for threatened loss of equal access to public facilities. 42 U.S.C. sec. 2000(b) (1988). Cross-burning to exclude persons from access to housing is covered under 42 U.S.C. sec. 3631(a), which prevents intimidation of "any person because of his race, color, religion, sex" from exercising rights to fair housing. 42 U.S.C. sec. 3631(a) (1988).

2. See, e.g., *NAACP* v. *Alabama*, 357 U.S. 449 (1958) (protecting voluntary group membership lists from state inspection); *NAACP* v. *Button*, 371 U.S. 415 (1963) (finding "impediments to the exercise of one's right to choose one's associates can violate the right of association protected by the First Amendment").

3. Respondent's (Saint Paul, Minnesota) brief before the United States Supreme Court offered the following two questions:

    1. May an enactment that has been authoritatively interpreted as proscribing conduct that constitutes fighting words and incites imminent lawless action be sustained, on its face, against claims that it is substantially overbroad and impermissibly vague?

    2. Is such an enactment narrowly tailored to serve the compelling interest of protecting victims of bias-motivated harassment against violation of their basic individual rights, which, on balance, far outweigh any minimally protected expression on the part of the accused?

    Brief for Respondent at 1, *R.A.V.* v. *City of St. Paul*, 112 S. Ct. 2538 (1992) (No. 90-7675). Similarly, the brief amicus curiae of the Anti-Defamation League supporting the respondent, stated as a question, presented:
    May a local government criminalize the act of burning a cross on the private property of a black family under an ordinance limited by the state's highest court to prohibit only fighting words or conduct directed to inciting or producing imminent lawless action and likely to incite or produce such action?
    Brief Amicus Curiae of the Anti-Defamation League of B'nai B'rith in support of Respondent at i, *R.A.V.* (no. 90-7675). Not surprisingly, the ACLU argued as amicus that the issue before the court was that "[t]he ordinance, as written, sweeps within its ambit whole categories of free speech," *R.A.V.* (no. 90-7675). Brief Amicus Curiae of the American Civil Liberties Union, Minnesota Civil Liberties Union, and American Jewish Congress, in Support of Petitioner at 7, *R.A.V.* (no. 90-7675).

4. Justice White's concurring opinion captures the way in which the majority transforms an act of coercion and intimidation into high-value political speech. He observes that "the Court's new 'underbreadth' creation serves no desirable function. Instead, it permits, indeed invites, the continuation of expressive conduct that in this case is evil and worthless in First Amendment terms. . . . Indeed, by characterizing fighting words as a form of 'debate,'

. . . the majority legitimates hate speech as a form of public discussion." Ibid. at 2553-54.
5. Ibid. at 2550.
6. Justice Taney held that African Americans were not included and were not intended to be included under the word "citizen" in the Constitution, and could therefore claim none of the rights and privileges which that instrument provides for and secures. He opined, "[the colored race] had for more than a century before been regarded as being of an inferior order, and altogether unfit to associate with the white race, either in social or political relations; and so far inferior, that they had no rights which the white man was bound to respect." *Dred Scott*, 60 U.S. at 407.
7. In rejecting plaintiff's argument in *Plessy* v. *Ferguson* (163 U.S. 537 [1896]) that enforced separation of the races constituted a badge of inferiority, Judge Brown stated, "If this be so, it is not by reason of anything found in the act, but solely because the colored race chooses to put that construction upon it." *Plessy*, 163 U.S. at 551. Justice Scalia's opinion contains this same dismissive argument. Responding to the city's argument that the ordinance is intended to protect against victimization of persons who are particularly vulnerable because of membership in a group that historically has been discriminated against, Justice Scalia stated that "it is clear that the St. Paul ordinance is not directed to the secondary effects. . . . 'The emotive impact of speech on its audience is not a secondary effect.' " *R.A.V.*, 112 S. Ct. at 2549. The argument here, like that in *Plessy*, is that the only injury here is in black folks' heads.
8. See Charles R. Lawrence III, "If He Hollers Let Him Go: Regulating Racist Speech on Campus," *Duke L. J.* (June 1990), p. 431, and Lawrence, "The Id, the Ego, and Equal Protection: Reckoning with Unconscious Racism," *Stan. L. Rev.* 39 (1987), p. 317.
9. Charles R. Lawrence, III, et al., *Words that Wound: Critical Race Theory, Assaultive Speech, and the First Amendment* (1993); Catharine A. MacKinnon, *Sexual Harassment of Working Women: A Case of Sex Discrimination* (1979), p. 27 (explaining why sexual harassment from men silences female victims); Kimberlé Crenshaw, "Beyond Racism and Misogyny: Black Feminism and 2 Live Crew," *Boston Rev.* (December 1991), pp. 6, 33 (illustrating how the debate over 2 Live Crew plays a role in rendering black women voiceless); Richard Delgado, "Words that Wound: A Tort Action for Racial Insults, Epithets, and Name-Calling," *Harv. C.R.-C.L. L. Rev.* 17 (1982), pp. 133, 135–49 (indicating that hate speech victims often suffer anti-social behavioral and psychological problems); Robert V. Guthrie, "White Racism and Its Impact on Black and White Behavior," *J. Non-White Concerns* 1 (1973), pp. 144, 146 (illustrating how overt discrimination forced black parents to accept that black children used inferior educational facilities); Jean C. Love, "Discriminatory Speech and the Tort of Intentional Infliction of Emotional Distress," *Wash. and Lee L. Rev.* 47 (1990), pp. 123, 159 (recommending a rebuttable presumption that certain categories of discriminatory speech constitute outrageous conduct for the purposes of the tort of intentional infliction of emotional distress); Mari J. Matsuda, "Public Response to Racist Speech: Considering the Victim's Story," *Mich. L. Rev.* 87 (1989), pp. 2320, 2337 (detailing the adverse effects that hate speech has on its victims).
10. Lawrence, "If He Hollers," pp. 438–41, 462–66.
11. See also *Plessy* v. *Ferguson*, 163 U.S. 537, 560 (1896) (Harlan, J., dissenting) (stating that the social meaning of racial segregation in the United States is a designation of superior and inferior caste, and segregation proceeds "on the ground that colored citizens are . . . inferior"). For a discussion of the "cultural meaning" of segregation, see Charles L. Black, Jr., "The Lawfulness of the Segregation Decisions," *Yale L.J.* 69 (1960), pp. 421, 427.
12. *U.S. Const.* Amend. 14, sec. 1; see also *Washington* v. *Davis*, 426 U.S. 229, 239 (1976) (holding that a law is not unconstitutional solely because of racially disproportionate impact); *Brown*, 347 U.S. at 495 (holding that the "separate but equal" doctrine has no place in field of public education).
13. See, e.g., the Civil Rights Act of 1964 secs. 201–207, 42 U.S.C. secs. 2000a-2000a-6 (1988) (public accommodations); ibid. secs. 601–606, 42 U.S.C. secs. 2000d-2000d-7 (1988) (federally assisted programs); 42 U.S.C. secs. 2000e-2000e-17 (1988) (equal employment opportunities). None of these regulations has been struck down as an unconstitutional infringement of an individual's speech or association rights.
14. See generally Delgado, "Words that Wound," pp. 133–34, 150–65 (arguing that an in-

dependent tort action for racial insults is permissible and necessary); Matsuda, "Public Response," pp. 2320, 2327–30. See also *Bailey* v. *Binyon*, 583 F. Supp. 923 (N.D. Ill. 1984) (cook sued employer for emotional distress damages for calling him "nigger" and menacing him repeatedly, under 42 U.S.C. sec. 1981); *Wiggs* v. *Courshon*, 355 F. Supp. 206 (S.D. Fla. 1973) (a black family, called a "bunch of niggers," and the father, called a "black son-of-a-bitch" by waitress, sued for intentional infliction of emotional distress and received a reduced verdict of $2,500); *Gomez* v. *Hug*, 645 P. 2d 916 (Kan. Ct. App. 1982) (a Mexican American sued an individual for intentional infliction of emotional distress for calling him a "fucking spic," a "Mexican greaser," and a "pile of shit"); *Dominguez* v. *Stone*, 638 P. 2d 423 (N.M. Ct. App. 1981) (a Mexican national residing in the U.S. sued an individual for intentional infliction of emotional distress when that person publicly questioned her employment and suggested that she should be a janitor due to her ethnic origin).

15. *Robinson* v. *Jacksonville Shipyards, Inc.* 760 F. Supp. 1491 (M.D. Fla. 1991).
16. Mike Graham, "Sexism in Shipyards Sets Off Legal Battle," *The Times* (London), 24 November 1991.
17. Laurence H. Tribe, *American Constitutional Law* (2d ed. 1988), pp. 785–89.
18. See Henry Louis Gates, Jr., "Frederick Douglass and the Language of Self," in *Figures in Black: Words, Signs, and the "Racial" Self* (1987), pp. 98, 104 (noting that the absence of a collective black voice effectively allowed European philosophers to deprive African slaves of their humanity).
19. See Kendall Thomas, "A House Divided against Itself: A Comment on 'Mastery, Slavery, and Emancipation,' " *Cardozo L. Rev.* 10 (1989), pp. 1481, 1510–12 (explaining that a black slave's humanity was destroyed when he or she was silenced).
20. For a more detailed discussion of the ways in which racist speech infects and disrupts the marketplace of ideas, see Lawrence, "If He Hollers," pp. 467–72.
21. See generally Eric Nesser, "Charging for Free Speech: User Fees and Insurance in the Marketplace of Ideas," *Geo. L. J.* 74 (1985), p. 257; Mark A. Rabinowitz, "Nazis in Skokie: Fighting Words or Heckler's Veto?" *DePaul L. Rev.* 28 (1979), p. 259; Geoffrey R. Stone, "Content Regulation and the First Amendment," *Wm. and Mary L. Rev.* 25 (1983), p. 189.
22. *Red Lion Broadcasting Co.* v. *FCC*, 395 U.S. 367, 385–86 (1969) (upholding FCC's "fairness doctrine," requiring that both sides of public issues be given fair coverage).
23. *Cf.* Thomas C. Grey, "Civil Rights vs. Civil Liberties: The Case of Discriminatory Verbal Harassment," *Soc. Phil. and Pol'y.* 8, no. 2 (Spring 1991), pp. 81, 82, 104.

> Under the civil-rights perspective, defense of basic human rights is by no means simply a matter of limiting state power. Government may deny equal protection by omission as well as by action—for example, by refusing law enforcement protection to minorities. . . . [T]he civil-rights approach, with its roots in anti-discrimination law and social policy, is centrally concerned with injuries of stigma and humiliation to those who are the victims of discrimination. . . . The point is not so much to protect a sphere of autonomy or personal security from intrusion as to protect potentially marginal members of the community from exclusion—from relegation, that is, to the status of second-class citizens.

By contrast, for civil-libertarians

> [t]he active state is traditionally conceived as the sole or dominant threat to civil liberties. Civil libertarians do not spend much of their time or energy seeking ways to positively empower dissenters, deviants, and nonconformists against the pressures brought on them by unorganized public opinion, or by private employers or landlords.

Ibid.
24. Catharine A. MacKinnon, *Toward a Feminist Theory of the State* (1989), p. 206.
25. See Martha R. Mahoney, "Legal Images of Battered Women: Redefining the Issue of Separation," *Mich. L. Rev.* 90 (1991), pp. 1, 93. "The most conservative figures estimate that women are physically abused in 12 percent of all marriages, and some scholars estimate that as many as 50 percent or more of all women will be battering victims at some point in their lives," ibid, pp. 10–11. See also ibid., pp. 18–19 (exploring women's response of silence

and denial to husbands' abuse in order to protect themselves from societal disapproval).
26.   Mari Matsuda, "Who Owns Speech?" address at Hofstra School of Law, 13 November 1991.

MICHELLE J. ANDERSON

1.   Naomi Wolf, *The Beauty Myth* (1991), p. 17.
2.   Ibid., p. 79.
3.   John Hubner, "In Love with Porn," *San Jose Merc. News*, 22 January 1989, p. 14 of the magazine.
4.   Ibid.
5.   Address by James Check, University of Chicago Law School conference, 5–7 March 1993. See also p. 89 herein.
6.   Edward Donnerstein and Daniel Linz, "Mass Media, Sexual Violence and Male Viewers: Current Theory and Research," in Michael S. Kimmel, ed. *Men Confront Pornography* (1990), pp. 224–25.
7.   As in traditional pornography, studies reveal that people become habituated to images of sexual violence in slasher films, and end up evincing less sensitivity to real sexual violence, Donnerstein and Linz, p. 225. After five days of viewing slasher films, the men rated the movies as less graphic, less gory, significantly less degrading to women, more humorous, and more enjoyable than they had on the first day; they also estimated fewer violent scenes, p. 226. In addition, they rated a rape victim as more worthless, assigned to her more blame for what happened, and deemed her injury significantly less severe, p. 227.
8.   Wolf, *Beauty Myth*, p. 162. See also Dolf Zillmann and Jennings Bryant, "Pornography, Sexual Callousness, and the Trivialization of Rape," in *Men Confront Pornography*, p. 208 (noting that young teens are increasingly likely to be exposed to pornography prior to becoming sexually active).
9.   Michele Landsberg, "Canada: Antipornography Breakthrough in the Law," *Ms.* (May/June 1992), p. 14 (citing the LEAF Brief to the Canadian Supreme Court).
10. Catharine MacKinnon, *Only Words* (1994), p. 10; Andrea Dworkin, *"For Men, Freedom of Speech; For Women, Silence Please,"* in Laura Lederer, ed., *Take Back the Night* (1980), p. 257.
11. Deborah Tannen, *You Just Don't Understand* (1990), p. 213 (citing the short story "You're Ugly Too" by Lorrie Moore).
12. Bent Preisler, *Linguistic Sex Roles in Conversation* (1986), p. 7.
13. David Graddol and Joan Swann, *Gender Voices* (1989), pp. 74–94; Philip M. Smith, *Language, the Sexes and Society* (1985), pp. 154–69. Cf. Tannen, *You Just Don't*, pp. 191, 196, 202, 205, 208 (arguing that interruptions do not always indicate conversational bullying), and pp. 18, 95 ("male dominance is not the whole story. . . . The effect of dominance is not always the result of an intention to dominate"). But cf. Katha Pollitt, "Are Women Morally Superior to Men?," *Utne Reader* (September/October 1993), p. 103 ("Tannen is quick to attribute blatant rudeness or sexism in male speech to anxiety, helplessness, fear of loss of face—anything, indeed, but rudeness and sexism").
14. Candace West and Don H. Zimmerman, "Small Insults: A Study of Interruptions in Cross-Sex Conversations between Unacquainted Persons," in Barrie Thorne, Cheris Kamarae, and Nancy Henley, eds., *Language, Gender, and Society* (1983), pp. 106–7.
15. Ibid.
16. Tannen, *You Just Don't*, pp. 75–76.
17. Ibid.
18. Coates, *Women, Men*, pp. 117, 131.
19. Tannen, *You Just Don't*, pp. 69, 167–68. Women also tend to phrase their comments as questions and speak at a lower volume than do men.
20. Preisler, *Sex Roles*, p. 284.
21. Tannen, *You Just Don't*, p. 238. Tannen asserts that this is due partially to the way women present their ideas in mixed-group settings.
22. Ibid., pp. 240, 244.
23. See, e.g., Muriel Schultz, "The Semantic Derogation of Women," in Barrie Thorne and Nancy Henley, eds., *Language and Sex: Difference and Dominance* (1975), pp. 64–73.

24. Deborah Cameron, *Feminism and Linguistic Theory* (1985), pp. 77–78.

25. Smith, *Language*, pp. 37–38, 153; Mary Ritchie Kay, *Male/Female Language* (1975), p. 129.

26. Doug McKenzie-Mohr and Mark P. Zanna, "Treating Women as Sexual Objects: Look to the (Gender Schematic) Male Who Has Viewed Pornography," *Pers. & Soc. Psych. Bull.* 16 (1990), p. 296.

27. Ibid., p. 304.

28. Ibid., p. 304.

29. Zillmann and Bryant, *Sexual Callousness*, pp. 213–4; Donnerstein and Linz, "Mass Media," p. 230.

30. Donnerstein and Linz, "Mass Media," pp. 220–21.

31. See chap. 1, p. 91: 71 percent of girls and 35 percent of boys think it is not okay for a boy to hold down a girl and force her to have sex if she gets him sexually excited.

32. See Jane Gross, "Suffering in Silence No More," *New York Times*, 13 July 1992, p. A1; Katharine Lampher, "Reading, 'Riting, and 'Rassment," *Ms.* (May/June 1992), p. 90. Katy Lyle finally filed a complaint with the Minnesota Department of Human Rights against the school for sexual harassment that interfered with her ability to receive an equal education. In a groundbreaking victory, she won a $15,000 damage award and a revision of the sexual harassment policy, which was posted throughout the school system.

33. *D.R. by L.R. v. Middle Bucks Area Vocational Tech. School*, 972 F. 2d 1364 (3rd Cir. 1992).

34. Just think. If he had gotten them to sign release forms, and had mass-produced the tape and sold it to peep shows or video stores, his right to "express" the abuse that it documents would have been protected by the First Amendment.

35. 972 F. 2d at 1366. In this 1983 suit, the court concluded that, based on *DeShaney v. Winnebago County Dept. of Social Services*, 489 U.S. 189 (1989), the school owed no duty to the girl, despite the state's enforcement of compulsory school attendance.

36. For just a few examples of the use of pornography as sexual harassment, see *Andrews v. City of Philadelphia*, 895 F. 2d 1469; 1472 (3rd Cir. 1990) (the only two women police officers in their squads subjected to, inter alia, routine, obscene comments about women and the placement of pornography in their desks and on the walls); *Dwyer v. Smith*, 867 F. 2d 184, 188 (4th Cir. 1989) (female police officer subjected to, inter alia, pornography and sexual conversations about the victims of sex crimes); *Waltman v. International Paper Co.*, 875 F. 2d 468, 471 (5th Cir. 1989) (only female powerhouse worker subjected to, inter alia, over thirty pornographic notes, extensive pornographic graffiti, and demeaning verbal remarks); *Rabidue v. Osceola Refining Co.*, 805 F. 2d 611, 615 (6th Cir. 1986), cert. denied, 481 U.S. 1041–42 (1987) (female worker subjected to work environment pervaded with pornography); *Contardo v. Merrill Lynch, Pierce, Fenner & Smith*, 753 F. Supp. 406, 408 (D. Mass. 1990) (female broker hired only after winning initial sex discrimination suit subjected to, inter alia, female strippers brought to the workplace, lewd comments, and pornographic pictures placed in her desk); *Sanchez v. City of Miami Beach*, 720 F. Supp. 974, 977–78 (S.D. Fla. 1989) (female police officer subjected to, inter alia, numerous pornographic posters, pictures, and graffiti); *Ross v. Twenty-Four Collection, Inc.*, 681 F. Supp. 1547, 1549–50 (S.D. Fla. 1988) (female employee subjected to, inter alia, pornography and repeated requests for sex); *Barbetta v. Chemlawn Services Corp.*, 669 F. Supp. 569, 572–73 (W.D.N.Y. 1987) (female employee subjected to, inter alia, pornography in the workplace, pornographic comments from coworkers, and the requirement that she wear skirts because the management "liked to look at women's legs"); *Egger v. Local 276, Plumbers and Pipefitters Union*, 644 F. Supp. 795, 797–98 (D. Mass. 1986) (female plumber subjected to, inter alia, pornography, lewd comments, and a request to pose for pornography); *Arnold v. City of Seminole*, 614 F. Supp. 853, 858–59 D.C. Okl. 1985) (lone woman police officer subjected to, inter alia, repeated pornographic deliveries to her mailbox and pornography posted on the walls with her name written on it).

37. Robert L. Allen, "Out of the Bedroom Closet," *Ms.* (January/February 1992), p. 95.

38. James E. Gruber and Lars Bjorn, "Women's Responses to Sexual Harassment: An Analysis of Sociocultural, Organizational, and Personal Resource Models," *Soc. Sci. Q.* 67, (1985) pp. 814, 822.

39. Morrison Torrey, "We Get the Message: Pornography in the Workplace," *Sw. U. L. Rev.* 22 (1992), pp. 68–69.
40. Ibid., pp. 69–70.
41. Diana E. H. Russell and Karen Trocki, "Evidence of Harm," in Diana E. H. Russell, ed., *Making Violence Sexy: Feminist Views on Pornography* (1993), p. 195. Approximately 14 percent of women have been asked to pose for pornographic pictures, ibid.
42. Wendy Stock's address at conference.
43. Russell and Trocki, "Evidence of Harm," p. 213.
44. Wolf, *Beauty Myth*, p. 165 (citing Greenlinger and Byrne study).
45. Zillmann and Bryant, "Sexual Callousness," p. 217.
46. Ibid., pp. 213–4; Donnerstein and Linz, "Mass Media," p. 222 and also p. 230 (men had a propensity to continue to trivialize rape three weeks after exposure to nonviolent pornography).
47. Donnerstein and Linz, "Mass Media," p. 220.
48. Ibid., p. 221.
49. Ibid., p. 221.
50. See "Looking Behind Rape Statistics," *Chri. Sci. Mon.*, (5 May 1992), p. 20; Bella English, "Beware of Law, Rape Victims," *Boston Globe* (8 February 1993), p. 13.
51. Gail Hanlon, "Introduction to an Honorable Ethic: An Interview with Andrea Dworkin," *Woman of Power* (Summer 1992), p. 52.
52. Their opponents will declare that pornography has not hurt them, and may offer pictures as proof. See, e.g., *State v. Zamora*, 803 P. 2d 568 (Kan. 1990). Defendant kidnapped, gagged, tied up, and raped a sixteen-year-old three times, and then threatened to photograph her *to prove that the sexual acts were consensual*. He testified to reading pornographic magazines that celebrated bondage and rape.

LAURA J. LEDERER

1. Mari Matsuda, "Public Response to Racist Speech: Considering the Victim's Story," *Mich. L. Rev.* 87, p. 2322 (1989).
2. See Charles Lawrence III, "The Id, the Ego, and Equal Protection: Reckoning with Unconscious Racism," *Stan. L. Rev.* 39, p. 317 (1987). See also "If He Hollers," *Duke Law Journal* (1990), pp. 431–483.
3. Address by Richard Delgado, State Historical Society, Madison, Wisconsin, 24 April 1989: I believe that racist speech benefits powerful, white-dominated institutions. The highly educated, refined persons who operate the University . . . would never ever themselves utter a racial slur. . . . Yet they benefit, and on a subconscious level they know they benefit, from a certain amount of low-grade racism in the environment. . . . This kind of behavior keeps non-white people on edge, a little off balance. We get these occasional reminders that we are different and not really wanted. It prevents us from digging in too strongly, starting to think we could really belong here. It makes us a little introspective, a little unsure of ourselves; at the right low-grade level it prevents us from organizing on behalf of more important things . . .
Quoted by Lawrence in *If He Hollers*, pp. 475–476.
4. Jacques Ellul, *Propaganda: The Formation of Men's Attitudes* (New York: Vintage Books, 1965), pp. 9–17.
5. The Center for Democratic Renewal notes that many of these groups also stockpile weapons, rob banks, and are tax resisters.
6. Conversation with Evelina Giobbe, Executive Director, WHISPER, 26 March 1993. Giobbe notes that the most violent pornography magazines and videos are produced underground in basements, warehouses, and garages and are very difficult to document, and that new technological developments promise pornographic virtual reality.
7. Dorchen Leidholdt, in Dorchen Leidholdt and Janice G. Raymond, eds., *The Sexual Liberals and the Attack on Feminism* (Pergamon Press, 1990), p. xi. Leidholdt describes how "a symbiotic relationship was formed" between civil libertarians and pornographers, with the ACLU using pornographic films to raise money for its local chapters. Interestingly, Playboy

Foundation helped found the National Network of Grantmakers, a group of funders who meet yearly to discuss support for progressive issues. They rarely discussed women's organizations or women's issues, and women members became so frustrated with this definition of "progressive" that they left and formed their own organization, the National Network of Women's Funds. This network brings together women funders from all over the country, and it is the first funder's organization that has specifically addressed the issue of pornography in workshops and meetings.

8. See Playboy Foundation grants lists from 1980 to 1993, available from the Illinois Secretary of State. Radical feminists theorize that pornographers support abortion rights because it heightens women's sexual availability for men (Leidholdt, *Sexual Liberals*, p. xv). See also Twiss Butler, "Abortion and Pornography: The Sexual Liberals' 'Gotcha' against Women's Equality," in Leidholdt, *Sexual Liberals*, p. 114. Butler argues that Playboy picked abortion as its women's issue because it benefits men and male exploitation by allowing pregnancies that result from men using women to be quickly terminated. Abortion thus serves the purposes of pornographers as well as women.

9. *When Hate Groups Come to Town: A Handbook of Effective Community Responses* (Center for Democratic Renewal, P.O. Box 50469, Atlanta GA 30302, 1992), pp. 118–122.

10. Ellul, *Propaganda*, pp. 17–24: "To give [propaganda] . . . continuity, duration an organization is required that controls the mass media, is capable of using them correctly. . . . There must [also] be an *administrative* organization. It can be a party organization (Nazi, fascist, Communist). . . . Or such physical organization can be the integration of an entire population into cells; in that case it operates inside a society by integrating the whole social body . . . or effective transformation can be made in the economic, political, or social domain."

11. Ellul notes (ibid.) that each of these media is suited to a different type of communication (slow infiltration, progressive inroads, overall integration, etc.) and must be used in concert for "total orchestration." Thus, Playboy does not just publish a magazine that reaches 2 million readers; it has also branched out into cable television, video, prerecorded phone messages, Hollywood movies, books, mail-order catalogs, clothing, eyewear, and air fresheners.

12. Ibid., pp. 25–33.

13. Doug McKenzie-Mohr and Mark P. Zanna, "Treating Women as Sexual Objects: Look to the (Gender Schematic) Male Who Has Viewed Pornography," *Pers. Soc. Psychol. Bull.* 16 (1990), pp. 296. See also Morrison Torrey, "We Get the Message: Pornography in the Workplace," *Southwest University L. Rev.* 22 pp. 53, 89: "Behavioral and social scientists have discovered over and over again in a multitude of studies that pornography affects male attitudes about rape, desensitizes men, sexually arouses them, and reduces their general inhibitions against sexual aggression." (Torrey also lists and summarizes the most important social science research.)

14. James A.C. Brown, *Techniques of Persuasion* (New York: Penguin Books, 1963).

15. See Beverly LaBelle, "The Propaganda of Misogyny," in *Take Back the Night*, p. 168, for the first analysis of pornography as propaganda. Andrea Dworkin also examines propaganda techniques in "The Power of Words," in *Letters from a War Zone* (New York: E. P. Dutton, 1988), pp. 27–30, comparing Joseph Goebbels' anti-Semitic propaganda campaign against a Jewish police official with U.S. propaganda campaigns against women. Dworkin notes that there is a similarity between the libel suits that the Jewish police official brought against Goebbels (both of which he lost) and the defamation suits brought by Dworkin, Steinem, Brownmiller, and others whose names, faces, and bodies have been used without permission by pornographers in the U.S. See also *Hustler Magazine* v. *Falwell*, 485 U.S. 46 (1988), regarding a *Hustler* magazine parody portraying Jerry Falwell in an "interview saying that he first had sex with his mother in an outhouse in a drunken rendezvous." Falwell brought suit for libel and intentional infliction of emotional distress and lost on First Amendment grounds.

16. For example, see Hugh Hefner, "Who Says Pornography Harms Society?" *Chicago Sun Times*, 13 March 1993: "The main thinkers of this group [of radical feminists organizing a conference on pornography and hate speech (Hefner conveniently left out the "hate speech" part of the conference title)] refuse to see women as sexual beings. They view romance as

exploitation, desire as domination, intercourse as rape. They have a pathological fear of anything that causes arousal."

17. See "An Intelligent Woman's Guide to Dirty Words: English Words and Phrases Reflecting Sexist Attitudes toward Women in Patriarchal Society, Arranged According to Usage and Idea," vol. 1 (Chicago: The Feminist English Dictionary, 1973), which documents over 400 derogatory words used to describe women.

18. "The Propaganda of Misogyny," by Beverly LaBelle, in Laura Lederer, ed., *Take Back the Night: Women on Pornography* (William Morrow, 1980), p. 170.

19. Interview with Judith Reisman, July 1978.

20. Susan Brownmiller, *Against Our Will*, p. 392.

21. *When Hate Groups Come*, p. 18.

22. *Beauharnais v. Illinois*, 343 U.S. 250 (1952).

23. In *The Propaganda of Misogyny*, by Beverly LaBelle, pp. 170–71.

24. Andrea Dworkin, *Woman-Hating* (1974), pp. 51–91. See also Dworkin, *Pornography: Men Possessing Women* (New York: E. P. Dutton, 1979).

25. "What Whites Think about Non-Whites," in *When Hate Groups Come*, p. 18.

26. Ibid., p. 41.

27. See "The Propaganda of Misogyny," p. 172. See also Sam Keen, *Faces of the Enemy: Reflections of the Hostile Imagination—The Psychology of Enmity* (San Francisco: Harper & Row, 1986), p. 13: "To mass produce hatred, the body politic must remain unconscious of its own paranoia, projection and propaganda."

28. See *Propaganda of Misogyny*, p. 172. See also Dworkin, *Woman-Hating* and *Pornography*; Susan Griffin, *Pornography and Silence*; and Susan Lurie, "Pornography and the Dread of Women: The Male Sexual Dilemma," in *Take Back the Night*, p. 152.

29. See Sam Keen, *Faces of the Enemy*.

30. Simone de Beauvoir, *The Second Sex* (New York: Vintage Books Edition, 1989; originally 1952), p. xxii.

CHRISTOPHER N. KENDALL

1. An expanded version of this article, entitled "Real Dominant, Real Fun!: Gale May Pornography and the Pursuit of Masculinity" can be found in 57 *Sask. L.Rev.* 21 (1993).

2. *R. v. Butler*, 1 S.C.R. 452 (1992).

3. Ibid., p. 493.

4. C. Bearchell, "In Harm's Way: A Calculated Campaign Takes Aim at Sexual Imagery and Free Speech," 37 *XS: a Supplement to Xtral Magazine* 1 (1992).

5. Some of the information about the gay male pornographic industry provided in this speech is derived from research conducted in 1985 by a student at the UCLA School of Law. This study was not published (for reasons that are perhaps obvious in light of the risks associated with the industry studied and the circumstances surrounding the interviews obtained). The author's research consisted of observing the filming of two gay male pornographic films, reviewing gay male pornographic publications, and interviewing both "actors" and producers. Much of the information obtained was obtained in the strictest of confidence. As such, the name of the young man interviewed will remain confidential. I have also, at the request of the author, agreed to withhold the author's name.

6. Andrea Dworkin, *Pornography: Men Possessing Women* (New York: Putnam, 1980), p. 61.

7. John Stoltenberg, "Gay and the Propornography Movement: Having the Hots for Sex Discrimination," *Men Confront Pornography* (New York: Crown Publishers Inc.), p. 250.

8. S. Pharr, *Homophobia: A Weapon of Sexism* (Little Rock: Chardon Press, 1988).

ROBIN D. BARNES

1. Richard Delgado, "Words that Wound," *Harv. C.R.-C.L. L.Rev.* 17 (1982), p. 133. Governing bodies must compare the values sought to be enhanced with those at risk in a decision to remain silent on issues of racial and sexual harassment and violence. Frank I. Michelman, "Conceptions of Democracy in American Constitutional Argument: The Case of Pornography Regulation," *Tenn.L.Rev.* 56 (1989), pp. 291, 307.

2. All of these incidents actually occurred on a university or college campus in the United States between 1980 and 1988.
3. See generally Charles H. Jones, "Equality, Dignity and Harm: The Constitutionality of Regulating American Campus Ethnoviolence," *Wayne L.Rev.* 37 (1991), p. 1383. This essay provides an insightful overview of the rise in ethnoviolence on college campuses by defining some of the causes and proposed remedies from a historical perspective that lends credibility to Jones's analysis of the public/private dichotomy and his moral vision for student participation in university life. Jones asserts that freedom and equality are the ultimate goals in this setting, even as he acknowledges the structural strain inherent in placing together (for perhaps the first time) students from widely divergent world and cultural perspectives.

TWISS BUTLER

1. Sally Kempton, "Cutting Loose," *Esquire* (July 1970), p. 57.
2. Alice Rossi, ed., *The Feminist Papers*, 1988, p. 9.
3. Ibid., p. 11.
4. Ibid., p. 5.
5. Ibid., p. 6.
6. Larry Green, "Book Censorship Wave Seen in the Wake of Conservative Political Victories," *Los Angeles Times*, 12 November 1980, p. 18 (an interview with Judy Krug, director of the American Library Association's Office of Intellectual Freedom; the article was included with a 1981 direct-mail funding solicitation by People for the American Way).
7. Frederick Schauer, "Uncoupling Free Speech," *Columbia L. R.* 92 (1992), p. 1321.
8. A 1993 Indiana University study shows that women have been kept at 34 percent of the journalism work force for the last ten years. D. Weaver and G. C. Willhoit, "The American Journalist in the 1990's," cited in *The Forum*, p. 7, a Freedom Forum Foundation insert in the *Washington Journalism Review* (January 1993).
9. Brae Canlen, "The Editorial They," *San Diego Reader*, 6 December 1987.
10. Saundra Saperstein, "Publishers Joining Playboy in Attack on Group's Letter," *Washington Post*, 7 June 1986, p. A2.
11. Media/Professional Insurance, *National Underwriter*, 19 October 1992, p. 47.
12. Bill Bauer, "Media Liability Coverage," *Best's Review*, August 1992.
13. *Washington Post*, 11 February 1993, p. A20.
14. Claudia A. Haskel and Jean H. Otto, eds., *A Time for Choices*, First Amendment Congress, 1991.
15. *Harvard Magazine* (January/February 1993), p. 74.
16. Clarence Page, "Restriction on Pinups Raises Another Issue," *Harrisburg Patriot News* (Pennsylvania), 11 November 1991.
17. Howard Kurtz, "Pornography Panel's Objectivity Disputed," *Washington Post*, 15 October 1985.
18. Catharine A. MacKinnon, speech to the National Press Club, Washington, D.C., 22 November 1993.
19. Isabel Wilkerson, "Foes of Pornography and Bigotry Join Forces," *New York Times*, 12 March 1993, p. B16.
20. *American Booksellers Association* v. *Hudnut*, 771 F. 2d 323 97th Cir. (1985), aff'd, 475 U.S. 1001 (1986). Routine cases heard, for example, *City of Renton et al.* v. *Playtime Theatres, Inc. et al.* 475 U.S. 41 (1986) (zoning regulations) and *Bethel School District No. 403 35 al.* v. *Fraser, a minor et al.* 478 U.S. 675 (1986) (regulating student speech).
21. Catharine A. MacKinnon, "Not a Moral Issue," in *Feminism Unmodified* (Harvard, 1987), pp. 147–48.

JOHN STOLTENBERG

1. The mayor of Minneapolis vetoed the ordinance both times it was passed there; see my history of the ordinance in *Refusing to Be a Man: Essays on Sex and Justice* (New York: Penguin USA/Meridian, 1990), pp. 137–171.
    A Media Coalition challenge to the Indianapolis ordinance resulted in a November 1984 decision by District Court Judge Sarah Evans Barker—a Reagan appointee—that the or-

dinance was unconstitutional. Barker based her ruling on the viewpoint that sex-discrimination interests never outweigh First Amendment interests—despite Supreme Court rulings to the contrary. The City of Indianapolis appealed to the Seventh U.S. Circuit Court of Appeals in Chicago, where another Reagan appointee, Judge Frank Easterbrook, ruled the ordinance unconstitutional because, in his view, although pornography does indeed harm women, this simply proves its power as speech. See *American Booksellers Association, Inc.* v. *Hudnut,* 771 F. 2d 323 (7th Cir. 1985), affirmed 475 U.S. 1001 (1986).

The Bellingham referendum drive was organized locally by Civil Rights Organizing for Women (CROW). An ACLU suit challenging the Bellingham ordinance resulted in a district court ruling that essentially repeated Easterbrook's 1985 decision.

With local organizing by Women's Alliance Against Pornography (WAAP), the ordinance was also placed on the ballot for popular vote in Cambridge, Massachusetts, in 1985. The ordinance won in all the working class and "ethnic" precincts but lost around Harvard University and in the wealthier, mostly white/Jewish precincts. Overall, 42 percent of voters supported the ordinance, an extremely high showing for a referendum initiated by a community petition drive.

2. Reprinted as "Pornography Is a Civil Rights Issue" in her book *Letters from a War Zone* (New York: E.P. Dutton, 1989), pp. 276–307.

3. *Final Report of the Attorney General's Commission on Pornography* (Washington, D.C.: U.S. Department of Justice, 1986), p. 756.

4. The Pornography Victims Protection Act and the Pornography Victims Compensation Act; both were amended into ineffectiveness.

5. The bill was never voted on in the Judiciary Committee within the time limit, so it expired.

6. *Pornography and Sexual Violence: Evidence of the Links* (London: Everywoman, 1988).

7. Confidential Gray and Company memo to the Media Coalition dated June 5, 1986, and somehow leaked. See Dworkin, p. 276.

8. Some money also came from *Penthouse.* Susan B. Trento, *The Power House: Robert Keith Gray and the Selling of Access and Influence in Washington* (New York: St. Martin's Press, 1992), p. 196.

9. Among parties to the Media Coalition suit against the Indianapolis ordinance (*Hudnut*) was a trade association for mainstream book publishers, the American Booksellers Association.

10. The phrase "chicks up front" originated in the sixties from a tactic used by lefty men who, in street confrontations with bayonet-wielding cops, would send bare-breasted women up front—on the theory that the women would offer some protection. I apply the phrase sarcastically to the spate of books and articles by so-called feminist women writing both popular and academic defenses of pornography, prostitution, and other institutionalized forms of women's oppression. New such book titles are displayed every month, even as radical feminist writings on these subjects are effectively excluded from publication. This pattern strongly suggests a viewpoint discrimination with links to the American Booksellers Association's official defense, in *Hudnut,* of pornographers' right to do harm through speech.

Chapter Four

ELENA KAGAN

1. *Wisconsin* v. *Mitchell,* 113 S. Ct. 2194 (1993).

2. See, for example, Cal. Penal Code sec. 422.7 (West. 1988 and Supp. 1993); N.Y. Penal Law sec. 240.30 (3) (McKinney Supp. 1993); or Rev. Stat. sec. 166.165 (1)(a)(A) (1991); Wis. Stat. Ann. sec. 939.645 (West. Supp. 1992).

3. The Supreme Court in *Mitchell* noted the precise analogy between Title VII and the hate crimes statute at issue in the case. See 113 S. Ct. at 2200. It is noteworthy that both laws apply not only irrespective of whether the discrimination at issue expresses a message, but also irrespective of whether the discrimination is caused by particular beliefs. If, for example, discrimination laws prohibited discharges or assaults motivated by racial hatred—rather than simply those based on race—they would pose a very different, and seemingly severe, First Amendment problem.

4. Cass R. Sunstein makes this point in "Words, Conduct, Caste," U. Chi. L. Rev. 60, pp.

827–28; his phrasing is that in such a case, the communication is merely evidence of, or a means of committing, an independently unlawful act. Sunstein, however, appears to think that this analysis fails to cover hate crimes, because there the state's interest arises from the expressive nature of the conduct. As stated in the text, I do not believe this to be the case. A state has a legitimate interest in preventing, say, assaults on the basis of race, even when they are wholly devoid of expression. The interest is the same as that in preventing discharges on the basis of race; it is an interest in eradicating racially based forms of disadvantage generally, whether or not accompanied by communication of a message.

5. See Catharine A. MacKinnon, "Pornography, Civil Rights, and Speech, *Harv. C.R.-C.L. L. Rev.* 20 (1985), pp. 1, 29 n. 52.

6. See, for example, Cass R. Sunstein, "Neutrality in Constitutional Law (with Special Reference to Pornography, Abortion, and Surrogacy)," *Colum. L. Rev.* 92 (1992), pp. 1, 23–24.

7. See, for example, *Police Department of Chicago v. Mosley*, 408 U.S. 92, 95–96 (1972); *Simon & Schuster, Inc. v. Members of the New York State Crime Victims Board*, 112 S. Ct. 501, 508–09 (1991); *Consolidated Edison Co. of New York v. Public Service Commission of New York*, 447 U.S. 530, 536 (1980).

8. See, for example, *Burson v. Freeman*, 112 S. Ct. 1846 (1992); *Greer v. Spock*, 424 U.S. 828 (1976); *CBS v. Democratic National Committee*, 412 U.S. 94 (1973). See generally Geoffrey R. Stone, "Restrictions of Speech Because of Its Content: The Peculiar Case of Subject-Matter Restrictions," *U. Chi. L. Rev.* 46 (1978), p. 81. R.A.V. might be thought to treat subject matter restrictions with the same distrust shown to viewpoint restrictions: the technical holding of the Court was that the St. Paul ordinance facially violated the Constitution "in that it prohibits otherwise permitted speech solely on the basis of the subjects the speech addresses" (112 S. Ct. at 2542). But elsewhere in the opinion, the Court made clear that its true concern related to viewpoint bias. What most bothered the Court was that the subject matter restriction operated in practice to restrict speech of only particular (racist or sexist) views. See, for example, ibid. at 2547–49.

9. See *FCC v. Pacifica Foundation*, 438 U.S. 726 (1978) (indecent radio broadcast); *Young v. American Mini-Theatres*, 427 U.S. 50 (1976) ("adult" theaters); and *City of Renton v. Playtime Theatres, Inc.*, 475 U.S. 41 (1986) (same).

10. 112 S. Ct. at 2550.

11. See *Chaplinsky v. New Hampshire*, 315 U.S. 568, 572 (1942). Of course, the application of the ordinance to any particular expression might well raise serious constitutional issues relating to the permissible scope of the fighting words category.

12. See Robert C. Post, "Racist Speech, Democracy, and the First Amendment," *Wm. & Mary L. Rev.* 32 (1991), pp. 267, 317–25, for a general discussion of the compatibility of speech regulation with the objectives of higher education.

13. 458 U.S. 747 (1982).

14. See Catharine A. MacKinnon, *Feminism Unmodified*, p. 147.

15. See ibid., pp. 174–75; Cass R. Sunstein, *Colum. L. Rev.* 92, pp. 20–21.

16. See MacKinnon, *Feminism Unmodified*, pp. 174–75.

17. *Paris Adult Theatre I v. Slaton*, 413 U.S. 49, 59–60, 61 (1973) (emphasis deleted), quoting *Jacobellis v. Ohio*, 378 U.S. 184, 199 (1964) (Warren dissenting), and *Roth v. United States*, 354 U.S. 476, 485 (1957).

18. 413 U.S. at 58–59.

19. For this reason, I think Catharine MacKinnon's statement that obscenity is "ideational and abstract," rather than "concrete and substantive," represents something of an overstatement, even as applied to the initial understanding and formulation of the category. See MacKinnon, *Feminism Unmodified*, p. 175.

20. One interesting proof (and product) of this reconceptualization is Senator Mitch McConnell's proposed legislation granting the victim of a sexual offense a right to claim damages from the distributor of any obscene work deemed to have contributed to the crime. Pornography Victims' Compensation Act of 1991, sec. 1521, 102d Congress, First session (22 July 1991). Whatever the merits of this legislation, which raises serious concerns on numerous grounds, it clearly presupposes a link between obscenity and sexual violence.

MARY BECKER

1. See Frederick Schauer, "The Political Incidence of the Free Speech Principle," *U. Colo. L. Rev.* 64 (1993) and J. M. Balkin, "Some Realism about Pluralism," *Duke L. Jr.* (1990), p. 375. For articles critical of free speech from the perspective of racial minorities, see, e.g., Mari J. Matsuda, Charles R. Lawrence III, Richard Delgado, and Kimberlé Crenshaw, in *Words that Wound: Critical Race Theory, Assaultive Speech, and the First Amendment* (1993); Richard Delgado and Jean Stefancic, "Images of the Outsider in American Law and Culture: Can Free Expression Remedy Systemic Social Ills?" *Cornell L. Rev.* 77 (1992), 1258.

2. *R.A.V. v. City of St. Paul, Minnesota*, 112 S. Ct. 2538 (1992) (striking as unconstitutional a criminal penalty for hate speech likely to cause harm).

3. See *Doe v. University of Michigan*, 721 Fed. Supp. 852 (E.D. Mich. 1989) (holding a policy unconstitutional as a violation of free speech; although the university argued that its policy did not apply in the classroom, the court stressed the possibility that it might be applied in classroom discussions); *UWM Post, Inc. v. Board of Regents of University of Wisconsin*, 774 F. Suppl. 1163 (E.D. Wis. 1991) (a similar holding; again, the university argued that the rule would not apply in the classroom); *IOTA XI Chapter of Sigma Chi Fraternity v. George Mason University*, 773 F. Supp. 792 (E.D. Virginia 1991) (the discipline of a fraternity for out-of-classroom events—including a "Dress a Sig" event in which a member dressed in blackface, with pillows for breasts and buttocks, and wore a black wig and curlers—was held unconstitutional), aff'd, 993 F. 2d 386 (4th Cir. 1993).

4. I use "he" because most teachers at most universities, especially those who are in the most prestigious positions, are men.

5. In two recent cases, lower federal courts have held unconstitutional unusual public university reactions to racist speech. See *Levin v. Harleston*, 966 F. 2d 85 (2nd Cir. 1992), and *Jeffries v. Harleston*, 820 F. Supp. 741 (S.D.N.Y. 1993).

6. See, e.g., *Guzwiller v. Fenik*, 860 F. 2d 1317 (6th Cir. 1988).

7. For a discussion of the need for such a standard, see Mary E. Becker, "Maternal Feelings: Myth, Taboo, and Child Custody," *Southern California Review of Law and Women's Studies* 1 (1992), p. 133.

8. *Webster v. Reproductive Health Services*, 492 U.S. 490 (1989) (upholding a state statute that limits the right to abortion in many ways).

9. 410 U.S. 113 (1973).

10. See chapter two in Mary Becker, Cynthia Grant Bowman, and Morrison Torrey, *Feminist Jurisprudence: Taking Women Seriously* (West Publishing Co., 1993).

11. See Louis Michael Seidman, "*Brown* and *Miranda*," *Calif. L. Rev.* 80 (1992), p. 673.

12. 349 U.S. 504 (1955).

13. Gerald N. Rosenberg, *The Hollow Hope: Can Courts Bring about Social Change?* (Chicago: University of Chicago Press, 1991).

14. See, e.g., *Shaw v. Reno*, 61 U.S.L.W. 4818 (1993) (concerning the striking of a legislative district drawn to ensure minority representation); *Richmond v. J.A. Cropson Co.*, 488 U.S. 469 (1989) (concerning the striking of a minority set-aside program adopted by a municipality).

15. For a fuller discussion of the political problems with binding judicial review from the perspective of women, see Mary Becker, "Conservative Free Speech and the Uneasy Case for Judicial Review," *U. Colo. L. Rev.* 64 (1993).

DORCHEN LEIDHOLDT

1. Peggy Crull and Marilyn Cohen, *Expanding the Definition of Sexual Harassment* (Working Women's Institute, 1982).

2. *Kyriatzi v. Western Electric Co.*, 461 F. Supp. 894 (D.N.J. 1978).

3. *Bundy v. Jackson*, 641 F. 2d 934 (D.C. Cir. 1981).

4. In 1972, women constituted 3.6 percent of skilled craftsworkers; by 1981 the figure had almost doubled, to 6.3 percent; and in 1986, 8.6 percent of skilled craftsworkers were female. The percentage of women in "protective services" (police, firefighters, guards, etc.) showed a similar climb, from 5.7 percent in 1972, to 10.1 percent in 1983, to 12.4 percent in 1986 (*Current Population Survey*, U.S. Department of Labor, Bureau of Labor Statistics).

5. Amicus brief on behalf of Women Against Pornography, et al., *American Booksellers Association* v. *Hudnut*, 771 F. 2d 323 (7th Cir. 1985).

6. Laura J. Lederer, ed., *Take Back the Night* (New York: William Morrow, 1980); Andrea Dworkin, *Pornography: Men Possessing Women* (New York: Putnam, 1980); Shere Hite, *The Hite Report on Male Sexuality* (New York: Knopf, 1981); Gloria Steinem, *Outrageous Acts and Everyday Rebellions* (New York: Holt, Rinehart and Winston, 1983); Catharine A. MacKinnon, *Feminism Unmodified* (Boston: Harvard University Press, 1987). Of equal importance in popularizing feminist criticism has been grass-roots activism on the part of such organizations as Women Against Pornography in New York City; Men Against Pornography in Brooklyn, New York; the Coalition Against Trafficking in Women, North Amherst, Massachusetts; WHISPER in Minneapolis, Minnesota; the Center and the National Organization for Women, by both the national headquarters and individual chapters around the country.

7. The cartoon is reproduced in the decision. See 461 F. Supp. at 934.

8. *Zabkowicz* v. *West Bend Co.*, 589 F. Supp. 786 (E. D. Wisc. 1984) at 782–783.

9. *Sanchez* v. *City of Miami Beach*, 720 F. Supp. 974, 977, FN9 (S.D. Fla. 1989); telephone conversation with Officer Sanchez, 1988.

10. *Robinson* v. *Jacksonville Shipyards, Inc.*, 760 F. Supp. 1486 (M.D. Fla. 1991).

11. Defendants' deposition of plaintiff Lois Robinson, *Robinson* v. *Jacksonville Shipyards, et al.*, Case No. 86-927 Civ. J. 12.

12. Plaintiff's Deposition of Lawanna Gail Banks, *Robinson* v. *Jacksonville Shipyards, et al.*

13. 641 F. 2d 934.

14. Catharine A. MacKinnon, *The Sexual Harassment of Working Women* (New Haven: Yale University Press, 1979), pp. 32–40.

15. *Henson* v. *City of Dundee*, 682 F. 2d 897 (11th Cir. 1982).

16. Ibid. at 904.

17. *Meritor Savings Bank* v. *Vinson*, 106 S. Ct. 2399 (1986).

18. Ibid. at 2404, quoting *Los Angeles Department of Water and Power* v. *Manhart*, 435 U.S. 702, 707, n. 13 (1978), quoting *Sprogis* v. *United Air Lines*, 444 F. 2d 1194, 1198 (7th Cir. 1971).

19. *Arnold* v. *City of Seminole, Oklahoma*, 614 F. Supp. 853 (E.D.Okl. 1985).

20. Ibid. at 867.

21. *Boyd* v. *Hayes Living Health Care Agency*, 44 F.E.P. Cases 332 (W.D. Tenn. 1987).

22. *Rabidue* v. *Osceola Refining Co.*, 805 F.2d 611 (6th Cir. 1986), cert denied.

23. *Harris* v. *Forklift Systems, Inc.*, 114 S. Ct. 367 (1993). *Rabidue* required plaintiffs to show that they sustained serious psychological damage from the harassment. This created a potential "Catch 22" for hostile environment plaintiffs. Those who could prove serious psychic injuries would have been discredited as mentally unbalanced while those who could not would have been unable to sustain their burden of proof.

24. See Dissent, *Thoreson* v. *Penthouse International Ltd.*, 583 N.Y.S.2d at 213, 223 (App. Div. 1992), aff'd, 606 N.E.2d 1369 (N.Y. 1992).

25. *Rabidue* at 615.

26. Ibid. at 624.

27. Ibid. at 615.

28. Ibid. at 618.

29. *Henson*, 692 F.2d at 904. For example, *Henson* required plaintiffs to prove that the harassment created abusive working conditions. *Rabidue* upped the ante considerably by requiring plaintiffs to prove, in addition, that the harassment unreasonably interfered with their work performance.

30. Ibid. at 620.

31. *Vaughan* v. *Menlove*, 1837, 3 Bing. N.C. 468, 132 Eng. Rep. 490.

32. Keeton et al., *Prosser and Keeton on Torts*, 5th Ed., p. 175.

33. *Rabidue* at 624.

34. Ibid. at 626.

35. 45 U.S.C.A., Section 54.

36. *Miller* v. *California*, 413 U.S. 15 (1973).

37. *Plessy* v. *Ferguson*, 163 U.S. 537 (1896).

38. *Meritor* v. *Vinson.*

39. Ibid. at 2405.

40. Ibid. at 2404.

41. *Comston* v. *Borden, Inc.*, 424 F. Supp. 157 (S.D. Ohio 1976).

42. *Katz* v. *Dole*, 709 F. 2d 251.

43. *Zabkowicz* v. *West Bend Co.*

44. *Roberts* v. *United States Jaycees*, 468 U.S. 609 (1984); *Pittsburgh Press Company* v. *Pittsburgh Commission on Human Relations*, 413 U.S. 376 (1973).

45. Ibid. at 675.

46. *Young* v. *American Mini-Theaters*, 427 U.S. 50 (1976).

47. *Miller* v. *California*, 413 U.S. 15 (1973).

48. *Central Hudson Gas* v. *Public Service Commission of New York*, 447 U.S. 557 (1980).

49. *FCC* v. *Pacifica Foundation*, 438 U.S. 726 (1978).

50. Ibid. at 438.

51. Feminists from Gloria Steinem to Susan Brownmiller and Alice Walker have long pointed out that pornography injures women as a class by using and portraying women as objects for male sexual abuse. How male workers can regard and treat women with whom they work as equals while they simultaneously embrace and participate in pornography's vision of women as sexual entertainment for men is a contradiction the *Rabidue* majority failed even to recognize, much less to grapple with. *Rabidue* also evaded the equally obvious fact that this conception of women takes on an exhortatory quality when pornographic pictures of women are displayed in public, like a hanging in effigy. In her deposition testimony taken by the defendants, Lois Robinson described this phenomenon precisely: "It is saying to the men that this is the way to view women here—as sex objects—and that's an acceptable thing there . . . having [the pinups] there is like saying that we can strip women anytime we want to."

52. There is a considerable body of evidence demonstrating that a large percentage of women find pornography offensive and intimidating. Sociologist Diana Russell conducted a random-sample survey of 930 California women and found that of those women exposed to pornography, 44 percent said that they were upset by it (Russell, "Pornography and Rape: A Causal Model," *Political Psychology*, vol. X). Gail Stevenson, a clinical psychologist, reports that "increasing numbers of women are entering psychotherapy with problems specifically related to the shame that results from their forced exposure to, but inability to counteract, pervasive pornographic denigration" (Stevenson, "Tolerance of Porn Traumatizes Women," *Los Angeles Times*, 28 May 1985, part 2, p. 5). Both Russell's and Stevenson's conclusions that significant numbers of women find pornography offensive or intimidating are supported by a 1986 *Time* magazine poll, which reported that 71 percent of the women in its sample believed that sexually explicit movies, magazines, and books encourage people to consider women as sex objects (compared to 50 percent of the men polled); 64 percent of the women believed that such materials lead people to commit acts of sexual violence (compared to 43 percent of the men); and 67 percent believed that magazines with nude pictures should be outlawed in local stores (compared to 49 percent of the men) ("Pornography: A Poll," *Time*, 21 July 1986).

53. Merrick T. Rossein, "Sex Discrimination and the Sexually Charged Work Environment," *New York University Review of Law and Social Change*, vol. 9, p. 273.

54. Nadine Taub, "Keeping Women in Their Place: Stereotyping Per Se as a Form of Employment Discrimination," *Boston College Law Review* 21, p. 370. See also, Employment and Training Administration, U.S. Department of Labor, *Women in Traditionally Male Jobs: The Experience of Ten Public Utility Companies* 76 (R & D Monograph No. 65, 1978).

55. Suzanne C. Carothers and Peggy Crull, "Contrasting Sexual Harassment in Female- and Male-Dominated Occupations," in Karen Sacks and Dorothy Remy, eds., *My Troubles Are Going To Have Trouble with Me: Everyday Trials and Triumphs of Women Workers* (New Brunswick, N.J.: Rutgers University Press, 1984).

56. Ibid., p. 224.

57. Communication with Sharon Wyse, of Women Against Pornography's Taskforce on Pornography and Sexual Abuse, 1988.

58. *Meritor* v. *Vinson.*

59. *Bundy* v. *Jackson.*
60. *Meritor* v. *Vinson.*
61. *Bundy* v. *Jackson.*

MARIANNE WESSON

1. Edward de Grazia, *Girls Lean Back Everywhere: The Law of Obscenity and the Assault on Genius* (New York: Random House, 1992), p. 10. In Ulysses, a character "leaned back and her garters were blue to match on account of the transparent and they all saw it and shouted to look. . . ." Leonard Bloom is among the observers and as the woman leans farther and farther back to watch the progress of a firework, he "could see her other things too, nainsook knickers, four and eleven . . . [and] he could see up high above her knee where no-one ever and she wasn't ashamed and he wasn't either to look in that immodest way. . . . ," quoted in de Grazia, pp. 9–10. Heap's statement was made to the readers of *The Little Review* in defense of the decision to publish the chapter. See Jane Heap, "Art and the Law," *The Little Review* 7, no. 3 (1967), pp. 5–6.
2. De Grazia, *Girls Lean Back,* pp. 581–86, 609–21.
3. Model antipornography civil rights ordinance, printed in Andrea Dworkin and Catharine A. MacKinnon, *Pornography and Civil Rights: A New Day for Women's Equality* pp. 138–39.
4. *American Booksellers Association* v. *Hudnut,* 598 F. Supp. 1316 (S.D. Ind. 1984), aff'd, 771 F. 2d 323 (1985), aff'd mem., 475 U.S. 1001 (1986).
5. Daniel Linz, Steven D. Penrod, and Edward Donnerstein, "The Attorney General's Commission on Pornography: The Gaps between 'Findings' and Facts," *Am. Bar. Found. Res. J.* (1987) pp. 713, 721–22.
6. Writers joining the *FACT Brief* included Rita Mae Brown, Rosemary Daniell, Betty Dodson, Vivian Gornick, Carolyn Heilbrun, Del Martin, Kate Millett, Felice Picano, Minnie Bruce Pratt, Adrienne Rich, Alix Kates Shulman, and Ellen Willis.
7. Sec. 1521, 102d Congress, First session, in *Cong. Rec.* 137 p. 10554 (22 July 1991).
8. Sec. 1521, 102d Congress, Second session, in *Cong. Rec.* 138 p. 12570 (12 August 1992).
9. Elsewhere I have called this material the "new hard core," a term that appealed to me because it reflects the shift in interest away from sexual explicitness and toward harm. See Marianne Wesson, "Sex, Lies and Videotape: The Pornographer as Censor," *Wash. L. Rev.* 66 (1991), pp. 913, 915. The Report of the Attorney General's Commission on Pornography used a similar definition for what it called sexually violent materials. U.S. Department of Justice, Attorney General's Commission on Pornography, *Final Report* (US GPO, 1986) pp. 323–24.
10. See Daniel A. Farber, "Foreword: Hate Speech after R.A.V.," *William Mitchell L. Rev.* 18 (1992), pp. 889, 894–95.
11. *Gertz* v. *Robert Welch, Inc.,* 418 U.S. 323, 347 (1974).
12. The most famous expression of this notion is in Justice Oliver Wendell Holmes's dissent in *Abrams* v. *United States,* 250 U.S. 616, 630 (1919) (Holmes dissenting). As others have observed, it borrows from John Milton's *Areopagitica* the idea that truth cannot be "put to the worse in a free and open encounter" (Milton, *Areopagitica,* in George H. Sabine, ed., *John Milton: Areopagitica and of Education* [Harlan Davidson, 1951], p. 50). The Supreme Court has consistently reinforced its own use of this metaphor. See, for example, *Board of Education* v. *Pico,* 457 U.S. 853, 866 (1984); *Citizens against Rent Control/Coalition for Fair Housing* v. *City of Berkeley,* 454 U.S. 290, 295 (1981). Defenders of free speech invoke the marketplace reflexively. See, for example, Kenneth L. Karst, "Equality as a Central Principle in the First Amendment," *U. Chi. L. Rev.* 43 (1975), pp. 20, 25 ("The advancement of knowledge depends on unfettered competition between today's prevailing opinions and those opinions that may come to prevail tomorrow"). It is the dominant paradigm invoked by the courts and by civil libertarians. See, for example, Stanley Ingber, "The Marketplace of Ideas: A Legitimizing Myth," *Duke L. J.* 1 (1984), pp. 2–3.
13. *Whitney* v. *California,* 274 U.S. 357, 375 (1926) (Brandeis concurring) ("[T]he fitting remedy for evil counsels is good ones"). But see Toni M. Massaro, "Equality and Freedom of Expression: The Hate Speech Dilemma," *William & Mary L. Rev.* 32 (1991), pp. 211, 218

(characterizing this sentiment as a "bromide") and Charles R. Lawrence III, "If He Hollers Let Him Go: Regulating Racist Speech on Campus," *Duke L. J.* (1990) pp. 431, 476 (characterizing it as an "empty ideal").

14. 968 F. 2d 1110 (11th Cir. 1992), cert. denied, 113 S. Ct. 1028 (1993).
15. The Court of Appeals inserted "[sic]" after the word *discrete*.
16. The punitive damages were later reduced to two million dollars *in remittitur.*
17. *Gertz v. Robert Welch, Inc.*, 418 U.S. 323, 347 (1974).
18. Compare Derrick Bell, "Foreword: The Final Civil Rights Act," *Cal. L. Rev.* 79 (1991), p. 597 (in which Bell proposes a law permitting, but taxing, racial discrimination).
19. See Mark Kelman, "The Necessary Myth of Objective Causation Judgments in Liberal Political Theory," *Chi. Kent. L. Rev.* 63 (1987), p. 579.
20. Compare Attorney General's Report, pp. 299–1035 (relying on Donnerstein's work to show harm of pornography) with Linz et al., "The Gaps between 'Findings' and Facts" (complaining that the commission misused their work).
21. See Daniel Linz and Edward Donnerstein, "Research Can Help Us Explain Violence and Pornography," *Chronicle of Higher Education*, 30 September 1992, p. B3.
22. See Edward Donnerstein, Daniel Linz, and Steven Penrod, *The Question of Pornography: Research Findings and Policy Implications* (Free Press, 1987), p. 160; Diana Scully, *Understanding Sexual Violence: A Study of Convicted Rapists* (Unwin Hyman, 1990), pp. 55–58.
23. See, for example, Richard Delgado and Jean Stefancic, "Pornography and Harm to Women: 'No Empirical Evidence?' " *Ohio. St. L. J.* 53 (1992), pp. 1041, 1048 ("[P]ornography is a *per se* harm, namely that of being derogatorily constructed as passive, hypersexual, masochistic, a sexual plaything, and so on") (emphasis added).
24. For the best description, see generally Robin L. West, "The Difference in Women's Hedonic Lives: A Phenomenological Critique of Feminist Legal Theory," *Wis. Women's L. J.* 3 (1987), p. 81. See also Cynthia Grant Bowman, "Street Harassment and the Informal Ghettoization of Women," *Harv. L. Rev.* 106 (1993), pp. 517, 518–20.
25. Catharine MacKinnon and others have proven this with their work on sexual harassment. See MacKinnon, *Sexual Harassment of Working Women* (New Haven, Conn.: Yale University Press, 1979) p. xi; Lin Farley, *Sexual Shakedown: The Sexual Harassment of Women on the Job* (McGraw-Hill, 1978). Their view was eventually adopted by the courts. See, for example, *Meritor Savings Bank* v. *Vinson*, 477 U.S. 57, 73 (1986) (recognizing sexual harassment as a form of illegal sex discrimination). Other once invisible harms that the legal system has, in some places, come to acknowledge through the efforts of law reformers and litigators are marital rape, *State* v. *Smith*, 85 N.J. 193, 426 A. 2d 38, 39 (1981), and domestic violence *Simmons* v. *Simmons*, 773 P. 2d 602, 603–04 (Colo. App. 1988).
26. I thank my friend Alison Jagger for educating me on the difficulty of this enterprise. See also Frederick Schauer, "Causation Theory and the Causes of Sexual Violence," 1987 *Am. Bar. Found. Res. J.* (1987), p. 737 (discussing meaning of causal conclusions in the Attorney General's report).
27. From the film *Field of Dreams*, this mysterious phrase makes a hero understand that he should build a ballpark, and that if he does so dead baseball players will come to life and compete there. He does and they do, of course. It says a great deal about some baseball fans that they did not find this film sappy.
28. See Anna Gronau, "Women and Images: Toward a Feminist Analysis of Censorship," in Varda Burstyn, ed., *Women Against Censorship* (Douglas & McIntyre, 1985), p. 91.
29. Audre Lorde, "The Master's Tools Will Never Dismantle the Master's House," in Lorde, *Sister Outsider* (Crossing Press, 1984), pp. 110–13.

Chapter Five

FREDERICK SCHAUER

1. See *Ocala Star-Banner Co.* v. *Damron*, 401 U.S. 295, 296 (1971) (plainly erroneous report of indictment for perjury); see also *Rood* v. *Finney*, 418 So. 2d 1, 2 (La. Ct. App. 1982)

(plainly erroneous report of drug addiction), cert. denied, 420 So. 2d 979 (La. 1982), and cert. denied, 460 U.S. 1013 (1983).

2. See *Herceg* v. *Hustler Magazine, Inc.*, 565 F. Supp. 802, 803 (S.D. Tex. 1983), motion to dismiss denied, 583 F. Supp. 1566 (S.D. Tex. 1984), rev'd, 814 F. 2d 1017 (5th Cir. 1987), cert. denied, 485 U.S. 959 (1988); *Olivia N.* v. *National Broadcasting System Co.*, 178 Cal. Rptr. 888, 892–93 (Ct. App. 1981), cert. denied sub nom.; *Niemi* v. *National Broadcasting Co.*, 458 U.S. 1108 (1982); *Walt Disney Prods., Inc.* v. *Shannon*, 276 S.E.2d 580, 582 (Ga. 1981). In all of the foregoing cases (and many others), the relationship between the publication and the injury would have satisfied standard tort requirements of negligence, foreseeability, and proximate cause. See generally Frederick Schauer, "Mrs. Palsgraf and the First Amendment," *Wash. and Lee L. Rev.* 47 (1990), p. 161. In some contrast to the above cases, however, is *Berhanu* v. *Metzger*, No. 8911-07007 (Cir. Ct., Multnomah County, Or., Oct. 22, 1990) (appeal pending). There, the victim of an attack by members of the White Aryan Resistance sued the leader of that organization for encouraging the attack, and the jury, finding specific intent, foreseeability, and proximate cause (although not imminence), found for the plaintiff against the leader in the amount of $12,479,000.

3. See *Brandenburg* v. *Ohio*, 395 U.S. 444, 448 (1969); *American Booksellers Ass'n* v. *Hudnut*, 771 F.2d 323, 333–34 (7th Cir. 1985), aff'd, 475 U.S. 1001 (1986). See Kent Greenawalt, *Speech, Crime, and the Uses of Language* (1989), pp. 262–63, and "Speech and Crime," *Am. B. Found Res. J.* (1980) pp. 645, 650–53.

4. 221 So. 2d 459 (Fla. Dist. Ct. App. 1969), case dismissed, 231 So. 2d 822 (Fla. 1970), rev'd, 401 U.S. 295 (1971).

5. 376 U.S. 254 (1964).

6. See 221 So. 2d at 461.

7. Justice Byron White added an even briefer concurrence, see 401 U.S. at 301, for the sole purpose of emphasizing that the toleration of harmful falsity was the unfortunate but necessary price that had to be paid in order to avoid the excess suppression of truth.

8. For my purposes it would have been nice were Leonard Damron a highly sympathy-inducing litigant. Alas, such an assumption may not be justified. See In Re Inquiry Concerning a Judge, Damron, 487 So. 2d 1, 2–3 (Fla. 1986) (approving recommendation of removal on the basis of charges of, inter alia, exchanging lenient sentences for political support, and discouraging defendants from exercising constitutional rights). For those looking for a somewhat more appealing libel plaintiff, see generally *Faulk* v. *Aware, Inc.*, 231 N.Y.S. 2d 270 (Sup. Ct. 1962), rev'd, 244 N.Y.S. 2d 259 (App. Div. 1963), aff'd, 200 N.E. 2d 778 (N.Y. 1964) (TV and radio personality won large damage award against entities involved in blacklisting him because of alleged Communist sympathies).

9. But maybe not. At least some editors maintain proudly that the threat of libel actions has no effect on their editorial judgments. See David A. Anderson, "Libel and Press Self-Censorship," *Tex. L. Rev.* 53 (1975), pp. 422, 434; David A. Hollander, "The Economics of Libel Litigation," in *Cost of Libel*, pp. 257, 258 n. 3; Barry F. Smith, "The Rising Tide of Libel Litigation: Implications of the Gertz Negligence Rules," *Mont. L. Rev.* 44 (1983), pp. 71, 87 (discussing views of counsel for the *Washington Post*). Assuming that such editor (manager) behavior is at least tolerated and perhaps encouraged by the publishers (owners), the explanation is likely to be complex. Part of the explanation may lie in publishers' being willing to pay for certain principles, part in publishers' believing that a given degree of editorial aggressiveness sells more papers, and part in publishers' valuing (for financial or nonfinancial reasons) a certain kind of newspaper reputation. But whatever the explanation, it seems plain that insofar as editors do operate without regard to potential legal liability, the premise that the *New York Times* rule is *necessary* is diminished *pro tanto*.

10. See, e.g., Norman E. Isaacs, *Untended Gates: The Mismanaged Press* (1986), pp. 164–65 (describing advertiser pressure on editors as "the worst kind of conflict of interest"); Tom Wicker, *On Press* (1978), pp. 181–82 (arguing that direct pressure from advertisers, while present, plays "a relatively small part in editorial decisions"). I describe this separation as a "tenet" rather than a "fact" because, as I will discuss shortly, I and others have substantial doubts as to whether the tenet is reflected in the reality of press practice. But my point here is only that one of the media's own tenets, whether adhered to or not, is seemingly at odds

with the major claim that the media itself makes with respect to the effect of defamation law on press practices.

11. On speech operating as the "but for" cause of physical harm, see note 2 above. Much of the analysis of defamation applies here as well.

12. This latter category resembles the concern at issue in R.A.V. v. *City of St. Paul*, 112 S. Ct. 2538, 2547–50 (1992). The Court's significant restriction on content-based remedies in R.A.V. suggests that the importance of uncoupling, of searching for nonrestricting forms of compensation, is now even greater.

   My definitions of both types of hate speech include intent to injure, though there could of course also be "negligence" versions of both—this latter would create differences of opinion as to whether the phrase "hate speech" should be used where negligence but not intent to injure exists.

13. See *Brandenburg v. Ohio*, 395 U.S. 444, 446–47 (1969) (per curiam).

14. This seems especially clear after R.A.V. v. *City of St. Paul*, 112 S. Ct. 2538 (1992). For examples of such laws in other countries and in international law, see Race Relations Act, 1976, ch. 74 secs. 30–31 (Eng.); Criminal Code, R.S.C., ch. C-46, secs. 318–319 (1985) (Can.); Brottsbalken (penal code), ch. 16, sec. 8 (Swed.), translated in Nat'l Swedish Council for Crime Prevention, *The Swedish Penal Code* 45 (John Hogg trans., 1984); International Convention on the Elimination of All Forms of Racial Discrimination, opened for signature 7 March 1966, art. 4, 660 U.N.T.S. 195. Additional examples are described in Mari J. Matsuda, "Public Response to Racist Speech: Considering the Victim's Story," *Mich. L. Rev.* 87 (1989), pp. 2320, 2341–48; Jordan J. Paust, "Rereading the First Amendment in Light of Treaties Proscribing Incitement to Racial Discrimination or Hostility," *Rutgers L. Rev.* 43 (1991), pp. 565, 565–68; Eric Stein, "History against Free Speech: The New German Law against the 'Auschwitz'—and Other—'Lies,' " *Mich. L. Rev.* 85 (1986), pp. 277, 281–87, 312–14, 322–24.

15. The claim is guarded in this way in large part because many other aspects of First Amendment doctrine may have had the effect of reducing the level of racism. I am thinking here of the propositions that First Amendment rulings in the 1960s had the effect of facilitating the efforts of the civil rights movement, see, e.g., *Gregory v. City of Chicago*, 394 U.S. 111, 112 (1969) (peaceful and orderly march to press desegregation claims protected by First Amendment); *Brown v. Louisiana*, 383 U.S. 131, 141–42 (1966) (First and Fourteenth amendments protect the right to protest "by silent and peaceful presence" in a "whites only" library); *Cox v. Louisiana*, 379 U.S. 559, 568–69, 574 (1965) (reversing the conviction of twenty-three student participants in a peaceful march near a courthouse); *New York Times Co. v. Sullivan*, 376 U.S. 254, 279–80, 282–83 (1964)—which in turn facilitated a decrease in what would otherwise have been the amount of racial violence and racial discrimination. (See generally Harry Kalven, Jr., *The Negro and the First Amendment* [1965].) These propositions are also empirical, and thus also could be or could have been otherwise, but I doubt it.

16. As I do. See Frederick Schauer, "Causation Theory and the Causes of Sexual Violence," *Am. B. Found. Res. J.* (1987) pp. 737, 767–70.

17. This way of thinking about the costs of the First Amendment is the general message of Catharine A. MacKinnon, *Feminism Unmodified: Discourses on Life and Law* (1987).

18. I use the word "harmful" rather than the word "offensive" because I believe that much of popular libertarian discourse about free speech uses the word "offense" to trivialize what someone else claims to be a harm. Thus, even if there is a sound distinction between harm and offense (see Joel Feinberg, *Offense to Others: The Moral Limits of the Criminal Law* [1985], pp. 1–5; Judith Jarvis Thomson, *The Realm of Rights* [1990], p. 354), the common use of the word "offense" is question begging, with "offense" being the label many people apply to utterances they have determined, on unarticulated grounds, to be harmless.

19. See *Collin v. Smith*, 447 F. Supp. 676, 686–87, 700 (N.D. Ill.), aff'd, 578 F. 2d 1197 (7th Cir.), stay denied, 436 U.S. 953, cert. denied, 439 U.S. 916 (1978).

20. See *Robinson v. Jacksonville Shipyards, Inc.*, 760 F. Supp. 1486, 1535–36 (M.D. Fla. 1991); see also Catharine A. MacKinnon, "Pornography, Civil Rights, and Speech," *Harv. C.R.-C.L. L. Rev.* 20 (1985), pp. 1, 39 (discussing interplay between pornography, civil rights, and the First Amendment).

21. See *United States* v. *Eichman*, 496 U.S. 474, 484–88 (1988).
22. See *Frisby* v. *Schultz*, 487 U.S. 474, 484–88 (1988).
23. See *Cohen* v. *California*, 403 U.S. 15, 21–22 (1971).
24. In particular, see *Hustler Magazine, Inc.* v. *Falwell*, 485 U.S. 46, 53 (1988).
25. See Mark Tushnet, "Political Correctness, the Law, and the Legal Academy," *Yale J.L. and Human.* 4 (1992), pp. 127, 149.
26. See Mary Ellen Gale, "Reimagining the First Amendment: Racist Speech and Equal Liberty," *St. John's L. Rev.* 65 (1991), p. 119.

Frank J. Michelman

Speaking at the Conference on Equality, Speech, and Harm, I offered some thoughts about two footnotes in Cass Sunstein's paper for the conference. See Sunstein, *Democracy and the Problem of Free Speech* (New York: The Free Press, 1993). This essay contains the substance of what I said, though the opening and closing paragraphs were composed more recently.
1. Ibid., p. 220.
2. Ibid.
3. See generally Cass Sunstein, *The Partial Constitution* (1993) and *Democracy and the Problem of Free Speech*.
4. Sunstein, *Democracy*.
5. *American Booksellers Association* v. *Hudnut*, 771 F. 2d 323, 329 (7th Cir. 1985), aff'd per cur., 475 U.S. 1001 (1986).
6. Charles Fried, "The New First Amendment Jurisprudence: A Threat to Liberty," in *The Bill of Rights and the Modern State* (1992), pp. 225, 250.
7. Sunstein, *Democracy*.
8. See, e.g., Sunstein, *Democracy*, p. 186.

Kathleen E. Mahoney

1. *McKinney* v. *Board of Governors of the University of Guelph* (1990), 76 D.L.R. (4th) 55 (S.C.C.) at pp. 582–583. See also *Reference Re Public Service Employee Relations Act* (Alta.) (1989) 1 S.C.R. 313 at 367 per Dickson, C.J.C.
2. Canadian Charter of Rights and Freedoms, part 1 of the Constitution Act, 1982, being schedule B of the Canadian Act, 1982, c. 11.
3. Section 15 reads:
   (1) Every individual is equal before and under the law and has the right to equal protection and equal benefit of the law without discrimination and, in particular, without discrimination based on race, national or ethnic origin, colour, religion, sex, age or mental or physical disability.
4. Subsection (2) of section 15 reads:
   (2) Subsection (1) does not preclude any law, program or activity that has as its object the amelioration of conditions of disadvantaged individuals or groups including those that are disadvantaged because of race, national or ethnic origin, colour, religion, sex, age or mental or physical disability.
5. Section 27 reads:
   This Charter shall be interpreted in a manner consistent with the preservation and enhancement of the multicultural heritage of Canadians.
6. Section 28 reads:
   Notwithstanding anything in this Charter, the rights and freedoms referred to in it are guaranteed equally to male and female persons.
7. For example, see *Attorney General of Canada* v. *Lavell* (1974) S.C.R. 349; *Bliss* v. *Attorney General of Canada* (1979) 1 S.C.R. 190 (where a narrow interpretation of equality resulted in the perpetuation of inequality for Native women and pregnant women).
8. See for example, Bertha Wilson, *The Making of a Constitution: Approaches to Judicial Interpretation* (Edinburgh, 1988). See also *R.* v. *Rahey* (1987) 1 S.C.R. 588 at 639, 57 C.R. (3d) 289, 33 C.C.C. (3d) 289, 39 D.L.R. (4th) 481, 33 C.R.R. 275, 78 N.S.R. (2d) 183, 193 A.P.R. 183, 75 N.R. 81 (La Forest, J.); *R.* v. *Keegstra*, [1991] 2 W.W.R. 1 at 37 (Dickson, C.J.C.).

9. Ibid.
10. Ibid., Wilson, J.
11. *Hunter* v. *Southam Inc.* (1984) 2 S.C.R. 145 at 155–6 (Dickson, J.) and *R.* v. *Big M Drug Mart Ltd.* (1985) 1 S.C.R. 295 at p. 344 (Dickson, J.).
12. Actual results of Charter litigation have been beneficial for disempowered or neglected groups in Canadian society. See *Re Singh and Minister of Employment and Immigration* (1985), 17 D.L.R. (4th) 422 (S.C.C.) (which benefited refugees); *Edwards Books and Art Ltd. et al.* v. *R.* (1986), 35 D.L.R. (4th) 1 (S.C.C.) (which benefited nonunionized workers); and *Morgentaler, Smoling and Scott* v. *R.* (1988), 44 D.L.R. (4th) 385 (S.C.C.) (which benefited women).
13. Bertha Wilson, "The Making of a Constitution," address to the Ninth Annual Conference of Women Judges, Seattle, Washington, October 1987, p. 12 (unpublished).
14. Brian Dickson, "Madam Justice Wilson: Trailblazer for Justice," *Dalhousie L. J.* 1 (1992) p. 17.
15. Rosalie Abella, "The Evolutionary Nature of Equality," in K. E. Mahoney and S. L. Martin, eds., *Equality and Judicial Neutrality* (Toronto: Carswell, 1987), p. 4.
16. *R.* v. *Big M Drug Mart* (1985), 18 D.L.R. (4th) 321 (S.C.C.).
17. *Andrews* v. *Law Society of British Columbia* (1989) 1 S.C.R. 143.
18. *Brooks* v. *Canada Safeway Ltd.* (1989) 1 S.C.R. 1219. This case was brought under provincial human rights legislation but Charter principles were applied.
19. *R.* v. *Lavallee* (1990) 1 S.C.R. 852.
20. *Regina* v. *Keegstra* (1990) 3 S.C.R. 697; *Regina* v. *Andrews and Smith* (1990) 3 S.C.R. 870; *Canada [Human Rights Commission]* v. *Taylor* (1990) 3 S.C.R. 892.
21. Canadian Human Rights Act, R.S.C., c. H-6, sec. 13 (1) as amended in 1985 reads:

    13. (1) It is a discriminatory practice for a person or group of persons acting in concert to communicate telephonically or to cause to be so communicated, repeatedly, in whole or in part by means of the facilities of a telecommunication undertaking within the legislative authority of Parliament, any matter that is likely to expose a person or persons to hatred or contempt by reason of the fact that that person or those persons are identifiable on the basis of a prohibited ground of discrimination.

    (2) Subsection (1) does not apply in respect of any matter that is communicated in whole or in part by means of the facilities of a broadcasting undertaking.

    (3) For the purposes of this section, no owner or operator of a telecommunication undertaking communicates or causes to be communicated any matter described in subsection (1) by reason only that the facilities of a telecommunication undertaking owned or operated by that person are used by another person for the transmission of that matter.

22. Sec. 1 reads:

    The *Canadian Charter of Rights and Freedoms* guarantees the rights and freedoms set out in it subject only to such reasonable limits prescribed by law as can be demonstrably justified in a free and democratic society.

23. *Irwin Toy Ltd.* v. *Quebec [Attorney-General]* (1989) 1 S.C.R. 927, 58 D.L.R. (4th) 577, 39 C.R.R. 193, 25 C.P.R. (3d) 417, 24 Q.A.C. 2, 94 N.R. 167.
24. *Beauharnais* v. *Illinois*, 343 U.S. 250, 96 L. Ed. 919, 72 S. Ct. 725 (1952) (rehearing denied 72 S. Ct. 1070).
25. The Court pointed to *Roth* v. *U.S.*, 354 U.S. 476, L. Ed. 2d 1498, 77 S. Ct. 1304 (1957) (obscenity); *New York* v. *Ferber*, 458 U.S. 747, 73 L. Ed. 2d 1113, 102 S. Ct. 3348 (1982) (child pornography); *Posadas de Puerto Rico Association* v. *Tourism Co. of Puerto Rico*, 478 U.S. 328, 92 L. Ed. 2d 266, 106 S. Ct. 2968 (1986) (commercial speech); *Cornelius* v. *N.A.A.C.P. Legal Defense and Education Fund Inc.*, 473 U.S. 788, 88 L. Ed. 2d 567, 1055 S. Ct. 3439 (1985) (political activity).
26. As set out in *Regina* v. *Oakes* (1986) 1 S.C.R. 103, 136.
27. *R.* v. *Keegstra* at 50.
28. The section reads:

    This Charter shall be interpreted in a manner consistent with the preservation and enhancement of the multicultural heritage of Canadians.

29. Citing Cory J. in *R.* v. *Andrews* (1988), 65 O.R. (2d) 161, 65 C.R. (3d) 320, 43 C.C.C. (3d), 193, 28 O.A.C. 161 (C.A.).

30. *Reference Re Alberta Legislation* (1938) S.C.R. 100; *Fraser* v. *P.S.S.R.B.* (1985) 2 S.C.R. 455 at 462.

31. *Rochet* v. *Royal College of Dental Surgeons of Ontario* (1990) 2 S.C.R. 232, 71 D.L.R. (4th) 68, 47 C.R.R. 193, 40 O.A.C. 241, 111 N.R. 161; *Edmonton Journal* v. *Alberta [Attorney General]* (1989) 2 S.C.R. 1326.

32. *R.* v. *Keegstra* at 56 (W.W.R.).

33. Ibid. at 60.

34. *R.* v. *Butler* (1992) 1 S.C.R. 432.

35. Citing Canada House of Commons Standing Committee on Justice and Legal Affairs, *Report on Pornography* no. 18 (22 March 1978), p. 4.

36. Agreement for the Suppression of the Circulation of Obscene Publications and the Convention for the Suppression of the Circulation and Traffic in Obscene Publications.

37. Citing *Royal College of Dental Surgeons of Ontario et al.* v. *Rochet and Price* at 177.

38. 771 F. 2d 323, Ind. Fed. Ct., 7th Cir. (1985).

39. *Butler.*

RICHARD DELGADO AND DAVID YUN

1. See Shawna H. Yen, "Redressing the Victim of Racist Speech after *R.A.V.* v. *St. Paul*: A Proposal to Permit Recovery in Tort," *Colum. J.L. and Soc. Probs.* 26 (1993), p. 589; Rhonda G. Hartman, "Revitalizing Group Defamation as a Remedy for Hate Speech on Campus," *Ore. L. Rev.* 71 (1992), p. 855; Jean Love, "Discriminatory Speech and the Tort of Intentional Infliction of Emotional Distress," *Wash. and Lee L. Rev.* 47 (1990), p. 105. For an earlier discussion of tort remedies, see Richard Delgado, "Words That Wound: A Tort Action for Racial Insults, Epithets, and Name-Calling," 17 *Harv. C.R.-C.L. L. Rev.* 17 (1982), p. 133.

2. Charles R. Lawrence III, "If He Hollers Let Him Go: Regulating Racist Speech on Campus," *Duke L.J.* 431 (1990); Mari Matsuda, "Public Response to Racist Speech: Considering the Victim's Story," *Mich. L. Rev.* 87 (1989), p. 2320. On the national ACLU position, see Nadine Strossen, "Legal Scholars Who Would Limit Free Speech," *Chron. Higher Ed.*, 7 July 1993, p. B1 (conceding that recent decisions may open the way to regulating hate speech).

3. E.g., Nadine Strossen, "Regulating Hate Speech on Campus: A Modest Proposal?" *Duke L.J.* 484 (1990); Nat Hentoff, *Free Speech for Me—But Not for Thee: How the American Left and Right Relentlessly Censor Each Other* (1992); Marjorie Heins, "Banning Words: A Comment on 'Words That Wound,' " *Harv. C.R.-C.L. L. Rev.* 18 (1983), pp. 585, 592. For a similar argument, see Nadine Strossen, "A Feminist Critique of 'the' Feminist Critique of Pornography, *Va. L. Rev.* 79 (1993), p. 1099.

4. By paternalism, we mean a justification for curtailing someone's liberty that invokes the well-being of the person concerned, that is, that requires that he or she do or refrain from doing something for his or her own good.

   Could it be argued that the opposite position, namely advocacy of hate speech regulation, is also paternalistic, in that it implies that minorities need or want protection, when many may not? No. The impetus for such regulation comes mainly from minority attorneys and scholars—and an argument emanating from the protected group cannot be paternalistic (although it may be misguided on other grounds). A gay person who finds it inoffensive to be gay-bashed or a Mexican who enjoys being called "spic" or "wetback" has an easy recourse—not to file a complaint under a hate speech statute.

5. E.g., Strossen, "Modest Proposal," pp. 111, 148, 162; Hentoff, *Free Speech for Me*; Marjorie Heins, "Banning Speech," *Harv. C.R.-C.L. L. Rev.* 18 (1983), p. 585; Strossen, "A Feminist Critique." These are not the only arguments that are made against regulating hate speech, of course, but they are an important set because (1) they are prominently and frequently repeated and (2) they are insidious—those who make them can pretend to be serving minorities' best interests.

6. E.g., Strossen, "Modest Proposal."

7. Denise K. Magner, "Blacks and Whites on the Campuses: Behind Ugly Racist Incidents, Student Isolation and Insensitivity," *Chron. Higher Ed.*, 26 April 1989, p. A1.

8. Deb Riechmann, "Colleges Tackle Increase in Racism on Campuses," *Los Angeles Times*, 30 April 1989, p. 36.

9. For a recent discussion of the international dimensions of hate speech and hate crimes, see Sandra Coliver, ed., *Striking a Balance: Hate Speech, Freedom of Expression, and Non-Discrimination*, International Centre Against Censorship, Human Rights Centre of the University of Essex, United Kingdom, 1992), article 19.

10. University of Texas, Institutional Rules of Student Services and Activities (1990–91), app. C, p. 174.

11. Diane Curtis, "Racial, Ethnic, Sexual Slurs Banned on U.C. Campuses," *San Francisco Chron.*, 27 September 1989, p. A1.

12. 721 F. Supp. 852 (E.D. Mich. 1989); quotation at 856.

13. 744 F. Supp. 1163 (E.D. Wis. 1991).

14. 112 S. St. 2538 (1992).

15. 113 S. Ct. 2194 (1993).

16. 3 S.C.R. 697 (1990) (Can.).

17. 89 D.L.R. 4th 449 (1992) (Can.).

18. See notes 1 and 2.

19. Additional arguments of course exist. This section focuses on the four principal ones that are paternalistic, as we define the term (see note 4). For example, the "martyrdom" argument (that penalizing hate speakers makes heroes out of them and gives them a further platform for their message; see Hentoff, *Free Speech for Me*, p. 559) and the "bellwether" argument (that racist speech raises and alerts public consciousness; ibid., p. 560) have both paternalistic and nonpaternalistic dimensions. We exclude from our consideration these and other arguments falling in the "gray zone"; their treatment awaits another day.

20. E.g., ibid., p. 134; Strossen, "A Feminist Critique," p. 1141.

21. Gordon Allport, *The Nature of Prejudice* (1954), pp. 62, 252, 460–61, 467–72 (rejecting the view that racist conduct serves as a catharsis and holding that laws and norms against discrimination change behavior for the better). See infra text and notes 27–30 (showing social science laboratory and field evidence corroborating Allport's observation). The mechanism probably consists of a combination of *habituation* (our tendency to repeat an action that is enjoyable and brings no penalty); *cognitive dissonance* ("he must deserve it—look how badly I treated him before"); and *social construction of reality* (the images we disseminate of and to minorities create a world in which they are always one down). See also Richard Delgado, "Rodrigo's Chronicle," *Yale L.J.* 101 (1992), p. 1357 (on a fourth mechanism, *perseveration*, a response to frustration and stress).

22. See Leonard Berkovitz, *Aggression: Its Causes, Consequences, and Control* (1993); "The Case for Bottling Up Rage," *Psychology Today* (July 1973), p. 24. On the role of desensitization, see Mari Matsuda, "Public Response to Racist Speech: Considering the Victim's Story," *Mich. L. Rev.* 57 (1989) pp. 2320, 2329–31 (each new repetition of a racial epithet increases the chance it will be resorted to again).

23. On this symbolic dimension and the part it plays in constructing racial reality, see Richard Delgado and Jean Stefancic, "Images of the Outsider in American Law and Culture: Can Free Expression Remedy Systemic Social Ills?" *Cornell L. Rev.* 77 (1992), p. 1258.

24. Stanley Milgram, *Obedience to Authority* (1974).

25. Haney, Banks, and Zimbardo, "Interpersonal Dynamics in a Simulated Prison," 1 *Int'l J. Criminol. and Penology* 1 (1973), p. 69 (the guards began to haze, browbeat, and even physically mistreat the prisoners).

26. The experiment was first done by a third-grade school teacher from Riceville, Iowa, on April 5, 1968, in response to the death of Martin Luther King. See generally William Peters, *A Class Divided: Then and Now* (1971).

27. Diane Sculley, *Understanding Sexual Violence* (1990), pp. 100–17.

28. E.g., Strossen, "Modest Proposal," p. 512; Strossen, "A Feminist Critique," pp. 1143–46; Hentoff, *Free Speech for Me*, pp. 109, 169.

29. E.g., "Race Bias Prompted Most Hate Crimes; FBI's First National Statistics Show Blacks as Main Target," *San Francisco Chronicle*, 5 January 1993, p. A1; Eugene H. Czajkoski,

Criminalizing Hate: An Empirical Assessment (Fed. Probation, September 1992), p. 36 (reporting Florida statistics).

30. Reichmann, "Racism on Campuses."
31. E.g., ibid.; "Race Bias." For an example of such a case, see *Wisconsin v. Mitchell.*
32. See Coliver, *Striking a Balance*, pp. 109, 138, 221, 223, 240, 259, 307 (describing the efforts of various countries at controlling hate speech).
33. Strossen, "Modest Proposal," p. 567.
34. E.g., Lawrence, "If He Hollers," pp. 466–67; Delgado and Stefancic, "Images of the Outsider," p. 1285.
35. Derrick Bell, *Race, Racism, and American Law* (2d ed. 1991), pp. 27–29.
36. Delgado and Stefancic, "Images of the Outsider," pp. 1276–82.
37. See Richard Delgado, "Campus Antiracism Rules: Constitutional Narratives in Collision," *Nw. U.L. Rev.* 85 (1991), pp. 343, 377–78 (reviewing these and other exceptions).
38. Hentoff, *Free Speech for Me*, pp. 101–02, 111, 159, 167.
39. Remarks by Benno Schmidt, then president of Yale University, at Campus Speech, a panel discussion and program, Yale Law School, 1 October 1991.
40. On the role of language and categories in constructing a world that reflects the empowered's sense of how things are, see Richard Delgado, "Mindset and Metaphor," *Harv. L. Rev.* 103 (1990), p. 1872.
41. E.g., Sally McGrath, "Student Denies Insulting Black During Scuffle," *Boulder Daily Camera* (Colorado), 28 August 1993, p. B1; Manning Marable, "No Longer As Simple As Black and White," *Boulder Daily Camera*, 12 August 1993, p. B3 (describing the Florida prosecution of assailants who murdered a black man who talked back following a racial slur).
42. Kenneth J. Dover, *Greek Homosexuality* (1978), p. 34.
43. Just as some out-and-out racists seem to believe that they may do or say anything toward members of minority groups with impunity, so some majoritarian commentators in the hate-speech debate appear to believe that they may employ the most caustic language toward those on the other side, secure in the belief that those who defend the minority position will not respond. See, e.g., Jonathan Yardley, "The Code Word: Alarming," *Washington Post*, 16 August 1993, p. B2 (calling the advocacy of campus hate-speech rules put forward by two authors "a peculiar blend of totalitarianism and phrenology"; dismissing allegations of harm as "pop psychology"; describing their position as evasion, euphemism, zealotry, newspeak, thought police tactics, fascism, doublethink, ludicrous reasoning, and an "Orwellian nightmare").

RICHARD DELGADO

1. "In the Defense of Freedom and Equality," *Harv. C.R.-C.U. L.Rev.* (forthcoming).
2. By this I mean that it is understandable and desirable for organizations to attempt to remain at peace and focused on common goals.
3. On legal realism, see Elizabeth Mensch, "The History of Mainstream Legal Thought," in D. Kairys, ed., *The Politics of Law* (1982), pp. 18, 26–29.
4. See Richard Delgado and David R. Millen, "God, Galileo, and Government: Toward Constitutional Protection for Scientific Inquiry," *Wash. L.Rev.* 53 (1978), pp. 349, 354–60.
5. E.g., Thomas Emerson, *The System of Freedom of Expression* (1970) and "Toward a General Theory of the First Amendment," 72 *Yale L.J.* 72 (1963), p. 877 (setting out functions of the First Amendment—the search for truth, promotion of social change, the self-fulfillment of the speaker, etc.).
6. E.g., Stanley Ingber, "The Marketplace of Ideas: A Legitimizing Myth," *Duke L.J.* 1984, p. 786.
7. On critical race theory in general, see Richard Delgado and Jean Stefancic, "Critical Race Theory: An Annotated Bibliography," *Va. L.Rev.* 79 (1993), p. 461; on the feminist critique of pornography, see, e.g., Andrea Dworkin and Catharine MacKinnon, *Pornography and Civil Rights: A New Day for Women* (1988).
8. For an example of vituperative writing by a mainstream columnist, see Jonathan Yardley, "The Code Word: Alarming," *Washington Post*, 16 August 1993, p. G2 (describing two

anti–hate speech writers as engaged in "euphemism," "evasion," "rank indifferences in constitutional meetings," "lunacy," "zealot[ry]," "totalitarianism," "phrenology," "New-speak," "Doublethink," and more).

9. See Steven H. Shiffrin, *The First Amendment, Democracy, and Romance* (1990), pp. 86–109, 140–69 (reevaluating some of these claims).

10. See Richard Delgado and Jean Stefancic, "Images of the Outsider in American Law and Culture: Can Free Expression Remedy Systemic Social Ills?" *Cornell L.Rev.* 77 (1992), pp. 1258, 1259, 1275–84.

11. Ibid., pp. 1261, 1275–84 (coining the term "empathic fallacy" to describe the belief that speech can dispel error embedded in one's own speech paradigm).

12. Ingber, "Legitimizing Myth"; Delgado and Stefancic, "Images of the Outsider," pp. 1284–88.

13. Delgado and Stefancic, "Images of the Outsider," pp. 1275–88.

14. On the way pornography constructs the social reality of women as sexualized, see generally Dworkin and MacKinnon, *New Day*; Richard Delgado and Jean Stefancic, "Pornography and Harm to Women: 'No Empirical Evidence?' " *Ohio St. L.Rev.* 53 (1992), pp. 1039, 1039–50; Frederick Schauer, "Uncoupling Free Speech," *Colum. L.Rev.* 92 (1992), p. 1321, parts of which appear in this volume, p. 259.

15. On these "aberrations" and exceptions to free speech (which number in the dozens) see, e.g., Richard Delgado, "Campus Antiracism Rules: Constitutional Narratives in Collision," *NWU L.Rev.* 85 (1991), pp. 343, 377–78.

16. Ibid., pp. 345–48; Cass Sunstein, "Words, Conduct, Caste," *U. Chi. L.Rev.* (1993), p. 795.

17. See Richard Delgado and David Yun, "Pressure Valves and Bloodied Chickens: An Analysis of Four Paternalistic Arguments for Resisting Hate-Speech Regulation," p. 290, this volume.

18. Delgado, "Narratives in Collision," pp. 383–86; Stanley Fish, *There's No Such Thing As Free Speech, and It's a Good Thing, Too* (1993).

19. See, e.g., Mari Matsuda, Charles Lawrence, Richard Delgado, and Kimberlé Crenshaw, in *Words That Wound* (1993); Kent Greenawalt, "Insults and Epithets: Are They Protected Speech?" *Rutgers L.Rev.* 42 (1990), p. 287.

20. Charles Lawrence, "If He Hollers Let Him Go: Regulating Racist Speech on Campus," *Duke L.J.* (1990), p. 431.

21. E.g., Mari Matsuda, "Public Response to Racist Speech: Listening to the Victim's Story," *Mich. L.Rev.* 87 (1989), p. 232.

22. See *Words That Wound*.

23. See Richard Delgado and Jean Stefancic, "Hateful Speech, Loving Communities: Why Our Notion of 'A Just Balance' Changes So Slowly," *Cal. L.Rev.* (Spring 1994).

24. Yardley, "Code Word"; see generally Nat Hentoff, *Free Speech for Me—But Not for Thee* (1992).

25. Hentoff, *Free Speech for Me.*

26. Ibid.; Nadine Strossen, "Legal Scholars Who Would Limit Free Speech," *Chron. Higher Ed.* (7 July 1993), pp. 1–3, and "Censuring the Censors of Free Speech," *Chicago Tribune*, 2 September 1993, p. 27.

27. Yun and Delgado, "Bloodied Chickens" (analyzing four such arguments).

28. Strossen, "Defense of Freedom." On the judiciary's somewhat tortured effort to come to grips with hate speech and hate crime, compare *R.A.V.* v. *City of St. Paul*, 112 S. Ct. 2538 (1992) (tolerating cross-burning) with *Wisconsin* v. *Mitchell*, 113 S. Ct. 2194 (1993) (permitting sentence enhancement for racially motivated crimes), and two recent Canadian Supreme Court decisions, *Regina* v. *Butler*, 89 D.L.R. 449 (1992) (upholding an antipornography law in the face of the objection that it limited speech, protected by the Canadian charter) and *Regina* v. *Keegstra* (1990) 3 S.C.R. 697 (upholding a federal hate-speech law in the face of similar objections).

JOHN A. POWELL

1. See generally L. Wittgenstein, *Philosophical Investigations* (1953); D. Cornell; N. Goodman, *Ways of Wordmakers* (1978). Although language is constitutive of the world, it would be a

mistake to believe that that is all there is. The world is also a reflection of power and material conditions.

2. R. Delgado, "Campus Antiracism Rules: Constitutional Narratives in Collision," *Nw. U.L. Rev.* 85 (1991), pp. 343, 345–46 (footnotes omitted).

3. See C. Baker, *Human Liberty and Freedom of Speech* (1989), pp. 47–69 and passim. Also see generally T. Emerson, "Toward a General Theory of the First Amendment," *Yale L.Rev* 72 (1963), p. 877; J. Mill, *On Liberty* (1859).

4. See generally K. Karst, *Belonging to America* (1989); M. Waltzer, *Spheres of Justice* (1983), pp. 31–40.

5. See generally R. Rorty, *Contingency, Irony, and Solidarity* (1989), pp. 3–22 for a good discussion of the lack of a metanarrative. Goodman also makes the point that a narrative cannot be judged as right or real by some objective language construct because there is none; see Goodman, *Ways of Wordmakers.*

6. I am not suggesting that I am neutral or that I have an equal interest or personal grounding in both sets of values.

7. See, e.g., N. Strossen, "Regulating Racist Speech on Campus: A Modest Proposal?" *Duke L.J.* (1990), pp. 484, 489.

8. See, e.g., C. Lawrence III, "If He Hollers Let Him Go: Regulating Racist Speech on Campus," *Duke L.J.* (1990), p. 431; Strossen, "Modest Proposal"; R. Post, "Racist Speech, Democracy, and the First Amendment," *William and Mary L.Rev.* 32 (1991), p. 267.

9. See, e.g., Emerson, *General Theory*; Baker, *Human Liberty*, J. Rawls, *A Theory of Justice* (1971).

10. See R. Post, "The Constitutional Concept of Public Discourse: Outrageous Opinion, Democratic Deliberation and *Hustler Magazine* v. *Falwell*," *Harv.L.Rev.* 103 (1990), pp. 601, 632–63.

11. Lawrence, "If He Hollers," p. 473, recounts a story I told demonstrating this type of privilege. I was at a Thanksgiving dinner. My family and I are vegetarians. My son Fon, while going through the line for food, noted that there was more than one type of stuffing. He turned to the person behind him and asked which of the stuffings was meat and which was vegetarian. The man responded by pointing to one of the dishes and said, "This is the regular stuffing and the other is the vegetarian." I spoke up for the benefit of my son and corrected the man that there is no regular stuffing—one was meat and the other vegetarian. Simone de Beauvoir was one of the first modern philosophers to point out that this move to make one thing essential and the other nonessential was a privileging move. See de Beauvoir, *The Second Sex* (The Modern Library, 1968), p. xxix.

    There is also a good discussion of this issue in M. Minow, "Foreword: Justice Engendered" *Harv. L. Rev.* 101 (1987), p. 10, and C. Gilligan, *In a Different Voice* (1982).

12. This is what Delgado has addressed in his discussion of the incommensurability of free speech and equality. See Delgado, "Campus Antiracism Rules: Constitutional Narratives in Collision."

    It is one of the major flaws in the analysis of *R.A.V.* v. *City of St. Paul*, 112 S.Ct. 2538 120 L. Ed. 2d 305 (1992). The Court assumed that the central issue in the case was the protection of free speech. But one could argue that it would have been at least as valid to look at the problem through a narrative of equality; it may or may not have produced a different decision, but it certainly would have produced a different analysis.

13. See L. Bollinger, *The Tolerant Society* (1986), pp. 35–39; F. Schauer, "Slippery Slopes," *Harv. L. Rev.* 99 (1989), p. 361.

14. See Schauer, "Slippery Slopes." See also S. Winter, "Transcendental Nonsense, Metaphoric Reasoning, and the Cognitive Stakes for Law," *U. Penn. L. Rev.* 137 (1989), p. 1105, on the use of metaphor. Lakoff and Johnson show that a large part of our language, perhaps as much as 90 percent, is metaphorical. See Lakoff and Johnson, *Metaphors We Live By* (1980). What often passes for analysis is really metaphor. This problem becomes most acute when claimants are using different metaphors to describe their world.

15. See Lawrence, "If He Hollers," pp. 474–75.

16. There is a similar male narrative about rape cases. When women have reported rape to the police, the police often use a male narrative to determine whether there has been a "real rape." The white male narrative in particular tells the story of a white woman being raped

by a strange black man. If the white woman is raped by a white male friend, it may not be a "real rape." For a "real" account of this story, see S. Estrich "Rape," *Yale L.J.* 95 (1986), pp. 1087–88.

17. *Mashpee Tribe* v. *Town of Mashpee*, 447 F. Supp. 940 (D. Mass. 1978) *aff'd sub nom. Mashpee Tribe* v. *New Seabury Corp.*, 592 F. 2d 575 (1st cir.), *cert. den.* 444 U.S. 866 (1979).

18. G. Torres and K. Milun, "Translating Yonnondio by Precedent and Evidence: The Mashpee Indian Case," *Duke L.J.* (1990), pp. 625, 633–36.

19. Some commentators have assumed that if one can speak, one can participate in the discourse; Post makes this argument, e.g., Post, "*Hustler Magazine* v. *Falwell*," p. 634. But this is clearly not true, except in the most formal sense. If one carries this position to its logical conclusion, this assuredly becomes clear: one can speak or participate, even in the face of the threat of death, yet such coercion would destroy any legitimacy to the claim that one is participating by speaking. The ability to speak does not alone entail participation in a meaningful sense. A child and an adult can speak to each other, a master to a slave, or an employer to an employee.

20. The privileging that usually goes on in the debate about racist speech is often unconscious. There are times, however, when there is a deliberate effort to privilege and to silence. There was often an effort to destroy the language and narrative of newly captured slaves. See E. Genovese, *Roll, Jordan, Roll* (1976), p. 432.

21. See Lawrence, "If He Hollers," p. 435.

22. Ibid., p. 439 (emphasis in original).

23. Ibid., pp. 44–49.

24. Ibid., p. 452. One moment in the free speech debate is often repeated: whenever there is an effort to regulate or curb speech, there is an effort to argue that the affected subject matter is not speech. Of course, if this is correct, then the difficult question of whether it can be regulated or not is avoided for First Amendment purposes. But it seems to me that this is only part of the issue. If there is a real conflict between free speech and equality in constitutional terms, it is not at all clear that, once something is categorized as speech, even speech that would normally be protected under the First Amendment, the discussion is over. Where there is real conflict, one cannot say a priori that speech wins. This is part of the mistake that the Court made in *Doe* v. *University of Michigan* 721 F. Supp. 852 (E.D. Mich. 1989). Of course, neither can one say that because there is an injury to equality, equality must win. Either of these assumptions would privilege one narrative over the other. Many who do privilege their narrative will be alarmed at this position and see it as very radical. But the Court has correctly suggested as much; see *FCC* v. *Pacifica Foundation* 438 U.S. 726, 747–48 (1978).

25. Lawrence, "If He Hollers," p. 467.

26. Ibid., pp. 466–70.

27. See Strossen, "Modest Proposal," p. 488.

28. Ibid., pp. 549–54.

29. Ibid., p. 497. Strossen does at times acknowledge the injury speech can cause, but it is speech, she says, that must receive First Amendment protection; see ibid., pp. 539–541.

30. Compare, for example, the characterization of the speech in question in F. Haiman, "Speech v. Privacy: Is There a Right Not To Be Spoken To?" *Nw. U.L. Rev.* 67 (1978?), pp. 153, 180, with R. Delgado, "Words that Wound: A Tort Action for Racial Insults, Epithets and Name Calling," *Harv. C.L.-C.R. L. Rev.* 17 (1982), pp. 133, 143. See also Lawrence, "If He Hollers," pp. 461–62. Bollinger, *Tolerant Society*, pp. 58–75, is one of the few commentators who tends to embrace the speech narrative and nonetheless acknowledges that racist speech can do more than offend—it can indeed injure.

31. Strossen, "Modest Proposal," p. 497, but see ibid. at 539–41.

32. Strossen, "Modest Proposal," p. 518.

33. Ibid., p. 521.

34. *Doe* v. *University of Michigan*, 721 F. Supp. 862 (E.D. Mich. 1989).

35. 774 F. Supp. 1163 (E.D. Wis. 1991).

36. 484 U.S. 260 (1988).

37. 760 F. Supp. 1486 (M.D. Fla. 1991).

38. Baker notes that when one is coerced, one's expressions are not autonomous. See Baker, *Human Liberty*, pp. 56–60. A master and slave can participate in a conversation, but it is not the type that values equality and free speech. See Unger, *Passion: An Essay on Personality* (1984), p. 14.
39. Emerson, *General Theory*, p. 878; Baker, *Human Liberty*, p. 47.
40. See T. McCarthy, *The Critical Theory of Jurgen Habermas* (1978), p. 334.
41. See S. Benhabib, *Critique, Norm, and Utopia* (1986), p. 282. Communication is not limited to language, but includes acts. Our norms and values, and indeed our language, are produced through our intersubjective engagement with each other.
42. See Baker, *Human Liberty*, pp. 12–14.
43. Benhabib, *Critique Norm, and Utopia*, p. 315.
44. See Walzer, *Spheres of Justice* (1983), p. 31.
45. *Lois Robinson v. Jacksonville Shipyards, Inc.* 760 F. Supp. 1486 (M.D. Fla. 1991).
46. Because these are scarce goods, e.g., a place at a particular job or school, not all members of society can have them. But they still must be distributed in a way consistent with our notion of equality of opportunity, and this is not inconsistent with the value of participation.

NOTES ON CONTRIBUTORS

Michelle J. Anderson graduated in 1994 from Yale Law School, where she was notes editor on the *Yale Law Journal*.

Robin D. Barnes, professor of law at the University of Connecticut, is the author of many law-review articles on civil rights and hate speech.

Kathleen Barry is the author of *Female Sexual Slavery*.

Mary Becker, professor of law at the University of Chicago Law School, clerked for Supreme Court Justice Lewis Powell. She writes frequently about domestic violence and feminist legal theory.

Twiss Butler works at the National Organization for Women. Her publications analyze automobile insurance, pornography, and abortion as issues used to block constitutional equality for women.

Ben Nighthorse Campbell, Senator from Colorado, is the only Native American in the U.S. Senate.

James Check, professor of psychology at York University in Ontario, Canada, has conducted social science research on the negative effects of pornography on children.

Gloria Cowan, professor of psychology at San Bernardino (California State University), is the author of several articles on pornography and racism.

Kimberlé Crenshaw, professor of law at the University of California Los Angeles School of Law, lectures and writes on black feminist legal theory and on race and the law.

Richard Delgado, Charles Inglis Thomson Professor of Law at the University of Colorado, teaches civil rights law and writes frequently on hate speech, civil rights, and pornography. He was co-drafter of the University of Wisconsin's hate-speech regulation.

Andrea Dworkin's numerous books include *Our Blood, Pornography: Men Possessing Women, Letters from a War Zone*, and the novel *Mercy*. With Catherine MacKinnon, she drafted a pioneer civil-rights anti-pornography ordinance in Minneapolis.

Howard J. Ehrlich is executive co-director and principal social scientist at The Prejudice Institute in Baltimore, Maryland.

Devona Futch is articles editor for the *Colorado Law Review* and Jonathan Boyd Chase Human Rights Fellow at the University of Colorado School of Law.

Evelina Giobbe is founder and executive director of WHISPER, a non-profit organization of ex-prostitutes who have escaped prostitution. She writes and lectures widely on pornography, prostitution, and the sex industry.

Wanda Henson, a registered nurse with a master's degree in education, is the Action Project Coordinator of Camp Sister Spirit, feminist education folkschool.

Martin Kazu Hiraga is former director of the Anti-Violence Project at the National Gay and Lesbian Task Force in Washington, D.C.

Elena Kagan, assistant professor of law at the University of Chicago Law School, where she teaches First Amendment Law, clerked for Supreme Court Justice Thurgood Marshall.

Christopher N. Kendall is a lecturer in law at Murdoch University School of Law in Perth, Australia.

Barbara Larcom is a social science researcher at The Prejudice Institute.

Charles R. Lawrence III, professor of law at Georgetown University, writes frequently on hate speech, racism, and discrimination.

Laura Lederer is a Research Fellow at the University of Minnesota Law School, and director of the Center on Speech, Equality, and Harm. She edited *Take Back the Night: Women on Pornography*.

Dorchen Leidholdt, director of litigation at the Center for Battered Women's Services in New York City and co-director of the International Coalition Against Trafficking in Women, is co-editor, with Janice Raymond, of *The Sexual Liberals and the Attack on Feminism*.

Marshall Levin is founder and director of Imaginitis Interactive, and former executive director of Shaare Tefila.

Catharine A. MacKinnon, professor of law at the University of Michigan Law School, is the author of *Sexual Harassment of Working Women*, *Feminism Unmodified: Discourses on Life and Law*, and *Toward a Feminist Theory of the State*, as well as numerous articles. With Andrea Dworkin, she conceived ordinances recognizing pornography as a violation of civil rights.

Kathleen E. Mahoney is professor of law at the University of Calgary, Canada.

Frank I. Michelman, Robert Walmsley University Professor at Harvard Law School, teaches constitutional law, and writes frequently on pornography and hate speech as they relate to constitutional law.

john a. powell is professor of law at the University of Minnesota Law School and former National Legal Director of ACLU and is currently director of The Institute on Race and Poverty.

Robert Purvis is director of legal affairs and co-executive director at The Prejudice Institute.

Loretta J. Ross, national program director for the Center for Democratic Renewal, has been program director for the National Black Women's Health Project and director of Women of Color programs for NOW.

Frederick Schauer, Frank Stanton Professor of the First Amendment at the John F. Kennedy School of Government, Harvard University, served on the U.S. Attorney General's Commission on Pornography, 1985–86. He has written articles and books on free speech and the legal and constitutional aspects of obscenity and pornography.

Alan Schwartz is director of the Research and Evaluation Department of the Anti-Defamation League (ADL).

Ann Simonton, a former fashion model, is founder and coordinator of Media Watch, a national feminist organization.

Eleanor Smeal is president of the Feminist Majority and past president of the National Organization of Women.

Wendy Stock, assistant professor of psychology at Texas A&M University, conducts research on the impact of pornography on women. She has written a number of articles about pornography and women and is co-editing, with James Check, an anthology of the current social science research on the effects of pornography.

John Stoltenberg is author of *Refusing to Be a Man* and *The End of Manhood* and co-founder of Men Against Pornography, a New York–based organization.

Cass Sunstein is the Karl Llewellyn Professor of Jurisprudence at the University of Chicago Law School.

Barbara Trees, the first female shop steward in her carpenters' union local, and founder and leader of New York Tradeswomen, was an organizer of the 1990 hearings on racism and sexism in the construction industry before the New York City Commission on Civil Rights.

Fred Veilleux is a member of Concerned American Indian Parents Organization and of the National Coalition on Racism in Sports and the Media.

Marianne Wesson, professor of law at the University of Colorado, served as co-counsel in *Simmons* v. *Simmons*, the Colorado case that established marital domestic violence as a tort cognizable under Colorado law.

Olivia Young, a registered nurse, is a plaintiff in a lawsuit arguing that her exposure to pornography in the workplace constituted intentional and negligent emotional distress.

David Yun, a member of the Colorado bar, writes frequently on civil rights and hate speech.

Helen Zia, a journalist and former assistant editor of *Ms.* magazine, was a participant in a recent Center for Women Policy Studies Seminar on Hate Crimes and Gender Bias Crimes.